The Cambridge History of Modern France

5   The Decline of the Third Republic, 1914–1938

The Cambridge History of Modern France

This is an eight-volume textbook series on the history of France from 1815 to the present day, co-published with the Maison des Sciences de l'Homme. Each volume is a translation of a title or titles from the series 'Nouvelle histoire de la France contemporaine' which has been in the course of publication by Editions du Seuil, Paris, since 1972. Authors are either historians at the top of their profession, but actively writing works of research, or younger scholars keenly involved with the topics concerned. Each shows a clear awareness of work currently being undertaken in the field, in English as well as in French. The series as a whole will form a comprehensive, coherent and up-to-date history of France since 1815.

Titles marked with an asterisk are also available in paperback

The Decline of the
Third Republic,
1914–1938

PHILIPPE BERNARD
and
HENRI DUBIEF

Translated by
ANTHONY FORSTER

CAMBRIDGE
UNIVERSITY PRESS

Published by the Press Syndicate of the University of Cambridge
The Pitt Building, Trumpington Street, Cambridge CB2 1RP
40 West 20th Street, New York, NY 10011-4211, USA
10 Stamford Road, Oakleigh, Melbourne 3166, Australia
and Editions de la Maison des Sciences de l'Homme
54 Boulevard Raspail, 75270 Paris Cedex 06

Originally published in French as *La Fin d'un monde 1914–1929* and
Le Déclin de la IIIe République 1929–1938 by Editions du Seuil, Paris 1975 and 1976
and © Editions du Seuil 1975 and 1976

First published in English by Editions de la Maison des Sciences de l'Homme and
Cambridge University Press 1985 as *The Decline of the Third Republic, 1914–1938*

First paperback edition 1988
Reprinted 1989, 1993

English translation © Maison des Sciences de l'Homme and
Cambridge University Press 1985

Printed in Great Britain by the Athenaeum Press Ltd, Newcastle upon Tyne

Library of Congress catalogue card number: 84-17043

British Library Cataloguing in Publication Data

Bernard, Philippe
The decline of the Third Republic, 1914–1938. –
(The Cambridge history of modern France; 5)
1. France – History – 1914–1940
I. Title   II. Dubief, Henri   III. Series
944.081'4   DC389

ISBN 0 521 25240 7 hardback
ISBN 2 7351 0076 6 hardback (France only)
ISBN 0 521 35854 X paperback
ISBN 2 7351 0224 6 paperback (France only)

CE

Contents

PART IV FRANCE IN THE THIRTIES: CHANGE AND STABILITY

PART V THE FRONT POPULAIRE

Chronology

1914

28 June	Assassination at Sarajevo
29 July	Meeting of the Socialist International Bureau in Brussels
30 July	General mobilisation in Russia
31 July	Assassination of Jaurès
1 August	General mobilisation in France and Germany. Germany declares war on Russia
3 August	Germany declares war on France
4 August	The Chamber unanimously passes laws giving full powers to the government
18–22 August	Battle of the frontiers
23 August	Battle of Charleroi and Lanrezac's retreat
26 August	Broadening of the Viviani cabinet which was joined by two socialists, Guesde and Sembat
2 September	The government leaves Paris for Bordeaux
4–10 September	Battle of the Marne
October–November	Battles in the 'race to the sea'
1 November	The allied powers break with Turkey
8 December	Naval battle off the Falkland Islands
23 December	Extraordinary meeting of parliament in Paris

1915

12 January	The parliamentary session begins
4 February	Germany's announcement of the first submarine offensive
19 February	First Franco-British naval attack on the Dardanelles
25 April	Landing of an allied expeditionary corps on the Dardanelles
26 April	Treaty of London between Italy and the allied powers
7 May	The *Lusitania* torpedoed
9 May	Beginning of French offensive in Artois
18 May	Appointment of Albert Thomas as under-secretary for artillery and military equipment
23 May	Italy's entry into the war against Austria-Hungary
13 August	Passing of the Dalbiez law
September	Publication in France of Romain Rolland's *Au-dessus de la mêlée*
5–8 September	Zimmerwald conference
25 September	Beginning of French offensive in Champagne
1–6 October	Landing of a French expeditionary corps in Salonika
5 October	Entry of Bulgaria into the war
25–9 October	Resignation of the Viviani cabinet. Formation of the Briand cabinet. Galliéni appointed minister of war

2 December	Decree appointing Joffre commander-in-chief of the French armies

1916

21 February	Beginning of the German attack on Verdun
7 March	Galliéni leaves the ministry of war
20–4 April	Socialist conference at Kienthal
1 May	First issue of *Le Populaire*
31 May	Naval battle of Jutland
16–22 June	First secret session of the Chamber
1 July	Beginning of the Franco-British offensive on the Somme
29 July	Fixing of the price of wheat
28 August	Entry of Rumania into the war
1 September	End of the first German submarine offensive
6 December	Fall of Bucharest
12 December	Reshuffle of Briand ministry. Lyautey appointed minister of war
15–29 December	Parliament refuses to let the government rule by decree
26 December	Marshall Joffre removed from the High Command
26–8 December	Thirteenth congress of the SFIO

1917

31 January	American government told of launching of all-out German submarine offensive
3 February	Diplomatic relations broken off between Germany and the USA
8–17 March	First Russian revolution. The Tsar abdicates
12–13 March	German withdrawal on the front of the attack planned by Nivelle
18 March	Resignation of the Briand ministry
20 March	Ribot government formed
April	Peak of the submarine offensive (874,000 tons of shipping sunk)
2 April	US Congress approves declaration of war on Germany
6 April	Council of war at Compiègne
16 April	Offensive of Chemin des Dames
May–June	Big workers' strikes, especially in Paris
4 May	First mutinies in the French army
16 May	Pétain replaces Nivelle as commander-in-chief
19 May	The Russian government proposes a search for peace without annexations or penalties
27–8 May	The national council of the SFIO unanimously decides that French socialists should attend the Stockholm conference
2 June	The Ribot government refuses to give passports to the delegates to Stockholm
11–26 June	King Constantine leaves Greece under French pressure. Venizelos forms a pro-ally government
28 June	Landing of the first American division at Saint-Nazaire
22 July	Clemenceau violently attacks Malvy in a public session of the Senate
31 August	Resignation of Malvy

12 September	Resignation of the Ribot cabinet
13 September	Formation of the Painlevé cabinet
25 September	Conference at Boulogne (Painlevé–Lloyd George) on the unity of command
6 November	The bolsheviks seize power in Russia
13 November	Painlevé cabinet overthrown
16 November	Formation of the Clemenceau cabinet
15 December	Armistice on the Russian front

1918

8 January	Message of Wilson to Congress and statement of the Fourteen Points
2 February	Creation of an inter-allied executive committee led by Foch
March–April	Wave of strikes in Paris and the provinces
3 March	Treaty of Brest-Litovsk
21 March–5 April	Ludendorff's offensive at Saint Quentin
26 March	Inter-allied conference at Doullens
3 April	Inter-allied conference at Beauvais. Foch becomes generalissimo
9–25 April	German offensive in Flanders
25 May–11 June	German offensive on the Aisne
14–16 July	German offensive in Champagne
18 July	Mangin's counter-offensive at Villers-Cotterêts
8 August	British offensive on Amiens
15 September	American divisions in action at Saint-Mihiel. Beginning of Franchet d'Espérey's offensive in the Balkans
26 September	General allied offensive
29 September	The Bulgarians sign an armistice
6–9 October	Socialist party congress: change of majority: Frossard becomes secretary-general
24–9 October	Italian offensive on the Piave. Collapse of Austria–Hungary
3 November	The emperor Charles accepts the armistice of Villa Giusti
11 November	Signature of the armistice at Rethondes
13 December	Wilson's arrival in France

1919

18 January	Opening of the peace conference
19 February	Attempt on Clemenceau's life
13 March	Great Britain ceases to support the franc on the foreign exchange
16–19 March	Meeting in Paris of the Confédération Internationale des Travailleurs Chrétiens
19 March	Passing of the electoral law in the Chamber
31 March	Law on war pensions
17 April	Law on the repair of war damage
19–21 April	Mutiny on the French ships in the Black Sea
23 April	Eight-hour law
23–4 April	Socialist congress in Paris
1 June	Proclamation by Dorten at Aix-la-Chapelle of a short-lived Rhine republic
26 June	Electoral reform voted in the Senate

28 June	Signature of the treaty of Versailles
16 July	Ratification of the Banque de France convention
10 September	Treaty of Saint-Germain
15–21 September	CGT congress at Lyon
2–12 October	Ratification of the treaty of Versailles in the Chamber and the Senate
26 October	Publication in *Le Temps* of the programme of the Bloc National
1–2 November	Congress on the constitution of the CFTC. Zirnheld becomes secretary-general
16 November	Parliamentary elections. Success of the Bloc National
8 December	First session of the 'bleu horizon' Chamber

1920

8 January	Inauguration of the Conseil Economique du Travail, inspired by the CGT to study nationalisation
16 January	Clemenceau beaten in the preliminary meeting for the election of the President of the Republic
17 January	Paul Deschanel elected President
20 January	Formation of the Millerand ministry
23 February–4 March	Strike of the CGT railwaymen
25–9 February	National congress of the socialist party at Strasbourg. Rejection of the Second International
7 March	Beginning of the miners' strike in the Nord
18–26 April	San Remo conference
28 April	The CGT federation of railwaymen orders a strike for 1 May
15 May	Hythe conference
22 May	CGT cancels the strike order
31 May	Cachin and Frossard leave for Moscow
4 June	Signature of the treaty of Trianon
21 June	Conference at Boulogne
6–17 July	Conference at Spa
19 July–7 August	Cachin and Frossard attend second congress of the Third International
21–4 September	Resignation of Deschanel. Election of Millerand as President of the Republic
27 September–2 October	CGT congress at Orléans
16 November	Debate in the Chamber on the restoration of diplomatic relations with the Vatican
20–6 December	Congress of the PSU at Tours. Schism in the party

1921

16 January	Formation of the Briand ministry
27 February	Opening of the London conference
1 March	Passing of the rent law
27 April–5 May	Fixing of the total sum of reparations and of payment methods
6–7 October	Signing of the Wiesbaden agreements
20 October	Signing of the peace of Ankara
29 October–16 December	Washington conference
27 December	Administrative commission of the CGT admits union split

End December	First French communist party conference at Marseille

1922

5–12 January	Cannes conference
12 January	Briand's resignation
14 January	Foundation of the CGTU
15 January	Formation of the Poincaré ministry
6 February	Washington agreement on naval armaments
10 April	Opening of the Genoa conference
12 July	Germany asks for moratorium on reparation payments
October	The radical Young Turks found the Ligue de la République. Second congress of the PCF
December	Fourth congress of the Communist International. French communists forbidden to join Freemasons or the Ligue des Droits de l'Homme
29 December	The US Secretary of State proposes to submit the problem of reparations to a committee of experts
31 December	The SFIO and the CGT criticise the government's harsh policy towards Germany

1923

1 January	Frossard ceases to be secretary-general of the PCF
2–3 January	Paris conference
7 January	Manifesto of the French, German, Belgian and British communist parties against the Ruhr operation, called the Essen Manifesto
11 January	Beginning of the occupation of the Ruhr
22 January	Murder of Plateau, secretary-general of Action Française
2–6 February	SFIO congress at Lille
3 May	Léon Bérard's decree on the reform of secondary education
18 June	The communist Renaud Jean proposes the *bloc ouvrier et paysan*
12 October	Strike launched by the PCF against the Rif war
14 October	Millerand's speech at Evreux
26 October	Poincaré agrees to consider revision of the reparations treaty
5 December	Death of Maurice Barrès
7 December	Monatte and Rosmer excluded from the PCF

1924

January	Extraordinary congress of the socialist party in Marseille. Electoral alliance with the radicals approved
14 January	First meeting of the Dawes committee
12 February	Massacre of the Rhineland autonomists at Pirmasens
24 February	Vote of the *double décime* in the Chamber
8 March	Pound sterling at 125 francs. French government borrows from Morgan Brothers
18 April	French government accepts Dawes plan
11 May	Elections to the Chamber and success of the Cartel des Gauches
11 June	Millerand's resignation
13 June	Doumergue elected President of the Republic

15 June	Formation of the Herriot ministry
20–2 June	Herriot–MacDonald interview at Chequers
16 July	Opening of the London conference
1 October	Signature of the 'Geneva Protocol' at the League of Nations
29 October	French government decrees official recognition of the USSR
31 October	Dawes plan comes into force
November	Millerand creates the Ligue Républicaine Nationale
1 December	First issue of *La Révolution surréaliste*

1925

January	Creation of the Conseil Economique
9 February	Stresemann's Memorandum to the French government
12 March	Austen Chamberlain refuses Great Britain's support for the 'Geneva Protocol'
10 April	The breaching of the ceiling for the issue of notes made public. Fall of the Herriot government
17 April	Formation of the Painlevé government. Caillaux becomes minister of finance
End April	Abd-el-Krim attacks French posts in Morocco
20 September	Congress of the PCF in Strasbourg demands a plebiscite on Alsace-Lorraine
16 October	Signature of the Locarno pact
27 October	Resignation of the Painlevé cabinet
29 October	New Painlevé ministry. Bonnet becomes minister of the budget
14 November	Exhibition of surrealist painting at the Galerie Pierre
22 November	Fall of the Painlevé government
28 November	Formation of the Briand government, with Loucheur as minister of finance
16 December	Resignation of Loucheur, replaced by Doumer

1926

January	Congress of the revived Action Catholique de la Jeunesse Française
6 March	Fall of the Briand ministry
9 March	New Briand cabinet with Péret as minister of finance
15 June	Fall of the Briand–Péret ministry
24 June	New Briand cabinet. Caillaux vice-president of the Council
16–17 July	Caillaux asks for special powers. Fall of the Briand–Caillaux cabinet
20–1 July	Brief Herriot cabinet. Pound sterling at 240 francs
23 July	Formation of the Poincaré cabinet
26 July	Pound sterling at 190 francs
August	Youth congress at Marc Sangnier's house at Bierville
3 August	Vote of the fiscal measures demanded by Poincaré
10 August	Law creating the *caisse autonome d'amortissement*
8 September	League of Nations assembly votes admission of Germany
17 September	Briand–Stresemann interview at Thoiry
29 September	Signing of the Mellon–Béranger agreement on war debts
30 September	Cartel convention between French and German steel-makers

1 October	Decree creating unified schools from twinned colleges
December	*De facto* stabilisation of the franc at 124 francs to the pound

1927

5 January	*L'Action française* put on the Index
17 February	Franco-British agreement on war debts
March	French troops evacuate the Saar
May	Law introducing one-year military service. Definition by the Communist International of the 'class against class' strategy
June	Passing of an electoral law creating the *scrutin d'arrondissement* with two ballots
October	Radical congress at the Salle Wagram. Daladier president of the party
24–9 October	Fifth Solvay congress on physics
27 December	Introduction of free secondary schooling in twinned establishments
28 December	The US Secretary of State Kellogg proposes to Briand a pact outlawing war

1928

9 January	The 'class against class' strategy adopted by the central committee of the PCF
6 February	Signature of the Briand–Kellogg pact
22–9 April	Elections to the Chamber
7 June	Presentation of the new Poincaré government
24–5 June	Official stabilisation of the franc. Vote on devaluation in the Chamber and the Senate
13 July	Loucheur law on low-rent housing
16 September	Announcement at Geneva of negotiations on international financial settlements under Young's direction
6–11 November	The radicals leave the Union National and the Poincaré government

1929

26 July	Resignation of Poincaré cabinet
27 September	Costes makes world record long-distance flight
22 October	Fall of Briand's eleventh ministry
25 October	The Wall Street crash
29 December	The construction of a line of fortifications (the Maginot Line) is voted

1930

10 February	Mutiny of Annamese infantrymen at Yen Bay
17 February	Fall of Tardieu's ministry
12 March	Free secondary education introduced
29 March	Ratification of the Young plan
16 April	Pensions voted for war veterans
30 June	French evacuation of the Rhineland
1 July	Social insurance laws brought into force
2 September	Non-stop flight across the Atlantic, east to west, by Costes and Bellonte

4 November	Start of the Oustric scandal
4 December	Fall of the Tardieu ministry

1931

9 February	Weygand replaces Pétain as vice-president of the Supreme War Council
6 May	Opening of the colonial exhibition in the Bois de Vincennes
13 May	Paul Doumer elected President of the Republic
20 June	Hoover moratorium on reparations and war debts
21 September	Devaluation of the pound sterling

1932

12 January	Resignation of the Laval cabinet
21 January	Law on family allowances
10 February	Fall of Laval cabinet
24 February	Breakdown of Geneva conference on disarmament
6 May	President Doumer assassinated by a lunatic White Russian
8 May	Gains by the left in second round of elections for the Chamber
10 May	Albert Lebrun elected President of the Republic
9 July	Lausanne conference on reparations wound up
29 November	Franco-Soviet pact of non-aggression
14 December	Fall of Herriot ministry

1933

30 January	Hitler becomes German chancellor
16 February	Pact of Petite Entente signed
19 February	Loterie Nationale instituted
14 July	Four Power Pact signed in Rome
24 October	Fall of Daladier ministry
5 November	Déat, Marquet, Montagnon and Renaudel expelled from the SFIO
29 December	Start of the Stavisky affair

1934

8 January	Death of Stavisky
26 January	German–Polish pact
27 January	Resignation of Chautemps cabinet
6 February	Attempted *coup d'état* of the Ligues
7 February	Resignation of Daladier cabinet
12 February	General strike throughout France
22 February	Doumergue empowered to govern by *décrets-lois*
3 March	Inauguration of Comité de Vigilance des Intellectuels Anti-Fascistes
30 June	'Night of the Long Knives' in Germany
25 July	Assassination of Austrian chancellor Dollfuss
27 July	French socialist and communist parties agree on pact for joint action
2 August	Death of Hindenburg
18 September	Soviet Union joins the League of Nations
9 October	King Alexander of Jugoslavia and foreign minister Barthou murdered in Marseille by Croat terrorists in the pay of Mussolini

8 November	Resignation of Doumergue cabinet
24 December	Law controlling distillation of excess wine and subsidies paid for ploughing up vines

1935

7 January	Franco-Italian agreement signed in Rome
13 January	The Saar votes to join the German Reich
18 January	Gamelin replaces Weygand as vice-president of the Supreme War Council
16 March	Germany introduces compulsory military service
2 May	Franco-Soviet pact of mutual assistance
5–12 May	Left-wing gains in municipal elections
31 May	Fall of Flandin ministry
12 June	The *Normandie* wins the Blue Riband of the Atlantic
14 July	Procession and oath of the Rassemblement Populaire
16 July	Laval introduces severely deflationary policy
4 October	Mussolini invades Abyssinia
16 November	Bloodshed in Limoges in clashes between Croix-de-Feu and left-wing militants
6 December	Suppression of paramilitary organisations

1936

January	Suppression of Action Française gangs
12 January	Manifesto of Rassemblement Populaire
20 January	Daladier replaces Herriot as leader of radical party
24 January	Resignation of Laval cabinet
7 March	Hitler denounces the treaty of Locarno and remilitarises the Rhineland
25 March	Unification of communist and socialist trade unions
5 May	Electoral triumph of the Front Populaire
26 May	Occupation of factories
5 June	Beginning of the Blum experiment
7 June	Matignon agreements
12 June	Laws on collective agreements, holidays with pay and the forty-hour week
18 June	Suppression of the Ligues
19 June–1 July	End of sanctions against Italy
21 June	Creation of the PSF (Parti Socialiste de France)
2 July	School-leaving age extended to fourteen
18 July	Spanish Civil War breaks out
24 July	Reform of the Banque de France
1 August	Blum proposes policy of 'non-intervention' in Spain
11 August	Nationalisation of the arms industry
15 August	Office National Interprofessionel du Blé set up
9 September	Vienot agreement between France and Syria
27 Sepember	Devaluation of the franc
18 November	Death of Salengro
4 December	Communist deputies abstain in foreign policy debate
31 December	Law on compulsory arbitration

1937

13 February	Blum announces the 'pause'

12 March	Loan for national defence launched
16 March	The 'fusillade' at Clichy
24 May	Opening of the great international exhibition in Paris
22 June	Fall of the Blum government
30 June	Further devaluation of the franc
31 August	Creation of the SNCF (nationalisation of the railways)
11 September	Fascist violence
15 December	Arrest of the Cagoulards

1938

15 January	Resignation of Chautemps cabinet. Chautemps forms new ministry
10 March	Resignation of Chautemps cabinet
12 March	Hitler invades and annexes Austria
24 March	Wave of strikes in France
8 April	Fall of Blum ministry
13 April	Daladier ministry wins almost unanimous confidence in the Chamber

PART I

From invasion to victory

1

The Union Sacrée

When general mobilisation was declared on 1 August 1914, the political right and the military authorities had much to fear from the socialists and trade unionists. The former had just demonstrated their growing influence at the recent parliamentary elections. Their fight against the three-year military service law and the meetings that they held with the social democrats from Germany gave serious grounds for anxiety. As for the trade unions, their leaders had, from the very beginning of the crisis, dared more than ever before to advocate recourse to strikes in order to sabotage mobilisation. They would certainly be the first enemy to be dealt with.

The question of the 'carnet B'

The ministry of the interior was much preoccupied by the danger threatening from union action, which could only help Germany. Repressive measures against the socialist unions would be tricky, for their main leaders being members of parliament enjoyed an immunity which could prove awkward. The government could act with fewer constraints against the leading figures of the CGT (Confédération Générale du Travail), whose anti-militarist and anti-nationalist reactions were far more emphatic. So a list of those who should be arrested on mobilisation had been prepared, based on reports from the prefects. This was the famous *carnet B* in which all dissidents knew that they were listed. On the evening of 29 July 1914 most of the joint committee, whose imminent arrest had already been announced by *L'Intransigeant*, fled to take refuge with good friends who were not on the police files, while Jouhaux talked of 'going to buy four centimes worth of tobacco in Brussels'.

That same day the general staff, who had no doubts that general mobilisation was imminent, demanded the immediate application of the measures planned. At the council of ministers Messimy backed this policy, but Malvy was against it. The reports he received from the informers, whom his ministry had infiltrated even into the highest ranks of the working-class movement, and the remarks of many of his socialist friends in parliament made him doubt the wisdom of allowing free rein to the bitter feelings

3

openly expressed by the supporters of strong-arm action. Malvy had just got his way when Jaurès' assassination was announced to the dismayed ministers, and the panic-stricken prefect of police declared that the revolutionaries would converge on Paris next day.

The change of heart

Yet on 1 August, at one o'clock in the morning, Malvy sent the prefects a telegram ordering the suspension of all planned arrests, for he had 'every reason to believe that he could trust all those who had been listed on the *carnet B* for political reasons'. During that day he made contact with Jouhaux, the secretary of the CGT, and, after promising that he would free the militants imprisoned here and there by over-zealous prefects, was assured that the trade unions would not hinder the general mobilisation that was now inevitable. Indeed, on 2 August, an appeal from the CGT 'to the workers of France' signalled the collapse of the joint committee's efforts for the cause of peace and a surrender to the march of events.

Finally, on 4 August, the decisive step was taken when Jouhaux, in an improvised speech before the coffin of Jean Jaurès, proclaimed his support for a war which for the people of France was a war for justice and republican liberty against the tyrants of the central powers, acting as the puppets of the military caste. He thereby spontaneously re-discovered *girondin* language and sentiments long since excluded from his consciousness by his persistent and certainly sincere attachment to the doctrines of proletarian internationalism. The secretary-general of the CGT, to the applause of a mixed crowd, in which Paul Déroulède's successor as the head of the Ligue des Patriotes, Maurice Barrès himself, was to be seen, publicly proclaimed that the working-class movement would do its duty in the just war that was breaking out.

As for the socialists, they rallied round even more rapidly. It is true that during the extraordinary congress of the party held in Paris from 14 to 16 July 1914 Jaurès had defeated Jules Guesde by getting a motion adopted which recommended 'a general strike organised simultaneously and internationally' as a particularly effective way of 'anticipating and preventing wars and obliging governments to have recourse to arbitration'. From then onwards Jaurès had not spared himself in berating the ministers and chancellories and threatening them with a pacifist movement of growing dimensions. He had met German socialists during the conference of the Socialist International Bureau in Brussels. He had returned from there on 30 July very optimistic about the chances of concerted action to avert disaster. On 31 July he again denounced Russia's warmongering and clung to the idea that British proposals for conciliation might lead to warding off the storm. But around 10 o'clock in the evening he succumbed to the shots of Raoul Villain, a mentally unbalanced youth, whose reading of the nationalist press had led him to gun down the man who was described in the papers as Germany's most dangerous accomplice.

The session of 4 August

The day after Jaurès' assassination, which was unanimously condemned, none of the journalists whose spiteful articles had gone to Villain's head would accept any responsibility for the outrage. The leaders of the socialist party, for their part, urged their supporters to be calm, given the gravity of the situation. On 2 August a meeting of Parisian socialists in the Salle Wagram saw a succession of their most respected leaders (except Guesde who was ill) mount the platform. All of them already accepted war and the party's share in the defence of the country – but on condition that France, the victim of aggression, should keep right on her side by eschewing all territorial conquest once Alsace-Lorraine had been restored to the motherland, and by moderating, if need be, the appetites of her Russian ally. So said Longuet, Marx's son-in-law, Marcel Cachin and the much-admired Edouard Vaillant.

At the session of the Chamber of Deputies on 4 August 1914, not a single discordant voice was raised. First of all Paul Deschanel, president of the Chamber, paid a tribute to Jaurès 'assassinated by a madman'. Then, in a religious silence, the Chamber listened to the message of the President of the Republic read by the president of the Council, Viviani. The Union Sacrée was launched. The government was granted the extraordinary (and excessive) authority it demanded, which amounted to giving it discretionary powers for the conduct of the war during an undetermined period. The Chamber adjourned *sine die* in stormy mood. Old Edouard Vaillant, the communard revolutionary, was seen to fall into the arms of Albert de Mun, the former *versaillais*, with whom he had never been on speaking terms. Not a single voice was raised against the war. The whole country backed the Union Sacrée wholeheartedly. And if certain militants, especially among the anarcho-syndicalists, continued after 4 August to harbour the sentiments about the army and the war which had inspired them a few weeks earlier, they kept them to themselves. 'The workers', Merrheim, the secretary of the Fédération des Métaux, was to say, 'were swept by an irresistible wave of nationalism and would not have left it to the police to shoot us. They would have shot us themselves.'

How did this collapse of an internationalist and pacifist movement, which a short time before had seemed so strong and determined, come about?

A treacherous aggressor

The first explanation suggested by reading the source material lies in the way French public opinion interpreted the mounting crisis of July–August 1914. Although they were looking desperately for means to avert that crisis, the socialist leaders, despite their critical attitude, did not really cast doubts on the government's desire for peace. Jaurès himself, at a meeting in Brussels which followed on the deliberations of the Socialist International Bureau of 29 and 30 July, stated clearly: 'I have never hesitated to draw upon myself the hatred of our diehard patriots by my wilful obstinacy, and I will never relax my efforts for a Franco-German reconciliation; but I have every right to say that at this moment the French government wants peace.'

Therefore, when on 2 August 1914 the German government, the day after declaring war on Russia, addressed an ultimatum to Belgium requesting free passage for its armies, French public opinion could only interpret this as deliberate aggression. On 29 July the French government had arranged for the withdrawal of forward troops to a distance of ten kilometres behind the frontiers, which made the incidents cited by Germany in justification of their aggression highly improbable. The invasion of Belgium could only strengthen the feeling among the French that they were the victims of an action that had been planned for years and was totally unjustifiable. So, for the socialists resistance to an attack of this kind constituted a 'just' war to which France was entitled to resort.

One should also add the disappointing results that attended the efforts of the French pacifists to achieve joint action with their opposite numbers within the Socialist International. On 1 August 1914, the day after Jaurès' death, a socialist deputy of the Reichstag, Hermann Müller, accompanied by Camille Huysmans, the secretary of the Socialist International, and Henri de Man met the leaders of the French party in Paris. After declaring that it would be 'out of the question' for his colleagues to vote the credits which his government might request for war purposes, he had obtained similar assurances from his French partners. When the latter learnt that on 3 August the socialist party group in the Reichstag had decided by seventy-eight votes to fourteen to vote such military credits, they could legitimately feel deceived and no longer bound by their promises.

An out-of-date concept

Many internationalists, forced to change their minds by the enemy's treachery and cruelly disappointed by the faintheartedness of the German socialists, could not resist the strong current of patriotism on the outbreak of war. However, these explanations are inadequate to explain on the one hand the unanimous strength of this attitude, and on the other hand the fact that the first signs of this attitude only appeared at the beginning of the crisis. Annie Kriegel has shown the anachronistic basis of French doctrine on proletarian internationalism. (In *Aux origines du communisme français, 1914–1920*, and in *1914, La Guerre et le mouvement ouvrier français*, written in collaboration with J.-J. Becker.) This doctrine, dating from the nineteenth century, arose out of the idea that the all-conquering bourgeoi-

*Internationalism = outdated because
the Bourg has effectively welcomed
the WC into the national community
(Bernard & Dubief?)

The Union Sacrée   7

sie expelled the working class (which it hated, exploited and feared all at
once) from the national community, and this idea was reinforced by the
cruel and bloodthirsty way in which that bourgeoisie had suppressed the
attempts at revolution of the working-class in 1848 and 1871. It stated as a
principle that this working class, cast out from all bourgeois nations, would
be able by a concerted effort to overthrow those nations and establish a new
international society of producers in their place.

The slide of the French socialists towards full participation in the Union
Sacrée of August 1914, the sudden complete reversal of the CGT's attitude
in the very last days of the crisis, above all Jouhaux's oration at Jaurès'
funeral, all go to show that the integration of the workers into the national
community had irrevocably taken place without anyone having clearly
noticed it. (For a new look at French public opinion at the beginning of the
war, see J.-J. Becker, *1914, Comment les Français sont entrés dans la guerre.*)

War and justice

However, one should not imagine that trade-union and socialist
membership of the Union Sacrée meant that they subscribed to the views of
their former opponents. If they went to war, it was to construct a new
Europe after destroying the criminals who had led the Germans to the
abyss; a new Europe in which reconciliation would be possible with an
enemy finally liberated by the establishment of a democratic republic. So
the left would always have to be vigilant to see that France did not succumb
to imperialist dreams, or that the rich and powerful did not make the
necessities of war a pretext for eroding liberties that had been won and for
increasing their grip on the workers. This was the special concern of all
working-class action organised during this testing time.

There were striking examples of this attitude in the very first days of the
war. In almost all the press hatred of the enemy was quickly expressed in
terms of rabid anti-German racism. Maurras developed the theme of 'the
instinctive savagery of German flesh and blood'. Even Bergson denounced
'a regression into the state of barbarism in the brutality and cynicism of
Germany, in its contempt for all justice and truth'. Alone (or very nearly
so), the trade-union and socialist press continued to insist that it was not the
German people but their arrogant masters who were the enemy, and to
express strong hopes of a reconciliation. The same press were also the only
ones to denounce the pogrom-like looting of allegedly German shops by
hysterical ruffians and the wave of xenophobia that shook the capital for a
while. In joining the Union Sacrée the socialists and trade unionists did not
automatically give up their attitudes and views. This meant that, once the
nation had settled down to war, the political game could not fail to come
back to life with all its controversies, whether they concerned the conduct of
military and diplomatic policy, the economic and social organisation of the
country, or national war aims.

2

The military stalemate

War plans thwarted

In both camps the general staffs had long since worked out the development of hostilities, readjusting their plans to the diplomatic situation and, to a much smaller extent, to the changing weaponry and the lessons of recent conflicts, e.g. the Sino-Japanese war and the wars in the Balkans.

The Schlieffen plan and plan XVII

There is no doubt that the German plans were better prepared. They envisaged a lightning attack on France, who would be knocked out of action within a few weeks. To that end a considerable numerical superiority was assured by reinforcing the German armies of western Europe at the expense of those of eastern Europe and giving the reserves an active role in the battle. Furthermore, the Germans were to outflank the bulk of the French army by reinforcing their right wing and making it push as far north as possible; this was found to involve the invasion of the whole of Belgium. The surrender of the Belgian strongholds would be brought about by using heavy artillery that was both effective and mobile. The German armies would be able thereby to encircle the French armies massed on their eastern and north-eastern frontiers and to force them to surrender, laying siege to Paris on the way.

On the lightly held Russian front the Germans hoped for a respite of two months, for they expected the mobilisation and concentration of the Russian armies to be a slow business. This would give them time to eliminate France and then to concentrate all their forces into battle on the eastern front. Everything would be settled by the autumn, and Germany would impose a peace whose conditions were already prepared: the annexation of Briey, Longwy, Belfort, the west slope of the Vosges and the French coast as far as Boulogne; the annexation of Luxembourg and subjugation of Belgium; the establishment in western and central Europe of a customs union dominated by Germany and embracing France, Belgium, Holland, Denmark and Austria-Hungary. To the east security would be assured by a

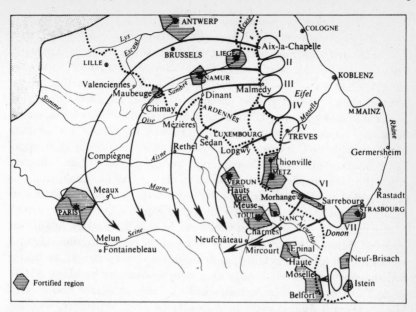

The German plan in 1914. (Ministère de la Guerre, Ecoles militaires, *Cours d'histoire.*
III. *La Guerre mondiale (1914/18)*, Maps and sketches, Paris, Imprimerie nationale,
1920.)

buffer-state under German protection, keeping the Russians at arm's
length. Finally, thanks to the French and Belgian colonies, Germany would
be guaranteed a dominant position in Africa.

The French general staff for their part had made many wrong forecasts.
They failed to take account of the use the Germans would make of their
reserves and badly underestimated the enemy strength on the western
front, reckoning it at forty-six instead of sixty-eight divisions! The general
staff's plan XVII proposed to break up the enemy's manœuvre by a double
attack on their centre, in Lorraine and north of Verdun, although these
were not regions suited for such operations. The forward drive of the troops,
galvanised by the offensive spirit recently and unanimously preached at
headquarters and supported by superior numbers, would alleviate the
difficulties of the terrain. Beaten in the west, the enemy would then have to
face invasion in the east; for the Russians would attack on the sixteenth day
of their mobilisation, offering their enemy no other choice but to let them in
so as to avoid a disaster in the west, or to accept such a disaster in order to
try and stop them in the east. Matters would be settled in the autumn at the
latest, and the allied powers would impose its peace. For the moment the
French had no other war aim but the return of Alsace-Lorraine, and on that
point they were unanimous.

The battle of the frontiers and the retreat

For a few weeks God seemed to be on the side of the Germans. The Schlieffen plan was carried out with clockwork precision. Ten days, from 6 to 16 August, were enough for the German armies to capture the stronghold of Liège and force the Belgian army to take refuge in the fortified town of Antwerp. The manœuvre planned for the German right flank could now go forward. The French attacks, on the other hand, were a disaster. In spite of their numerical superiority the armies of Castelnau and de Langle de Cary were forced to retreat, decimated by their opponents' machine-guns and field artillery. They did indeed withdraw in good order, but the 'battle of the frontiers' was lost. As for Lanrezac, who commanded the French left flank, he did not receive the reinforcements requested and waited in vain for the 'contemptible little British army'. Making then for the Sambre at Charleroi, he met there on 21 August the forces of Bülow, who were superior in numbers (thirty divisions against nineteen). All his attacks failed, so he in his turn beat a retreat, as did the British army under French, who were soundly trounced at Mons. Meanwhile Pau's army, which had attacked in southern Alsace and entered Mulhouse on 8 August without encountering much resistance, was also forced to clear out when the VIIth German army reacted in the direction of the southern slopes of the Vosges.

In the meantime Joffre had not lost his calm. He now intended to launch his attack further down, where the ground and especially the railway system (in the use of which he was an adept) would be favourable to him, i.e. to the south of the Seine. So the French armies withdrew by forced marches and concentrated towards the east. In this plan Paris was to be abandoned. However, Joffre accepted that the command there should be given to the old general Galliéni, who with scratch troops immediately set about organising the defence of the city. His job was made easier by the government's acceptance of the general staff's recommendation to leave the capital and make for Bordeaux on 2 September. In these conditions the German advance continued without much resistance apart from the rearguard action launched on 29 August by Lanrezac's army at Guise, where success ensured an orderly retreat.

Public opinion had no clear idea of these disasters, and the government was hardly better informed. Flags were put out on the capture of Mulhouse, and it was generally thought that the war was won. There was no word from the general staff and the press painted a rosy picture of imaginary enemy defeats. The Germans gave themselves up for a piece of cake (story in *L'Intransigeant*, 16 August), their shells and bullets were no use (*ibid.*, 17 August), while the Cossacks were only 'five days' march' from Berlin (headline in *Le Matin*, 24 August). It was a horrible surprise when the general public learnt in the communiqué of 28 August that the situation was unchanged 'from the Somme to the Vosges'. Panic seized the Parisians and five hundred thousand of them fled towards the south in one week.

The miracle of the Marne

Meanwhile things went too well for the Germans. A few mistakes were to rob them of the decisive victory which they thought was theirs at the beginning of September. The first mistake was made by Moltke, the commander-in-chief, who established his headquarters much too far from his armies and so found it harder and harder to keep himself informed. When he learnt that the Russians, contrary to all expectations, had entered East Prussia on 15 August, he thought it prudent to reinforce his eastern armies and so ward off invasion. He removed two army corps from the right flank of the German forces in the west, thus dangerously weakening the element on which depended the success of the Schlieffen plan. Thanks to this assistance Hindenburg was able to crush the Russians, but these troops were badly missed at a critical moment on the western front. The Russian ally had kept his word, but at the cost of a heavy defeat. The second mistake was made by von Klück, the commander of the 1st German army, who thought it was more important to conform to the rules of the *Kriegspiel* than to the orders which he had been given. He had been told to direct his troops to the southwest in the direction of Pontoise and to invest Paris. But how could he resist the temptation to encircle the bulk of the French forces by cutting down to the south-east? On 3 September Galliéni was informed that the 1st German army was heading south-east, avoiding Paris and presenting its right flank to the French 6th reserve army. In addition, von Klück, by advancing more rapidly than had Bülow on his left, had exposed his other flank to attacks from the British, who were exhausted but had arrived in good order in the region situated between Mormant and Tournan. Furthermore, as the allied armies now enjoyed superiority in numbers (fifty-six divisions against forty), Galliéni judged that he could launch a counter-attack. On 4 September he won over Joffre, who had been thinking of joining battle further south. Joffre in his turn persuaded French, who was at first very unwilling. The battle started on 5 September with Maunoury's attack on von Klück, and it became general on 6 September following Joffre's famous order of the day which enjoined everyone 'to let themselves be killed on the spot rather than retreat'. It took a decisive turn on 8 September when French and Franchet d'Espérey, taking advantage of a gap between the armies of von Klück and Bülow, broke through on the Ourcq causing a general withdrawal of the German right flank. On the 9th and the 10th the Germans looked for a success on their left flank, but Sarrail held on at Verdun in a desperate situation, and the manœuvre failed. On the 10th Moltke ordered a general withdrawal to a line running from Nancy to the Vesle.

The 'race to the sea'

However, the allied powers were unable to exploit the results of this undoubted victory to the full. The troops were exhausted and, above all, there was a shortage of munitions. Settling on well-sited ground such as the hills of Champagne, Chemin des Dames and the disused quarries of the Soissonnais, the retreating German armies were able to establish themselves in trenches and could not be dislodged. The allies on their side began to dig in, and the front became immovable. There remained the possibility of turning the flanks on the west. Each side attempted it, but the attacks of one came up against the trenches of the other, and the decision had to be sought further north. So there followed, between 12 September and 13 November, a series of engagements, the 'race to the sea', after which a continuous line of trenches was consolidated from the Oise to Ypres and Nieuport. A double line of trenches, protected by barbed wire, prevented all movement over seven hundred kilometres. Contrary to all forecasts, neither side had won. In spite of terrible casualties on both sides (in five months the French army lost more than 900,000 men, of whom 300,000 were known to have died; the German army lost 750,000), the struggle had to be continued, new troops equipped and new ways of combat invented.

'*All quiet on the western front*'

In 1915 the forces of the Anglo-French enjoyed numerical superiority in the trenches, which extended altogether from Belfort to Nieuport. The German general staff, in its efforts to achieve a decisive victory in the east, had removed troops from the west, relying on material superiority, e.g. in artillery and concrete emplacements.

On the French side, adaptation to this siege warfare was carried out haphazardly. Their trenches were far less well maintained than the enemy's for want of materials such as appropriate timber and cement. Mud, rats and vermin added to the appalling discomfort of the troops, who also lacked suitable weapons. The Saint-Etienne machine-gun was fragile and jammed easily. Mortars and small trench cannon, the *crapouillots*, became available far too slowly.

In these conditions, attacks made on the enemy lines without destroying their barbed wire and their machine-gun nests could not lead to any result, however spirited the attack. In places where the attackers had the good fortune to capture the first line of trenches on a narrow front, they then found that there was a second impenetrable line a few hundred yards further on.

The wisest plan would perhaps have been to wait until a great effort on the part of the war industries had produced powerful enough weapons to shatter the defensive capacity of the enemy on a broad front. This would

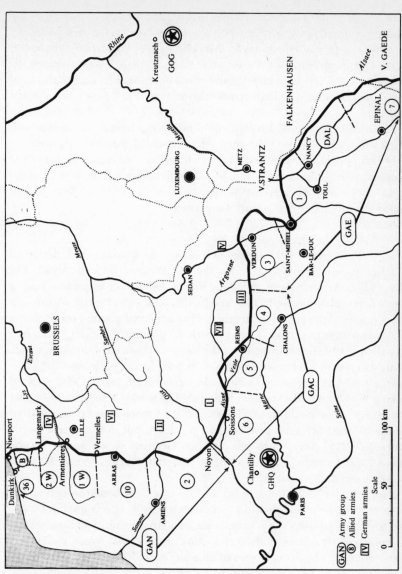

The organisation of the front on 1 July 1915. (Ministère de la Guerre, Ecoles militaires, *Cours d'histoire. III. La Guerre mondiale (1914/18),* Maps and sketches, Paris, Imprimerie nationale, 1920.)

have involved much heavy artillery and a prodigious quantity of shells, mortars, grenades, etc. New weapons would probably have been found, for there was no lack of inventors. In this sphere the French were outstripped by the Germans, who used poison gas from April 1915 onwards against the British at Ypres (without any decisive result once the surprise wore off) and also flamethrowers. The British were also getting ahead, producing the first tanks.

Meanwhile Joffre and his staff could not resign themselves to inaction. Their argument was that the enemy had removed many troops from the west to supply their needs on the eastern front, so it was up to the French to support their Russian ally and to take advantage of their substantial superiority in numbers. Above all they believed in 'the breakthrough' and hoped thereby to resume a war of movement.

'*I'm nibbling at them ...*'

Throughout 1915 a series of fresh attacks was launched, first of all in Champagne (January–March), then in Woëvre (March–April), but above all in Artois, where on 9 May it was thought for a moment that 'a breakthrough had been effected', and finally, on a wider front, in Artois and Champagne at the end of September. They achieved no solid result. News of this spread into the back areas where the obstinacy of GHQ, who had launched costly attacks on south of the Vosges at the end of the year, struck many as criminal. This sentiment was echoed in the parliamentary commissions and in ministerial offices. In defending himself Joffre stopped talking big about a 'breakthrough' and said he simply wanted to 'nibble at the enemy'. How could this be believed when French losses (four hundred thousand dead or taken prisoner and a million put out of action in the course of 1915) were much heavier then German losses, and when the morale of the troops, which had been high at the beginning of the year, began to sag dangerously?

However, Joffre did not give up the idea of a clear breakthrough on the western front, believing that this was the only way to a decision. But he was prepared to wait until the accumulation of a large quantity of armaments, and particularly of heavy artillery worthy of the name, would give him a better chance. The French were to attack on a widened front with thirty-nine divisions and 1,700 pieces of heavy artillery; the British would attack with fifty-two divisions on a forty-kilometre front, while the Russians would attack in the east. As the British would not be ready before the summer because of the slow progress of conscription, which had been adopted on 25 May 1916, this great offensive was postponed until the beginning of July.

Verdun

The next German initiative seemed to put everything into question. Falkenhayn gave up the eastern offensives, much to Hindenburg's disapproval, for fear of getting lost in the vast Russian spaces without a conclusive result. Instead, he decided to launch an attack on Verdun. No doubt he also counted on achieving the breakthrough that had so far proved impossible; and at least the results would be spectacular. The fortified zone, which formed a wedge in the German front, was surrounded on three sides and would be difficult and costly to defend. Yet the French would be obliged to defend it, for the fall of such a symbolic place would have a disastrous effect on public opinion. The French could only defend it at the price of such losses that their army would wear itself out, thereby becoming incapable of launching the attack which they had planned for the summer.

Once again the action was better organised by the enemy. French GHQ, which was taken up with preparations for the Somme attack, did not believe in this German offensive in spite of corroborative information. The Verdun sector of the front was neglected and even the heavy artillery was removed from the forts. Parliament was informed of this, for the deputy Driant, a lieutenant-colonel in the *infantry* at Bois des Caures, had at the end of December alerted the army commission, of which he was a member. When comments on the subject were made to Joffre, he replied loftily that everything had been provided for. When the first German attacks occurred on 21 February 1916, it was obvious that the High Command had been continuously misinformed. Furthermore, ugly rumours were going around about its responsibility for the first setbacks and the slowness of its reactions. However, the defenders of Verdun, left largely to their own devices in this inferno, weathered the first shock without any disastrous breakdown. On 24 February Joffre gave Pétain the difficult task of holding the ground without excessive casualties, so that the planned offensive should not be compromised. For the first time an important battle was being directed by a 'top general', who was anxious to spare the lives of his troops and to assure himself of the equipment that was necessary for such an operation. Pétain was able to hang on by dint of protesting at the meanness of GHQ in the matter of troops and munitions, and by assuring supplies for the front-line troops by an intensive use of road transport – the famous *Voie sacrée*. He also learnt through experience to perfect certain tactical manœuvres, especially by a rational use of artillery barrages with the help of observation planes. However, the French losses up to July were enormous and exceeded those of the attacking Germans. As Pétain had insisted, in spite of Joffre's doubts, regular relief of the defenders on the spot was organised, so that practically the whole of the French army had some experience of the miseries of Verdun. Finally, the demands of this battle forced GHQ to reduce the scale of the operations planned on the Somme.

The Somme

Joffre, however, decided to stick to his plan, with less troops and on a reduced front. After a continuous bombardment of unprecedented vio-

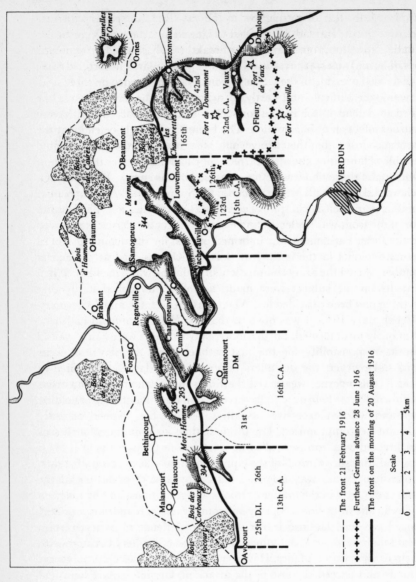

The victory at Verdun, 20–6 August 1917. (Ministère de la Guerre, Ecoles militaires, *Cours d'histoire*. III. *La Guerre mondiale (1914/18)*, Maps and sketches, Paris, Imprimerie nationale, 1920.)

– – – – The front 21 February 1916

✛ ✛ ✛ ✛ Furthest German advance 28 June 1916
✛ ✛ ✛ ✛

───── The front on the morning of 20 August 1916

Scale

0   1   2   3   4   5 km

lence, thanks to the heavy artillery that was at last adequate and to air forces that controlled the sky, the allied infantry with superior equipment (grenade launchers, machine-guns, mortars and thirty-seven cannon) achieved some important results in the first days of the offensive at fairly low cost. Yet from 10 July onwards the enemy pulled their forces together and recovered themselves. However, to achieve this, the Germans, just like the French at Verdun, had to 'plug' the line in a manner that led to the exhaustion of most of their forces. For them the 'hell of the Somme' was the equivalent of the 'hell of Verdun' for the *poilus*. But they hung on, and the war of attrition was resumed over the whole front, with the troops, again decimated, becoming a prey to fatigue and disillusionment. In the autumn the slaughter had to cease without any of the objectives (e.g. Bapaume, Péronne, Nesle) having been won. The allies had lost 615,000 men and the Germans 650,000. The only comfort was that Verdun seemed definitely to have been saved and there were even some successful counter-offensives in that sector during October and November which enabled nearly all the ground lost since February to be re-won. But there was no sign of an end to a conflict that was becoming more and more murderous.

Useless diversions

Meanwhile the campaigns on the 'secondary fronts', as the French were pleased to call them, met with the same disappointments. The idea of starting a new theatre of operations, which was mooted here and there before the end of 1914, arose from two considerations – strategic and diplomatic. For instance, Turkey, Bulgaria, Rumania, Greece and Italy were liable to join the side which could boast of promising successes somewhere in the Balkans.

But the idea came up against many obstacles and contradictions. Diplomatic complications were inevitable because Russian, and later Italian, war aims in the Balkans seriously worried the British, the Bulgars, the Greeks and the Serbs. Above all, operations of this kind involved removing men and material from the main front. Furthermore, geography favoured the central powers as they were well placed to reply to attacks on their periphery; their geographical situation enabling them to operate on interior lines, whereas their allies would encounter very serious logistical problems.

The Dardanelles expedition

Nevertheless, at the beginning of 1915, the British got agreement for a first operation against Turkey. However, in the face of the opposition of Joffre and French and doubts on Kitchener's part, it was decided to launch an essentially naval expedition directed against the Dardanelles straits, which among other things would open up an important route for supplying the Russians. After a first attack on 19 February 1915 against the Turkish batteries on the Dardanelles, the allied fleet arrived on 18 March to force the straits; but these were better protected than expected and were successfully defended by the Turks, who sank one-third of the allied ships engaged in the operation. The High Command then obtained the despatch of a Franco-British expeditionary corps, which secured a foothold on the Gallipoli peninsular in an unbelievable confusion of disorder and improvisation. The invaders were severely mauled by the Turks and, after hanging on until December without any noticeable result, had to re-embark in a hurry. The straits remained closed and, on top of it all, the episode aroused the suspicions of the Russians, who detected a menace to their own ambitions on Constantinople. At least the operation helped to bring about the entry of Italy into the war against Austria-Hungary.

Salonika

In the meantime an imbroglio was developing in the Balkans, which led to another disappointing expedition. In September 1915, just as Falkenhayn was preparing an Austro-German operation against Serbia, Bulgaria appeared to rally to the side of the central powers. The Greeks had certainly promised help to the Serbs against the Bulgars, but on condition that they stationed 150,000 men on the Vardar – an impossible task if they were crushed in the north! The allies however thought they would play a very clever game. They made contradictory promises to the Greeks and the Bulgars and then, violating Greek neutrality, began to land an expeditionary corps at Salonika, which was to rush from there to the help of the Serbs. The results were worse than mediocre. On 5 October the Bulgars joined the central powers, thus ensuring the defeat of the Serbian army. As for the expeditionary corps in Salonika, it found itself isolated, in deplorable sanitary conditions and amid Greeks who were now hostile. It could only stay put and impotently witness the crushing of the Serbian army. The remains of the old King Peter's forces, after a painful retreat across Albania, arived at Corfu which was occupied by the French. They were then shipped to Salonika where Sarrail, under Joffre's watchful eye, was reduced to a demoralising inaction. This led Clemenceau, who had always opposed far-flung expeditions, to denounce loudly, and not without justice, 'the shirkers of Salonika'.

Similar disappointments followed in 1916. In the spring the Austrian offensive against Italy, after initial successes, lost momentum so that there too the front was static. Following on the success of the Russian offensive launched on 22 May in Galicia under General Brussilov, the Rumanians decided to enter the war on the side of the allied powers on 27 August. But by that time the Russians were already exhausted and the German reply was like lightning. In a few weeks the Rumanian army was crushed without any possibility of a Russian or an allied reaction.

All this contributed to a poisoning of the atmosphere in France wherever discussions in political and military circles were taking place and decisions being worked out. The military chiefs disagreed amongst themselves. Each had his own clique in the commissions and in the government. Intrigue followed intrigue, and gradually Joffre and his entourage became less convincing in their replies, especially as events were often contradicting their forecasts. The result was that, after the Somme, while GHQ still talked of a decisive offensive, all those who were worried by this apparent lack of realism banded together and challenged the commander-in-chief. After a series of humiliating discussions, Joffre accepted his removal from command, somewhat cheered by the award of a marshal's baton.

The economic and naval war

From the outbreak of hostilities the belligerents sought to strangle their opponents economically by using the blockade weapon, which had played such an important role in the Napoleonic wars.

As soon as the front stabilised, largely as the result of supplies running out, the two camps resumed their international trade with feverish activity. For the allies who controlled the seas, this only posed financial problems. The Germans on the other hand were subjected to the effects of the blockade imposed by their adversaries – a blockade made all the more vigorous by the allies deliberately flouting the international conventions, which regulated this form of warfare in defence of neutral rights. For the central powers would have been able, through Sweden and Holland, to keep up their foreign trade without much difficulty if these conventions had been respected, and that would have nullified the effects of the blockade. The Americans, however, protested vigorously against this violation; and, as there could be no question of breaking with a power on whom they largely depended for supplies, the allies could not push their contempt for international law too far. There were gaps therefore in the blockade of Germany, rendering it largely ineffective.

In February 1915 the central powers thought they could take advantage from the discontent provoked among the neutral powers by the behaviour of the allies by crippling in their turn the whole of their opponents' merchant fleet through the use of submarines. This type of vessel was only vulnerable on the high seas if it surfaced; so the Germans announced that they would sink without warning all merchant ships sailing in British waters. It meant risking the lives of the passengers and crews, i.e. civilians, including neutrals. This violation of human rights was much more brutal than what the allies had done. So there was a reversal of public opinion in

America, especially after the torpedoing of the *Lusitania*, a British liner, on 7 May 1915, which cost the lives of about two thousand civilians, among them 118 Americans. After an extremely tough note from President Wilson had been delivered to the central powers on 13 May, the Kaiser was forced in June to promise an end to such practices. From that moment the submarine war lost much of its effectiveness.

The allies on the other hand had profited from these events to reinforce the blockade of Germany, which had hitherto been far from watertight. The British in particular decided to limit the entry into European countries of certain strategic materials to the quantity which those neutrals might reasonably require for their own use. To arrive at such rationing, reference was made to pre-war deliveries. The blockade of Germany became more effective thanks to this rationing system. Not only were strategic metals such as copper soon in short supply, but also foodstuffs, e.g. meat, fertilisers and cotton. Yet American pressure still prevented a total embargo. German chemists, well served by a powerful industry, learnt how to perfect *ersatz* materials, and recovery of non-ferrous metals was organised. It became evident in 1916 that, thanks to these German measures, the blockade could never be a decisive weapon, however much damage it inflicted on the feeding and economy of Germany.

At the same time the huge naval armaments that had been built up before the war, causing considerable international tension, had achieved nothing. After the rapid sinking of a few German ships on the high seas in 1914, the bulk of the *Kriegsmarine* stayed in port. It ventured out at the beginning of 1916 to fight an indecisive battle at Jutland on 31 January; then it settled once again in its bases.

Both the economic and then the naval war showed themselves incapable of obtaining the decisive results expected of them

3

The birth of the war economy, 1914–16

The belief current everywhere, in government as well as in military circles, that the war would only last a very short time, was largely based on the reasoning of the economists. Nothing had been prepared for a long conflict. There had been a thorough general mobilisation, production was at a standstill, and external trade was slowed up all the more because the seas were no longer safe. Moratoria decreed by the special powers granted to the government on 4 August had stopped the general course of business. As for the day-to-day needs of the army, these had to be satisfied by the requisitioning system, which now applied to the whole country by the extension of the state of the siege. But once the 'race to the sea' was over and the front had stabilised, once the prospect of a military decision at the most optimistic estimate had been postponed to the following spring, a restoration of economic activity had to be improvised.

It was a task that was all the harder because in this respect geography worked especially in France's disfavour. Deprived of territory in the north and east where many of her modern industries were to be found, she had to replace from scratch certain basic elements of her war production, e.g. ninety-five blast-furnaces out of a total of 123, half the mines of the Nord and the Pas-de-Calais as well as a large number of her engineering, chemical and textile plants had fallen into enemy hands. So above all it was important, outside the occupied zone, to put France back to work.

Special postings and 'shirkers'

To this end it was necessary to bring indispensable personnel back from the front – factory workers, managers and contractors. There was no lack of conflict between the war industries and the general staff on the subject of 'special releases'. The general staff was inclined to think that the home front authorities were exaggerating their needs in order to get 'cushy' jobs for those who had good connections, so doing harm both to the troops' morale and to military efficiency by reducing excessively (in their view) the numbers at the front. The industrialists on their side tended to criticise bitterly a High Command that at the same time demanded ample supplies

21

and was reluctant to release from the front the specialists that were essential for the war factories. One also noticed friction between the peasants and the rest of the social categories, e.g. managers, civil servants and qualified operatives. The presence of farm workers did not seem to be necessary in the back areas for the revival of production. In case of need it was easier to fill their places with women, old people and children. On the other hand, factory workers and managers seemed more and more indispensable in the back areas, i.e. in safety.

As a result there was general bad feeling, first of all at the front, where the departures of specially posted personnel could not fail to be noted with disfavour by those who remained in the hell of the trenches – for the latter very much tended to suspect the real reasons for these postings. Indeed, even when the reasons were clear and obvious, there was often much difficulty in arriving at a foolproof criterion for choice. Take for example a coalmining foreman. Who could be more indispensable and harder to replace at a moment's notice in a mine than a worker of this sort? But also what service a specialist of this kind could render in the front-lines with their trenches, their saps and their dug-outs!

Of course, an operation on this scale could not be carried out without many abuses that were as often the result of unintentional administrative mistakes as of wangling by scroungers – all of which made for an uneasy atmosphere. The unexpected presence of a solicitor or a pharmacist in a workshop making shells (it actually happened) could not help causing eyebrows to rise.

The bad feeling that resulted was all the more dangerous for the morale of the country at war in that it soon took on a political aspect. In order to speed industrial recovery an appeal was naturally made to those who, as trade unionists or socialists, enjoyed wide influence in working-class circles and who, because of their adherence to the Union Sacrée, were well disposed to use their influence to help the war effort. In the spring of 1915, an old *normalien* Albert Thomas, who was an *agrégé de philosophie* and disciple of Jaurès, was appointed to the ministry of war as under-secretary in charge of artillery and military equipment. From the autumn of 1914 onwards he had shown real qualities as an organiser. He wielded strong influence in socialist and trade-union circles, and he managed very quickly to build up a good relationship with the leaders of industry, which was vital for the effective revival of the economy. Everyone, both on the staff and in the government, was at the outset unanimous in congratulating themselves on this happy choice.

Albert Thomas

However, it was not to be expected that a socialist would also take over Millerand's ideas. For the latter thought that the specially posted conscripts, being still mobilised, should not enjoy any of those rights so grudgingly granted to industrial workers by pre-war social legislation. 'There are no more workers' rights, no more social laws. There is nothing now but war', he proclaimed on 13 January 1915. This position was all the more untenable morally because not only was not the slightest thing done to reduce the enormous profits which contractors derived from the special conditions, but, worse still, these same contractors were offered vast subsidies and captive markets. And it was unrealistic seeing that the working-class movement was functioning again with its traditional structures intact, especially the trade unions, and could move into action to defend workers' rights.

Unlike Millerand, Albert Thomas sought the support of the workers. He negotiated wages and conditions of work with them. Even better, he requested and obtained their support in the search for qualified workers to bring back from the front. As it was often among these workers that the unions had found the most willing recruits before the war, it looked from the outside as if the under-secretary was going about his special postings in a thoroughly partisan fashion. Such remarks were indeed made from spring 1915 onwards, especially in political circles hostile to the socialists. This happened all the more easily because Alphonse Merrheim, secretary of the Fédération des Métaux in the CGT, i.e. a union much involved in the war industries, was one of the first leaders of the working-class movement to shift away from the position adopted by the CGT's leadership in 1914. He recommended and obtained more vigorous union action which took the form of renewed strikes. The government and employers could only keep this action under control by granting the workers' claims. It should be noted in passing that the movement was on a modest scale: there were ninety-eight strikes in 1915 as compared with 1,073 in 1913. Going even further than that, Merrheim set up within the central committee of the trade-union organisation a movement, albeit a minority one, which proposed to act in the summer of 1915 in favour of the cessation of hostilities.

A disastrous collapse of national unity might have resulted from all this. It was avoided first of all, it must be admitted, by the existence of the censorship, which prevented the inevitable controversies from becoming widely known and potentially dangerous in the current state of public opinion. The worst was also prevented by parliamentary action. From the beginning of 1915 the army commissions in the Chamber, and especially in the Senate, whose members drawn from all parties worked in relatively discreet conditions, gave priority to their search for rules that would be both effective and fair. They were able to work out legislation whose main enactment was *la loi Dalbiez*, named after the radical parliamentarian who steered it through the Chamber in 1915. This law remedied the worst faults of the action already taken to re-organise production. Unfortunately, in assuming responsibility for actions which were bound, as we have seen, to include mistakes and injustices that were evident to a sensitive public opinion, parliament was inevitably providing ammunition for an anti-parliamentarism that was already powerful. One can only ascribe the relatively easy way in which such a delicate operation was carried through to a generally felt desire not to create bad feeling. This moderation could only be explained by a persistence of most of those sentiments which had inspired reasonable behaviour at the outbreak of hostilities.

Whatever the explanation, it was now possible to obtain for industry, and notably for the war factories, some of the manpower and management that were indispensable. However, for the heavy tasks the government decided to resort to colonial labour, and even to coolies press-ganged in China. That was how the future minister Chou En-lai spent time in the Saint-Etienne region, and how Ho Chi-minh arrived in France. Above all, one could call on female labour to serve in occupations that were not usually theirs – women tram-conductors and shell-makers soon became commonplace. In rural areas women, hitherto confined to the humble work of the kitchen, the farmyard and the gleaning, now learnt the masculine tasks of ploughing, sowing and harvesting. There is no doubt that this development counted a great deal in the movement for female emancipation which began to develop after the war.

It was very often necessary to build completely new factories for this labour force, because the conversion of existing firms in the unoccupied parts of the country was far from being able to satisfy the enormous requirements of a war that was becoming more and more industrial.

Here again there were possibilities of serious disagreement and friction. To begin with, there were the arsenals, which were state enterprises run by military managements which often included outstanding technicians. Their personnel professed great contempt for private contractors, whose honesty they challenged, if not their competence. In return the industrialists readily accused these civil servants of narrow-mindedness, bureaucratic ways of thought and even an excessive perfectionism in their work. In spite of the extremely trying circumstances they did not hesitate to denounce to the government attitudes which they considered criminal. The Michelins and the Renaults, for instance, besieged politicians and ministers and even the President of the Republic himself. They carried all the more conviction in these government circles because many politicians had very long-established relations with the world of business, not to mention important common interests. Furthermore, in their strictures on the nationalised establishments, the industrialists could often denounce their socialist doctrines, which they were very ready to confuse with what remained of the *colbertiste* tradition in France's war industry.

The war factories

After an initial period of confusion, the systems began to function smoothly. Albert Thomas, who was in charge, won a very good reputation. There was now only the question of dealing with experienced industrialists, but these usually did not have the necessary financial resources to build the new plant which the situation required. So of course the state came to the rescue, on terms that were extremely advantageous to industry. The products were bound to be profitable because their sale, at prices that were often very favourable to the vendor, was obviously without risk of any sort. So the suppliers of war materials made fabulous profits. This was acceptable when the recipient of these favours was capable of introducing mass-production methods suited to the army's needs, e.g. a young *polytechnicien* called Citroën, owner of a small gear-making business, who built up a factory to make shells on the Quai de Javel in Paris. However, only too often the production of these firms, which cost the public a great deal of money, was a cruel disappointment. Throughout 1915 there were complaints of shells which failed to explode or, worse still, which exploded too soon, killing the battery crews.

There were even graver failures in the more complex industries, especially in aircraft manufacture. Before 1914 the ministry of war had followed a policy of spreading very small orders among all the aircraft and engine manufacturers who were more or less efficient. None of them, with the possible exception of Renault, ran a firm that was capable of supplying the steady output that the developing warfare needed in the second year of the war. Furthermore the excessive variety of models was a serious handicap from every point of view. So the supply services tried to limit the number of models by presenting chosen industrialists with the means of building up full-scale firms, and asking them to allow their rivals to build their engines against the payment of high royalties. There then followed a long series of intrigues and feuds with each aircraft manufacturer trying to create a ring of clients in the armed services and using politicians to boost their products and play down those of their rivals. Meanwhile those who got the contracts showed the greatest reluctance to pass on their industrial secrets to the sub-contractors who had been foisted on them.

All this explains how the public got the idea that every 'war contractor' was also a 'war profiteer', whose quick riches seemed all the more scandalous because they were shown off with vulgar ostentation. Meanwhile the infantryman received a few centimes a day, and this fact was shamelessly used as an argument to denounce the immorality of workers asking for increases in wages.

It is worth noting that it was the deliberate choice of the socialist Albert Thomas to keep profit as the essential motive for industrial effort and to exclude all levy on profits. Although most of his political colleagues favoured the latter policy, Thomas decided to confine himself to a strict control of prices, with hard bargaining in individual cases.

It is also worthy of remark that, whatever the political and moral problems posed by this policy, the results in practice were undeniable. The French industrial machine, whose directors were thus able to combine patriotism and profit in an easy partnership, responded more than adequately to the formidable demands imposed by the war. (On this, and on the importance of Albert Thomas, see an interesting collection of articles in P. Fridenson (ed.), *1914–1918, L'Autre Front.*)

Recourse to borrowing

The war effort required an enormous increase in state expenditure. Already in 1915 the budget deficit had reached eighteen billion francs, whereas in 1913 the whole of the state's receipts amounted to five billion francs, of which only three and a half billion came from taxes. This very modest levy did not enable the state, even in times of peace, to meet its expenses, and it had to resort to undated loans. Meanwhile the floating debt increased dangerously. It was to remedy this situation that Joseph Caillaux had recommended an income tax, which was unknown in France. We know how unpopular he became as a result of this move. Income tax was eventually approved in July 1914 by the Senate, who had for a long time refused to follow the Chamber in this matter. However, it was very soon decided that circumstances, in particular the mobilisation of the tax inspectors, prevented the launching of this tax before the end of hostilities. Therefore, as there could be no question of increasing existing taxes, other expedients had to be found.

The imposition of a forced currency decreed by the government on 5 August 1914 made recourse to Banque de France loans easier. It was a very dangerous policy and could lead to currency depreciation, of which the French collective memory could recall a famous example – the promissory notes of the French Revolution period. Besides, it could endanger external payments, which were absolutely vital. True, the Banque de France by an agreement dated 21 September 1914 had authorised new loans to the state, which brought the total up to six billion francs. But everyone agreed that it could only be a temporary palliative.

In these circumstances the finance minister Ribot decided on a policy of raising loans. But the success of such a policy in the form of undated stock, either non-repayable or only gradually repayable at a remote date, was not at all assured, either because savers had little confidence in it or because they could not tie up money for the long periods required. The failure of a loan of eight hundred million francs launched on 7 July 1914, which had only drawn in 380 million francs by the beginning of September, tended to confirm these forecasts. In addition, the moratoria voted at the beginning of the war made these loans difficult. For all these reasons the loans could only be offered with much higher rates of interest than in the past. So Ribot and Pallain, the governor of the Banque de France, devised a means of short-term borrowing in the form of treasury bonds with very early maturity, underwritten by the banks with the deposit funds they held. These treasury bonds, which became national defence bonds (giving the subscriber a feeling of having done his patriotic duty), carried a high interest rate of 5 per cent. They were perpetually renewable every three months. Finally, they were available to the general public at tax offices and post offices in denominations of 100, 500 and 1,000 francs. The issue of these short-term bonds, first approved by parliament in November 1915, provided a very large portion of the resources necessary for the financing of the war, though it led to a mounting burden of debt. Of the 157 billion gold francs of estimated public expenditure between August 1914 and October 1919, forty-five billion came from tax receipts as against sixty billion provided by defence bonds, while other borrowing provided the rest. It is true that part of this debt was carried by an upward price movement, which was largely the result of the increase in the fiduciary note issue. The latter increased from an index of 107 in January 1915 to 147 in January 1916 (100 = 4th quarter of 1914), while the wholesale price index went up in the same period from ten to sixty-three points. This is a rate of inflation which we would consider moderate nowadays, but its social effects were then considerable because it especially affected the very many people living on fixed incomes and a large proportion of wage-earners, who in the current situation could not obtain incomes corresponding to the rise in living costs.

Purchases abroad and external debts

However much increase there was in national production as a result of these actions, it could never be enough. There had to be recourse to imports from abroad for raw materials, foodstuffs and a large variety of machines. In spite of the strictest control the value of these imports did not cease to increase, rising from 6.4 to 11 billion francs between 1914 and 1915.

A state-run organisation proved necessary to rationalise and keep control of these purchases. Agreements concluded between the allies in August 1914, then on 15 January and 5 February 1915, arranged a system of financial co-operation. This however did not exempt France from increasing indebtedness vis-à-vis Great Britain. Even more money was owed to the United States, where France's purchases were always on the increase. The stock of foreign investments held by French financiers included few that were acceptable to the Americans, who refused the Russian, Ottoman and Austro-Hungarian bonds so well loved of French banks. France had to resort to private borrowing in the United States so as not to lose all her reserves of gold. However, the loan which Ribot tried to place through

Morgan Brothers in April 1915 was a failure, and the franc started a dangerous slide in New York. The allied finance ministers met at Boulogne on 21 August 1915 in anxious mood and decided to give an inter-allied mission the task of getting a better deal. In October a syndicate of important New York banks arranged a loan of five hundred million dollars at 5 per cent, of which 193 million was allotted to France. Other borrowing, on more and more onerous terms, followed soon after.

One must conclude therefore that, although the French continued in the 1914–18 war to give their own and their children's blood freely, they were the most reluctant of all nations to give their money. The systematic recourse to borrowing in order to finance the war was not matched by a fiscal effort such as occurred elsewhere. The idea of income tax continued to provoke horror, and the parliamentary commissions continued to study ways and means of implementing it with a measured slowness that looked very much like deliberate stonewalling. The policy of taxing the super-profits of war contractors ought to have been adopted in view of mounting scandals. Instead it gave rise to interminable discussions in those same commissions, where the ardent defenders of liberalism launched vigorous rearguard actions, not without success, against everything which in their eyes smacked of a hated fiscal inquisition.

At the end of 1916, in spite of the prodigious cost of errors and prejudices, the rich and powerful had not made the very necessary examination of their consciences, nor had they revised their pre-war values as they should have done.

4

The different forms of wartime government

On 4 August 1914, after having voted the laws introduced by the government, which amounted to delegating very wide powers to the executive, the two chambers rose, leaving their presidents the option of recalling them if the occasion demanded. In fact the government saw itself as possessed of quasi-dictatorial powers – very temporary, it was thought, since it was everyone's opinion that matters would be sorted out by the end of the year.

The 'dictatorship' of GHQ

The first signs of this suspension of normal powers were the ministerial changes that were made without consulting parliament on 26 August 1914. It was a question of giving concrete form to the Union Sacrée, the ideal to which both parliament and public opinion had so spectacularly given support. The result was far from perfect because one of the policital leaders victorious at the recent general election, Joseph Caillaux, remained outside the government. This was partly because of the sudden unpopularity of his pacifist politics and partly because of the dramatic aftermath of the Calmette affair. Furthermore, Clemenceau, another personality of the first rank, who did not spare his criticism of the civil and military authorities, peremptorily refused to take any part in the coalition government. So, paradoxically, one saw the losers in the last elections coming back to power. Ribot took over finance, Delcassé foreign affairs and Briand justice. The socialists pursued their outright support for the Union Sacrée to its logical conclusion, and one saw Marcel Sembat (public works) and Jules Guesde himself (minister without portfolio) entering the government, which would have been inconceivable a month earlier. Finally, Messimy, the minister of war, had several times shown signs of emotional instability since mobilisation and was replaced by Millerand, This appointment was of considerable importance at the time because the new minister saw his role as subordinate to that of the commander-in-chief. The result of this was that the enormous powers granted to the government by the extension of the 'state of war' to the whole country from 8 September onwards were in fact passed to the military authorities. So one can rightly talk of a real dictatorship of Joffre, which was reinforced by the government's departure to Bordeaux.

The victory on the Marne removed most of the criticism that had been directed at the commander-in-chief, thanks to the enormous prestige which he now enjoyed. But the strictures revived once the 'race to the sea' was over, once the front had stabilised and there was disturbing news of errors by the service ministries, especially in connection with the artillery and medical services. Furthermore, as it was clear that the war was going to last, it became intolerable and dangerous that the dictatorship of GHQ should continue.

The return of parliament

On 20 December the government returned to Paris, followed by the deputies. On 22 and 23 December an extraordinary session of parliament was held and the budget credits were voted. Then, as laid down in the 1875 constitution, the ordinary session opened on the second Tuesday in January 1915. There was therefore a return to the legal forms of the parliamentary regime. This did not mean that there was to be a return to pre-1914 practice. In any case, the state of the war and the Union Sacrée put a brake on political infighting, and a sort of truce prevailed. Furthermore, the public powers, both government and parliament, found themselves in an entirely novel situation. In the first place a certain anaesthesia of public opinion was evident. This was mainly due to the censorship, which was theoretically military but in fact was also political, for the necessity of keeping up the nation's morale was invoked to prevent the publication of news that could excite dangerous controversy. This anaesthesia was reinforced by the fact that a large number of the most active citizens were mobilised. The ones who remained in the towns and villages of the back areas were mostly old people, women and children, and these were all from the start submitted to the 'brainwashing' of the press.

Moreover, the situation helped to bring discredit on the civil powers. The military was now king. The great chiefs like Joffre and Galliéni became the objects of a real personality cult, often projected by naive and puerile propaganda. Opinion was widespread that they were the real leaders of the country, and it was up to the politicians to be at their service. The war gave an added force to an anti-parliamentary feeling that was always latent in France; and this was actively encouraged by certain military chiefs who were anti-democratic by family tradition or caste feeling. These officers, who despised the civilian (*le pékin* as they called him) were particularly hostile towards professional politicians, the embodiment of evil in their eyes. At the beginning of 1915, Lyautey deplored the return of parliament which, he thought, would spoil the new 'moral health' regained during the silence of parliament in 1914. This did not prevent each 'big chief' from having a certain number of faithful friends in government circles, his 'gang', whose job was to fight for his career and glory and to denigrate the actions of his rivals. In these conditions parliament tended to become no more than a rubber-stamping operation.

The elimination of Millerand

At the beginning of 1915 the number of politicians who were aware of serious mistakes in the organisation and running of war services was enough to stir parliament into action. The deputies who came back from the front (Tardieu, for example) had desperate stories to tell about the lack of guns and munitions and the failures of the medical services. Constituents in the army wrote in the same vein.

So it was against the ministry of war that parliament first acted, considering not without justice that it bore most of the responsibility for the failures. Or rather the parliamentary commissions acted, for their discussions took place in a relatively small circle and behind closed doors, which avoided the embarrassments of a public debate. These commissions very soon demanded to send investigators into the relevant offices to see the necessary documents. In the case of establishments which were not in the war zones, it was impossible to refuse these requests, for which there were well-established precedents, at least in the case of the great finance, army and health commissions. Thus certain deficiencies in the administration of the war ministry came to light, notably in the artillery section. Its chief, General Baquet, persisted in neglecting the heavy artillery, as he did not believe in its effectiveness. So the ministers and the president of the Council, invoking the necessity of leaving elbow room to the High Command, tended to deny or cover up the shortcomings of their services. Certain deputies and senators, therefore, who were members of the important commissions, very soon decided to intervene, to shake up the administrators, to propose remedies and to replace the inefficient or recalcitrant. The left was quick to invoke the example of the French Revolution, with its missions of the Convention, to justify this procedure.

Millerand was, at first, the main target of attack. The dismissal of General Baquet was eventually obtained, not by a public debate, but by a ceaseless harassing of ministers, the president of the Council and Poincaré himself. Albert Thomas, who, as we have already seen, had been appointed under-secretary, took Baquet's place on 20 May 1915. The deputies were driven to a pitch of fury when Millerand awarded Baquet the cross of a commander in the Legion of Honour. But his ministry started to slip out of his grasp, especially when new under-secretaries were imposed on him.

Behind Millerand, Joffre became the real target, especially of the army commission run by Doumer, Charles Humbert, Freycinet, Jules Jeanneney and, above all, Clemenceau. Joffre was criticised mainly for refusing all parliamentary control in the military zone, where he aimed at continuing to exercise the same dictatorship as in 1914; but there were some who deplored his way of handling the military operations, e.g. his brutal and ineffective offensives. They condemned, too, his assumption of total control of the war effort. It was felt that this was a government responsibility, but the commander-in-chief did not seem to agree. A parallel government, which was said to be the only effective power, had installed itself at Chantilly, sovereign and untouchable.

Meanwhile the press, with a few exceptions such as *Le Journal* and, above all, Clemenceau's *L'Homme enchaîné*, vied with each other in praising the army leaders and abusing the politicians, who did not get nearly enough protection from the censorship. Furthermore, in parliament, and even in the commissions, there were plenty of politicians ready to speak out, as did the deputy Colliard, before the army commission: 'Beware! If you create an incident, you will have neither the chamber nor the nation with you. In the back areas you already enjoy every liberty. As for the army zone, I know only one thing: if you want to go there, you'd better take your guns and your arms with you.' By their constant recriminations and their repeated demands for interviews with ministers, the commissions were wearing the government down. Viviani complained to Poincaré: 'Even physically I can no longer keep going. I spend three or four hours every day in the commissions .... I return exhausted to my office where the senators and deputies get at me. I haven't a moment to work in peace.' (R. Poincaré, *Au service de la France* ... , vol. VI, p. 277.)

The entry of Bulgaria into the war, which was a serious setback for Delcassé's policy, completed the discredit and exhaustion of the cabinet. Viviani yielded to the pressure brought by a delegation to Poincaré led by Combes, handing in his resignation on 25 October 1915. The new cabinet led by Briand reflected a widening of the Union Sacrée. One of the most representative of the deputies of the Catholic right, Denys Cochin, was now added to the socialists Guesde, Sembat and Thomas, who retained their portfolios. In compensation a post of minister of state was given to Combes. But the most important change was that Millerand left, being replaced by Galliéni, who was flanked, like his predecessor, by four secretaries of state. The Chamber unanimously gave its vote of confidence to the new government.

The main points of parliamentary criticism

However, this new striking example of the Union Sacrée was not going to prevent the birth of an opposition that varied in its motivation and was nourished by disappointment with the conduct of the war. If we simplify matters, we can detect three themes that provoked these defections:

government attempts at a certain amount of social reform, the relations of this government with the High Command, and the problem of war aims.

The reforming tendencies of Albert Thomas

As regards the first theme, the controversy essentially centred on the activities of Albert Thomas. There is little doubt – and the papers of this statesman preserved at the national archives clearly prove it – that Thomas intended to use his tenure of a key national defence post to promote the reforming socialism which he favoured. He sought to bring about a new relationship between workers and their employers; and he managed to keep on good terms with the latter. He set up commissions on conditions of work, housing, female labour, hygiene, etc., in which employers and union representatives worked out new rules. He favoured the creation of co-operatives to reduce the cost of living, believing that these would be one of the main elements of a socialist society. As we have already seen, it became clear by 1916 that the liberal mechanisms of the economy could not be left to work by themselves and that food distribution and production would have to be controlled. This could only please Thomas as it was a practical demonstration of the excellence of socialist ideas. He devoted much attention to the building of a large arsenal at Roanne in which, besides new methods of management and manufacture, a new style of relationship between the managing director, the technicians and the workers was to be created. With great enthusiasm the young minister hoped, as did the other socialist ministers, 'to be able to convince the nation of the excellence and fertility of his ideas, so that, at the hour of victory, French democracy, having confidence in the socialists and stimulated by their efforts, would blossom out in new and just institutions' (*The Times*, 6 September 1916).

This way of turning the Union Sacrée to good account provoked some opposition. In the socialist party there were murmurings against the betrayal inherent in the doctrine and actions of the minister, and they made fun of his jingoistic speeches delivered from the top of piles of shells in war factories. However, the authority of Albert Thomas, backed up by the excellence of his management, was such that up to 1917 this opposition had little importance, especially in the parliamentary group. The criticism of the defenders of liberalism, from the radical party to the extreme right, was to prove more worrying, for they were full of apprehension about this minister's 'collectivism'. In certain criticisms of his management, usually hardly justified, there emerged real fear of the future consequences of those practices which he had initiated.

Parliament and the High Command

The second theme of recriminations in parliament, and the most important one, was the question of the High Command and its relations with the civil authority. From this point of view, the arrival of Galliéni at the war ministry was greeted with hope. He was known to be on fairly bad terms with Joffre, and it was thought that the latter would not be able to treat his enquiries and directives with the hauteur of a specialist dealing with an amateur. In addition, the new minister was on the best of terms with parliament (whose role he publicly commended) and the commissions. However, Joffre, threatening periodically to resign, always refused to accept parliamentary control at the front, but the events at Verdun were going to force him to make a few concessions. We have seen how Driant, a deputy and lieutenant-colonel, had in 1915 warned parliament of the defence weaknesses in that sector. On receiving this information Galliéni asked Joffre for details. The generalissimo replied drily that all was for the best at Verdun, and that it was intolerable to be censured on the basis of tales told by members of parliament serving at the front, who thereby showed a serious lack of discipline. This was distasteful to Galliéni, who, as minister, meant to keep for himself the general direction of the war. The first successes of the German attack came at the end of February 1915 and confirmed in a startling way that Driant (who had been killed in the first assaults) was right in his strictures. It needed all Briand's skill to protect the commander-in-chief from these renewed criticisms. First, there was Galliéni, who on 7 March read a note to the Council denouncing the encroachments on government prerogatives, both in internal and in diplomatic affairs. He demanded that these abuses should cease and that there should be a clean sweep of 'generals who are weighed down by out-of-date ideas'. However, the minister of war was by now very ill (he died on 27 May) and he was not in a position to keep up the struggle with the agile Briand. He resigned on 16 March and was replaced by General Roques, another soldier and an ally of Joffre.

Recriminations in parliament did not thereby cease. Briand was forced to grant a secret session (June 1916) in the course of which the High Command was often criticised. To calm the atmosphere the president of the Council had to accept an order of the day stating clearly the principle of parliamentary control at the front. The parliamentary delegates could: 'while not interfering in the conception, direction and execution of operations, exercise on the spot effective control of all services which minister to the needs of the army' (22 June 1916). However, the establishment of this control kept alive the tension between the minister and GHQ on the one hand, who always tried to limit as much as possible the incursions of parliamentarians into the war zone, and on the other hand the commissions, whose demands became more and more pressing and indiscreet.

The quarrel was further inflamed by the Salonika expedition. The government thought they had found an elegant solution to the problem by putting General Sarrail, a 'republican' heartily disliked by Joffre and his entourage, in command of the expeditionary corps. Sarrail was commander-in-chief in the new theatre of operations and was not under Joffre's control, taking his orders direct from the government. However, in Salonika he immediately requested reinforcements which GHQ at Chantilly firmly refused, pleading the needs of the main front. Joffre complained of the manœuvres of Sarrail's political supporters which, he said, damaged his reputation and liberty of action. As soon as Briand took over, he let himself be convinced by this argument and, on 2 December 1915, a decree established the unity of command over all forces, which meant that Sarrail was subordinate to Joffre. The aftermath of the incessant bickering between these two leaders embittered the intrigues and debates in parliament.

War aims

Finally, with the prolongation of the conflict, a growing number of politicians began to ask themselves why the war was being waged. (On this question, cf. P. Renouvin, 'Les Buts de guerre du gouvernement français', *Revue historique du monde contemporain (RHMC)*, January–March 1966, pp. 1–38.) In this they were merely following certain expressions of opinion outside parliament where in 1915 there arose a desire to define more clearly the objectives to be aimed at. The question was important because on the answer depended France's choice of a compromise peace or a German capitulation. This obviously affected the future conduct of the war. At the beginning of hostilities a sort of tacit agreement was arrived at between all parties, based on a programme defined by Viviani on 22 December 1914. This insisted on three conditions following on an allied victory: 'the restitution of violated rights', i.e. the integrity of Belgium, the return 'to the French motherland of provinces that were seized by force', and finally the annihilation of 'Prussian militarism'.

This last condition could give rise to many interpretations. Maurice Barrès, in a series of articles in *L'Echo de Paris* between February and April 1915, put forward an interpretation which gave a frankly imperialist look to France's war aims. In order to ensure his country's security against a new German aggression, he proposed to detach from the Reich all the provinces to the west of the Rhine. Similar ideas were taken up by historians of the Sorbonne, particularly by Lavisse and Aulard. The latter made a special point of recalling the attitude of the Rhine peoples during the French Revolution, which gave a more republican tinge to this point of view. Certain parliamentarians, especially Antonin Dubost, the president of the Senate, advocated annexation. A Comité de la Rive Gauche du Rhin was formed which propagated these views by distributing tracts and postcards.

For different reasons, certain leading elements of industry also furthered annexation programmes. In October 1915 Robert Pinot, the secretary-general of the Comité des Forges addressed a note to the economic expansion commission of the Senate, pointing out that large amounts of iron ore would result from the return of Lorraine to France and that this would lead to a shortage of coal. He therefore advocated the annexation of the Saar coalfield.

However, these schemes for annexation met with fierce opposition in left and extreme left circles, in spite of their acceptance of the concept of a victorious peace. In fact, the socialists had, despite pressure from foreign colleagues, given up the idea of a referendum, among the peoples concerned, on the return to France of the provinces lost in 1871. But there was total rejection of new annexations or the dismemberment of Germany. They hoped rather that the war would deliver that country from its military caste which had imposed aggression on her, and would make her a reliable member of an international society, restored to peace by the establishment of collective security.

The civil power for a long time preferred to remain vague about their attitude to these various proposals. The censorship forced Barrès to stop his campaign and parliament also quietened down without much protest.

However, the debate was resumed in the middle of 1916. First, Poincaré, in the course of a visit to Nancy in May, mentioned in a speech the necessity of not being content to exact from Germany 'a peace that would leave her strong enough to go to war again and would allow a threat to hang constantly over Europe'. He clearly showed himself favourable to projects that incorporated the Rhine left bank and the Saar. This move did not fail to stir the Caillaux radicals and the socialists, amongst whom a pacifist minority was now particularly active. Then, towards July 1916 Briand, who up to now had shown himself very reticent on these questions, came out into the open, probably as the result of an optimism arising from an improvement in the military situation. The censorship relaxed its grip and campaigns for annexation started up again in the press. Then Poincaré asked Joffre to give him a report on the military conditions of an armistice. The commander-in-chief replied in August with a memorandum on peace terms which advocated the formation of a Rhineland state integrated with France in a customs union. Finally, on 7 October Briand sounded out the presidents of the Chambers, Dubost and Deschanel, as well as Léon Bourgeois and Freycinet, on a policy for the Rhine.

It is true that matters moved slowly. On 19 January 1917, when questioned by a socialist deputy on war aims, the president of the Council obtained the postponement of the discussion *sine die* by a crushing majority (437 votes against 57). In the opinion of most parliamentarians the moment had not yet come to discuss peace problems in public. The government on the other hand was more preoccupied by the subject than ever and adopted as its policy the aims of the groups who sought to annex the Saar and the left bank of the Rhine, intending to give these provinces the status of neutrality.

Briand was in agreement with the Council and gave a mission led by Gaston Doumergue the task of getting the Russians to accept this policy, which they did in general terms at the beginning of February. In exchange, on 10 March 1917, Briand left Russia 'total freedom as regards the fixing of their western boundaries'. Naturally these negotiations and agreements remained secret for the moment.

The failure to create a war government

Meanwhile parliament was applying more and more pressure on the government. It blamed it openly for its inertia in the conduct of the war and for the excessive liberty of action allowed to the 'government of Chantilly', i.e. to Joffre's GHQ. These criticisms were fuelled by the difficulties which the High Command continued to put in the way of parliamentary control of the war zone, not to mention the setbacks of the Somme offensive, which did not achieve its expected success. In the face of mounting attacks, the government had to accept some new secret committees. After the one that met between 28 November and 7 December Briand had to bring himself to reshuffle his cabinet and also to undertake a thorough reform of the war direction. Imitating Lloyd George he tried to strengthen government action by concentrating it in the hands of a war committee consisting of the president of the Council and only four ministers – war, finance, navy and armaments. It was hoped that this would lead to frequent and effective meetings of a sort that were not possible for over-crowded government committees. Almost at once the government asked parliament for a wide delegation of powers, allowing it to take by special decrees 'all the measures which, by addition to or dispensation from existing laws, will be required by the exigencies of national defence' (14 December 1916). Finally, the government proposed a change in the High Command which was intended to disarm all critics. Joffre became technical adviser to the government and a member of the war committee. Nivelle became commander-in-chief of the armies of the north and north-east, and Sarrail commander-in-chief of the army of the Orient. These two were in sole charge of the operations of their armies and quite independent of Joffre.

However, these reforms hung fire. Joffre soon resigned, with a marshal's baton to sweeten his retirement. Parliament showed such hostility to the delegation of powers demanded by Briand that the government gave up the plan and confined itself to the adoption of a rapid voting procedure for laws that concerned national defence. The war committee remained, but, contrary to what happened in London, it had no powers of its own and was restricted to preparing the decisions that had to be taken at the Council. In short, neither the government nor parliament was disposed to accept fully the reforms which would have brought a real war government into being. The feebleness of the executive, which had characterised political life before the war, was again becoming apparent, and the government was rapidly losing strength. It could not survive the upheaval provoked by Lyautey, the minister of war, who publicly expressed his doubts about the discretion of the deputies. On 18 March Briand handed in his resignation. As if to show a return to the habits of the past, Poincaré called on one of the oldest members of the previous cabinet – Ribot. It was to fall to the lot of this president of the Council, an old hand of the Third Republic, to face the gravest crisis of the war.

5

The civilians' war, 1914–16

Those remaining in civilian life had to adapt themselves gradually to the war, which seemed unending. In spite of the upheaval to society and behaviour, the population behind the lines adjusted itself to circumstances as best it could. Fighting soldiers on leave from the front were often bitter at the apparent ease with which civilians ignored the front and its miseries. 'The nation has adapted itself, the war could last for a hundred years!' was the sardonic comment of Captain Delvert, when passing through Paris on 4 August 1916. (Charles Delvert, *Carnets d'un fantassin*, cited by A. Ducasse, J. Meyer and G. Perreux, *1914–18, Vie et mort des Français*, p. 289.)

The resigned attitude of the peasants
It was in the rural areas that there seemed to be the least change. Of course the men, almost without exception, went off to the front in August 1914. They were generally expected back for the grape harvest. Disillusionment soon followed, and the farms had to do without them. Old men, women and children learnt to take their place and managed this without too much difficulty. However, it is true that shortage of labour was the most serious problem of the countryside throughout the war. One partial remedy was increased foreign labour, which was attracted by the inevitable wage rises brought on by the situation. In 1915, the civil powers sought to control the flow of immigrants by creating a special office. Refugees from the invaded zone, prisoners of war and soldiers on leave also provided valuable help. Here and there, but in a limited way, there was recourse to motorisation and machinery. Nevertheless, the amount of fallow land increased and crop yields diminished. The wheat harvest was eighty-eight million quintals in 1913 and seventy-seven million in 1914, sixty million in 1915 and fifty-eight million in 1916. The loss of harvests in occupied territory was not enough to explain this drop, which continued after the stabilisation of the front. It is true that crops were damaged by harmful wildlife which flourished as a result of the ban on shooting decreed in August 1914. The right to 'destroy game' had to be restored in September 1916, which was a fresh sign of a return to normal.

In spite of these difficulties the general situation favoured the farmers, for the rise in food prices amply made up for certain increased costs, e.g. wages and materials. The needs of the army and the industrial towns, where full employment and rising wages led to an increase in consumption, were such that demand was assured. The state even had to intervene and to fix the price of wheat at thirty-two francs a quintal in 1915 and fifty-three francs a quintal in 1916. The prices of other foodstuffs, whose production was much harder to control, rose even more. This relative material prosperity speeded up certain changes in the rural world that were foreshadowed before the war. Not that patterns of consumption were much altered – it was still very rare for peasants to buy luxury goods, such as the silk stockings that they occasionally liked to acquire. Most profit gained, when it was not simply put by, was spent by tenant farmers and sharecroppers buying up the land that they worked. Small landowners bought up modest plots to round off their properties and, much less often, improved their equipment or animal stock. There was, therefore, movement of property, which was shown up by the continuous increase in tax revenue from sales of real estate. As for day labourers, who were so numerous before the war, some of those who had not been called up were able to leave the land, drawn by what seemed to them very high wages in the war industries, while others, profiting as we have seen from the labour shortage, were able to improve their earning power considerably.

The calm and resignation with which country people on the whole accepted the continuing conflict was partly attributable to the general prosperity that flowed from it. But the war brought its losses too. To realise this one only has to look at the war memorials in the humblest villages. By the end of 1916 there were few families in the country who had not received a visit from the mayor awkwardly and mournfully announcing bad news. However, the great sorrows, in the country more than elsewhere, went unexpressed. Widows, who in any case were usually dressed in black, did not parade their bereavement. Their loss was shared because 'shirkers' hardly existed in rural communities. The parents, wives and children of the dead had already got used to their absence. Everything conspired to muffle the effects of the slaughter, terrible though it was. It took a lot to make the cup run over. Yet in 1916, or even earlier, there were signs of painful weariness and repressed fury. How could these sentiments be usefully expressed? In places where there existed an ancient tradition of the political left combined with agrarian structures (e.g. sharecropping or *fermiers généraux*) that were particularly unfavourable to most country people, one came across an echo of 'pacifist' ideas. This was the case in the Haute-Vienne, where there was a demonstration in May 1915 which led to the formation of a minority pacifist group in the socialist party. This situation in the Haute-Vienne is probably explained by widespread support among the popular masses. 'A sense of weariness that is hard to define is being felt in certain worker and peasant circles, particularly among the latter' wrote an informer of the ministry of the interior. This was also the sentiment in the Allier where the activities of the deputy Brizon, who early on became a critic of the Union Sacrée and a partisan of peace by negotiation, aroused more enthusiasm among the sharecroppers than in working circles. But on the whole, up to 1916, the countryside remained quiet and orderly.

The urban population: workers and middle classes

In the towns, on the other hand, the changes caused by the war were often felt much more directly. General mobilisation had at first suspended nearly all production. We have seen how Albert Thomas was able to organise the release of essential personnel by a system that was controlled by parliament. Thus industrial workers, who had spilt as much blood as the rest in the first year of the war, were now to some extent spared. They also benefited from the wages policy, likewise the work of Albert Thomas. Even so the increase in wages, moderated by this policy until 1916, did not generally compensate for the increase in the cost of living. Relative affluence often came to working-class families as a result of full employment, which automatically boosted consumption. However, wages varied enormously according to sectors and regions, and many workers complained, not without reason, of the high cost of living. For example, women working at home were disgracefully exploited until the beginning of 1916, when a regulation dated 10 July 1915 fixing minimum rates of pay for these workers started to apply. However, the situation of the working classes in the towns was such that, thanks to Albert Thomas' social policies, conflict was almost non-existent until the end of 1916 in spite of difficult economic conditions.

But, for a large section of the middle classes, the situation was disastrous. People living on unearned incomes, members of the liberal professions and even civil servants were very badly hit by the consequences of the war. They were often called up and had to leave their families badly provided for, especially as their social status prevented them from claiming the allowances which for a long time were only paid to the 'needy' who were not liable to direct taxation. Civil service salaries remained static as did income from fixed interest investments. In varying degrees, therefore, the high cost of living was disastrous for this class. Furthermore, members of the middle classes, unlike the workers, were not often recalled from the front; and as their level of education often meant that they were subalterns of the reserve, they had a strong chance of becoming casualties. Often the loss of the father meant that there was very little hope of the family regaining a 'normal' condition of life once the storm was over. Hard times, not to mention destitution, often came to those bourgeois homes whose relative prosperity, saving habits and prudence were a mainstay of the centre parties that enjoyed so much power before the war.

Defeatism

It was not, however, from the ranks of the middle classes that were recruited those who, after 1915, were called 'the defeatists'. These were the people who came to desire a negotiated peace, to put an end to the slaughter, even if it meant abandoning the war aims, e.g. the return of Alsace-Lorraine, that had been unanimously accepted in 1914. There was, indeed, a bourgeois opposition to the war, which first appeared in 1915 and grew in 1916, but it remained limited to restricted circles of intellectuals without wide influence. The same was not true of the working classes.

Certain trade-union leaders, as early as the end of 1914, started to criticise the consequences of the Union Sacrée policy and inter-class collaboration practised by their organisation. Merrheim and Bourderon, in particular, worked to form an opposition inside the CGT, centred on *La Voix ouvrière*. Within the socialist party the criticisms, voiced particularly in the Haute-Vienne federation at the beginning of 1915 and taken up by the Isère and then the Rhône federations, led to a 'pacifist' opposition at the party congress of July 1915 with Jean Longuet, Marx's grandson, at its head. However, no French socialist dared to respond to the invitation put out by the Swiss Grimm to the heads of workers' movements in the belligerent countries, asking them to take part in a conference to discuss ways of bringing about peace. Only the trade unionists Merrheim and Bourderon, who were used to semi-illegal activities, took part in the work of the Zimmerwald conference (5–8 September 1915). On their return, in order to promote the resolutions in favour of a peace without annexations and against belonging to the Union Sacrée, they founded a committee with certain socialists to work for the resumption of international relations. At first, the response was very feeble. However, as the war dragged on and worker discontent increased, this minority group grew in importance. At the socialist congress of 16 April 1916 a motion proposed by them attracted nine hundred votes, against 1,800 for the majority. From May of that year they had in *Le Populaire*, edited by Longuet and printed in Limoges, a press organ with a national readership. But the majority remained unmoved. This was demonstrated when Raffin-Dugens, Alexandre Blanc and Pierre Brizon came back after taking part in the Kienthal conference, which had been organised by a commission set up at Zimmerwald. *L'Humanité* condemned in outraged terms 'the pilgrims of Kienthal', and in *Le Populaire* Longuet himself indicated that, in spite of the conference's conclusions, he would continue to vote for war credits. So there arose a split in the minority between the 'Zimmerwaldians' and the centrists. In August 1916 the party conference condemned 'the dangerous deviationism of Kienthal'.

However, all this did not hinder the progress of pacifism. The military defeats of 1916, the example given by a minority of German socialists and President Wilson's diplomacy in favour of a compromise peace furthered its growth. Brizon's *La Vague* reached the trenches, sowing doubt about the wisdom of a continuation of the struggle. From then onwards defeatism began seriously to worry the country's leaders because its spread among the workers was all too obvious.

The pleasures of the back areas

This mood of defeatism spread all the more easily because in the towns the fortunes made by war profiteers were not only becoming evident but were being openly flaunted. First, there were the profits of tradespeople, large and small, who constantly increased their margins and usually operated in a guaranteed market. Second, there were the manufacturers. We have already seen the facilities granted to them by the armaments and supply policy, but there were no serious restraints on their profits. Finally, there were the middlemen of all sorts, the 'sharks' using their influence and audacity to open up profitable markets to a wide variety of businessmen, in return for fabulous fees. As always, these *nouveaux riches* longed to display the wealth they had so quickly acquired. They shamelessly tore up the rules, whether they were written or tacitly agreed, that had imposed a grey puritanism on civilian life ever since the beginning of the war. Stressing the importance of keeping up the nation's morale and showing the enemy that the country was not sinking, they went in for wartime styles of the most vulgar bad taste and led a life of ostentatious pleasure, with expensive mistresses covered in jewels, late suppers, 'houses of pleasure' and gambling clubs to provide them with amusement.

Such people had been criticised in Bordeaux during the first months of the war when the government had taken refuge there for a while. In the wake of the ministers, their staffs and their mistresses, the town had received a disreputable crowd of people, among whom were the smart set, the *demi-monde*, politicians without much to do and swindlers in search of profitable deals. Bordeaux seemed to wallow in debauchery while catastrophe threatened the rest of the country. The minister Malvy had even seen his reputation tarnished, in spite of the Union Sacrée and the censorship, because of the blatant way in which he was said to have profited from the special circumstances.

During this time Paris had emptied itself in a strange way. On receiving the first bad news from the front, the inhabitants of the smart quarters, anxious to avoid the horrors of a possible siege or a Commune, were seized by violent panic that was reinforced by the pitiable sight of destitute refugees coming from the occupied zones with their tales of horror. Prosperous Parisians jumped on trains and into taxis regardless of cost and fled the capital. Galliéni, on becoming governor of the beleaguered city, was keen to get rid of useless mouths and encouraged as much as he could the departure of Parisians. The town, deserted and without light at night, seemed almost dead to those who stayed behind. But after the battle of the Marne, the stabilisation of the front and the return of the government, everyone felt reassured. The smart set returned and business revived in a remarkable way. The town changed in appearance, for the railway system made it the focus of large-scale movements of people. There were men passing through on leave and ready for adventure; members of the civil service and the censorship, whose numbers were swollen by increased state activity; airmen making frequent trips to the nearby capital, whose rowdy celebrations met with amused indulgence, thanks to their immense prestige; allied servicemen in various uniforms, equally keen to profit from their stay in France and taste the delights of 'Gay Paree'. By 1916 the town had become the capital of pleasure to the great scandal of those who were suffering from the war. And, following the example of Paris, the traditional centres of pleasure regained their lustre. Deauville became even more fashionable than before, in spite of the closure of the casino. The Côte d'Azur welcomed in winter its crowd of well-heeled holiday-makers. In short, while grief and real suffering hid themselves, luxury and pleasure made a vulgar display.

It was in the provinces of France that the war weighed most heavily and most directly. First, the towns and villages in the combat zone, which suffered destructive bombardment. But those who remained there also had opportunities to enrich themselves, supplying goods and services to the troops in the back areas. Traders, both large and small, made quick profits in this way. The French who suffered most were those in the occupied departments. From the very start they had to put up with curfews, arbitrary requisitioning and forced labour. They were menaced with sanctions and exploited by an enemy who was determined to get the most out of them. They suffered appalling hardships, and it was certainly the collective memory of all this that led to the gigantic exodus of May–June 1940. But what could one do for these unfortunate people, except pity them and hope that they would soon be delivered from the enemy?

To sum up, the country settled into the war without excessive upheavals. The necessary disciplines were not imposed. On the economic side the state had only reluctantly, and in an *ad hoc* manner, taken the most urgent measures. It did not manage to impose a more just sharing of sacrifices or a more rational organisation of resources which would have led to economies and greater efficiency. In the last resort the rulers remained loyal to the values of a liberalism that was incompatible with the sort of war that they were trying to wage. Furthermore, in two and a half years external assets were sold to stave off catastrophe, but without much thought of what would happen once credit was exhausted. The spectre of a military dictatorship was in the end dispelled, and the civil powers gradually regained their rights and prerogatives, but instead of a firm direction of the nation one saw a resumption of futile political games, even in the conduct of the war. The country, proud of its unexpected resistance to a powerful and pitiless enemy, still had little idea of its precarious position and the risks it was running.

6

The 1917 crisis

In the course of 1917 the allies met with a series of reverses, some of which were so serious that some thought that the war was lost.

Military reverses

The dismissal of Joffre in December 1916 opened the way to Nivelle. This general had won sudden popularity after some successful actions fought by his troops against the forts of Douaumont and Vaux, which he recaptured from the Germans without excessive losses. His protestantism won him the confidence of lay circles, who were often suspicious of 'Jesuit generals'. His perfect knowledge of English encouraged the hope of excellent relations with the allies. He had prepared a plan which he expounded with great verve to anyone who cared to listen. This plan, which owed a lot to that of Joffre, depended on coordinated offensives by all the allies. On the western front operations could start on 1 February. The French would attack between the Somme and the Oise and the British between Bapaume and Vimy, aiming by the 'Nivelle tactics' tried out at Verdun at an effect of surprise, which would lead to a breakthrough and a rapid exploitation of success. The plan then counted on Russian and Italian offensives to complete the rout of the enemy.

However, an exceptionally cold winter forced the postponement of the intended offensive. The temperature dropped to −20°C at the beginning of February. The effects of the freeze, and the ensuing thaw, paralysed the armies for a time. Then, in mid-March, came the news of the first Russian Revolution. It is true that the provisional government installed after the Tsar's abdication stated clearly that the struggle would continue; but the soviet in the capital demanded the end of hostilities, and anarchy spread through the army. It became obvious that, whatever the outcome of events in Russia, no planned offensive could seriously be counted on from that quarter. The Italians reacted at once to this news and let it be known that, as they feared an Austro-German attack reinforced by Russia's defection, they had decided to wait a while and to postpone the proposed operations.

Chemin des Dames

In the meantime, the French, with some surprise, watched a German manœuvre that completely changed the map of the front in the sector where the attack was planned to take place. Counting on all-out submarine warfare to achieve victory, Hindenburg decided to adopt a purely defensive attitude on the western front, shortening the line from south of Arras to a point east of Soissons. After constructing a remarkable series of fortifications, called the 'Siegfried Line', from Cambrai to Chemin des Dames in positions particularly well suited to defence, the Germans withdrew from the old front-line, starting on 24 February, carrying out systematic demolitions in the evacuated area to a depth of fifteen to forty kilometres. This made the occupation of the new front-line very difficult for the French and British. Incredulous at first and taken completely by surprise, Nivelle regarded the withdrawal as a victory and saw no reason to modify his plan.

This blind recklessness eventually alarmed the government. Lyautey, the minister of war, did not conceal his sceptical attitude to the Nivelle plan, contemptuously calling it 'Kriegspiel'. Painlevé, who replaced him on 20 March, incompetent though he was, also had his doubts. He arranged a meeting of the Supreme War Council on 6 April, with Poincaré in the chair, which was attended by all the corps commanders. He proposed that they should cancel the agreed action and wait for the arrival of American help. Pétain was the only military commander to add his frank scepticism. Nivelle reaffirmed with vigour his complete certainty that a decisive success would result, and at one stage he threatened to resign if he was contradicted. The rest kept silent or supported the plan, so the offensive was approved. However, the commander-in-chief promised, in the case of failure, to stop the action after three days.

On 9 April the British launched a diversionary attack and captured Vimy ridge at heavy cost. On the other hand, another similar operation attempted by Franchet d'Espérey's army in the Saint-Quentin region was a failure. What did this matter to Nivelle, who had decided to launch a decisive assault on 16 April against one of the enemy's strongest positions between the Oise and the high ground of Reims, all along a line of hill-tops where ran the 'Chemin des Dames'? He was so sure of success that he invited a group of parliamentarians to watch the battle.

It was a bloody disaster. There was no effect of surprise because plans of the attack had been circulated long before among troops in the forward positions, and some of these had fallen into enemy hands. The artillery preparation, which had been short but very intensive, was very far from being as effective as at Verdun the year before because the enemy occupied a wider and better fortified front. So none of the conditions essential for the success of 'Nivelle tactics' were present. As at the beginning of the war, the assault troops came up against an enemy that was securely entrenched in pill-boxes and helped by icy fog, which made artillery control and liaison difficult, if not impossible. On 19 April Nivelle called off the main attack in accordance with his promise of the 6th. The French casualties were forty thousand killed and eighty thousand wounded, and the medical services revealed themselves as woefully inadequate. Yet the High Command refused to draw lessons from these events. Believing that the Germans had suffered badly and had hardly any reserves, it continued to order attacks 'of attrition' on different points along the Siegfried Line. These were just as futile and even more costly (if that was possible) than the attack on 16 April. This was enough and Parliament claimed the head of the commander-in-chief. On 16 May, after defending himself for five days against Painlevé's invective, Nivelle gave up his command to Pétain, who on 28 April had been named chief-of-staff of the war ministry. It was already too late. Mutiny had broken out in the French army at the front where the offensives had taken place.

The mutinies

On 4 May one company refused to proceed to Laffaux where an attack was planned for the 5th. The movement spread quickly and refusals to go into action increased. The men said that they did not want to get killed for twenty-five centimes a day, or they repeated a strange rumour that women in the outskirts of Paris were being massacred by Indo-Chinese. At Cœuvres red flags were waved and the *Internationale* was sung. On 29 June two regiments stationed at Soissons suddenly decided to march on Paris to force parliament (which was in fact sitting in secret session to discuss the events) to seek an end to the war. A total of some thirty thousand to forty thousand soldiers during May and June took part in collective acts of disobedience. As for the causes of the movement, most of the generals thought it was the work of secret organisations, which had been allowed to go about their work by the incompetence, inertia and even the connivance of the authorities, especially of Malvy the minister of the interior. According to the generals these organisations worked closely with revolutionaries of every type; they were more or less financed by the enemy and, like their Russian models, sought to bring about France's defeat and the revolution at the same time. Their decisions, passed on by men on leave, had begun to be put into practice by the men at the front. The best of these had already been killed. Among the survivors there were too many cowards, too many weaklings, reluctant to follow the paths of glory. Franchet d'Espérey in particular was an ardent promoter of this idea of a bolshevik plot. This interpretation of the events enabled a direct link to be established between the mutinies and the failure of the Nivelle plan, which protected the High Command from too severe criticism. Certain politicians had talked of dragging Nivelle before the High Court, but he ended up by becoming governor-general of Algeria.

In fact the mutinies were simply a vast protest movement against the disastrous way in which the war was being waged. This explanation was voiced at the time by observers of various political persuasions and has since been confirmed by the research of Guy Pedroncini. (See *Les Mutineries de 1917.*) They were simply a kind of strike on the part of soldiers who had experienced in person the uselessness of the attacks that incompetent leaders were continuing to order. It is true that the pacifist movement, which was rampant among civilians, had succeeded in infiltrating certain front-line regiments, especially through schoolteachers converted to socialism; but it reached precisely those regiments who were not involved in the mutinies. On the contrary, Guy Pedroncini has shown irrefutably that there was a very close correlation, both in time and space, between the mutinies and the launching of attacks in May or June. It is a remarkable fact that the mutineers never tried to fraternise with the enemy and, thanks to the maintenance of discipline in the front-line, never let him get an idea of the gravity of the situation. They simply refused to march and hoped that those in charge would put an end to a war that they clearly could not control. The evidence of the troops' mail, as analysed by the postal censorship, is conclusive on this point.

We can therefore more easily understand how Pétain was able to put an end to the mutinies in an apparently miraculous way. For a long time he had openly supported the continuation of defensive tactics while the French had no clear material superiority, so he was in profound agreement with the basic demands of the fighting soldier. By deciding on 19 May to call a halt to crazy attacks, he gave profound satisfaction to exhausted troops.

With this to his credit, Pétain was able to start taking the army in hand with a mixture of stern, but limited, punishment and various new forms of welfare. By way of the stick, he made military justice take its course: but at the end of 1916 this had been re-organised so that the rights of the defence against arbitrary and subjective judicial decisions were better guaranteed than at the beginning of the war. The number of sentences pronounced totalled 3,427, covering 10 per cent of the mutineers, among which there were 554 death sentences. Forty-nine of those sentenced to death were executed. The repression was harsh enough to give rise to various legends at the front, in particular the rumour of a 'massacre'; for usually the troops never knew what had happened to their comrades who were deported or pardoned. By way of the carrot, Pétain showed the fighting soldier that he appreciated his value, and that he was concerned with his comfort and morale. Open discussions with officers at the front, a fairer distribution of rest periods and leaves, improvements of billets, speeding up of leave trains, etc. were measures that won Pétain the hearts of the army and earned him an amazing and lasting popularity.

Allied reverses

By 20 June the mutinies were no more than a bad memory. But the French army was bogged down again, and looked like remaining so. And the offensives of the other allied armies were hanging fire. In Russia, Kerensky, the head of the provisional government from April 1917 onwards, canvassed the idea of a peace without annexation or sanctions. This was a concession forced on him by the Petrograd soviet, whose influence was as decisive at home as in the army. He was thus able, by a campaign of persuasion, to revive the patriotic spirit for a while. An offensive was launched in Galicia on 1 July. On their side, the Italians were preparing an attack on the Carso front for the beginning of August. Finally, the morale of the British had not cracked at the same time as that of the French, and their commanders were keen to prove it by showing the fighting spirit of their troops. They undertook to carry on, from Cambrai to Passchendaele, the attacks that their allies had abandoned. Nothing positive resulted from all this. The Russian offensive was stopped almost at once by a German counter-offensive. The disintegration of the Russian army became more evident every day. To make matters worse the bolshevik party seized power in Russia between 3 and 7 November. It favoured the immediate conclusion of peace and at the same time the redistribution of all land, which encouraged the mass desertion of soldiers keen to take part in this redistribution. As he had promised, Lenin, now in charge of the new council of people's commissars, immediately opened up talks with the central powers, who could now virtually strip their eastern front to reinforce others. In addition the Germans laid hands on the Ukraine, where they protected the anti-bolshevik government of Petlioura, who gave them a free hand.

Meanwhile the Italians had captured Monte Santo in August at very heavy cost, but without achieving a decisive result. The High Command in that campaign, too, showed a complete disregard of danger. Yet the increase in the number of deserters and soldiers absent without leave was a sign of a poor morale that was perpetuated by the brutality and haughtiness of the commanders. When the Austrians and Germans launched a lightning attack on 23 October with forces that were only slightly superior in strength (forty-four divisions against forty-one), the Italian retreat after the battle of Caporetto turned into a rout. Eight, and then twelve, Anglo-French divisions had to be sent with all speed to restore the situation on the Piave as best they could.

As for the British attacks, doggedly pursued by Douglas Haig throughout the summer and autumn, they achieved no result of importance. Yet tanks, used on a massive scale on 20 November without artillery preparation, did open a breach in the enemy's front at Cambrai, which would not be exploited because the success exceeded expectations. A German counter-attack was able to nullify the gains. At enormous cost of life the British High Command in its turn learnt the futility of traditional offensives. In his turn, also, the British soldier began to know weariness and discouragement.

Submarine warfare

These reverses were all the more serious in that the submarine war, launched by the German High Command at the beginning of 1917, looked for a time like being successful. Their idea was not a new one. It was that by sinking without warning all ships of all nationalities encountered in the waters surrounding the countries of the Entente, they could strangle their economies, and especially Great Britain's, and force them to capitulate. The German chancellor Bethmann-Hollweg, who was frightened of an American intervention in the conflict, was for long opposed to this policy. But the insistence of the general staff finally convinced the Kaiser. On 9 January 1917 the Germans announced the start of all-out submarine warfare, beginning on 1 February.

Admiral von Capelle had stated that it would be enough to sink 600,000 tons of shipping a month in order to succeed. German submarines sent 450,000 tons to the bottom in February, 578,000 in March, 870,000 in April. German hopes were exceeded, panic seized the British admiralty and government. Lord Lansdowne openly advocated suing for peace. Yet gradually answers were found. Anti-submarine mines were manufactured in massive quantities and the dangerous sea-lanes were filled with them. Pressure was applied to secondary powers that were still neutral to make them declare war on Germany. This manœuvre, which had the support of American diplomacy, resulted in the allies obtaining tonnage that the Germans had not bargained for. But, above all, with a slowness which once again showed how leaders could not overcome glaringly obvious pre-judices, a technique was perfected that was to win the submarine war decisively – the convoy system.

This system was suggested by civilians, particularly by mathematicians using the theory of games. They demonstrated that losses would be much less heavy if ships were grouped together, whereas common sense seemed on the contrary to require that they be dispersed to profit from the expanse of ocean. This tactic supposed that warships, rather than pursuing at all speed submarines that were practically invisible, would hang around convoys of cargo ships in order to defend them.

Lloyd George organised a few convoys that were so successful that the admirals had to admit their efficiency. From May onwards the tonnage of ships sunk became less and less, to such a point that the Germans were bound to admit that, although they might be seriously increasing the food supply difficulties of the Entente by this form of warfare, they could no longer expect a decisive victory from it.

At this point the intervention of the United States, provoked as Bethmann-Hollweg foresaw by all-out submarine warfare, was called to play its part. It was probably this error of calculation that cost the central powers their victory at a moment – the terrible winter of 1917 – when all the other events of the war seemed to assure them success.

Rifts in the back areas

The military situation of the Entente could only confirm in their opinions those who for over a year, and for various reasons, had been taking the view that this pointless massacre should be stopped as soon as possible. The historian finds himself in the difficult position of having to distinguish between simple treason, dictated by gain and the pacifist approach, which was inspired both by despair and by the feeling that the nation could not benefit from a prolongation of the conflict. In the 'fight to the finish' camp there were people who mixed the two very different attitudes, which enabled them to discredit the pacifists and more easily to use against them the repressive measures that were available to the state in time of war.

Treason

Fortunately the publication since 1965 of archives that were secret hitherto, especially German archives, now enables us to make the necessary distinction in many cases. (Notably by A. Scherer and J. Grunewald, *L'Allemagne et les problèmes de la paix pendant la première guerre mondiale*, Paris, Presses Universitaires, 1962–78, 4 vols.) These archives show, first of all, that treason for financial gain spread to circles relatively close to the government and, in particular, to parliament. This was true of the activities of an obscure radical deputy called Turmel who, having been rash enough to hide a sum of Swiss money, fruits of his espionage, in his desk, was unmasked almost by accident and eventually executed. Then there was the senator Charles Humbert, who was well known for his pre-war indictment of the deficiencies in the French artillery, was an influential member of the Senate's army commission and far removed from parliamentary circles that were favourable to peace. He had to resign his seat when it was discovered that the newspaper which he ran, *Le Journal*, had been bought by German money.

Another press scandal concerned *Le Bonnet rouge*, for it was established that this paper also was financed by German money, and this was even more serious. For one thing, at the time of the 1914 elections, the director of the paper, Vigo, also called Almeyreda, a former anarchist turned radical, supported the campaign of Joseph Caillaux. True, the latter always denied having retained links with the suspect *Le Bonnet rouge* gang, and not a shred of proof was adduced to refute this claim. However, the affair gave useful ammunition to those who wanted to damage the former president of the Council. For another thing, the enquiry held after Almeyreda's arrest made it clear that the minister of the interior, Malvy, had received him and had even made certain advances to him from secret funds. In his own defence he argued, as was certainly true, that in this way he hoped to exercise more control on leftist circles, where *Le Bonnet rouge* carried influence. However, this was all grist to the mills of those who wanted Malvy's downfall.

But, nothing was known until recent years of the activities of the radical deputy Accambray, former *polytechnicien*, artillery officer and from the outbreak of war, member of the Chamber's army commission. German sources have now proved that he passed information to the enemy.

However, not all 'pacifists' were enemy agents in 1917. Their motives were diverse, as were their objectives, but they all agreed that means must urgently be found to put an end to the war.

'Bourgeois' pacifism

Joseph Caillaux's past was bound to lead him to condemn the war as absurd. Before the war he had supported Franco-German concord at a time when mounting jingoism made this attitude difficult to sustain; and his role in the Moroccan crisis of 1911 was significant. At the time of the crisis of July 1914 he was unable to intervene despite the success won by his supporters in the recent parliamentary elections. We have already mentioned the disreputable press campaign by the journalist Calmette, which had driven Caillaux's wife, at her wits' end, to assassinate her husband's persecutor. Caillaux was forced to withdraw from politics by this scandal, which suited his opponents very well. But he was still very much of the opinion that the war was a catastrophe both for France and for the whole of Europe. He thought that the continent would lose its position in the world and, what is more, would be submerged by revolutionary movements, to which he was vigorously opposed.

For all these reasons Caillaux had in 1915, by the choice of his contacts and confidants, recklessly expressed his belief in the necessity of ending the war and seeking a compromise peace. Furthermore, he was convinced (wrongly, as we now know) that he could find currents of opinion in the enemy ranks that resembled his own, and that were strong enough to lead to peace. Finally, he was convinced, and not without reason, that a section of the 'fight to the finish' party belonging to the right and the extreme right was preparing, thanks to the prolongation of the conflict, to overthrow the Republic and seize permanent power. In the hope of checking this move, Caillaux had envisaged a constitutional reform, strengthening the powers of the executive and severely punishing this type of intrigue, in the event of his coming to power. Imprudently he had noted these ideas on some documents that he had locked up in a bank safe in Rome.

However, Caillaux remained an isolated figure, both in parliament and in the opinion of the public. The Ligue Républicaine which he formed only managed to recruit personalities of the second rank, in particular the socialist Pierre Laval and the radical Augagneur; most of the socialists were highly suspicious of him.

Yet, when the events of 1917 made many politicians doubt eventual victory, it was towards Caillaux that they turned. In the autumn, when Poincaré was saying that at least one-third of the deputies were hoping for peace without daring to say so, Caillaux looked like the man capable of finding that peace, and people almost openly talked of a ministry being given to him.

Pacifism and the working class

As for the working class, it found itself deeply divided. The events and difficulties of 1917 helped to swell the numbers of those who listened to the supporters of a rapid peace. They were brought to this point of view by a general feeling of capitalist exploitation. This was fuelled by the rapid rise in the cost of living, by poor working conditions, particularly in the war factories that had been hurriedly built (long hours, discomfort, defective equipment that often led to accidents, etc.), and finally by the rationing of certain foods and of coal, which had become scarce because of the harshness of the winter.

Strikes were much more numerous and more serious than in the previous years: 696, involving 293,810 strikers of whom 104,589 were in the Seine department alone, against 314, involving 41,000, in 1916. And the suppression of the strikes was difficult, especially when women were among the workers. Unlike their male colleagues they could ignore threats of mobilisation and drafting to the front. Pacifist slogans often appeared in the meetings and demonstrations that followed the strikes. They showed the growing influence exerted by the trade-union minority that was hostile to the Union Sacrée and its consequences.

The 'Zimmerwald' party, whose influence so far had been slight, won more and more recruits. Merrheim had for two years, in spite of various threats, shown his hostility to a war that he considered to be the work of greedy capitalists, and his wish for a peace without strings won by the combined action of proletarians in the nations at war. He now inspired within the Fédération des Métaux a movement of opinion that was much strengthened by the events of 1917.

Jouhaux, who kept aloof from the politically most advanced elements in the trade unions, was now forced to take this minor but real current of opinion seriously. He did not give up his policy of union presence in the organisations that ran the economy, which were getting more numerous as difficulties mounted; not did he stop union participation in the work of national defence. However, he did use his good standing with the government to dissuade them from exercising the sanctions on Merrheim and his colleagues that the right and the extreme right, i.e. Maurras, Daudet, Clemenceau and others, were demanding.

The Stockholm conference

The minority support for an unconditional peace was also gaining ground among the socialists. It was, above all, the developing situation in Russia that was shaking the party. The February revolution, which brought to its knees an autocratic regime that was unanimously condemned, was bound to win general sympathy. At first the majority of the party even thought that the Entente would be strengthened by an enthusiastic rallying of the Russian people to their country's defence. This was the thesis of *L'Humanité* when the Tsar's fall was announced. At this junction the Petrograd soviet on 14 March 1917, in defiance of the provisional government, launched an appeal to the peoples of all countries at war for a peace without annexations or sanctions. The provisional government under Kerensky, wishing to block the progress of the bolsheviks, who were using this appeal as a springboard to power, felt bound to take over the manœuvre as their own. The menshevik Tseretelli at this point became the theoretician of an action which, in dissociating the Russian government from all ambitions of annexation, would (he hoped) gain the support of the socialist parties in all countries at war. These would bring pressure to bear on their respective governments, and a way to peace would be found on the lines of the 14 March manifesto. To achieve this a meeting of the Socialist International would be necessary. On a Dutch initiative the secretary of the Socialist International convened such a conference of national party representatives at Stockholm on 15 May.

The Petrograd soviet's manifesto of 14 March was bound to cause embarrassment to many French socialists because of the Alsace-Lorraine problem. In their eyes this war aim was in no sense imperialist or annexationist. It simply restored lands seized by Bismarck contrary to international law. The German socialists generally expressed just the opposite view: the annexed territories of Alsace and Lorraine had in the end become German lands, and their acquisition by France would be pure robbery. Albert Thomas on the one hand and Moutet and Cachin on the other were despatched to Russia with the government's blessing to present the problem, and in reply the Russian socialists suggested a plebiscite to find out the views of the peoples concerned, to be carried out after the evacuation of all armed forces from the territories.

In spite of this thorny problem, Tseretelli's idea could not fail to win support among many socialists, because it rendered possible the conclusion of a peace without defeat arranged with the Socialist International's help, and it would certainly bring great prestige to the party. The discussion on the merits of sending French socialist delegates to the conference brought about a regrouping of tendencies, with minority members like Longuet and majority members like Cachin united in favour of participation. From that moment a centre group came into existence supporting a peace without winners or losers, and this soon became the majority group within the party. They asked the government to grant passports to their delegates. At one moment, at the beginning of the summer, there were vast hopes in the air. In parliament Pierre Laval announced to everyone the approach of peace. But disappointment soon followed. It became clear that in no country except Russia were the socialists united or influential enough to impose such a revision of war aims on their respective governments. The British government was the first to demur, followed by Pétain who stated clearly that he would be unable to control the army if the conference took place. Finally, Ribot too decided against it. Although they maintained a formal request for the passports, the socialists accepted the rebuff. Their acquiescence was encouraged by the absence of public support.

These moves did at least lead a few months later to the break-up of the Union Sacrée. Within the party, a majority now emerged to condemn socialist participation in the war government. After Ribot's fall on 12 September 1917, Albert Thomas, to his great regret, had to give up his ministry, and no other socialist took his place.

This pacifism was not specifically working class. The country people, whose morale had on the whole been very high so far, were also inclined in that direction. As there has been no special research on the subject, we can only take note of some symptomatic details. For example, an informer reported on the situation in the Allier in March 1917, saying that Brizon, a minority socialist deputy, was strangely enough winning more support in the villages than in the industrial centres of Montluçon and Moulin (Archives Nationales, Albert Thomas Papers, 94 AP 258). In a quite different region where there was no leader of Brizon's stature to give this pacifism an aspect of cohesion, a letter of the historian Albert Mathiez to Albert Thomas on 3 October 1917 reported: 'The women of this region do not want to sow the fields because of an absurd belief they have that by refusing they will bring the war to an end.' (*Ibid.*)

But the French supporters of a compromise peace did not find the public support that would have helped them to overcome their own divisions and suspicions. And it has been asserted that, even if they could have got this support and taken power, the war was going so well for the central powers that only a heavy defeat suffered by the Entente could have moved the

Reich to end the conflict. It is true that the same did not apply for Austria-Hungary, the Reich's main ally, who was very hard-pressed; but this power only played a secondary role in the conduct of the war.

Secret negotiations

This weakness was to be shown up by the various attempts at secret negotiation made in the course of 1917. These negotiations were suspected by the public and aroused hope at times, but they all ended in failure because the various points of view were utterly incompatible.

The most coherent of these attempts was the one made at the beginning of 1917 by the young Charles I, who had only just become emperor and was well aware of the dangers that beset the Double Monarchy. He used as his intermediary with the French and British governments Prince Sixtus of Bourbon-Parma, at the time an artillery officer in a Belgian regiment. The proposals which the prince handed to Poincaré on 31 March were accompanied by a commentary that hinted that Austria would be ready to force Germany's hand if necessary. They seemed worthy of serious consideration by the President of the Republic, by Ribot and by Lloyd George. The emperor agreed to support 'by all available means' the French claims affecting Alsace-Lorraine. He agreed also to the complete restoration of Belgium. But he said nothing about Italy. When in April Sonnino, the Italian foreign minister, was informed of the 31 March proposals, he demanded that the secret treaty of 1915 be respected and he refused all concessions on this point. Furthermore, it soon emerged that Prince Sixtus, when he mooted a possible separate peace with Austria, had probably only consulted Charles I's views, and that in any case Prince Czernin, the Austrian foreign minister, was unequivocally opposed to this idea. What was more, Charles I's soundings of the German government turned out very disappointing. At first the chancellor Bethmann-Hollweg had indeed planned to restore a few southern cantons of Alsace to France, but in exchange for the Briey basin, which was of course unacceptable to the French. Charles I then laid siege to his powerful ally and, using the argument of his armies' extreme exhaustion, proposed a swap of Alsace-Lorraine for Poland, which Austria would give up entirely to Germany, renouncing all territorial claims in that country, including those in Galicia. In mid-April, being convinced that the success of the submarine war and the collapse of Russia guaranteed a victory in the near future, Wilhelm II took up an uncompromising position and was quite unmoved by Austria's veiled threat of a separate peace. The negotiations petered out in May with Ribot not even replying to Charles I's last notes.

In this whole affair the young emperor seems to have sought a compromise peace in all sincerity. But he ran up against Italian intransigence and, above all, against the opposition of Germany, who at the time was convinced of gaining victory before long.

One can gather from this failure, and others that are not worthy of note here, that the gulf still separating the war aims of the two alliances was such that a pacifist policy pursued by the French government could certainly not have succeeded. The German general staff, who carried more and more weight, had given up none of their war aims in the west and would only cease fighting after France had been reduced to secondary power status by the loss of all its industrial regions in the north and east. French renunciation of the one war aim on which its citizens were agreed – Alsace-Lorraine – did not strike their opponents as a concession. In such conditions no outright peace was possible and no compromise conceivable. There was only a choice between defeat, which some saw as imminent after the reverses of 1917, or victory which would be won in a final effort, made possible in these last months of 1917 by American help and the moral recovery of the army.

The political crisis

The crisis affecting the army and the nation's morale was bound to lead to a political crisis, which was now a possibility thanks to the return of the political game. It would continue until the end of the year. More than ever before, the government seemed to be dangerously feeble, and this at a time when energetic action on the part of the executive was called for. However, Painlevé, minister of war in the Ribot cabinet, knew how to resolve the command crisis caused by the failure of Nivelle's offensive.

On 29 April he promoted General Pétain, whom he had supported in political circles, to be chief of the general staff. The latter was charged with the general running of the war within the government, while the commander-in-chief was in control of military operations. It was not a solution that was likely to last, for Pétain had never lost a chance of expressing his poor opinion of Nivelle's grandiose operations. The result was that on 15 May the Council, in spite of Malvy's objections, decided to request the resignation of the commander-in-chief. This was obtained the next day, but not without difficulty.

Pétain, 'asked for by the whole army' according to Painlevé, became commander-in-chief of the armies of the north and north-east, while Foch, recalled from the disfavour into which he fell after Joffre's eclipse, replaced him as chief of the general staff. This solution, based on the system adopted by the British, was to prove lasting and succeeded in calming ruffled feelings in parliament. But the problem of government control in the war zone, which GHQ continued to oppose, still persisted until a circular of 28 October settled the matter by insisting on the demands of the commissions and by laying down the rights and duties of their delegates in the war zones.

However, the government was losing its support. The right-wing parties in the Chamber listened sympathetically to the campaigns against Malvy, particularly those of the Action Française, who blamed him for the reverses of 16 April and for the mutinies. His 'feebleness' in dealing with the left was unpopular with the right-wing, especially as it proved expensive for the employers, who were forced to give way to the strikers. It was also unpopular with the middle classes and the peasants, who were often shocked by the workers' claims. Clemenceau in a Senate secret committee led the final assault and forced Malvy, and then Ribot, to resign. Painlevé's ministry, which followed in September, was not joined by the socialists. It was torn by internal dissension and shaken by the Italian disaster at Caporetto, so that it was turned out of office on 13 November by a mixed collection of socialists, who counted on the crisis to bring them back to power, and right-wing deputies, who thought that excessive concessions had been made to these same socialists.

On 15 November 1917 Poincaré, hoping perhaps to wear out a man whom he disliked, called on Clemenceau to form a government.

The entry of Clemenceau on the scene
'The Tiger' was at once ready to take command. The day after his arrival he formed his government team and he presented it to the Chamber on 19 November. In a moving and vigorous speech he laid down his aims for a victorious peace: 'we present ourselves to you with one thought – total war'. On recovery at home: 'There have been mistakes. Let our sole thought be to repair them.' On the fight against all defeatism: 'Alas, there have also been crimes, crimes against France, which call for prompt punishment. We solemnly undertake before you that justice will be done strictly according to the law ... No more pacifist campaigns, no more German intrigues, no treason, no semi-treason. Just war, war, and nothing but war.'

The Chamber, mesmerised, gave him a vote of confidence by 418 votes to sixty-five. The new president of the Council was an old man; yet, for all his seventy-six years, he was in astonishing physical condition and kept himself fit by daily Swedish drill. He was a born fighter. As he had a caustic tongue and superb skill in banter and repartee he had for a long time been the terror of successive governments, whom he turned out of office by his savage speeches. He had started his political career at the time of the disastrous siege of Paris and the Commune, and he had been on the extreme left of the parliaments which followed. A native of the Vendée, unshakeably republican, anti-clerical to the marrow, a passionate *dreyfusard* (he founded *L'Aurore* at the time of the affair) he felt nothing but loathing for collectivist doctrines and detested pacifism, as much through his temperament as his beliefs.

The outbreak of war found him a senator for the Var. From the start, he never ceased denouncing all those, civil or military, who held the controls of power. He gave himself free rein in his violent attacks on ministers and on the army staff. He condemned all blunders in his paper *L'Homme libre*, which became *L'Homme enchaîné* after the censorship had in vain tried to quieten him down. His criticisms had certainly not increased his number of friends; all the more so because, whenever invited to enter ministerial coalitions, he always refused in no uncertain terms, letting it be known that he was awaiting the moment when he would have to be put in charge of affairs. But how could he expect an invitation from Poincaré, against whom he had fought stubbornly in the presidential elections and upon whom he heaped his sarcasms?

The Senate's army commission had in the end made him their chairman. The fact was that he was gradually becoming as popular in the country as at the front, in spite of the attacks of his enemies – the socialists, trade unionists, clerics and monarchists. He had been one of the few to oppose excessive brainwashing and to make the country aware of the truth, however disagreeable it might be. So much so that people complained that, because of his pessimism, he was quoted at length in the press that the Germans ran in the invaded regions. But, in the end, people admired him for his attitude which events had justified and which had not caused him to despair – indeed quite the contrary. Furthermore, he had made a habit of visiting the trenches, hustling the army leaders, frowning at the encroachments of the army chaplains, joking with the troops and jeering at the enemy when he came in sight of their lines. Thus he had made a reputation with the soldiery for fearlessness and drive, which was not shared by other politicians who ventured into the war zone.

In the summer of 1917, Clemenceau had led the attack on Malvy's feebleness towards defeatists and traitors. In 1914 he had not approved of the minister of the interior's gamble and the scrapping of the *carnet B*. He wanted at that time to arrest a few agitators and make the socialists feel the weight of suspicion caused by their pacifism. The revival of the working-class movement in 1916 and 1917 infuriated him. His attitude found support in the public at large, not only in the traditional right but also in the middle classes, even those of a radical persuasion, and among socialists still imbued with a concern for national defence.

A new phenomenon was appearing in political life. A man without much parliamentary support, and politically isolated from the important groups in the Chamber, was enjoying in the country a popularity which gained strength without his depending, as Boulanger had done, on a critique of the regime and the institutions. The events of 1917 handed him power against all parliamentary arithmetic. This power was all the more 'personal' in that, in forming his cabinet, he guarded against doling out the usual favours. He became minister of war himself and replied to Painlevé's suggestion that some of his colleagues should be kept: 'I'm burning everything, even the furniture!' The foreign affairs portfolio, another key post, was awarded to a fairly unknown parliamentarian but a faithful friend of long standing, Stephen Pichon. The ministry of the interior went to the insignificant Pams, whom Clemenceau had unsuccessfully supported as candidate for the Elysée against Poincaré.

Thus he kept all important decisions for himself. The meetings of the council of ministers lost all importance and indeed became very infrequent. The President of the Republic was thus isolated. In this manner the problem of the war government was solved.

7

Dealing with the crisis, then victory

The elements of recovery

Among so many disasters afflicting the Entente there was one new element whose importance, as we have seen, had been most unwisely ignored by the leaders of the Reich and which was to be of the first importance – American intervention. The entry of the world's greatest economic power into the fray was a decisive factor, and it largely compensated for Russia's defection. But the military leaders were generally unaware of this because America, who had no military tradition and practically no arms, was not considered a factor of much importance.

American aid and economic mobilisation

From the economic and financial point of view, American support was to enable the Entente powers at the beginning of 1917 to extricate themselves from an almost hopeless situation. In fact, on the eve of American entry into the war, the state of the allies' finances was such that it was becoming impossible for them to buy supplies and food in the United States. France had run up a debt of eight hundred million dollars to pay for her purchases, to which had to be added a two hundred million dollar advance from the British treasury. The latter, who had an overdraft of four hundred million dollars in New York banks, declared that no more credit was available without cover or the surrender of gold. The cash holding of the Banque de France was gravely depleted and fell to 3,252 million francs at the end of March 1917. Furthermore, the bank had guaranteed the foreign operations of French firms to the tune of more than five hundred million francs. The fiduciary note issue amounted to 18.5 billion francs. Ribot maintained at this time that there could be no question of reducing the cash holding any further if catastrophe were to be avoided. As no new loan was possible in the United States without guarantees, which France was unable to provide, one could see how well justified was the pessimism of the minister of finance before the parliamentary commissions in March 1917. However, immediately after the declaration of war against Germany,

President Wilson made the necessary arrangements to provide the Entente powers with the financial assistance most urgently needed. In April 1917 a law authorised the federal government to issue five billion dollars' worth of long-term bonds and two billion dollars' worth of one-year debentures. Three billion dollars could be lent to the allied governments with the money gathered in this way. So there came into existence a system of agreements between governments, instead of private loans that were becoming more and more onerous and hard to find. At the end of April, a delegation with Viviani as chairman managed to obtain a loan of two hundred million dollars from the United States for current purposes, then, starting in July, a loan of 160 million dollars per month.

These enormous demands (which were likewise made by Great Britain and the other allies) did not fail to arouse the fears of the American treasury, who were careful to impose conditions which had to be accepted. The first was that this money had to be used solely for purchases from American industry and agriculture. However, the Americans ended up by agreeing provisionally to support the franc, which would have crashed without this help. In addition, the proclamation of a state of war in that paradise of free enterprise had been attended by the granting of exceptional powers to the President. He made use of these powers at once to effect an economic mobilisation, taking charge of it himself. He proceeded to requisition the merchant fleet and the naval dockyards, to acquire powers of requisition and price-fixing and to adopt the principle of a single purchaser for specified products under government control. In a word, what the allied governments in the course of two and a half years of war had not even planned was achieved within a few weeks in the United States.

The Washington government wanted this effort to be imitated by the allies. The system of one purchaser for each basic product was to become general practice. In France up to this time it was only purchases of wheat and iron and steel products that followed this system. Now there appeared a mass of consortia: for cotton in July, then for oils, glass, pulp, petrol etc. They consisted of companies with fixed capital, and the members were the traders concerned. These companies had a monopoly of imports under state control and sold to their members at prices fixed by the state. In this way *laissez-faire* was more and more openly rejected, and the movement for control now grew apace. On 10 February 1918 the French government was given the right, which had been refused to Briand the year before, 'to regulate or suspend, in order to ensure national supplies, the production, circulation, sale, hoarding or consumption of foodstuffs necessary for feeding men and animals'. By the very end of the war, the government found itself with exceptional powers which enabled it to proceed to a vigorous economic mobilisation.

Clémentel's activities

For some of the leading supporters in this policy, in particular the minister for commerce Clémentel, these were not simply *ad hoc* measures. They foresaw that peace would not bring an end to the difficulties besetting a country that was financially and demographically much weakened. They therefore thought it essential, in order to face up to a future that looked difficult, that the state should retain the capacity to help with reconstruction problems by its encouragement and advice. Furthermore, they had at long last woken up to the real power and dynamism of the German economy. Conversely, they recognised France's relatively poor performance in the same sphere.

Already in 1916 Clémentel was denouncing the weaknesses of the chemical industry before the budget commission of the Chamber. He proposed that the state should take on the permanent role of promoter, whether it was to encourage technical education, to facilitate the regrouping of firms that was essential for standing up to the German cartels, or to encourage scientific research. This was the opposite of Albert Thomas' attitude, for Clémentel was a man of the centre who did not want to turn the state into an entrepreneur, except in special circumstances. He wanted it to be a stimulus for the greater good of the cartelised industries controlled by the state.

This way of looking at things was not general, and Clémentel ran up against the supporters of 'freedom without limits or restraints'. Would France, after the self-examination imposed on her by the difficulties of war, be able to acquire a new spirit of organisation and economic expansion? In any case the mobilisation of the economy was now an established fact. In spite of the criticism which state control encountered, there is little doubt that it enabled American aid to be used to the best advantage. In the situation of shortages created by the submarine war, the freight crisis and the financial difficulties of the country, it meant that the expansion of the war industries could continue and an excessive rise in prices be avoided.

However, there were real difficulties in many spheres. Rationing had to be instituted for certain foodstuffs, particularly bread and sugar. In several regions of France the shortage of domestic coal was serious, especially as the winter of 1917–18 was hardly less severe than the preceding one. But these sufferings were in no way comparable to what was being endured by the countries of the central powers, and, above all, by people in the invaded regions, in spite of the relief organisations of the neutral countries.

Military recovery

We have seen how, even in the crisis of the army mutinies, the army held together. The front remained intact and, thanks to a series of measures that satisfied the troops, morale was restored. But the mad extravagance with which manpower had been wasted in the early years of the war meant that, by the end of 1917, some divisions had to be disbanded. This was all the more worrying because the development of events on the Russian front was to allow the central powers to strip this front to a large extent and reinforce their armies in the west. Moreover, the British, having decided to achieve in Flanders, if not a decisive victory, at least an important success, were refusing quite logically to weaken themselves by accepting a widening of their front, which would have considerably eased the French army's situation. To cap it all, at the end of the year troops had to be withdrawn and sent to the Italian front after the Caporetto débâcle.

Pétain's command

To counter these difficulties Pétain, now commander-in-chief on the north and north-east front, who made a habit of facing facts and was also acquiring a reputation for pessimism, now launched a new tactic that he had been pondering for a long time. It was revealed on 19 May in the famous directive No. 1. In it he started by proclaiming the impossibility of breaking through the enemy front at present and of following this up with a strategic exploitation: therefore, no more of those attacks in depth on distant objectives, which had always failed up to now. But the front was not to remain inactive. There would be further attempts to wear down the enemy, but by a completely new tactic consisting of attacks on limited objectives. There would be 'will o' the wisp offensives' (Pedroncini) after careful preparation, so as to achieve maximum surprise. Armaments rather than men would be used to the full by concentrating it on these limited fronts. Special use would be made of new forms of armament: tanks, which would operate in close liaison with the infantry so as to eliminate obstacles, e.g. barbed wire and machine-gun nests; and planes, which would operate directly on the battlefield and its immediate rear, so as to prevent or hamper the movements of enemy reserves. Economy of manpower would be assured because, as soon as the enemy's reaction was seriously felt, the attack would not be pressed home. One would stop dead and perhaps launch an immediate attack on another sector of the front. One would hope in this way to wear down the enemy more than oneself.

However, one could foresee also that the enemy would not remain passive. He was assured of numerical superiority until the Americans arrived, and it was not expected that they would be up to strength or properly trained before the end of 1918. Germany would not fail to look for a decision by large-scale offensives which everyone, both at GHQ and in the government, expected in the spring of 1918.

Pétain devised a new defensive tactic to resist these expected attacks. It consisted in organising a defence in depth along the whole front. Only a few troops would be kept in the front-line, but they would be sufficiently well equipped to disorganise the enemy if possible. The latter would be awaited on the intact second-line positions, where the effect of surprise would not be felt. It would be necessary also to strengthen the links between the front-line formations in order to avoid a situation in which the enemy could fan out by lateral movements after a breakthrough.

To reinforce this defence tactic, there would be more dependence than before on both traditional and novel armaments, which implied a more intensive 'industrialisation of the war' (Pétain). As for armour, the heavy Schneider tanks proved both too unmanœuvrable and too vulnerable, so GHQ gave its preference to the small Renault tank and requested that it be produced in large quantities. In aviation a big effort was made in the production of the Breguet 14, a tactical bomber that was most appropriate for the missions in mind.

These innovations were only accepted with difficulty. The supporters of attack at all costs had so dominated the first three years of the war that it was difficult suddenly to make them approve of Pétain's ideas, which appeared to them to be too cautious. In addition, it seemed very hard to abandon still more French territory to an enemy who already occupied so much of it simply to comply with Pétain's directives. Finally, people began to ask when the end of the war would come by this method.

Strategy: differences in the Entente

The commander-in-chief also had a strategic vision of the war. He wanted to confine himself in the first half of 1917 to a few limited attacks mounted according to his method. These were carried out with conspicuous success at Verdun in August and, above all, at La Malmaison in October. Tanks were used very effectively, and the enemy positions on the Chemin des Dames were overrun without excessive losses, which gave the troops, as the postal censor noted, 'a winning spirit'. Pétain wanted the British to take up a similar tactic, which would have enabled them to extend their front and allow an even better disposition of the French army. As we know, nothing came of this. The British wanted to fight their own war in Flanders. Pétain was concerned that they might move further and further away from the coalition, for we must remember that the British government did not include the restitution of Alsace-Lorraine to France among its declared war aims. He was obliged therefore to take part in these British operations.

The commander-in-chief was particularly worried that the French armies, who had provided the main effort so far, were so exhausted that they would only be able to achieve victory thanks to the help of their British and American partners. But, if the Anglo-Americans played a decisive role in the final phase of the war, they would be in a position to dictate their conditions and the French point of view would be very secondary. In order to prevent this happening Pétain suggested a policy of guarantees. He had in mind an offensive in Alsace for the end of 1918, a sort of Turenne campaign, which would place the French in a favourable position when the peace treaty was being worked out. From such a position, the French could exploit success in the direction of central Germany, if the material and moral state of the army allowed it and if American help also relieved French troops of part of their responsibilities.

This strategy indicated a certain indifference to the war which the British were waging in Flanders. At a meeting with Field-Marshal Haig at Amiens on 18 October 1917 Pétain suggested to him that he abandon this remoteness and return to planning combined operations with his allies. Pétain did not hide his opinion that the general direction of operations should be entrusted to him. He asked Clemenceau at the time of Caporetto to support his candidature to the supreme command of the allied armies in Europe. Rejected in this ambition, he fell back on his policy of guarantees, hoping to win the support of the government and the chief of the general staff.

These vicissitudes showed up, if proof was needed, one of the weaknesses of the Entente. While the central powers had long since arrived at a unified command on all fronts, each of the allied armies continued to fight the war in its own way.

But how could suspicions, clashing interests and national susceptibilities be surmounted? At the conference of Rapallo (5–7 November 1917), which assembled to examine means of bringing help to Italy after Caporetto, Painlevé proposed to Lloyd George the formation of an inter-allied staff with Foch at its head. The only result was the formation of a permanent inter-allied military committee. However, because of a wish expressed by Lloyd George, article Five of the agreement stipulated that none of the military members of this committee would depend directly on a minister or a national general staff. This being so, the committee, without much information and without real power, 'scratched a lot of paper' according to Weygand, who represented France on it.

Therefore no choice was made between a defensive and a counter-offensive policy, or between continuing to look for a decision on the French front and embarking on an operation in the east.

The offensives of Ludendorff

It was in fact Ludendorff who disentangled the situation by his initiatives. On 21 March 1918 he attacked the British army, already weakened by the abortive offensives of the year before, in the Saint-Quentin region. As the British had not adopted the tactic of defence in depth preached by Pétain and were not expecting a blow on this scale, they gave way under the pressure, and their retreat after forty-eight hours began to look like a rout. Haig announced that he was withdrawing to cover the Channel ports, which were key strategic points for England. But Pétain wanted to protect Paris, which the Germans were already bombarding with 'Big Bertha', a very long-range gun. There was obvious dissension among the commanders-in-chief. The idea of a single command started to gain ground at this point. On 26 March the French and British heads of government and chiefs of staff held a meeting at Doullens. Pétain remained cautious, even rather pessimistic. On the other hand, the optimism and dash of Foch charmed his British allies. Above all, his tactical and strategic concepts seemed to show a good understanding of British aims, while Pétain, as we have seen, favoured a very different strategy of guarantees. Finally, Foch was not commander-in-chief of the French forces, which in British eyes was an additional safeguard. They also agreed that the coordination of the armies on the western front should be entrusted to him. Foch at once complained that he was being put in command of a battle that was already lost. In fact the Doullens meeting took place at a moment when the German offensive was running out of steam. The best German assault troops were due to be relieved. Furthermore, the reinforcements which Pétain had sent off without delay had now arrived and were restoring the continuity of the front. In the race to the Somme, Pétain had thrown in nearly half the French army. Ludendorff had to halt his offensive on 5 April, but he could congratulate himself on a considerable success: he had pushed forward sixty kilometres at the point of his attack. He had not achieved a decisive victory, nor had he even separated, as he had hoped, the British and French armies. However, he intended to take advantage of the British army's loss of strength. In August he again launched an offensive between Armentières and La Bassée, which shook the British considerably. But, after an initial real success, Ludendorff had to call a halt to his losses without gaining the results he had hoped for.

So far events had justified General Pétain – with the troops at their disposal the allies showed themselves incapable of building up reserves large enough to reply to German attacks by a counter-offensive. These German attacks, which were mounted in accordance with a new tactic, succeeded in breaking through front-line positions which were supposed to be defended. However, the lessons were not clear enough for several French army chiefs, and some of them failed to prepare the defence of their sectors in depth in accordance with the commander-in-chief's directives.

This disobedience had in fact been tolerated by General Foch whose powers, which were inadequately defined at the end of the Doullens meeting, were reinforced at the Beauvais conference on 3 April 1918. Foch was charged by the British, French and American governments with 'the strategic direction of military operations', each commander-in-chief retaining 'the tactical direction of his forces in full' and the right of appeal to his government 'if, in his opinion, his army seemed to be endangered by any instruction received from General Foch'. Thus the single unified command was realised to the advantage of a commander who had never hidden his reservations about the doctrines of Pétain and his entourage. Foch's directives forbade the abandonment of territory and so were opposed to defence in depth.

On 27 May, in the Chemin des Dames sector, Ludendorff launched a very violent attack which turned out to be a disaster for the French and the British. The first positions were carried and, as there was no further resistance, the German advance was pursued with a swiftness that surprised even the German High Command. On 30 May German troops arrived on the Marne and began to cross it at Dormans and Château-Thierry. Disaster was so near that Pétain was forced to envisage a general retreat and asked the government to think of leaving Paris, where there was a short outbreak of panic.

However, Ludendorff did not manage to widen the front of his attack. On the flanks the bastions of Reims and the Soissons plateau held firm. As with earlier attacks, the ground gained was harassed and bombed by allied aircraft and became an obstacle to the exploitation of success. On 9 June he tried a thrust in the direction of Compiègne, but it was halted and on 11 June Ludendorff had to order the front to be stabilised on the positions gained. Once again these positions indicated the scale of the tactical success – an advance of sixty kilometres in a vital region, considerable booty and the capture of fifty thousand prisoners.

However, the allies held good. Events had now so far borne out Pétain's doctrines that no one thought of arguing with them any more. He and Foch were now in agreement. The tactical ideas of the commander-in-chief would be applied in the face of any German attack until the arrival of American troops restored numerical superiority to the allies. In order to forestall such an attack, the two commanders agreed to prepare a clearing operation. It was planned for 18 July and entrusted to Mangin's army, which formed up under cover of the forest of Villers-Cotterêts. When German troops attacked the French front in Champagne on 15 July, they did not achieve the surprise effect of their earlier successes. Their assaults broke up nearly everywhere on the French second positions. It is true that the Marne was reached between Jargonnet and Bassy, and that Epernay was threatened. In order to counter this danger, Pétain had even ordered the preparations for the Mangin offensive to be postponed and troops to be switched to cope with the German offensive. Foch refused to approve this move.

In fact the German menace to the south of the Marne diminished in the days that followed, and Mangin, operating with his full complement of troops and assisted by a morning mist, directed his attack on the west flank of the German pocket at Château-Thierry. His success was such that Ludendorff was suddenly forced to evacuate nearly all the ground won since 27 May. The German army was beaten, and the balance of power was gradually altering. The French and British armies were now assured of a considerable superiority in modern armaments, for the Renault tanks, the aircraft and the new guns were pouring in. They were also receiving American reinforcements every month, which were an immense help in view of the exhaustion of the reserves.

So it seemed as if Germany could no longer look forward to the total victory which Ludendorff had rashly promised before the summer. But his army was still enormously powerful. His geographical position allowed him to build up withdrawal positions outside his national territory, and he lost no time in strengthening them. Indeed, the allies expected at least another year of war.

Morale holds up

The divisions of the socialists

It was thought that in 1919 the onrush of Americans would submerge the enemy. But before this juncture the allied camp came close to disaster on several occasions. It needed all the energy of a war government that was at last solidly based to face the darkest moments of the first half of 1918. Clemenceau had in fact discovered how to deal with the problems that resulted from the inertia and then the fall of his predecessors. Yet he did not have the benefit of the theoretical advantages that arose from the Union Sacrée. The socialists, whom he invited to join his team, refused to take part in the government and even turned into an established opposition. On the one hand, their members harboured resentment against the man who as minister of the interior before the war had carried on an often murderous feud against the working-class movement. Thus the minority group had little difficulty in persuading the unions to vote against supporting the government. On the other hand, Albert Thomas, like many others, did not believe in the ultimate success of Clemenceau, for his wayward behaviour made Thomas think that his administration would not last. His departure would leave the door open to a new line-up, in which the socialists would have their place. This miscalculation on the part of the former minister for armaments had important results. The socialist party, once again in opposition, was paralysed still further because the bolshevik revolution brought new reasons for dissension. Meanwhile, the minority group within the socialists gathered strength throughout 1917. It denounced the bogus nature of the Union Sacrée, the refusal of successive governments to let a French delegation go to Stockholm, and the secretive imperialism of the government's war aims. Even if the minority did sometimes condemn the methods of the bolsheviks and criticise the Brest-Litovsk capitulations, they also put up a lively resistance to the allied government's behaviour towards Russia, which in their eyes was actuated more by social fears than by the interests of the country. Most of the majority in the socialist party was in fact ready to agree with the minority on all these points. From January 1918 onwards they laid stress on the Wilsonian thesis as detailed in the President's Fourteen Points. At the national council meeting on 28 July 1918, Renaudel's majority motion, which accepted western intervention in Russia 'as much for the struggle against German imperialism as for the destruction of the treaty of Brest-Litovsk' only gained 1,172 votes, against 1,544 votes for Longuet's 'centrist' text, which demanded open support for the Fourteen Points, opposed all intervention in Russia and refused to vote for military credits until passports for a conference of the Socialist International had been granted.

Renaudel had to resign his management of *L'Humanité* on 13 September. It was the end of the reformist socialism of Albert Thomas. 'Political developments in the last year of the war robbed him of the political and social gains which he expected from the Union Sacrée and which could have produced a renovated France after 1918.' (B. W. Schaper (ed.) *Albert Thomas, trente ans de réformisme social*, p. 172.)

These upheavals, however, did not have the weakening effects on public opinion which might have been expected. Apart from the small 'Zimmerwaldian' fringe, the ex-minority group, while continuing their search for peace, did not deny the necessity of pursuing the national defence effort without giving in.

The strikes of 1918

These events explain the comparative ease with which the government, between March and May, was able to put an end to a strike movement comparable in size to that of 1917, but different in character. In that year wage claims were the basis of the movement, and the government only had to give broad satisfaction to those claims to stop the strikes; but this time there was spontaneous action in the ranks, there was little control by union leaders, and political motives quickly became the leading factor. Exploiting the discontent caused by the call-up of young specialist workers, who were replaced by foreigners, a union minority thought it could launch a movement that was at once defeatist and revolutionary, like the one that had broken out in Russia. At least this is the impression one gets from the turn of events, especially in the Saint-Etienne region where in March a meeting of the minority group advocated a general strike. As it turned out, Clemenceau got the support of Merrheim, the director of the union defence committee, although he had publicly denounced him the year before when he was attacking Malvy. Merrheim had never supported revolutionary defeatism: 'we did not want to subject France to the treaty of Brest-Litovsk' he was to say at the CGT congress in 1919, in order to justify his behaviour at this time.

Thanks to this support and also to severe measures (e.g. arrests, censorship, despatch of ringleaders to the front), but without resorting to the extreme action advocated by the right (e.g. the requisition and general militarisation of labour), the government managed to avoid the worst. In the second half of May, work was resumed generally, and the trade unions took up positions that closely resembled those of the socialist centre. As a result, Merrheim and Jouhaux were able to come to terms.

Clemenceau's government

These disturbances, although important in themselves, did not stir the country to its roots for it felt itself to be firmly governed. Clemenceau knew how to make use of his popularity and he made his opponents feel it. Whenever there were rumblings in parliament, he proposed a vote of confidence and always won it. He thus managed to increase his power, and everyone acquiesced, even though they grumbled about his 'dictatorship'. Indeed he was clever at granting favours to those who opposed the previous governments. Above all, he made it clear that he alone was in charge of the conduct of the war; and this was not empty talk. From now onwards the High Command knew not only that the civil power counted for something, but also that all final decisions rested with it. The government for its part assumed its responsibilities. When parliament demanded sanctions against Foch and Pétain after the disaster of 27 May, he defended them vigorously (4 June). Furthermore, he put no further obstacles in the way of parliamentary control in the war zone. The new president of the Council had long made a habit of going up to the front, and he was still often seen in the trenches. He even authorised parliamentary missions to go up during operations, which scandalised Poincaré. Better still, when the storm died down, he allowed the creation of a court of enquiry to investigate the mistakes made during the offensive of May 1918 and he appointed to it, at General Guillaumat's side, the presidents of the army commissions of both the Chamber and the Senate. In this way, the criticisms of those who, from the beginning of the war, had been complaining of the civil powers' impotence in the face of military power, were effectively silenced at last. Furthermore, in the composition of his cabinet, Clemenceau avoided those 'clever' mixtures which had been one of the reasons for his predecessors' weakness. As most of the parliamentary stars had either quarrelled with him, or had been very anxious not to compromise themselves in an adventure that might not last long, Clemenceau was generally content to call on second-rank or as yet unknown personalities, which strengthened his own authority. He also attracted the sympathy of rank-and-file deputies and senators. To reinforce this he would distribute the jobs of 'government commissioners' who proliferated through the establishment of a new administration organising the war economy. This policy had the advantage of disarming the criticisms of those who foresaw in this swelling of the bureaucracy a diminution of parliamentary control. By this method even the socialist party was more or less neutralised. When the socialists Compère-Morel (agriculture), Bouisson (merchant navy) and Diagne (overseas recruitment) accepted the posts proposed to them, the national council of the party gave them the authorisation which was deemed necessary (February 1918).

In contrast, the general conduct of the war was run by Clemenceau without any distribution of favours. He was both president of the Council and minister for war. He was assisted by a cabinet run by Georges Mandel for political affairs and by General Mordacq for military affairs, two men who were entirely devoted to him.

Clemenceau obtained from parliament a vast delegation of power in order to be able to act with more energy. As we have seen, the law of 10 February 1918 gave him a considerable extension of regulation where food and trade were concerned. In this way a sort of government of public safety came into being, reminding the left of the government of the Year II of the Revolution and reassuring the right by the elimination of the socialists.

There still remained the task of crushing 'defeatism', i.e. the search for a compromise peace that had been widely canvassed in 1917. Its leader was undoubtedly Caillaux, but he no longer had the ear of the public. Besides Clemenceau had decided to destroy him politically.

Poincaré, vindictive as ever, wanted a military tribunal, where the silhouette of a gibbet would loom up on the way out. The High Court was good enough for the president of the Council. Although the evidence was slight he easily obtained parliament's authority for proceedings against Caillaux (11 December 1917). That was enough to give Clemenceau a free hand where the diplomatic conduct of the war was concerned. As for the parliamentary majority, it practically gave the president of the Council *carte blanche* to run the war as he liked until victory was assured.

Victory

Clemenceau's 'dictatorship' increased its grip from the summer of 1918 onwards as the military balance of strength changed irrevocably in favour of the allies. Both Foch and Pétain, even in the worst moments of the spring, had been concerned to take advantage of this change when it occurred. Pétain's directive No. 5, which drew conclusions from recent battles, laid down tactical rules for offensive operations. It emphasised the necessity of achieving surprise by the siting and violence of the artillery preparation, such as Ludendorff had practised with success. But it also gave a considerable role to tanks and aircraft, which was a new departure. Also, when Foch assembled the commanders-in-chief at his headquarters at Bombon near Melun, he told them: 'The moment has now come to abandon the defensive attitude which has been imposed on us up till now by our numerical inferiority. We must now pass to the offensive.' This attitude won everyone's support. The German army still looked formidable, but a few head-on blows could wear down its resistance and lead to decisive battles, which were now foreseen for 1919.

It was the same with the operations that were getting under way on the other fronts. In Italy the full-scale defeat of an Austro-Hungarian offensive (15–20 June 1918) proved that the Italian army had overcome the weaknesses that had led to the rout at Caporetto. However, the Italian supreme command declined Foch's invitation to mount an offensive in the summer. In Salonika, Franchet d'Espérey, the new commander-in-chief, had high hopes of the attack planned by his predecessor. However, he had to wait until 3 August for his plans to be approved, for the British feared failure and counted more on making Bulgaria change sides by diplomacy. As for Clemenceau, he insisted that an operation in this region should in no way affect the supply of arms and troops to the French front.

The allied operations proved to be even more successful than expected. On 8 August Foch, newly promoted *maréchal de France*, launched a Franco-British offensive in Picardy under Haig's command, which was to break up the front in this sector. On three occasions, it succeeded in the Ludendorff style of attack and forced the latter to use his reserves without effect. The result was that, at the beginning of September, Ludendorff had to order a general withdrawal to the Hindenburg Line, while he quickly fortified a new withdrawal position, the 'Hermann Line'. For the first time German troops showed signs of exhaustion. Ludendorff was forced to admit to the emperor and the chancellor that he had no hope of obtaining the victory which he had promised the month before. He could only hope to break the enemy's will to pursue the war by carrying out an energetic defence of occupied territory.

Could Germany now hold on to the territory won in the east by restoring the pre-war situation in the west? In this event France would find herself deprived of Alsace-Lorraine, which was unacceptable. However, despite Lloyd George's tardy statements on the matter, and despite the eighth of Wilson's Fourteen Points, with all their imprecision ('the wrong done to France by Prussia in 1871 in the matter of Alsace-Lorraine ... should be righted'), the German government was convinced that the allies would not give very energetic support to the French claim for the simple restoration of the lost provinces.

To have a chance of success, all designs on Belgium would have to be abandoned. The allied general staff ruled it out, and the approaches made to the king of Belgium and the queen of Holland at the beginning of September came to nothing. So, after American troops had reduced the bulging Saint-Mihiel salient on 15 September, Foch unleashed a triple offensive, starting on 26 September, with the French and Americans attacking between the Meuse and the Suippes towards Mézières, the British between Cambrai and Saint-Quentin towards Valenciennes, and the Belgians, with the French, in Flanders towards Bruges. The Germans managed to hold on in spite of certain allied successes, but on 28 September the German High Command learnt of the disasters which had overtaken the central powers in the Balkans. Franchet d'Espérey's offensive of 15 September had completely demoralised the Bulgarian army so that Bulgaria demanded an armistice on 26 September, which was concluded on the 29th. This laid the country open to the allied forces.

Austria-Hungary was suddenly menaced with invasion. Hindenburg and Ludendorff then decided to sue for an armistice with all speed in order to save the German army. On 29 September they made a plain announcement of this decision to the emperor and the chancellor, who bowed to their request and agreed that the Reichstag's support should be obtained so as to lessen the bad moral effect on the German army and people. Chancellor Herbling resigned and the emperor put in his place Prince Max of Baden, who was reputed to be a liberal and a supporter of a compromise peace. On 3 October Prince Max sent President Wilson a message saying that the German government accepted the Fourteen Points as a basis for peace negotiations and asked for an immediate armistice to avoid further bloodshed.

In spite of all this the German army continued to resist Foch's offensive and only withdrew step by step. It was hoped in Germany that the armistice conditions would leave the Reich's fighting power more or less intact and would allow peace to be negotiated in as favourable conditions as possible. This fact makes the strategic plans being worked out at GHQ by General Pétain most interesting. From 3 August onwards he planned a large-scale operation in Lorraine aimed at the enemy's weak spot to the east of Verdun. This menace to German communications would lead to the 'defeat of the enemy's main forces' and would give France 'bargaining assets' once the annexed territories were entered. Finally, the success of the operation would bring the war into German territory, bringing home to the people of the Reich their defeat more clearly. The operation was at first only planned for 1919, but the events of September and October made GHQ prepare to launch it at the beginning of November.

Meanwhile the exchange of notes between Wilson and the German government all through the month of October made the Germans lose all hope of dividing the allies and obtaining an armistice that was militarily acceptable. The American president exacted conditions that would make resumption of hostilities by Germany 'impossible'. He added that peace could only be negotiated with the 'representatives of the German people' and not with 'those who have been their masters up till now'. It was an invitation to the Germans to start a revolution. At the same time Germany's allies were finally collapsing. In mid-October the Turkish government requested an armistice through General Townshend, who was their prisoner-of-war. This treaty was signed on 31 October at Mudros without the French, to their great annoyance, being called to the discussions. Austria-Hungary was falling apart through the activities of the Czech, Polish and Croat national movements. This was the moment chosen by the Italian High Command to launch an offensive, which broke through the Austrian front on 30 October after the occupation of Vittorio Veneto. On 3 November the government in Vienna, who had lost all authority over the empire, accepted the very harsh terms of an armistice that allowed the allies free passage to attack Germany through Austria.

The Reich lost all hope of prolonging its resistance and from 3 November onwards there were the first signs of revolution. On 7 November a delegation led by the minister of state Erzberger crossed the lines to negotiate the inevitable armistice, whose conditions would certainly be severe. On 9 November a republic was proclaimed in Berlin amid scenes of disorder, while the Kaiser was abandoned by his most loyal troops, who were now forming soldiers' councils. He finally decided to abdicate.

The Entente powers and their American 'associate' had reached agreement on the conditions of the armistice. There were no great difficulties as far as the military clauses were concerned. Foch's point of view, which demanded solid guarantees, prevailed on the whole. Germany had, of course, to evacuate all the invaded territories and to accept the occupation of the left bank of the Rhine, together with certain bridgeheads on the right bank. She was forced to surrender a large part of her armaments and railway equipment. She also had to give up all her submarines to the victors, while her fleet had to be interned in a neutral port.

Discussion had been livelier on the political clauses. Wilson put forward his Fourteen Points, of which the second (on the freedom of the seas) was not accepted by the British because it robbed them of the blockade weapon for the future. The French on their side were worried about the inadequate provision (in their view) for war damage reparations, while the Italians feared the obstacles which the ninth point placed in the way of what had been promised them in 1915. As Wilson demanded the allies' acceptance of his programme, the governments of the Entente sent him a note on 4 November in which they accepted the Fourteen Points, but with reservations on the principle of the freedom of the seas and on the interpretation to be given to the 'restoration' of the invaded territories. When Erzberger met Foch, he encountered what appeared to be a united front; he therefore had to give in, obtaining hardly any of the mitigation he asked for. He signed the capitulation during the night of 10–11 November 1918.

Later on, certain students of the period would come to regard the armistice as premature. They would be led to this point of view by the very rapid birth, on the German side, of the 'stab in the back' legend, which maintained that the unbeaten Germany army was brought to its knees by revolution at home. This legend would serve to maintain the prestige of the army and its leaders, who of course encouraged it; but it does not stand up to historical analysis.

It is probable that the Lorraine offensive, planned by Pétain and his staff, would have inflicted a military disaster on the enemy if it had been launched on time. That at least was the opinion of the French commander-in-chief. It was not the opinion of Foch, who took a long time to approve the operation so that its start was put off until 14 November. In his view this offensive was just one like all the others, and no decisive results could be expected of it, for, as Pershing and Clemenceau were to say later, the German capacity to resist was still overestimated by the allies. But, in any case, would a more obvious military defeat have prevented a spirit of revenge from growing in Germany? Did the very heavy defeat of 1870–71 incline France towards pacifism at any price?

However much people may have later discussed the timeliness of the armistice, one can easily understand the joy and relief with which it was greeted in the country. This victory, which had at various times seemed remote, appeared now to be complete. As, of all the allies, France was the one who had suffered far the most from the war, and as the military leaders of the alliance were French, there were very few to doubt that the victory was French. The forthcoming peace was expected to guarantee that no such ordeal could recur. It was also expected to provide means, at the enemy's expense, to heal all France's wounds and bring back quickly the pre-war world, which had begun in the collective unconscious to take on the appearance of a golden age.

The era of illusions was about to begin for the majority of French people.

8

The year 1919

The human losses

The France that was victorious in November 1918 was a country gravely weakened. From the demographic point of view she had for a long time been relatively feeble, but on top of this she had spilt her blood in a way that had no parallel among the other belligerents, the exception being Serbia. She had lost 1,310,000 killed or missing, i.e. 10.5 out of 100 active men, as compared with 9.8 for Germany and 5.1 for Great Britain. To this figure had to be added 1,100,000 severely wounded, most of whom would only be able to live a restricted life. According to Alfred Sauvy, this was equivalent to an additional loss of 360,000 men; and to this have to be added the victims of the world-wide Spanish influenza epidemic that struck at the end of 1918.

The war situation and its effects had of course caused a considerable fall in the birth-rate, which could not be made good in the immediate post-war period by the steep rise in 'postponed' births. Demographers estimate the loss of population due to this factor at 1,400,000 souls. This was a far-reaching phenomenon, carrying through one generation after another those 'hollow' groups of the 1914–18 war.

In addition, this reduced population deteriorated in quality. The most measurable phenomenon was the increase in aged persons, which was already evident before the war and was now even more marked. The proportion of over-sixties increased from 12.6 per hundred to 13.6 (Sauvy). This new imbalance not only increased the charges on the active population, but also, in an unhealthy way, encouraged in the community those pessimistic and cautious attitudes that are typical of old people. It is also probable that the weariness following on the tension and violence of the battlefield rendered certain soothing myths attractive, e.g. a return to the pre-war 'belle époque', illusions about international security, and blaming mysterious plotters for every kind of difficulty caused or aggravated by the war.

The human losses of the war

Occupation	Active male population in 1919	Deaths			Deaths per 1,000	Injured
		Deaths	Missing	Total		
Agriculture	5,400,000	397,500	140,500	538,000	996	161,200
Industry	4,730,000	306,900	108,500	415,400	877	123,300
Transport	580,000	35,100	12,400	47,500	810	13,400
Commerce	1,300,000	90,900	32,100	123,000	940	37,000
Liberal professions	310,000	24,500	8,700	33,200	1,070	10,000
Domestic work	160,000	12,100	14,300	16,400	1,025	5,100
Civil servants	520,000	40,500	14,300	54,800	1,055	15,900
Regular Army	100,000 }					
Others	}	50,000 }	16,800 }	66,800 }	– }	22,900 }
Total	13,100,000	957,500	337,600	1,295,100	990	388,800

Source: A. Sauvy, *Histoire économique de la France entre les deux guerres*, vol. I, p. 442.

Material and financial damage

Enormous material harm was added to these human and moral losses. France entered the war a rich nation, but she came out of it ruined. The whole production machine was shattered. In the areas where the battles had raged for nearly four years, the destruction was so great that the soil itself was rendered barren, sometimes irreparably. Whole villages, indeed whole towns (e.g. Reims, Lens, Saint-Quentin) had been razed to the ground. About eight million acres had become desert and would have to be completely rehabilitated. As for the invaded regions, they had been exploited without thought for the morrow by an enemy who in the end very often wrecked their industrial potential. Mines had been flooded, coal production reduced to practically nothing and ore production to about 40 per cent. Other industrial installations, particularly textile factories and steel plants, had been systematically destroyed. The production of iron and steel in the invaded departments had decreased by 95 per cent compared with 1913. In the country districts a large part of the stock had been pillaged (840,000 head of cattle, 400,000 horses, 900,000 sheep and 330,000 pigs).

The transport system – roads, canals, railways – had to a large extent been put out of use. It is true that, in the rest of the country, industrialisation connected with the war had given rise to new activities and new plant, but these still had to be adapted to meet the needs of peacetime. Furthermore, the communication network in these areas had often been overused to the point of disrepair, especially the railway system. The merchant navy was largely destroyed. Overall, the rehabilitation of the production machine in many areas required considerable investment; for, as a direct or indirect result of the war, a large part of the national wealth had been affected.

France had before the war obtained an income from some forty billion francs invested in foreign countries. As we have seen, many of these investments had been sold to pay for imports, and it appeared that much of the rest would never be paid because of the financial difficulties of the borrower states. In addition, part of the public and private gold reserves had left France. Most important of all, necessity had required considerable overseas borrowings to be made.

As taxes had hardly increased, the state had been forced to finance much of the war effort by enormous loans, which had to be repaid, and also by the issue of paper-money. This was to cause relatively fast inflation, especially after the beginning of 1917, accompanied by a rise in the cost of living which was dangerous for its possible social consequences. Finally, part of the population (war wounded, orphans and widows) was going to be financially dependent on the state, either entirely or partially.

It is of course very difficult to estimate the total amount of these losses and debts. Estimates are often unreliable. If we take for example the case of French loans abroad, we see that they were often highly artificial, as the payment of interest was only assured in so far as the states concerned could arrange further loans. So it is not reasonable to base losses on the total of defaulting loans. In another respect one can see that destruction of the production machine could have certain positive advantages because reconstruction meant modernisation. The productivity and profitability of the rebuilt plant would be much improved.

Alfred Sauvy has attempted the difficult task of making an overall estimate, and he suggests that there was a loss of fifty-five billion francs (1913 value), or fifteen months of national income based on this same year, or again the loss of the wealth accumulation of eleven pre-war years. So one can see the effort and sacrifices which the exhausted French would have to make simply to restore the pre-war position. Most of them were in no doubt that they should not be the only ones to bear the enormous cost of paying the country's external debts and repairing the damage suffered. The French were unanimous in their belief that Germany should pay.

Germany shall pay

Yes, pay, but how much? First, the cost of the country's heritage destroyed in the war. This had to be evaluated with some degree of accuracy, and this is where important differences began to arise, not only with the Germans, but also with the British and Americans, who were always ready to believe that the French were deliberately exaggerating the value of their losses. This was the view in August 1919 of the American secretary of the treasury, Glass, who wrote to Wilson: 'The needs of Europe have been greatly exaggerated.' Above all, this was what was stated to the peace negotiators by the economist John Maynard Keynes, a man of unorthodox views who was well known, if not very influential, across the Channel. The French saw in these criticisms only shameful slanders actuated by evil designs and sordid interest.

It was thought in France that the total pensions and indemnities to be paid by the allied governments to their own war victims should be added to the reparations. The Americans viewed with disfavour the mounting total of these reparations. Faced with the enormous expenses incurred by the state as an immediate consequence of the war, and with the interest payments on the vast internal debt caused by systematic borrowing, the French government was determined to discuss an increase in taxes. Klotz even went so far as to talk of an extraordinary tax on capital. From 19 February onwards the press thundered against such plans: 'Did we win the war? A plan for a tax on capital indeed! First of all German capital must be hit' cried *La Liberté*'s headline, soon to be followed by most newspapers. The press thus led public opinion to believe that to ask the country for a tax effort was out of the question, even though other countries imposed such taxes.

At the same time the foreign affairs commission of the Chamber voted a resolution demanding 'the total repayment of war costs', which amounted in effect to requiring the Germans to pay all France's debts. As it was clear that Germany in her ruined condition could not pay at once, the budget commission put forward the idea that for the moment France should receive from her allies, especially the United States, 'a sort of revolving credit'. (See P. Miquel, *La Paix de Versailles et l'opinion publique française*.) The American government received this suggestion very badly, especially as the unfortunate Klotz had been forced to withdraw his tax proposals post-haste in face of the uproar they provoked; and he even gave up a substantial tax on excessive war profits which had been proposed by Vincent Auriol on behalf of the socialists and already approved.

Many of the French held the comforting belief that, as their country had suffered more than the other opponents of Germany, they might be let off some or all of the debts contracted in England and America, especially as they viewed with some apprehension the enormous growth in the economic and financial power of 'Uncle Sam'. In the more immediate future they hoped for the continuation of the inter-allied solidarity born of the war. So the French government proposed the maintenance of the different assistance organisations set up in 1917 and 1918 and continued support for the franc both in London and New York.

Both the Americans and the British very soon showed that they intended to return to the traditional rules of economic liberalism. In particular, they stopped supporting the franc in March 1919, which immediately caused a dramatic fall. As for the cancellation or reduction of France's debts, the treasury department in Washington made it clear to Klotz in November 1918 that he should not count on it. In their view commercial morality precluded it absolutely.

This was the beginning of long-lasting bad feeling between the Americans and the French. The words 'Germany must pay', endlessly repeated, summarised France's economic and financial hopes; and if her allies, through blind selfishness, assisted the Germans in their manœuvres to avoid paying their just retribution, those allies in their turn should not expect to be repaid debts which, after all, were contracted for the better defence of the common cause.

Security: the problem of the Rhine

Similarly, in the matter of security, the year 1919 saw the birth of certain great illusions, whose common characteristic was that final solutions were sought without regard for the realities of the time. The 'nationalists' – i.e. not only the right but also a fair contingent of radicals, not to mention a socialist fringe – sought a solution in the elimination of Germany as a power. To achieve this the left bank of the Rhine would have to be detached from Germany, either by annexing it to France and Belgium, or by encouraging the birth of an independent state under the military protection of the French army. The wilder spirits even dreamt of a new treaty of Westphalia which would break up German unity. To such moves were added the suppression of the Russian menace, for the bolsheviks were considered to be the agents of Germany and the enemies of society.

But how could anyone think such solutions possible when Wilson, who played a decisive role in the coalition, proclaimed principles in his Fourteen Points which ruled them out? In any case they rode rough-shod over German national sentiment.

For the internationalist left it was collective security, with the active participation of a 'good' Germany, which would bring about the abolition of war. The 'peace of justice' would have to accompany the 'peace of victory', together with international reconciliation and universal disarmament. The workers' organisations would have to be associated with the realisation of these ideals – this was a view strongly held by Jouhaux at the beginning of 1919. The supporters of collective security were not a united block. Some socialists were entirely in favour, taking up certain ideas current before the war, but other socialists and radicals were against collective security, having reservations about admitting Germany and even more Russia. In any case both groups were misguided about Wilson's real intentions and the state of mind of the defeated Germans.

It was in this atmosphere of contradictory illusions that the clauses of the peace treaty were going to be discussed. Clemenceau did indeed keep great freedom of manœuvre. Brushing aside Poincaré's hesitations, he assumed command of the French delegation and refused in the preliminary stages to keep parliament informed of the progress of the negotiations. This won him the declared hostility of the socialists as well as the scarcely concealed enmity of Briand's supporters, who began to intrigue against him. However, just as in wartime, he easily overrode this opposition. On 16 April 1919 the Chamber of deputies, by 345 voices to 121, confirmed the freedom of action which he had asked for in January.

In what state of mind did Clemenceau come to the negotiating table? He had no sympathy whatsoever for the ideas of the 'internationalists', whether of the Wilsonian or socialist kind. The essential problem in his eyes was to neutralise a Germany that was bound to be filled with the spirit of revenge. But he was also very well aware of the weakness of an isolated France. He was determined, therefore, to preserve the entente between the victors, even to the point of agreeing to necessary compromises. He did not share the dreams of those who gambled on the autonomist tendencies of various parts of Germany; and he refused all annexation of German populations. On 26 November, in a memorandum addressed to the British government, he made his proposals: acquisition of Alsace-Lorraine within the 1814 frontiers (i.e. with Saarbrücken and Sarrelouis); surrender to France of the production of the mines of the Saar; constitution of a strong Poland to whom Upper Silesia and the Polish districts of East Prussia would be given, and who from then onwards would be capable of dealing with the double German and Bolshevik danger; free choice for the Germans of their own government, but with the Allies trying to favour any federalist tendencies that might show themselves. In a supplementary note of 3 December he added that the frontiers of Czechoslovakia ought to respect the 'homogeneity' of that state, which meant the integration of Sudetenland, although it was inhabited by a German majority.

His views were less clear-cut in the matter of reparations, and he left it to the 'experts', Klotz and Loucheur in particular, who were in agreement with the idea of total reparations expressed in parliament and in most of the press.

Clemenceau in action: the treaty of Versailles

Clemenceau had to rest for a short time after the attempt on his life on 19 February by an anarchist worker called Cottin; but he then spent most of the first six months of 1919 in difficult negotiations with Lloyd George, Wilson and Orlando, who made up the Council of Four. Its role was essential, especially after the end of March.

Acting with his usual mixture of authority and flexibility, Clemenceau came near to dominating the situation at critical moments. On one occasion, however, he had to deal with opposition from his own side, which complicated his task. Marshal Foch, supported by a section of parliament and public opinion, vigorously criticised the results of the negotiations on Germany's western frontier. At first Clemenceau had supported the claims of the Comité de la Rive Gauche du Rhin. He proposed the annexation of the Saar and the fixing of France's 'military frontier' along the Rhine, which would involve permanent occupation of the German Rhineland on the river's left bank. Lloyd George and Wilson would not agree to these moves which, in their opinion, would be contrary to the principles laid down in the Fourteen Points; so Clemenceau had to give way. The Saar would be administered by the League of Nations for fifteen years and its mines would be transferred to France, on the understanding that, at the end of the period, the populations concerned would choose their own status by plebiscite. As for the Rhineland, Clemenceau had to give up the idea of detaching it from Germany. He also had great difficulty in getting approval for the occupation of the region for fifteen years by an allied force, its evacuation to be dependent on the enemy's strict respect of the treaty. On the other hand, subject only to parliamentary approval, Lloyd George and Wilson offered immediate military assistance to France in case of 'unprovoked action' by Germany. Finally, the left bank of the Rhine and a strip fifty kilometres wide on the right bank were to be permanently stripped of all military equipment and buildings.

Marshal Foch opposed Clemenceau's concessions vigorously. One of the consequences of this was that General Mangin towards the end of May 1919 gave considerable encouragement to a Rhineland separatist movement, which was to persist for a long time. The British and Americans saw in this an attempt to face them with a *fait accompli*, and Clemenceau had to rebuke severely these military rebels, who were backed by the nationalist press. As Foch could find no supporters in the political world, he in his turn had to give in.

Other difficulties in the negotiations gave rise to limited outcries, notably in the matter of reparations. The builders of the treaty could not reach agreement on this point, either as regards the total that Germany would have to pay or on the distribution of the payments. So the treaty limited itself to making the losers admit the moral and legal force of the reparations, and also Germany's sole and exclusive responsibility for the outbreak of the war (article 231). As for the rest, it was decided that an advance payment of twenty-five billion gold francs should be made within two years, after which Germany would accept the conclusions of a commission which would fix the total of these reparations, the methods of payment and the respective shares of the allies.

Another controversy arose over the German disarmament clauses. Foch favoured a small army conscripted for very short military service, which in his view was the only way to avoid creating the nucleus of a large army that might come into being if Germany violated the treaty. The negotiators, however, followed the British line and opted for an army reduced to one hundred thousand men, recruited from volunteers for a service of twelve years.

The other clauses of the treaty did not stir up public opinion, apart from the discussion over the constitution of the League of Nations. As Clemenceau was highly sceptical about this institution, he left Léon Bourgeois and his friends to defend the French point of view, whose main feature consisted in the creation of an international army capable of enforcing the organisation's decisions. However, the British and Americans rejected this proposal. The League of Nations, the only body fitted to take action, would not be able, therefore, to do much against erring states. It could apply mandatory economic sanctions, whose effectiveness remained to be proved, and it could also order military sanctions, though their application was optional for each member state. In these circumstances one can understand why many people felt doubtful about the effectiveness of an organisation whose authority was only moral; yet it was intended to intervene in conflicts where moral rules carried little weight. As for the admission of Germany, which the socialists had demanded since the beginning of the year, this was postponed to an unspecified date, and in practice was left to the discretion of the victors. So the peace treaty took on much more the appearance of a permanent alliance than of an international organisation, which had been the dream of pacifists ever since Kant.

On the other hand, the ideas of certain French socialists and trade unionists, notably Jouhaux and Albert Thomas, were taken up, and the principle of international coordination of social legislation was accepted. The idea was to harmonise as much as possible the attitudes of the different states and so avoid excessive disparities in the working conditions of the labouring classes. Thus the cause both of social justice and of peace would be served. It was decided to create the International Labour Office, whose main task would be to prepare international agreements, more particularly on working conditions. But there again the League of Nations was without the means to enforce its agreements.

The altercations, both on the left and on the right, that attended the negotiation of the treaty did not prevent Clemenceau from easily obtaining its ratification by parliament with a crushing majority (372 votes to 53, including only fifty-one socialists, with seventy-four abstentions), despite the sharp criticism of Barrès, Louis Marin and Barthou. Public opinion felt that, given the circumstances, no one could have done better than Clemenceau; so his position remained very strong. Furthermore, the approach of the elections silenced criticism on the left, for the socialists were not keen to contradict the arguments of the nationalists and the right, who on their side were organising their campaign under the banner of 'Clemencism'.

Two different attitudes towards the peace treaty soon revealed themselves. Some thought that direct agreement should be sought with Germany. This presupposed a revision of the treaty with certain clauses toned down, and it would demand considerable sacrifices of France as most of the intended reparations would be cancelled. It would also lead to a policy of austerity and effort in the economic and financial domain, especially as the American debt would continue. It was a very optimistic attitude, for it supposed the disappearance of all spirit of revenge in a defeated Germany.

According to others, France must count only on her own efforts to keep for as long as possible the advantages over Germany gained at the time of the capitulation. Every possible advantage must be extracted from a treaty that was certainly imperfect, but had great value all the same. This attitude also was dangerous in the current state of exhaustion of the country, because it underestimated the opposition that it would encounter in the world. However, it was certainly the more popular in 1919 when opinion was marked by hatreds kept up through four years of war, and was ready to preserve the illusion that Germany could and should repair all the ruin caused by the war.

Electoral reform

This spirit of nationalism was doubtless one of the factors in the success of the right in the elections of 16 November 1919, but it was certainly not the only one. Some important changes were happening in the political world.

The first change was in the voting system, which had been unaltered for a long time. In certain right-wing circles, as well as on the extreme left, there had been growing criticism of the one-name, two-round *scrutin d'arrondissement*. It was said, on the second round, to lead to circumstantial alliances on vague programmes. Furthermore, they added, it left too much scope for petty personal influence, and this was exercised widely by local magnates in the smaller constituencies. All this made the establishment of solid majorities very difficult and gave too much importance to petty local interests in the parliamentary debates. Finally, the system prevented the fair representation of minorities. Campaigns were waged, therefore, in favour of proportional representation, though there was by no means unanimity on the subject. In the end the reform voted on 7 July was a compromise between the majority principle and proportional representation. There would be voting on a list covering the department, the distribution of the seats being effected on a proportional basis, but with an advantage to those lists which picked up the greatest number of votes. And if one of these lists obtained an absolute majority, it took all the seats. In fact these modifications of the proportional principle had been adopted to favour the coalition that was being formed against, what many leaders of parliament and public opinion regarded as the main danger, socialism, and behind it the dreaded spectre of bolshevism.

The working-class movement: hopes and isolation

Since the armistice, there had been a great leap forward of the working-class movement, which could be seen by the progress of both the socialist party and the CGT.

All through 1919, and in spite of serious internal quarrels, which we shall discuss later, the socialist party had increased its number of members in a spectacular manner. These rose, according to party figures, from 36,000 in December 1918 to 133,000 in December 1919. Contemporary observers attributed this to an influx of young people, often with revolutionary tendencies. Annie Kriegel has shown that this explanation is wrong, stressing at the same time the impossibility of ascribing this exceptional growth to any one factor. It was often due to diverse reasons, each peculiar to the union in which it occurred. However, this progress certainly reflected, once the war was over and the victory won, the desire of a section of the proletariat to restart the class war and 'to have the war paid for by the people responsible'. As for the CGT, it had an even more spectacular growth, for its members in 1919 numbered about one million (as compared with less than seven hundred thousand before the war) according to a critical study carried out by Annie Kriegel. (*La Croissance des effectifs de la CGT, 1918–1921.*) This growth was caused both by the adhesion of professional organisations, e.g. the post office and the teachers, and by larger numbers joining existing unions. It was certainly favoured by the ever more rapid rise in prices, which was not accompanied by corresponding rises in wages. All this inflamed the fighting spirit of the trade unionists. It did not, however, turn French trade unionism into a mass movement, such as existed in Germany and Great Britain. In only eight departments did the membership go over 5 per cent. Yet the progress made was enough to rouse the fears of the wealthy classes and the anxiety of the police. In order to defuse the wave of foreseeable unrest as much as possible, the government passed certain social measures, in particular the law on collective agreements (25 March 1919) and the law inaugurating – albeit with some postponements – the eight-hour day (23 April 1919). All this did not prevent street demonstrations on 1 May, which had been forbidden by the government. In Paris there were some very violent clashes with the forces of the law, and one worker was killed. Feelings ran all the higher because the situation was greatly exaggerated, for the censorship had driven people to mistrust official information. However, contrary to what the revolutionaries had hoped, there was no move towards a general strike. Members of the Paris metal-workers union, who embarked on a strike in spite of the collective agreement signed by their unions, were not supported, and at the end of June they had to resume work unconditionally. This enabled Jouhaux to win a victory against the revolutionary minority at the general trade-union congress held in Lyon (15–21 September).

As we have already seen, the leaders of the socialists during the war period had lost control of the party because of their attitude towards events in Russia. Nearly all members of the party agreed in condemning all foreign intervention that was aimed at destroying the bolsheviks, whereas the allied governments had several times thought during 1919 that they could drive out Lenin and his followers by supporting one or other of the 'white' generals.

In March, Clemenceau allowed an expeditionary corps under French command to start an offensive towards the Ukraine, but a mutiny broke out in the fleet led by a young engineer called André Marty. In April, Odessa was abandoned. From June onwards these indecisive interventions ceased and a policy was adopted of isolating bolshevik Russia, which was by now plunged in chaos. Meanwhile Germany had been shaken since January by outbreaks of revolution, incited by Spartacists and independent socialists. The social democrats and centre Catholics, whose coalition was put in power by the constituent assembly at Weimar, had called in the Reichswehr to deal with these disturbances, which they gladly proceeded to do in a brutal manner, both in Berlin and Munich. In the same way Hungary for 123 days, beginning on 21 February, was the scene of efforts by Béla Kun to install a soviet republic. The attempt was finally crushed by intervention from Rumania.

This series of events made many socialists think, as it did Lenin himself, that the hour of general revolution had struck. Although they were profoundly ignorant about events in Russia and about the theories of the bolsheviks, most French socialists believed in a revolutionary outcome of this kind. So the influence of the old 'majority' socialists, who had been discredited by their 'socialist–jingoist' attitude, was on the wain. Some of them left the party and, on 2 July 1918, founded La France Libre, and then the Parti Socialiste Français, which joined up with the socialist republicans. However the great majority of socialists were not ready to encourage the birth of a soviet republic in France. Yet a Comité pour la Troisième Internationale, founded by Monatte and Loriot, assembled the extreme left elements in the SFIO (Section Française de l'Internationale Ouvrière) and the CGT and aimed at steering the majority of the party gradually towards revolution. It soon received the backing of Lenin, but the cautious attitude adopted by the committee was in fact dictated by the limited support it commanded. The doctrine of its members was allied to the ideas of revolutionary trade unionism rather than to Marxist Leninism, about which they knew very little.

In fact most of the party followed the leaders of the centre group, which was created at the end of the war by a grouping of 'minority' socialists like Longuet and by 'majority' socialists like Cachin, who were disappointed by the national defence policy of the Union Sacrée. They sympathised with the Russian revolution and, at the congress of the Second International Bureau at Berne in February 1919, they countered the severe criticism of the bolsheviks made by the Swede Branting and by Kautsky. However, although they readily preached the revolutionary destiny of the party, they adapted themselves provisionally to the parliamentary political system and remained attached to the gains of bourgeois democracy.

The 'bleu horizon' Chamber

However, it was also decided unanimously by the socialists that no alliance would be concluded with the 'bourgeois' parties. With the current voting system this could have been suicidal. Yet, by comparison with the elections of 1914, the party made solid progress. With 1,700,000 votes against 1,400,000 it held its traditional bastions (the Nord and the Pas-de-Calais, the 'red crescent' of Burgundy and Limousin, Mediterranean France and the Paris suburbs). It also inherited the relative strength of the German social democrats in Alsace, especially in the Upper Rhine. But, as the majority principle worked in favour of their opponents, the parliamentary representation of the party diminished considerably – sixty-eight deputies against one hundred and three in 1914 when, in a *scrutin d'arrondissement*, the socialists had often benefited from agreements with the radicals.

Because of this the new Chamber was the most right-wing of any which the Republic had known since 1875. In many constituencies there had been Bloc National lists, and frequently the radicals had deemed it wiser to join them. On the extreme right only the avowed opponents of the Republic were excluded. Supported by most of the press and endowed with ample funds, the Bloc National had concentrated its campaign on the bolshevik danger, as illustrated by the famous poster of the man with the knife between his teeth. The enormous popularity of Clemenceau was also exploited. With 417 seats the Bloc National had a crushing majority in the Chamber, which came to be known as the 'bleu horizon' Chamber after the many army veterans who were there to carry the flag. The non-socialist left was reduced to a hundred or so deputies.

The dominating presence of Clemenceau at this point began to weigh on the leaders of this new majority. It was then that those close to the president of the Council let it be known that 'the Tiger', although he had often fought shy of it in the course of the year, would gladly let himself be elected President of the Republic in 1920. They also declared that he would know how to use the constitutional powers attaching to this function, powers which preceding presidents had not chosen to use. So Clemenceau was accused of secretly aiming at a dictatorship, and people were especially worried when, on 4 November at Strasbourg in the course of a policy speech, he recommended a programme of financial austerity based on a more just tax system, e.g. a rising scale of income tax and the establishment of industrial consultative bodies with worker representation. It was Briand who undertook to get rid of the danger. He was particularly careful to point out to the Roman Catholics, who were numerous among the new deputies, that the president of the Council adhered to a strict interpretation of secularism.

This underground campaign was a great success. On 16 January 1920 the traditional preparatory gathering of the republican groups in the Chamber and Senate held at the Palais du Luxembourg, on a trial vote, gave 408 votes to Paul Deschanel, the president of the Chamber, and only 389 to Clemenceau. 'The Tiger' then threw in his hand and refused irrevocably to present himself as candidate to the presidency.

On 17 January the National Assembly elected Deschanel as President of the Republic, and at once Clemenceau handed in the resignation of his cabinet. On the 20th Millerand formed the new government, most of whose members were connected with business and only too ready to profit from the situation. With the left crushed and Clemenceau removed from the scene, the right took in hand the destiny of the country.

PART II

After the war

9

Monetary illusions: the fall of the franc: reparations and war debts

The right had hardly settled down in power when it found itself grappling with a monetary phenomenon which was incomprehensible to nearly everyone, even the 'experts'; for the franc had been stable for more than a century. Even in the war, and despite the prodigious expenses incurred by that war, the franc kept its exchange value. We have already seen how and why on 13 March 1919 the allies refused to support the currency any longer, so that it began at once to decline in the foreign exchange markets. In December the pound was at forty-two francs (against twenty-five in 1914) and the dollar was at eleven francs (against five in 1914). The fall continued in 1920, which we now can see was inevitable because France, drained by the war, had to import large quantities of raw materials, even foodstuffs, and could only cover 53 per cent of her imports by her exports. By April the dollar cost more than sixteen francs, and in December more than 17; the franc had lost more than two-thirds of its value.

The first crisis of the franc
Suddenly saddled with a falling currency the French saw prices rise steadily. In April the wholesale price index (on the usual forty-five articles) was at six hundred, and in October the retail price index reached 412 (as compared with one hundred in July 1914).

People could only attribute this disaster to a vast conspiracy on the part of the powerful nations, Great Britain and the United States, probably encouraged by defeated Germany. Or, alternatively, they could blame the carelessness and improvidence of the government and the spendthrift tendencies of parliament. In any case there were few who dared to assert that the collapse of the currency was the logical result of war expenditure.

In the autumn of 1920, however, France was affected by a cyclical world crisis, whose first effect was to cause a fall in the price of imported raw materials. At the same time, the trade balance recovered spectacularly and exports managed to cover 87 per cent of imports. After a short delay, French prices followed suit and settled at around 310 for retail and 350 for wholesale prices during the last half of 1921 and throughout 1922. The crisis, like others before it, recovered most of the inflation unleashed in the preceding period. Many farmers found their incomes shrinking suddenly as a result, and there was a sudden increase in unemployment, which reached half a million in 1921.

This crisis at least led to a shake-out on the exchange scene. The pound fell back to forty-eight francs and the dollar to eleven francs in April 1921, so that the final depreciation of the franc was only about 50 per cent. This respite was widely interpreted as a first step towards the pre-war situation; for no one really believed that those days would not come back.

The monetary crisis of 1924

The situation was made even more unstable because public opinion did not understand the real character of an inflation that resulted from the imbalance between global supplies and solvent demand. In its ignorance it confined itself to examining anxiously the purely financial aspects of the problem, i.e. the balancing or non-balancing of the state budget, and the proportion of paper-money in circulation related to the gold reserves of the Banque de France. In these departments the position was particularly disquieting. On the one hand, as it was still hoped that the Germans would pay reparations for war damage to the economy, the government thought it possible to have, besides the usual budget, a second budget of 'recoverable expenses' (30 July 1920). But if the Germans ceased their payments, a gaping hole would appear, considerably worsening the budget deficit. On the other hand, much of the internal debt contracted since the beginning of the war was made up of national defence and treasury bonds, which were repayable in the short term. If the bearers of these bonds lost confidence and wanted to exchange them for less hazardous investments, e.g. gold or foreign currency, the treasury would be in no position to pay the state's outgoings, even if the budget were balanced. If the treasury, to meet its obligations, asked the Banque de France to increase its advances, the equilibrium between the gold cover and the number of notes in circulation would be threatened. The efficient management of public finances was thus constantly at the mercy of the holders of treasury bonds, while a careful watch had to be kept on the budget and the balance between the gold stock and the number of notes in circulation.

Then in 1923, for reasons that we shall analyse later, Poincaré as president of the Council decided to launch a costly operation in the Ruhr. The Germans, who were already in the grip of runaway inflation and had suspended payment of reparations, did little to prevent the mark from crashing, which could only increase the anxieties of the French.

The situation deteriorated all through 1923. In January the dollar was at fifteen francs: it passed seventeen francs in August and 19 francs in December. In the first six months of 1924 there was the threat of a real panic. On one day in March the dollar reached 28.74 francs and the pound 122.06 francs. The financial indicators, on which specialists based their judgments, showed nothing to justify such speculation against the franc: 'Everyone wonders', said *Le Temps*, 'what are the causes of this depreciation, which is obviously exaggerated. Economic and financial realities do not justify it' (9 March). Once again the idea of an international plot against the French currency was vigorously canvassed by the press, and it was all the more plausible because the British, like the Americans, did not conceal their dislike of Poincaré's policy towards Germany, which they found too severe. The plot theory was readily believed on the political right, where the return to balanced budgets practised since 1919 was considered most praiseworthy. The deficit, which had been twenty-six billion francs in 1919, was only ten billion francs in 1922, thanks to an increase in tax receipts (income tax, and especially indirect taxation), which had been accepted only with much grumbling. Furthermore, at the end of 1923, just as a hard electoral campaign was in prospect, the government embarked on a rigorous budget policy. There would be an end to the easy-going policies that allowed a supplementary budget for recoverable expenditure. The latter would be reinstated in the normal budget and, to deal with the resulting increase of the deficit, the minister of finance proposed a general increase in taxes of 20 per cent, which would bring in six billion francs. This plan for financial stabilisation was placed before parliament on 17 January 1924 and was passed by the Chamber on 24 February, but the Senate was reluctant to follow suit. Meanwhile the exchange crisis gathered pace and amounted to a real panic. The government in its efforts to fight against it resorted to the bankers Morgan Brothers in New York, who let it be known that any loan would be conditional on a stabilisation of the nation's finances. On 14 March the Senate finally decided to pass the government's measures. A loan of one hundred million dollars from Morgan Brothers was then announced, which the Banque de France rather grudgingly agreed to guarantee with its gold.

By now the clearly speculative nature of the recent excessive fall of the franc became obvious. The economist Alfred Sauvy has worked on the problem using Cassel's law, according to which, when two currency systems suffer from inflation, the normal exchange rate after this inflation should equal the old exchange rate multiplied by the two countries' coefficient of inflation. The result in this case shows that in March 1924 the franc–dollar rate ought to have stabilised at twelve or thirteen francs so as to bring wholesale prices into balance. One can tell from this how artificial, and therefore speculative, were the rates recorded on 8 March, i.e. around twenty-two francs. (A. Sauvy, *Histoire économique de la France entre les deux guerres*, vol. I, p. 53.)

Even in the great days of the gold standard before the war, exchange operators indulged in speculation on small fluctuations between top and bottom prices. However, now that all currencies, except the dollar, had left the gold standard, the rates depended solely on the laws of the market. Speculation was no longer a cottage industry, but the source of enormous profits.

But who was it who speculated? It is hard to arrive at reliable figures in the absence of proper exchange control – always difficult to set up in a liberal democracy. (J. Bouvier, 'Les Maladies monétaires de l'entre-deux-guerres', *Politique aujourd'hui*, November 1971; and J.-N. Jeanneney, 'De la spéculation financière comme arme diplomatique à propos de la première "bataille du Franc"', November 1923–March 1924', *Relations internationales*, 13, 1978, pp. 5–27.) However there is no doubt that syndicates of foreign banks, many of them based in Amsterdam, worked together to speculate against the franc, and that enormous quantities of floating capital, once tied up in profitable central European operations, were released on the weak point in the chain. Moreover, it has been maintained that the British government thought of using this means to put pressure on Poincaré's diplomacy, which it criticised for the occupation of the Ruhr. In the end London refrained from action, but was not displeased by the discomfiture in Paris. It may well be that the cabinet in Berlin covertly encouraged its bankers in their attacks on the franc, pressing them to combine patriotism with profit in a most agreeable manner.

However, it is important to stress that French capitalism also played its part against the franc, particularly at the beginning of the squall. Was the run on the franc, as has been suggested by certain analysts especially on the right, the work of a mass of small bondholders, who were worried by muddled public finances, exhausted by fiscal inquisitions and tortured by the rise in prices? Were they showing their mistrust of their rulers by exchanging their few French bonds for foreign currency, even at inflated prices? This explanation, which was often put forward later when the left was in power, did not fit the facts of the time. These small capitalists 'too nervous to play the big game, too ignorant to use the financial machinery at the proper time' (J. Bouvier, *ibid.*) were not in a position to provoke such swift and dramatic movements. One must conclude therefore that the bulk of the speculation on the French side came from the obvious source – the rich, the big traders, the industrialists, the bankers – in short, all those who owned enough to speculate profitably 'with funds and stocks and shares in large quantities'. In short, a section of the well-to-do gambled against a right-wing government – and it would not be for the last time.

The simultaneous announcement of stabilisation measures and the Morgan loan was enough to restore the situation and show the 'blown-up' nature of the speculation. The dollar came down to seventeen francs. The government had at one time hoped to arrive at a rate of fifteen francs, but had to admit failure, so that on the whole this second crisis ended up with an overall depreciation of the currency. The uneasy atmosphere which resulted was no doubt partly responsible for the reverse suffered by the government at the May elections. But the Cartel des Gauches, which then came into power, had no more grip on monetary realities than their predecessors of the right.

The third monetary crisis (1925–6)

The left were to make the worst possible mistake in the circumstances. The socialists in the winning coalition had long advocated severe measures against capital, but the other element in the Cartel des Gauches, the radicals, were much less in favour of such action. Measures were announced to satisfy the socialists' demands, but without precise details being given, and at the same time men were put in positions of power who were determined to resist such measures. Yet it is a department of politics in which it is more important to act than to talk. Anxiety was sown among the large number of bondholders, and their worries were carefully fed by the dire predictions of the right-wing press. So very soon the government was faced with the treasury's difficulties arising from the fact that people refused to renew their treasury bonds. There had to be recourse to advances from the Banque de France, and the fiduciary note issue had to be increased. A 1919 law had fixed the ceiling of the money in circulation at forty-one billion francs, and in January 1925 this was exceeded. Deceptive action had to be taken so that this state of affairs should not come to light in the weekly report of the Banque de France. At the end of December the council of regents, whose job was precisely to guarantee the truth of the bank's reports, learnt with horror about this fraudulent manipulation. From that moment the council found itself burdened with a moral responsibility and political power that it had never expected.

If the Cartel government on arrival in office had listened to the treasury experts, and particularly Pierre de Mouij who was in charge of the movement of funds, it could have explained to the country that it had inherited a difficult situation, and that it made no economic sense to try and contract the note circulation to the 1914 level simply to regain the pre-war gold-parity of the franc. The government could have carried out, to the left's benefit, the stabilising programme which Poincaré later conducted – to the right's benefit. Instead of this, Herriot refused to face reality and hoped to retrieve the situation by speeches, swearing by all the gods that he would forbid any increase in the note circulation – whereas in fact this had already happened! He was fiddling the thermometer instead of fighting the illness.

The Cartel paid a very heavy price for this gross initial error. Herriot had delivered himself bound hand and foot to the regents, whom he now begged to give him a little time before publishing the real accounts. From then onwards he lived from hand to mouth, alternating menaces and blandishments. Meanwhile the leakage of information started, confidence melted, the holders of matured bonds did not renew them, the franc crumbled and the net tightened.

Finally, at the end of March, one of the regents, François de Wendel, president of the Comité des Forges and a right-wing deputy, dealt the final blow by announcing that he would resign from the Banque de France if the true accounts were not published – which he knew would be fatal for the government. His colleagues, through the governor, presented an ultimatum to the cabinet.

Well might Herriot, knowing the fatal outcome, announce a capital levy as a final grand bluff. It was no more than shadow boxing. All that the Cartel did was to compromise in their fall an important idea in their programme and tarnish the image of the left as financial managers – a heavy historic responsibility. (See also J.–N. Jeanneney, *Leçon d'histoire pour une gauche au pouvoir, la faillite du Cartel 1924–1926.*) On 10 April Herriot, vigorously denounced by Poincaré and criticised by the Senate, had to hand in the resignation of his cabinet. On 16 April parliament accepted the lifting of the note circulation ceiling. The same day the pound was quoted at one hundred francs. The French currency began to lose value in spite of a favourable economic situation and a trade balance that was comfortably positive.

Herriot's fall was followed by a series of short-lived governments, who were thwarted in every course of action. On the one hand, Caillaux favoured a restoration of confidence by launching a loan that was highly advantageous for the subscribers – but they ignored it. Georges Bonnet, on the other hand, tried to force the bondholders to renew their loans – and failed. Mounting anxiety led the extreme right, largely financed by Coty the scent-manufacturer, to denounce the negligence of the administrations and, through them, the flaws of democracy as compared with the successes of Italian fascism. The opportunity was also seized to blame the eight-hour law for general idleness and drunkenness, to blame high wages for wastage and high prices, and even to affirm that the mild social laws which were introduced by the Cartel, by protecting people from life's risks, would deprive the economy of all motivation. (M. Perrot, *La Monnaie et l'opinion publique en France et en Grande-Bretagne, 1924–1936.*) Meanwhile the purely speculative fall of the franc gathered momentum. In July 1926 the pound rose to 243 francs.

Poincaré's stabilisation

Up to now various political solutions had been tried and rejected, except one: with Poincaré, who could count on a majority which went from the radicals to the right, and who thus restored, under the name of the Union

Nationale, the old majority of the Bloc. He obtained this majority in the Chamber after Herriot's final defeat. The Cartel surrendered unconditionally while disorder threatened round the Palais-Bourbon.

Confidence returned almost miraculously. 'Once the Poincaré cabinet was set up on 22 July, capital movements changed direction. On the 23rd the pound fell to 208 francs, on the 26th to 199, and on the 27th to 196. The return flow of funds continued to grow. On 30 October the pound was at 194 francs and on 19 November at 174 francs. The capital that had previously gone abroad flooded the market. Those who yesterday had sought foreign currencies now wanted francs at any price.' (J. Rueff, preface to *Souvenirs . . . du gouverneur de la Banque de France Moreau*, cited in J. Bouvier, 'Les Maladies monétaires de l'entre-deux-guerres', *Politique aujourd'hui*, November 1971.)

On 3 August 1926 the new government announced from the start that it would respect all undertakings; and it increased the discount rate to 7.5 per cent. It also passed through parliament a group of fiscal measures designed to complete the recovery. Concessions were made to the rich by a sharp drop in the rate of income tax and a flat 2 per cent turnover tax, but there was a general increase in direct taxation, e.g. scheduled taxes on income from stocks and shares, and indirect taxation, e.g. levies on alcoholic drinks, motor-cars and even bicycles. Furthermore, the government did not hesitate to hit large fortunes more directly by levying a 7 per cent tax on first real estate transfers.

In addition, on 10 August the two Chambers sitting at Versailles voted for the creation of a *Caisse autonome de gestion des bons de la défense nationale* according to the constitutional procedure, so as to make any revision of the law harder. This *Caisse* was charged with the redemption of the public debt, using income received from taxes on real estate, etc., more especially from the manufacture of tobacco. Thus the treasury, by renewing their bonds, was protected from short-term fluctuations and so from the whims of public opinion.

There was nothing very original in these measures, but Poincaré was able to obtain what none of his predecessors could win, not even the clever Caillaux – the confidence of the holders of wealth, great and small. Between June and December 1926 the value of the franc went up faster than it had fallen, to such an extent that there was considerable disquiet. Both the world of business and of labour began to fear a crisis of production and employment – in fact Jouhaux sought out Poincaré to warn him of the dire dangers to employment of too obvious recovery of the franc. The number of unemployed reached nearly half a million at the end of the year. Underemployment on this scale had been unknown since the crisis of 1921. Poincaré also decided to support the pound by buying foreign currency so that it should stabilise at 124 francs.

The stability of the franc, which lasted until mid-1928, was the subject of heated discussions between those who would have preferred an attempt to restore the 1914 parity, if necessary by stages, and those who argued for keeping the present rate. The unfortunate example of Great Britain, who had in 1925 opted for a return to the parity and had been unable ever since to profit from the general prosperity, was an argument in favour of devaluation. Poincaré's temperament and ideas inclined him to side with the revaluers, but he was prudent enough to wait. People (including Poincaré) gradually got used to the idea of devaluation, which by relieving the public debt and absorbing the rise in domestic prices since 1914, would allow a fairly painless return to the gold standard. Of course creditors, especially those of the state, would lose out; but they were under no illusions and were in fact resigned to their fate. The law of 25 June 1928 was passed, therefore, fixing the new value of the franc at 65 milligrams of gold, or one-fifth of its original value. To mark the return to the gold standard the compulsory acceptance of banknotes was abolished; but they could only be exchanged against gold bars of at least 215,000 francs in value, which would prevent any panic movements. Thanks to the revaluation of the gold holding which resulted from the new rate, the state's debts to the Banque de France were wiped out.

The rate of devaluation adopted was the subject of argument at the time, and afterwards. It appears from Alfred Sauvy's calculations that the level of the franc was pitched a little lower than was required by a strict alignment on purchasing power. (*Histoire économique de la France entre les deux guerres*, vol. 1, p. 97.) This left a certain margin for prices, which could as easily be devoted to vote-catching measures as to extra spending of a productive character. In addition – and Poincaré certainly could not have foreseen this – the advantage which the French economy, and its foreign trade in particular, enjoyed was to put her in a favourable position at the beginning of the world crisis of 1929. This was undoubtedly advantageous in the short term, but it delayed France's awakening to the gravity of the situation.

On the whole, however, amid all the errors and illusions of the immediate post-war period, this devaluation of the franc seems to have been a wise move. It enabled the French to face facts and stop dreaming of an impossible return to pre-war conditions. It also reduced to a tolerable minimum the undeniable loss of wealth caused by the war. In short, it was 'an island of reasonableness in an ocean of error' (A. Sauvy, *ibid.*). Poincaré, the incarnation of 'petit-bourgeois' France, the solid pillar of the Third Republic, had managed to choose the middle way with the consent of most of the country. He avoided the social risks likely to result from an excessive inflation such as occurred in Germany, which would have reduced to nothing the incomes of the middle classes, on which the regime depended; and he also avoided a brutal deflation, such as the British had experienced, with its attendant high unemployment and business slump. This middle way was the only one capable of preserving unearned incomes and savings and of giving the nation productive strength not only to repair the ravages of war, but also to adapt the archaic economy to the new world promised by swift technical progress. Only in this way could France assure her wealth and her place in the world. (See P. Miquel (ed.), *Poincaré*, p. 513.)

Unfortunately this wisdom did not persist without serious blows being dealt to public morality in general and respect for institutions in particular. For the rich, and notably for the minor bourgeoisie, to accept the loss of four-fifths of the value of the franc ('a nice little bankruptcy', said Léon Daudet contemptuously), they had to be allowed for years to express all their rancour against the state as destroyer of property, against its ravenous financial lacqueys and against the lazy and improvident working classes. All serious social reforms, which could have brought a better share-out of eventual growth, had to be jettisoned. In addition, public opinion developed the myth of the 'man sent by Providence', which was to make people in times of crisis look for a solution of this unhealthy type.

10

The illusion of power

A precarious peace: from Versailles to the Dawes plan

The American retreat and its consequences

As we have already seen, the French attributed the financial crisis and the troubles of the franc to the machinations of all the great world powers. For hardly was the ink dry on the signatures to the treaty of Versailles than the French began to be conscious of their isolation. The precious Anglo-American 'guarantees', in exchange for which Clemenceau had thought he need no longer demand a solid military presence on the Rhine, soon vanished. American public opinion, which President Wilson, isolated by his illness, had ignored far too much, promptly returned at the end of hostilities to its traditional isolationism. The Versailles treaty, which the White House presented very clumsily to Congress, picked up only 49 votes on 20 March 1920, i.e. much less than the two-thirds majority demanded by the American constitution. The hostile senators wanted to show their disapproval of the League of Nations, which entangled the United States in a system of permanent alliances that went against all American tradition. The withdrawal of the Americans took Great Britain in its wake. The promise of automatic intervention on France's side in the event of German aggression, which had justified Clemenceau's concessions on the Rhine problem, was now a dead letter. French public opinion felt that it had been duped. It felt its isolation all the more because of what was happening in the east. In the solution of problems arising from the collapse of the old central European powers and of Turkey, French diplomacy on several occasions came into almost headlong collision with the British.

Difficulties in the east

In the Middle East the treaty of Sèvres, signed on 10 August 1920, confirmed the dismemberment of Turkey, which was reduced in Europe to Constantinople with its surroundings and in Asia to Anatolia. In the old possessions of the Sublime Porte in the Middle East – Lebanon, Palestine, Syria, Iraq and Arabia – the French and the British indulged in complex struggles for influence, which were sharpened by the presence of oil. However, the French ended up with a protectorate not only over Lebanon but also over Syria, where the British had to give up the idea of installing an Arab Kingdom (24 April 1920). Furthermore, they obtained control of quarter of the oil in the Mosul region, as well as the right to move it towards the Mediterranean by a pipeline which would be built in territory under French influence (8 April 1919). Meanwhile in Anatolia itself the treaty of Sèvres handed over vast regions to Greek, Italian and also French ambitions. Posing as protectors of the Armenians, the forces of General Gouraud established themselves in Cilicia.

This carving up of what had undoubtedly been Turkish in the old empire inflamed Ottoman national sentiment and gave Mustafa Kemal, a rebel general and head of the revolutionary government, the popular support he required. In the course of 1921 he was able to crush the Greeks, who had rashly ventured into the heart of Anatolia, and at the same time to chase the last sultan out of Constantinople. It was clear that the treaty of Sèvres would have to be revised, and a new conference was called at Lausanne for this purpose. By the treaty that was signed there on 24 July 1923, Kemal obtained the suppression of capitulations and the end of all financial control. The presidency of the commission charged with supervising the demilitarisation and neutrality of the Straits was entrusted to Turkey, who thereby recovered her sovereignty in full. In addition she recovered eastern Thrace in Europe and kept her authority over the whole Anatolian peninsula from which the Greek population had been expelled.

This outcome was a serious reverse for British diplomacy, which had dreamt of gaining the support of a 'Greater' Greece within her sphere of influence in the eastern Mediterranean. Kemal had been most opportunely helped by France at a crucial moment in his fight against the Greek armies; for France had then agreed to abandon all her designs on Cilicia (October 1921) and to stop all military action against him. The Foreign Office was outraged by this French desertion and as a result harboured some resentment.

Central and eastern Europe

In central Europe the collapse of the Austro-Hungarian empire had created a situation that was both highly unstable and absurd. The geographical tangle of peoples made the principle of nationality impossible to apply in practice. Each of the new states born of the disappearance of the double monarchy was the object of irredentist claims from his neighbour, who in his turn was accused of enslaving minorities. The allies, divided amongst themselves as to their aims, could only leave the antagonisms to gain strength, while Austria had by treaty to be protected against the attractions of joining up with Germany, a move that was favoured by the socialists of the time.

Finally, in eastern Europe, the fixing of the frontiers of Poland gave the allies much trouble. The French government was anxious to find east of Germany the ally it had lost by the bolshevisation of Russia, and it was also influenced by the traditional sentimental attachment which public opinion periodically showed for poor Poland. On the whole, therefore, it sought to support the claims of the new state. But suddenly Poland showed signs of vast ambitions both to the east and to the west – ambitions which the British and Americans were anxious to contain. Some feeble compromises had been reached in the treaty of Versailles, particularly concerning Polish claims in Upper Silesia. Pending a plebiscite this province was put under the control of an inter-allied commission, presided over by a French general and attended by a considerable military force (February 1920).

At this juncture Poland took a risk that might have ended in disaster. She was dissatisfied with the eastern frontiers proposed by the allies – the Curzon Line – and thought she could take advantage of Russia's exhaustion. On 5 April 1920 Polish troops entered the Ukraine and captured Kiev. However, a Red Army counter-attack soon threw them back, and their retreat turned into a rout. In August the Russians were in the outskirts of Warsaw. The French government promised help and sent money, munitions and military advisers, among them General Weygand. Meanwhile, Pilsudski managed to defeat and pursue the bolsheviks, who had advanced most rashly. This retrieval of the situation allowed the Poles, by the peace of Riga (12 March 1921), to fix their frontier 150 kilometres east of the lane planned by the Foreign Office, who were much displeased by this forwardness.

There remained the problem of Upper Silesia. On 21 March 1921 the plebiscite gave the majority to the supporters of rejoining Germany; but the Poles were the majority in the eastern and southern districts. Poland, backed by France, claimed a partition, which Germany refused and Great Britain opposed. Procrastination resulted from these disagreements until Korfanty, the son of a Polish miner in Silesia and former Reichstag deputy, thought he could force the pace by fermenting an insurrection, which delivered the province into his hands. The French troops on the spot did not react. So the Germans sent along some irregular forces and the British let it be known that in their eyes Korfanty, backed by the Polish government, was an aggressor. Relations between Paris and London became very strained, and Briand had to use all his tact to smooth things out. Finally, it was agreed to give the League of Nations the task of fixing the frontier, which was done with some difficulty on 12 October 1921.

The Petite Entente

As a result of these events the Foreign Office developed a deep and lasting dislike of the Poles, while in this same year, 1921, French diplomacy started to build a 'Petite Entente' in eastern and central Europe – with Poland as one of its corner-stones.

The operation was in fact an attempt to unify irreconcilable opposites. States who had always been jealous of one another were being asked to cement alliances. The first steps had been taken in 1920 by an agreement signed between Czechoslovakia and Jugoslavia, and it had raised few difficulties as they had no grounds for dissension and both feared the Hungarians. A more delicate matter was the bringing together of the Rumanians and the Czechs, who both had designs on Sub-Carpathian Russia. However, the adventures of the ex-emperor Charles in Hungary, by the fears it provoked, helped on an alliance which up till then would have been impossible (April 1921). In June, for the same reasons, the Rumanians and the Jugoslavs in their turn signed an agreement. A common hatred of the Magyars thereby allowed a network of alliances to be built up under the protective wing of France. The latter wished to add Poland, to whom since February 1921 she had been linked by a formal alliance. All the prestige France enjoyed was necessary to achieve this as there were many points of dissension between the Poles and the Czechs. With great difficulty a commercial agreement was concluded by the two states; then, in November 1921, a vague political entente was signed.

With this network of alliances France hope to have found in central Europe a decent substitute for the old Russian alliance. But, from the start, the worm was in the fruit. Not only did the rivalries, ambitions and hatreds within this Petite Entente make the alliances extremely fragile, but also France could not, as she had so often done before the war, reinforce her influence by financial assistance. This used to take the form of placing in her market the bonds which the new states issued in their thirst for development; but the French market was now too weak to absorb these bonds. Furthermore, for this network of alliances to be credible, the French army would have had to organise itself in such a way that it could go to the rescue of its allies in an aggressive manner, whereas the French, even those who were most 'nationalist', were inclined to espouse defensive doctrines. This attitude was typical of a public opinion that had been traumatised by the war and had no thoughts of territorial expansion, and of a general staff that was obsessed by the legacy of four years of trench warfare. Finally, and not least important, France's policy in this part of the world put a strain on her links with Great Britain. Yet no one in France seriously contemplated a rift with an old ally, who showed her frank contempt for France's new 'barbarian' associates.

Two policies for security

The settlement of the German question also stirred up growing dissension between France and her Anglo-American allies. Yet the return of Alsace-Lorraine to the mother country, repairing the 'injustice' of 1871, was greeted with satisfaction by nearly all shades of opinion. The extreme nationalist right led by Jacques Bainville and Charles Maurras, who had re-discovered the old theory of natural frontiers and dreamed of annexing the Rhineland, did not rally substantial support. The desire for peace constantly expressed by the politicians and echoed by nearly all the public was perfectly genuine and could easily be explained by the gruelling ordeal which the French had recently undergone.

But how could one be quite sure that this desire for peace was shared by the nation who lost the war? There were plenty of signs in Germany of the spirit of revenge. A section of French opinion therefore deemed it essential to be on guard, to watch the eastern neighbour very closely and see that the conditions of the Versailles treaty were closely adhered to, especially those clauses that concerned disarmament and reparations; and there should be no hesitation to use force, if necessary, on a recalcitrant neighbour. So one can understand how the cancelling of the American and British guarantees strengthened the idea that, in the interests of peace, France ought to preserve a military and strategic superiority, in order to enforce the strict application of the treaty and stifle any German attempt at revenge. Poincaré was the oracle of this outlook, which at first was shared by the 'nationalists', many of the 'moderates' and a section of the radicals. Having left the Elysée in February 1920, the senator from Lorraine became a stickler for the strict application of the Versailles treaty, making speeches on Sundays and writing bi-monthly articles in the *Revue des deux mondes*. Untiringly he denounced the duplicity of the defeated Germans and their broken promises. He also attacked the dishonesty of the British and Americans who were always ready, in their quest for lucre, to tolerate the recovery of a Germany who would provide them with profitable markets. Finally, he lashed the feebleness and impotence of the institutions for collective security.

However, in opposition to this policy of 'security through force' (see J.-B. Duroselle (ed.), *A la recherche de la France*, Paris, Editions du Seuil, 1963) there were those who bore in mind the isolation that would result and the weakness of the nation after the war; and they placed their hopes in a peace arising out of a *rapprochement* with Germany, and in recourse to international institutions and arbitration. This point of of view, which the socialists had defended unsuccessfully in 1919, gradually, amid the mounting difficulties, won over both the bulk of the left and a number of the moderates who were disappointed with the failure of the hard-liners. It soon found a champion in the person of Aristide Briand, even though he was one of the leaders of the

Bloc National and had for a time seemed to agree with the supporters of security through force. Having become president of the Council and foreign minister in January 1921, did he not in April promise to 'grab Germany by the throat' if she failed in her obligations? But his realism and flexibility soon made him feel that this attitude was incompatible not only with the survival of France's alliances but also with the modest means at the nation's disposal. 'I practise the policy of our birth-rate', he was to say later. So this former socialist, who had turned into a moderate, came back to the pacifism and internationalism of his early beliefs. He was not the only one to have high hopes of a policy of this kind. The socialists, encouraged by the arrival in power of the German social democrats, naturally believed in this policy, as did many of the radicals, including Edouard Herriot.

However, the supporters of this pacifism were not without certain *arrière-pensées* and contradictions, as indeed were their opponents. Briand was not ready to give up alliances in the east which, as we have seen, excited the suspicions of the British. Furthermore, the most ardent defenders of the League of Nations, and notably Léon Bourgeois, a leading thinker among the radicals, wanted to give the League an international military force, which was refused finally by the British and Americans at the time of the drafting of the charter. As Stanley Hoffmann has said: 'many of the heralds of the League of Nations were trying hard to turn the League into an instrument of, and a supplement to, French power' (in J. B. Duroselle (ed.), *A la recherche de la France*, p. 35). These moves could not fail to strengthen the feeling among the British and Americans that, whatever ideology was in power in France, one must be wary of the French and their inveterate militarism. Finally, certain French politicians, diplomats and businessmen saw in a policy of reconciliation with Germany the opportunity for a profitable alliance between complementary economies. Loucheur, for example, and Haguenin, head of the French information mission in Berlin, and Georges Seydoux, assistant director of trade relations at the Quai d'Orsay, all advanced the view at the beginning of the twenties that a *rapprochement* between the industrialists of France and Germany, notably in the coal and steel sectors, might contribute both to peace and to the prosperity of the two countries. (See on this, G. Soutou, 'Problème du rétablissement des relations économiques entre la France et l'Allemagne, 1918–1929', in *Francia*, 2, 1973.) In the eyes of the British, who were having considerable economic difficulties, a sort of continental coalition was looming up which threatened them and had to be thwarted at all costs.

The difficult fixing of reparations

Nothing however aroused the suspicion and even the hostility of France's partners so much as the obstinate way in which her governments, with almost the whole country's support, insisted on Germany paying for the losses caused by the war. J. M. Keynes' book *The economic consequences of the peace*, translated into French in 1920, was generally ignored by the daily press, but it met with stupefaction and general incomprehension in the specialist reviews, where the creators of opinion looked for their ideas. Moreover, this economist was thought to have considerable influence in British government circles, and he was therefore transformed into 'a sort of diabolical genius responsible for all France's troubles'. (F. Crouzet, 'Réactions françaises devant *Les Conséquences économiques de la paix* de Keynes', *RHMC*, January–March 1972.) Certainly the criticisms which dwelt on Keynes' low estimate of the damage suffered by France were justified. How could one accept, for instance, the method used by Keynes to estimate France's war damage? He simply divided the national wealth by the percentage of the country's surface that had been invaded, without taking into account the fact that these territories included the major part of France's riches. But, as François Crouzet has pointed out, the French objectors to Keynes did not reply to the main question raised in the book: Was Germany capable of paying the enormous reparations that were being demanded of her in the name of right and justice? This blindness seemed to outsiders even more inexcusable because, while France was demanding enormous payments, she was at pains to deny Germany all means of making those payments. Reminding the world of the Reich's real wealth, the French denied Keynes' thesis that, in order to pay its debts, it would have to declare a trade war against the allies, as well as against the rest of the world, in order to acquire the necessary amount of currency. In short, most French experts, despite the scruples of a handful of people like Charles Rist, had no idea of the crucial problem of transfers, which made their dreams impracticable.

The bitterness of these controversies went far to explain the slowness with which the reparations commission, chaired at first by Poincaré, laid down principles on which the total sum to be paid by Germany would be fixed. At San Remo in April 1920, then at conferences at Hythe and Boulogne in May and June, the British voiced without equivocation their desire not to crush defeated Germany under an intolerable load of debt. Poincaré then resigned from the reparations commission, denouncing in advance the concessions which he feared the French would make. 'The spectre of revision', he wrote, 'appears at every moment before our eyes.' (P. Miquel (ed.), *Poincaré*, p. 425.) In the event, at the Spa conference in July, the Germans were admitted for the first time to discuss the problem on an equal footing with the allies. The latter were able to agree on a distribution of the reparations among themselves, which slightly reduced France's share (52 per cent instead of 55 per cent) and also Great Britain's (22 per cent instead of 25 per cent) compared with what had been proposed in 1919. But the Germans showed a violent objection to accepting the figures put forward by 'experts'. This hostility intensified from conference to conference until the London meeting of May 1921, when the total of the debt was communicated to the Germans – 132 billion gold marks, a figure arrived at on 27 April by the reparations commission. The Germans were to pay two billion marks annually, to which would be added a sum equivalent to 26 per cent of their exports. In economic terms this amounted to asking them to pay the victors 14 per cent of their national revenue for thirty years. But in commercial terms it would oblige them to raise the volume of their exports by 65 per cent and therefore build up an economic strength that would be formidable in every way. (The figures are from A. Sauvy, *Histoire économique de la France entre les deux guerres*, vol. i, p. 143.)

As was to be expected, the Germans found this sum impossible. They declared that the conditions and methods of payment were impracticable. However, when menaced with an occupation of the Ruhr by the British and French (who were in agreement for once), they had to give in and start paying.

But the arguments about the revision of the treaty were by no means at an end. In a new book (*A revision of the treaty, being a sequel to 'The economic consequences of the peace'*, London, Macmillan, 1922) Keynes demanded an immediate revision, seeking to demonstrate that the Germans could only pay the sums demanded of them if the allies undertook to help the German export trade – to their own disadvantage. The liberal economists' reply to these arguments was that the transfers necessitated by these enormous payments would settle themselves by the interplay of gold movements and the variations of prices which would result – all this as if nothing, either in the monetary mechanisms or in the structures of international trade, had changed since 1913. Certain business circles with more sense and politicians more in touch with economic realities hoped to resolve the problems by seeking agreement with German industrialists, especially those of the Ruhr. After the disappearance of the monarchy, the failure of the revolution and the discredit into which the social democrats soon fell, the real masters of the German political scene in 1922 were the industrial leaders of the Ruhr, in particular Hugo Stinnes, who had built up an enormous empire there. In many ways Chancellor Cuno appeared as the docile representative of the business world. All this enabled Loucheur, minister of the liberated territories, to negotiate with Walter Rathenau, German minister for reconstruction, and to sign an agreement at Wiesbaden on 6–7 October 1921. This tried to facilitate in part the payment of reparations by deliveries in kind. In this way French citizens affected by the war could obtain directly from Germany those goods which they needed to set themselves up again. However, this arrangment aroused the suspicions of the British, who feared the establishment of lasting preferential links between the German and French economies; and so they withheld their approval until 11 March

1922. The hostility of many French industrialists was even more serious – they foresaw dangerous competition in a market where they had done good business – and in the end the deliveries in kind were very limited.

These efforts, and others besides, were unsuccessful for a long time. This was mainly because they met with the systematic hostility and suspicion of Great Britain, but also because the German steel industrialists were in fact pursuing a quite different policy. They hoped to obtain spectacular results at the cost of 'an economic cold war' (see J. Bariéty, 'Sidérurgie, littérature, politique et journalisme: une famille luxembourgeoise, les Mayrisch, entre l'Allemagne et la France après la Première Guerre mondiale', *Bulletin de la société d'histoire moderne*, 10, 1969) against the French iron and steel industry. They limited their deliveries of coke to France as much as possible, thereby restricting the mining of iron ore in Lorraine, and they built new blast-furnaces in the Ruhr, suitable for treating Swedish, Spanish and even Canadian ore. As a result of this, a weakened Germany had by 1922 recovered her pre-war iron and steel output, while French steelworks were in difficulties. Stinnes hoped that French industrialists in their anxiety would put pressure on their government to make important economic and political concessions to Germany.

Meanwhile, the collapse of the German economy followed soon after the first payment of the reparations decided in London. The dollar, which was worth sixty marks in May 1921, was worth eighty-four marks in August, and 268 at the beginning of September. In the eyes of the British this collapse proved the soundness of Keynesian ideas about the excessive size of reparations, and it led them to support the revision of the London agreement. Most of the French thought exactly the opposite – the collapse was desired by Germany's leaders, who were more prosperous than ever. They saw it as a case of bad excuses made by bad payers. Between the two views no compromise seemed possible.

Faced with the dilemma, Briand chose revision of the treaty. When he went to the Cannes conference on 4 January 1922 he already knew that he would be able to obtain some diplomatic guarantees from the British in exchange for solid French concessions in the matter of reparations. Lloyd George offered him in effect a pact of assistance in the event of German aggression on the Belgian or French borders. Briand on his side agreed to convene a fresh conference at Genoa to which the victors and the vanquished would be invited in order to work out together a grand re-organisation of the still troubled continent. But neither French public opinion nor the Bloc National in power was ready for such a revision. Called home by President Millerand (who had succeeded the ailing Deschanel in September 1920 and took a special interest in foreign affairs) Briand had to leave Cannes early. He had the support of Herriot but was condemned by those who accused him of being in the pocket of the British. Furthermore, the results of the conference which Harding as President of the United States had convened in Washington to examine the disarmament question (October 1921) did him considerable harm. He was badly informed by his secret services and thought he could play off the British against the Americans in the matter of naval armaments limitation. But he unexpectedly found himself faced with a united Anglo-American front. Finally, France had to accept a hierarchy of naval fleets which put her fourth in the world ranking, equal with Italy, which was interpreted as a humiliation by the French public. Under attack from all sides, Briand did not wait for a hostile vote in the Chamber. Leaving the Palais-Bourbon in full session, he handed in his resignation saying, 'Others will do better' (12 January 1922). The alternative leader in everyone's view was Poincaré who, as president of the senate commission on foreign affairs, had not restrained his criticism, setting himself up as champion of a strict and total application of the various treaties and their subsequent prolongations.

The Ruhr operation

The former President of the Republic at once formed a government which was supported by the whole right wing in parliament. Scorning to go to Genoa himself, he sent Barthou along, forbidding him to make the slightest concession on disarmament and reparations. So he seemed responsible for the failure of the re-organisation that the British hoped to achieve. Indeed, the only tangible result of the Rapallo encounter was the conclusion of a German–Soviet pact. This enabled the two powers to give support to one another and so break out of their isolation, opening up all sorts of possibilities (17 April 1922). Bonar Law, who had succeeded Lloyd George as prime minister, backed a German request for a moratorium following on the escalating collapse of the mark. The French government only reluctantly agreed to this moratorium as a temporary measure and demanded pledges in the Rhineland and the Ruhr, which the British refused to accept (London conference, August 1922). But the French premier had already announced publicly the possibility of unilateral action to secure such pledges. The arguments were not lacking. Not only were the Germans declaring themselves incapable of paying reparations, but throughout 1922 they were conducting an economic cold war against the French iron and steel industry. The industrialists of the Ruhr hoped by this campaign to bring France to a better frame of mind. The increasing number of paramilitary formations in the Reich that were being organised by the enigmatic General von Seekt were a violation of the treaty terms on German disarmament. Moreover, the internal debt of the German government was melting away thanks to inflation at the cost of middle-class ruin, and as she was being more or less excused from paying reparations, she would soon be the European country where taxation hit least hard. Her industry would be in a position to attack with success world markets in which the French economy, saddled with Poincaré's strict budgetary measures, would not be able to compete. What was more, and this was absurdly illogical, none of France's rich allies gave her any hope of a reduction in her enormous war debts; yet France continued to believe that account would be taken of the blood spilt by her more generously in the common cause than by all the other nations, and that her allies would wipe out the debts entirely or in part. On several occasions, and with some irritation, the Americans had made it clear that there was no question of letting France off. An attempt was made to link war debts to reparations, but Washington remained adamant in the name of strict commercial morality. The anger of Paris was understandable. France was being required to pay her debts while the United States, by their return to an ever stricter protectionism, were preventing her from earning the necessary funds by overseas trade. She was also being asked to accept a generous amnesty for those who for four years had consumed the country's substance. A military intervention was likely, therefore, to be popular in France, even if it increased her diplomatic isolation. It is not true, as has sometimes been alleged, that the forces of capital supported this intervention from the start. If François de Wendel, the president of the Comité des Forges, was in favour of force, it was more for action on the left bank of the Rhine than in the Ruhr. Furthermore, the Comité was, as so often, very much divided, and Poincaré was very careful to keep the industrialists at arm's length, rarely asking for their advice. As for the opposition on the left, it was a mixed bag. (J.-N. Jeanneney, *François de Wendel en République, l'argent et le pouvoir, 1914–1940*, pp. 148–75.) Certainly the socialists and some of the radicals vigorously criticised the operation, but less because of its objectives than because of the means used. They maintained that both security and payment of reparations would be obtained more effectively by a policy of agreement with France's allies and the democratic forces of the new Germany than by a policy of force, which would isolate the country. Only the communists went further and saw in defeated Germany (who incidentally had just recognised the Soviet Union) a victim of the bourgeois governments' greed for power.

Poincaré therefore put his operation into action. He got the reparations commission to list Germany's short deliveries of wood and coal. By the end of 1922 all was ready for an occupation of the Ruhr, fully in accordance with the letter of the Versailles treaty. Poincaré had made sure of the effective support of Belgium. The British made a final attempt to stop the move. At the Paris conference of January 1923 Bonar Law proposed an overall settlement, but Poincaré refused to be party to a plan that could offer no guarantees so long as France had no bargaining counters. This was also why he rejected American proposals outlined by Charles Hughes, the Secretary of State, in a speech made on 29 December 1922 at New Haven.

In Poincaré's view only the occupation of the Ruhr could supply the necessary bargaining element. It would touch the heart of Germany and bring her to her senses, particularly as regards the economic cold war on which she had embarked. It would also enable France to negotiate from strength in future on the problem of reparations and debts. The British and behind them the Americans could not help being anxious about a situation that could lead to a reorientation of the Rhenish economy, entirely to the profit of France. They too should be involved in the negotiations. Finally, by insisting on the support of the Czechs and Poles and requiring them not to deliver to Germany the coal which would be unavailable in the Ruhr, the French would reinforce the Petite Entente. The countries of this group were in fact the object of British intrigues that aimed at detaching them from France by the offer of loans. (D. Artaud, 'A propos de l'occupation de la Ruhr', *RHMC*, January–March 1970, pp. 14–15.) So it was above all a political manœuvre that France was launching by her occupation of the Ruhr.

This explains more clearly the subsequent events which took many of Poincaré's supporters by surprise. After careful preparation the Ruhr operation was launched on 11 January 1923. The government of the Reich, by way of reply, organised passive resistance in the form of a general strike in the Ruhr. It also secretly encouraged small groups of the extreme right to multiply attacks and sabotage in the occupied zone. The French and the Belgians on the spot were able to restart the railways and the mines which had been paralysed by the strike. At the same time, the German public finances, weakened by the expenses of passive resistance and obliged to assist millions of strikers, were very soon powerless to prevent a spectacular crash of the mark. The dollar was worth 4,620,455 marks in August, and four trillion two hundred billion marks in December. This astronomical inflation paralysed rather than favoured the national economy, as it had done before. Unemployment spread, the middle classes were ruined for ever, and political anarchy took over amid mounting distress. However, the passive resistance was failing. By August many German railway workers had gone back to work, and the miners followed.

Besides this, the occupation authorities expelled about one hundred thousand supporters of passive resistance, mostly civil servants of Prussian origin. They set up a customs barrier between the occupied territory and the rest of Germany, while, from August 1923 onwards, the inter-allied mission of factory and mine control (MICUM) did not confine itself to its original mission of verifying the real paying capacity of German firms, but passed delivery contracts to these firms thus forging economic links between the Rhineland, Belgium and France. There were even preparations within the entourage of Tirard, the high commissioner in the Rhineland, for the creation of a Rhineland monetary authority which would replace the collapsing mark with its own currency and mark a step forward towards the creation of a Rhineland state, autonomous and independent, keeping close links with its western neighbours. (J. Bariéty, 'Les Réparations allemandes, 1919–1924, objet au prétexte à une politique rhénane de la France', *Bulletin de la société d'histoire moderne*, 6, 1973, pp. 26–7.) A regionalist movement seeking autonomy was coming into existence in the Rhineland, with the mayor of Cologne, Konrad Adenauer, and a convinced separatist of uninspiring character, Dorte, well to the fore. In France, right and extreme-right circles, who since at least 1910 had dreamed of detaching francophil Rhineland from the rest of Germany, were living in hope: 'A Rhineland detached from Prussia and Bavaria means peace' wrote Barrès in a speech which remained undelivered because of his death on 5 December. (M. Barrès, *Les Grands Problèmes du Rhin*, Paris, Plon, 1930, pp. 354f.)

From August onwards the German government knew that the game was up. Stresemann succeeded Cuno and began to put an end to the passive resistance (26 September). Germany seemed to be beaten, and at this point France made no serious attempt at bilateral negotiations, which might have brought about a happy issue and a sort of second victory – she was soon to be criticised for not having made the attempt. But this was not what Poincaré was after. From the beginning of the affair he had felt that a general settlement could only be arranged with the co-operation of the British and especially of the Americans. They alone were capable, once the debt question had been settled, of bringing to Europe the capital necessary for reconstruction. He also hoped (in vain) that the Americans would consent to a reduction of the French debts due to them, if only he could come to the negotiating table with a trump card in his hand.

It was therefore from his Anglo-American allies that Poincaré awaited an initiative, and not from Germany. When on 20 October the British government proposed a meeting of experts, he thought he could accept it, because the Ruhr operation gave him a bargaining lever such as France had never had before in the numerous inter-allied conferences. It is true that at the end of 1923 this political bargaining counter lost much of its value. Faced with Tirard's monetary and political plans, the Bank of England flew to Berlin's assistance. As a result of support from the City, Dr Schacht was able to set up a new currency, the 'Rentenmark', while a strict budget policy rebuilt the minimum necessary confidence in Germany (November 1923). At one blow the project for a Rhenish monetary authority vanished, and with it the dreams of the autonomists and separatists.

In addition to all this, the French government found itself coping with the crisis of the franc which, as we have seen, amounted almost to a panic in January 1924. While the right was glad to attribute it to a foreign conspiracy, the left thought it was the result of the Ruhr operation, which now became the object of increasingly violent attacks. Cries of 'Poincaruhr' and 'Poincaré la Guerre' were heard, for the public debate on the origins of the war led certain people to point out the harmful role of the President of the Republic between 1912 and 1914. This all led to a request to the bank of Morgan Brothers for aid.

The Dawes plan

Everything was now ready for the liquidation of the operation. The conversations in October with the British and Americans ended in the formation of a committee of experts with the American banker-general Dawes at its head. The members were nominated by the reparations commission (30 November 1923). After three months of deliberation they presented their conclusions. They laid down as a governing principle the economic and administrative unity of Germany, which put an end to French business activities in the Rhineland. However, as Poincaré had insisted, the total amount of the reparations, as fixed in 1921, was left untouched. German payments in 1925 and 1926 would amount to 1,220 million gold marks, then 2,500 million gold marks in 1928–9. A 'prosperity index' of the German economy would allow these annual payments to be increased, if required, and there was no fixed date for their termination. As a guarantee, German industry and the German railways would be put under the control of boards on which the allies would be represented. An allied commission would receive certain indirect taxes and exchange control would be managed by a 'transfer committee'. Finally, the new Reichstag could only issue currency under the supervision of a general council, half composed of foreigners.

Poincaré accepted this plan in April. In the eyes of some of his supporters this was a surrender that could not be explained. It amounted to recognition of a long-lasting error for those who had opposed him, particularly for the radicals and socialists grouped in the Cartel des Gauches. They could point out that relations with their Anglo-American allies had been dangerously strained, and that in Germany the extreme nationalist elements had gained ground, helped by the anger caused by the Ruhr occupation; and all this was to end in a policy of conciliation which had been refused at first. This criticism was in fact pretty specious, for the Dawes plan was much more favourable to France than the Bonar Law plan of January 1923. It guaranteed the payment of reparations and thwarted Germany's hopes of finding an excuse to default because of a disturbed currency which she no longer controlled. Thus, the diplomacy of the Cartel, who had won the May elections, could take over from the diplomacy of Poincaré without apparent violent change. It was logical that the new government should promise the evacuation of the Ruhr at the London conference (July–August 1924), conditional on the implementation of the Dawes plan. But it was also in keeping with the new spirit of French diplomacy that an evacuation of part of the Rhineland was also accepted. It must be added that Edouard Herriot, in his obsession with preserving good relations with the Labour government in London, negotiated with very little skill and wasted several good bargaining points. However, despite all this, confidence was restored to such an extent that the first great international loan since the war was launched in the United States to enable the Reichsbank to stabilise the mark and allow the first payments to be made in accordance with the Dawes plan.

The illusions of security

In this way American capital, and behind it American technology, and finally the American way of life were now able to invade all Europe through Germany. Thanks to American loans Germany could now pay the reparations which in turn enabled her former enemies, notably France and Great Britain, to pay their war debts. This 'circular flow of paper' as Keynes called it, was going to give Europe as well as the United States an era of new expansion and prosperity, lasting right up to the end of the nineteen-twenties.

America and Europe

This system did, however, conceal two great dangers. In the first place it marked the triumph of American economic and financial imperialism. Public opinion in the United States might profess a taste for political isolationism, but this word did not generally apply to the realities of the twenties.

French governments, and Poincaré's in particular, had certainly encouraged this trend. They had realised that the European states, and especially the new ones that emerged from the treaty of Versailles, would need help and external credit to put their economies on a more or less sound basis. This was abundantly proved by the monetary disorders that periodically convulsed these states right up to 1926. France, by granting such credit, could have consolidated in pre-war style the alliance networks she had set up, particularly the Petite Entente. But her financial power had diminished, and investors in France had burnt their fingers in Russian, Italian and Turkish bonds, whose scrip was now languishing in their cupboards – valueless. They were succeeded by international, and particularly American, finance; for in the new capital markets governments, and especially the French government, had lost all their primacy. Resort to the financial institutions of the League of Nations had been ruled out for fear of British domination. Therefore, the French government favoured agreement between American, British, French and, after the mark's recovery, German central banks. This consortium, which was still informal, now started to organise the recent currency confusion. It insisted that governments who asked for its aid should put their own financial houses in order, only then would it agree to grant short-term loans, thereby bringing stability. Reassured by this, the private American banks began to invest. It is true that the Banque de France played a part in all this. One might have assumed that having replaced the private banks, which were now mostly out of the running, it would form part of a new banking diplomacy that would be able to help the government. (R. Mayer, *Bankers' diplomacy.*) In practice this was not so, both because, like all the other central banks, the Banque de France, whose statutes had been renewed in 1918 without any serious debate, aimed at maximum independence from the political power; and because this system perfectly suited the aims and ambitions of the great American bankers – the Youngs, the Morgans, the Parker Gilberts, etc. These bankers played a crucial role in the world of that time. They were thus the essential agents of a thrusting American imperialism against which Europe was poorly equipped to preserve its independence.

The second danger of this system, which was now firmly established through the Dawes plan, was that the whole economic edifice was fragile to an extent that few except Keynes and his disciples understood; and they criticised it accordingly. If Europeans could not cope with the formidable customs barriers put up by the United States, the pursuit of expansion depended more and more on new injections of American capital, and internal debt grew uncontrollably. The payments which Germany would now make had already been mortgaged for reconstruction. Paying war debts would demand in addition such a heavy sacrifice for the taxpayer and the worker that no government would be likely to persist in it for long.

However, the attachment of financial experts to liberal principles was so widespread that neither the man in the street nor the government were really aware of these weaknesses. The expansion that followed on the settlement of the Dawes plan appeared to nearly everyone as proof of a permanent return to normality.

The 'spirit of Geneva' and Locarno

This optimism was encouraged from 1925 onwards by the fact that the main role in foreign affairs devolved on Aristide Briand, 'the apostle of peace'. He was minister of foreign affairs in all the successive governments over nearly seven years, and he was now able to make a reality of security by arbitration, conciliation and the use of collective security. However, in this field the French government failed at once in a new attempt to give real force to the arbitration of the League of Nations, which was considered to be an essential prerequisite to any attempt at general disarmament. Edouard Herriot had been able on 1 October 1924 to obtain Ramsay MacDonald's signature to a text entitled 'the Geneva Protocol'. This proclaimed the principle of compulsory arbitration in the event of conflict and provided for sanctions of a rather imprecise kind against all violations of that protocol. However, MacDonald was defeated at the general election and was replaced by Baldwin, who listened to the loud protests of the Dominions and refused to ratify the text.

It was, however, in the fashionable 'spirit of Geneva' that the negotiations were conducted leading to an attempt at Franco-German reconciliation, the touchstone of European peace. In pursuit of this peace Briand found an attentive partner in the German minister of foreign affairs, the able Stresemann. This man of the right and ardent nationalist was far from sharing the pacifist ideals of his opposite number; but a realistic appreciation of the situation made him see that for the moment Germany was in no position to recover the provinces lost in 1919, either in the east or the west. So, after accepting the peace treaty, she had to recover as soon as possible full sovereignty over the territories of the Reich and take up her place again in the concert of nations, pursuing at the same time the economic recovery which the Dawes plan had made possible. Encouraged by the British, the foreign minister of the Reich proposed a general settlement of the Rhine question to the French government (9 February 1925). Briand was attracted by this idea and started long negotiations which ended in the meeting at Locarno on 5 October of all the powers 'interested in the Rhine', i.e. France, Belgium, Germany, Great Britain and Italy. A pact was signed on 16 October proposing 'to bring about a moral détente among nations ... to facilitate the solution of many political and economic problems ... to speed up in an effective manner the disarmament mentioned in article 8 of the League of Nations covenant'. The frontiers fixed at Versailles between Germany, Belgium and France were guaranteed by these three powers promising not to alter them by force and to have recourse, in the case of disagreement, to the League of Nations. Great Britain and Italy added their guarantee to this undertaking, promising to support the victim of the pact's violation. Thus France found recognition for her frontier on the Rhine and for the return of her provinces lost in 1871, not only by a Diktat imposed by force, but by an agreement freely negotiated and signed. In exchange, Germany was protected against an operation such as had recently ended in the Ruhr.

There was no debate over the eastern and southern frontiers of Germany. Yet the Reich's claims in Poland and Czechoslovakia were such as to cause anxiety to those two states. In spite of considerable efforts, Briand was not able to obtain in those regions the kind of guarantees that Stresemann had given for the Rhineland. The most he was able to get, when the pacts fixing the eastern frontiers were being signed, was an agreement whereby Poland, Czechoslovakia and Germany agreed to go to the League of Nations for arbitration in the event of conflicts over frontiers. Two treaties of defensive alliance, one between France and Czechoslovakia and one between France and Poland, which were mentioned in the proceedings of the conference, aimed at reassuring France's allies. The latter were uneasy about the vagueness of the arbitration agreements, especially as Great Britain and Italy had not guaranteed their frontiers.

French public opinion greeted the Locarno pact with relief and hope. Briand saw his position in parliament strengthened; he was thereby assured of his tenure at the Quai d'Orsay in spite of the high turnover of ministers, and so could hope to pursue effectively his search for international security through arbitration and conciliation. His policy readily won the support of leftist circles. The socialist and radical parties, the movements of opinion such as the Ligue des Droits de l'Homme and the Freemasons had no difficulty in exploiting their considerable influence to promote 'the spirit of Geneva'.

This spirit was also encouraged by the action of several groups who wanted to profit from the better international climate and advance towards a more solid reconciliation with Germany. One of the most interesting movements arose out of the initiatives of the Mayrisch family. This ironmaster of Luxembourg had, since the end of the war, tried unsuccessfully to work out an agreement between French and German industrialists. The economic cold war launched by Hugo Stinnes and his accomplices between 1920 and 1923 had wrecked all his efforts. Mayrisch resumed his role as intermediary between French and German industry after the Ruhr operation and succeeded, with Thyssen and Poensgen on the one hand and Laurent and de Wendel on the other, in creating an international steel cartel between France, Belgium, Luxembourg and Germany. It was signed on 30 September 1926 and brought an end to economic war. It used on a European scale the organisation methods which German heavy industry had used so successfully in her great days, and at the same time it put a stop to harmful competition. Every year a production programme would be drawn up on the basis of the previous year's production and the estimates for the following year; and this work would be distributed among the member states. France found herself allotted 31.18 per cent against 43.18 per cent for Germany, 11.56 per cent for Belgium, 8.30 per cent for Luxembourg and 5.78 per cent for the Saar. An annual general meeting would draw up a report, and those countries who had exceeded their quota would pay a fine (four dollars per tonne) which would be distributed among those countries who had fallen short of their quota.

Mayrisch was so encouraged by this success and so enamoured of the 'spirit of Geneva' that he wanted to go further. Thanks to Madame Mayrisch the couple were at the centre of a small group of writers, politicians and businessmen from France and Germany who had for some time been looking for ways towards a Franco-German reconciliation. Through this group and because of the development of the Locarno spirit they were able to form a Franco-German committee of information and documentation which had some success. It attracted the membership of Franz von Papen in Germany, while in 1928 Wladimir d'Ormesson published under its auspices an essay with a stirring title – *Confiance en l'Allemagne*. The same inspiration gave rise in France to a more specifically religious movement launched by Marc Sangnier after he had broken with the Bloc National. Encouraged by Briand he revived a moribund association, the Action Catholique de la Jeunesse Française (ACJF). At the 1926 congress a young *agrégé d'histoire* Georges Bidault paid a warm tribute to the Locarno policy. In the same year the movement organised an international meeting of young people on a pacifist theme. Not only Briand but also Painlevé and Herriot showed their interest in this meeting, where the bishops of Versailles and Arras were also to be seen. A motion was even adopted against compulsory military service and in support of conscientious objectors.

The general climate thus created led public opinion to greet as successes the various negotiations and pacts whereby Briand tried to round off the work of Locarno. On 31 January 1926 the French government accepted the early evacuation of the Cologne area, a first step towards the total evacuation of the Rhineland which the Germans awaited with more and more impatience. On 8 September France sponsored Germany's admission to the League of Nations. On this occasion Briand pronounced a paean of praise to the new spirit: 'Away with rifles, machine-guns and cannon!' he cried. 'Make room for conciliation, arbitration and peace!'

The agreements on war debts and the Briand–Kellogg pact

In 1926 and 1927 Briand's policy began to run out of steam. At Geneva the work of the preparatory commission for the disarmament conference mentioned in the 1924 Protocol had been dragging on for three years. This commission had been set up to prevent, not only in Germany but in the world at large, an armaments race such as had preceded and had largely been responsible for the First World War; but now it came up against the prevarications and hesitations of the leading powers, especially France. In practice the 'spirit of Geneva' had not dispelled suspicion of Germany, who was showing dynamism in every sphere. Commentators continually underlined the differing birth-rates of the two countries, the failure of the German authorities to apply the military clauses of the Versailles treaty, and the many signs of the spirit of revenge in the German populace. The French therefore insisted on the occupation of the right bank of the Rhine. Briand had difficulty in getting agreement to the evacuation of the Saar where, in accordance with a decision of the League of Nations council on 12 March, an international force of eight hundred men replaced the French troops and were to remain there until the plebiscite planned for 1935.

In another sphere – the thorny problem of war debts – relations between France and the United States were not of the best. Here the adoption of the Dawes plan marked a decisive turning-point. On the one hand, in ensuring in the long term and under international control the payment of reparations as fixed in 1921, it deprived the French government of one of its most solid arguments for avoiding the consolidation of its debts. On the other hand, France could not now hope to be allowed by its creditors, whether British or American, to link the problem of war debts to the problem of reparations. On this point, which had been one of Poincaré's aims, the Ruhr operation was a failure. Moreover, the annoyance of the British at France's aspirations only speeded Anglo-American negotiations, which led to an agreement (31 January 1923) on a consolidation of Britain's debt to the United States. Paris was forced to negotiate in her turn. The consolidation of her debt to Great Britain was established in July 1926 by an agreement which provided for the payment of 799 million pounds sterling in sixty-two annual payments, rising progressively from four million pounds in the first year to fourteen million pounds for the last thirty-one years. The negotiations with the United States were led on the French side by the Senator Henry Bérenger from January to May 1926. With considerable trouble a consolidation agreement was drawn up and signed on 26 April 1926. It provided for the payment of 4,025 million dollars in sixty-two annual payments, which would start at thirty million dollars and rise to 125 million dollars in the sixteenth year. The Americans felt that they had made a generous concession in agreeing to the reduction of the interest rate. The French, on the other hand, found these conditions very tough. There was talk of the 'American Shylock', and the parliamentary ratification of the agreement was delayed on various pretexts for more than three years. The disagreement between Washington and Paris was not settled. In the meantime, France found herself deprived of the generous American loans that were pouring into Europe at a quickening pace, and particularly into Germany. Stresemann had the idea that by letting Germany become indebted to the Americans he would be able to enjoy the favours granted by all wise lenders to their debtors if they wish to be repaid. This was a dangerous policy, and it explains in part the serious crisis that engulfed Germany in the thirties; but it did enable her to pay the reparations on time and also largely to re-equip herself.

All this went far to explain the disillusionment that began at the end of 1927 to take hold of the supporters of the 'spirit of Geneva'. Once again Briand took the initiative. With the intention of reinforcing the Locarno agreements, and in particular those concerning the Polish frontiers which had received no guarantees apart from those of France, he visited various capitals and proposed a solemn pact outlawing war, which was to be signed by all the countries represented. The American Secretary of State, Kellogg, finally came round to the idea and on 28 December in Paris proposed that the two governments should submit to the other nations a covenant renouncing war. On 6 February 1928 France and America signed an arbitration treaty in this spirit. London, after difficult negotiations, rallied to the plan which Berlin had accepted at once. Thus it was in Paris, where a German minister for foreign affairs was received for the first time since the peace of Frankfurt (1871), that the pact was signed whereby fifteen powers, soon to be joined by others (including the USSR), declared that they 'condemned recourse to war for the settlement of international differences', that they outlawed it 'as an instrument of national policy' and finally that they would look for the regulation of their conflicts 'by peaceful means only'. In a long note added as an appendix Kellogg laid down that this statement of principle would in no way exclude the right of legitimate defence, especially against any violator of the Locarno agreements. Furthermore, no guarantees of any sort and no sanctions were provided for. However, this rallying of the sceptical Briand to the purest Wilsonian idealism breathed life into a France that longed for security.

One more uncertainty in Europe was plain for all to see: the Dawes plan had not fixed the number of annual payments that Germany would have to make. This omission diminished the confidence of those capitalists, American for the most part, who subscribed to loans granted to individuals, companies and corporations in Germany. The idea of a revision of the Dawes plan loomed up, proposed in 1926 by Parker Gilbert, the American expert on the plan. It was turned down by the British, who could see no point in changing a system which worked well on the whole; but it got a good reception in Paris. In fact Poincaré, on his return to power, hoped to profit from this development to get the idea of a link between reparations and war debts accepted. This would make the ratification of the Mellon-Bérenger agreement on these debts easier to pass through parliament, a procedure which he knew would be difficult. Yet he had misgivings about the reductions in reparations which the Germans could not fail to demand on the occasion of this revision. Indeed at Geneva, a few days after the signature of the Briand–Kellogg pact, Chancellor Müller urged the necessity of barring the way to the Nazis, who had just obtained one million votes, and with brutal frankness now demanded both these reductions and the rapid evacuation of the Rhineland. In spite of Briand's unfavourable reaction at first, Müller on 16 September 1928 got a joint declaration from Germany, Belgium, France, Great Britain, Italy and Japan announcing, on the one hand, 'the opening in the near future of official negotiations on the early evacuation of the Rhineland' and, on the other hand, 'the necessity of a complete final settlement of reparations, and the establishment of a commission of financial experts appointed by the six governments to achieve this aim'. So there was hope of arriving at a lasting settlement of Europe's financial and economic problems, which would bring a new prosperity and would be shared by a Germany that was fully mistress of her own territory. The French government which accepted the pact was headed by Poincaré, that old champion of security by force, and included, besides Briand, politicians of widely differing opinions such as Herriot, Louis Marin and Tardieu. It was reasonable to believe, therefore, that a new era was really dawning, in which old divisions would melt away and enduring reconciliation would be sought by common effort.

This whole fragile edifice, however, rested on good faith, general optimism and prosperity. It would not be true to say that those responsible for French policy had no notion of this fragility. Proof of this could be found in the reluctance of successive governments to hasten the abandonment of the only serious guarantee of security as demanded by Foch – the military frontier of the Rhine. In the same way the maintenance of the Petite Entente alliances, which so complicated collective security, could well be seen as a desire to keep two irons in the fire. Finally, the constant and sometimes almost desperate efforts of Briand to bring the United States back into the concert of nations was a sign that in Paris the danger of France being isolated in a Europe fraught with uncertainty was keenly felt.

Military illusions

This state of mind did not, however, dislodge some fixed ideas that were full of danger.

Until 1928 the debates on national defence were among those which most stirred up public opinion. The left, taking up the old cliché of the 'nation in arms', favoured a very short military service and the organisation of a militia that could be easily mobilised behind an army stationed on the frontiers. These ideas were all the more attractive in that they claimed to spring from the lessons of the war, which had certainly been won by civilians. Furthermore, they fitted in admirably with the 'spirit of Geneva' since this kind of French army could only be strictly defensive. Even the right was not far from sharing this way of looking at things. It wanted a longer military service (its main point of disagreement with the left); but this policy was temporary, while it waited to see how the diplomatic situation developed, and was intended to ensure that there would be an adequate defence, in the event of a conflict, while the nation armed herself. In the course of the debates between March and June 1922, when military service was reduced to eighteen months, and the debate of May 1927, during which the minister of war Painlevé reduced it to one year, a general consensus on a purely defensive army was born.

It is true that the general staff shared this outlook. Foch, however, had different ideas. He believed that future international relations could lead either to incursions into Germany to prevent rearmament or to expeditions to help the European allies of the Petite Entente against possible Russian or German aggression. He wanted to maintain an offensive force for such emergencies. But his views soon appeared incompatible with the short military service which the military chiefs were beginning to accept. At the end of 1919, Pétain had raised the possibility of military service of one year in a speech he made at Béthune. Furthermore, the High Command had come round to a static concept of war, which was formulated in a 'Provisional instruction on the tactical use of large units'. The authorities preached the invulnerability of the continuous front and the idea of an army covering the frontiers, as well protected as possible and equipped with enormous fire-power. Any offensive action could come only after a long mobilisation of the human and economic forces represented by the 'nation in arms'. This was the spirit in which, from 1924 onwards, the idea of the future Maginot Line was worked out, and its construction was started in 1928. Although certain prophets like General Estienne pointed out the growing effectiveness of tanks, these machines were confined to secondary support roles. In the same way the lessons drawn from the role played by aircraft in the 1918 battles were forgotten, so that aeroplanes were completely excluded from land warfare. (P. Bernard, 'La Stratégie aérienne pendant la Première Guerre mondiale', *RHMC*, July–September 1969, pp. 374–5.) It was the infantry that remained the essential element.

The High Command and the army leaders refused all innovation. This is a state of mind typical of a nation that has won a war: all military thought is paralysed. Liddell Hart noted the same phenomenon in Great Britain: 'In contrast to the Germans, the heads of the British Army, and the French too, became more complacent as the result of their final success in 1918, and were thus all the more inclined to continue in the old rut without attempting any revolutionary change.' (B. H. Liddell Hart, *Memoirs*.) Matters were made worse in France by the fact that the year of reference in the collective consciousness was not 1918, but 1916, the year of Verdun. It was Verdun that was constantly evoked, even in the battle of the franc. So the lessons of the last year of the war, the time of recovered mobility and victory, were more or less forgotten. Everything conspired to extinguish the spirit of innovation in military circles. Leaders that were advanced in years, but covered in glory, naturally held all the posts of responsibility and decision. Behind them the careers of the most gifted young officers seemed blocked. Many of them, and often the most dynamic, lost heart and left the army, especially as their pay was whittled down by inflation and was no longer attractive. Economic prosperity enabled them to find many ways of using their talents in civilian life. With very few exceptions, those who remained, being forced to live a dead-end existence in barracks, brooded on their discontent and denounced the immorality of a society and epoch which they no longer understood. They were often ready to join the first fascist movements and to give vent to anti-parliamentary and anti-communist feelings, which only increased their isolation.

So military illusions, fed by the memory of the glorious days, added their disastrous effect to the political illusions, which an incoherent diplomacy encouraged in a nation that both longed for peace and also believed herself to be one of the powers that ruled the world.

Imperialist illusions

Wasn't France, through her colonial empire, present in all the corners of the world? During the war, this empire had provided raw materials, fighting men and workers to the nations at war. Because of the censorship people had been almost unaware of the few political movements which had threatened the peace of the colonies. These movements had been provoked in Indo-China, Madagascar and especially Algeria, by the increases in taxes, the conscription of labour and government propaganda. The hopes aroused here and there, and especially in Tunisia, by the Wilsonian principle of self-determination had caused little uneasiness in France, where the home country's duty was to promote the values and benefits of French civilisation through an administration that enjoyed absolute power. Even those who here and there denounced the excesses of this administration, or the cupidity of the companies that exploited the colonies, usually saw these excesses as blunders that a more thorough policy of direct administration and assimilation would correct.

Alone, or almost alone, the communists, faithful to Leninist doctrine on imperialism, indulged in fundamental and revolutionary criticism of French colonisation. They found an audience among certain natives of the colonies, particularly among the temporary immigrants who came to know communism in France. At the congress of Tours there was a young delegate from Vietnam who would later achieve fame under the name of Ho Chi Minh. In Algeria the communist movement l'Etoile Nord-Africaine was formed in 1926, which preached direct action for the independence of North Africa, and was soon to find a dynamic and charismatic leader in Messali Hadj, a former soldier. In France the communists did not hesitate to attack all the dogmas of colonialism, and during Abd-el-Krim's revolt (1924–5) they declared their solidarity with the rebels.

Yet even on the left and among most of the native élites in the colonies, these extreme positions met with alarm and disapproval. Although the socialists freely denounced the excesses of colonialism, it was to promote ideas that were even more imperialist than those held by French businessmen and residents overseas. The latter were accused by the left with justice of being opposed to all moves towards assimilation and therefore to all advancement for the native populations, so as to be able to exploit them more effectively.

These ideas gained support among the most developed colonial populations. In Algeria the movement of the Kabyle primary school teachers, expressing itself through the journal *La Voix des humbles*, demanded an extension of the policy of assimilation. The law of 4 February 1915 helped on certain natives towards French nationality and sharpened their appetites for assimilation to such an extent that they adopted a militant secularism very much like the outlook of their metropolitan colleagues. Similar ideas flourished among the few young intellectuals, as is well described in the writings of the young Ferhat ʿAbbās. In Madagascar a primary school teacher and former soldier Ralaimongo founded a league for the admission of the natives of Madagascar to French civil rights and demanded in his journal *L'Opinion* the granting of departmental status to the island.

It is true that such attitudes were unusual in the protectorates where the memory of national independence was still green. The movements, which in Tunisia and Indo-China demanded an end to the progress of direct administration and respect for the treaties of protection, often showed a desire for friendly association with France, whose civilisation and culture were much admired. But the French settlers were opposed to any concession. They always urged the home government to intensify its protective control, to suppress in a brutal manner all autonomist impulses and so leave the way clear for their business activities. The result was that in many of these colonies from 1926–7 onwards movements that were frankly revolutionary and hostile to all forms of colonisation took over from moderate movements that had been systematically suppressed. In Madagascar, after Ralaimongo had been convicted by the administration, a new native opposition began to organise itself and demand independence. In Indo-China, in spite of a few liberal measures introduced by the socialist governor-general Varenne, the Vietnamese national party, founded in 1927 by the schoolmaster Nguyen Thai Hoc, proposed direct action with independence as its aim, inspired by Sun Yat Sen.

People in France were all the more ready to believe that such movements had no future because the colonial administration actively boasted of the considerable efforts in equipment and modernisation that were being made in most colonies. In 1921 Albert Sarraut, minister for the colonies, proposed to improve these colonies and protectorates in a more rational manner than heretofore, and he allotted four billion francs for the task. Ports and roads were to be constructed, health and educational facilities were to be improved. However, in spite of general approval in principle, the Sarraut plan was only put into practice piecemeal although there was some progress, thanks to better credit facilities and more interest in colonial matters on the part of bankers and investors. In the valley of the middle Niger the ambitious irrigation plans of the engineer Bélime, which had been approved by parliament in 1928, aroused much hope for the future. Railways and ports sprang up in an often spectacular fashion in Morocco and Indo-China.

However the home country had few men to spare for this colonisation because of her own low birth-rate. The number of French nationals in North Africa did increase considerably in the period, but this was largely due to a generous policy of naturalisation for Spaniards in Morocco and the Oran district, and for Italians in Tunisia. Everywhere else there were few French smallholders and most Europeans lived off the exploitation of the colonies' riches by the large companies. These companies were very powerful and easily obtained vast concessions from the government, which they exploited with native labour. Scandalous abuses were not uncommon. In black Africa requisitions and forced labour continued to empty whole regions, the peasants being deported to the work sites. The native peoples, constantly increasing in numbers, saw their already miserable conditions deteriorate even further. There were very few expatriate Frenchmen who, by their reports or writings, alerted public opinion at home to the situation. Metropolitan France was more than ever convinced of the benefits and legitimacy of colonisation. (Cf. C. Coquery-Vidrovitch, 'L'Exploitation de l'Afrique équatoriale', *L'Histoire*, 3, July–August 1978, pp. 43–52.)

11

The limits of prosperity

Factors favourable to expansion

While the shifting currency and the twists of national foreign policy plunged most of the public into pessimism and anxiety, the return of peace made possible a restoration of the country's economy. It had been seriously damaged by the destruction of war and had up till now been entirely geared to supplying the military forces.

On the whole the nineteen-twenties were a favourable period for the economy. It is true that the return of the Republicans to power in the United States brought savage deflation and a general crisis in that country from the middle of 1920 onwards, and this event affected Europe. But it was much more sharply felt in Great Britain than in France, as the sterling countries experienced a dramatic fall in the price of their raw materials. This crisis did bring a drop in prices and share values in France and a considerable rise in unemployment, but on the whole it was well absorbed. (A. Sauvy, *Histoire économique de la France entre les deux guerres*, vol. I, p. 261.) The size of the demand, as a result of war privations and destruction, was such that activity was the order of the day even, as we have seen, at the price of marked inflation. From October 1921 onwards, recovery was evident and persisted up to the world crisis, apart from two short periods of anxiety in 1924 and 1927.

A favourable economic situation in the world at large is never enough to explain the pace of economic activity in any one country. This is borne out by the serious difficulties that were being experienced by Great Britain in this period. If France showed remarkable growth, this was due to several factors, among them inflation on the one hand and the modernisation of production structures on the other.

The effects of inflation

Although it was much deplored, the inflation of the twenties undoubtedly had a favourable effect on the progress of business, at least in the period which preceded the stabilisation of the franc in 1926. It helped to limit in France the effects of the world crisis of 1921. As events developed, this phenomenon was more or less recognised, as much in business circles, where some feared any deflationary policy, as on the left where the vocal elements pointed out the benefits that were accruing to capital from the situation. These attitudes came to the fore from 1926 onwards when Poincaré succeeded in stabilising the franc, and a lively debate ensued between the revaluers and the devaluers. Opinion divided even business circles. The supporters of devaluation feared the effects of excessive deflation on external trade, noting its consequences in Great Britain at the time. Even the public learnt to link inflation with expansion.

One could also attribute to the war and its consequences some valuable modifications to the country's economic situation.

Modernisation of the monetary system

First, we must take note of the modernisation of the banking system and of the way money circulated. In this sector people had to get used to bank money, a modern form of payment for which the French showed a great dislike throughout the nineteenth century, an attitude which put them in a position of inferiority vis-à-vis their rivals. If we compare the structure of the money supply in 1913 and 1929 (see p. 130), we notice on the one hand the almost total disappearance of specie, which has simply become fractional, and on the other hand the considerable increase not only in the fiduciary issue (banknotes) but also in deposit money, which now constituted over one-half of the money supply.

The state as banker

This development resulted largely from the fact that the state, either on its own or in association with private banks, had itself become a banker in order to make up for the inadequacies of the banking sector. In 1918, on Clémentel's initiative, the system of postal cheques was started. In 1919 the Crédit National was founded (law of 10 October 1919) to facilitate the payment of compensation for war damage and to make advances to industry in the devastated regions. In 1920 the Caisse Nationale du Crédit Agricole and the Banque Française du Commerce Extérieur were established, and the Caisse Centrale du Crédit Hôtelier followed in 1923. In addition, an older institution, the Caisse des Dépôts et Consignations developed its investment function, which up till now had been a secondary activity. The government used it more and more often for investments in capital programmes, e.g. electrification, transport development and building, whose financing was thus 'debudgetised'. This made it easier to present more balanced budgets to parliament. Poincaré made much use of the procedure. (J. Bouvier, *Un siècle de banque française, les contraintes de l'état et les*

Structure of the money supply, 1913 and 1929

Money supply (year end in billions of current francs)	Structure of the money supply (%)			Proportion of deposits/ species and banknotes
	Specie	Banknotes	Deposit	
1913 26.4	34.0	21.0	45.0	0.82
1929 153	0.9	43.4	55.7	1.22

Source: INSEE, *Bulletin hebdomadaire de statistique*, 8 December 1951, in J. Bouvier, *Un Siècle de banque française, les contraintes de l'état et les incertitudes des marchés*.

incertitudes des marchés, p. 141.) In 1921 grants to local authorities, to housing and to firms made up 12.8 per cent of the Caisse's business.

The state thus remedied the shortcomings of a banking system which had been largely responsible for the slow equipment and modernisation of the country before the war. But there was no question of nationalising this sector. The new organisations, in which the world of big business was generously represented, were intended to strengthen the private banks by plugging the gaps in the credit system. State banking was in no way trying to compete with private banking, and this was well illustrated when the privileges of the Banque de France were renewed in December 1918 without serious opposition: although the role of high finance had not ceased to decline since the middle of the nineteenth century, it retained its crushing supremacy in the Banque de France. This fact, combined with the treasury's request for advances, put the Banque de France in a position of strength and enabled it to play an obvious political role. This happened in May 1926 when it refused the minister of finance Raoul Péret its support for the franc in the exchange markets; and again in July 1926 when it prevented the formation of the second Herriot government by announcing the suspension of credit to the treasury, and so dealt the final blow to a Cartel that was already on its last legs. It is true that the clumsiness of the Cartel had done everything to place this unexpected power in the hands of the governors, a power which several of them regarded as a poisoned chalice. (See J.-N. Jeanneney, *François de Wendel en République, l'argent et le pouvoir, 1914–40*.) It is also true that similar glaring actions would later stir up suspicions on the left, which would make possible future reforms.

Scandals
This modernisation of the banking sector did not however go forward without blunders and scandals. In the general euphoria of pros-

perity, speculation ran wild, especially after 1926 when stable exchange rates and the general clearing of the international situation by the application of the Dawes plan, freed even the most nervous characters of the constraints which had held them back hitherto. One saw the birth of various investment companies, who claimed to help small savers share in the bonanza reserved up till now for the world of big business, and especially to enjoy the large profits accruing from the sudden boom in ordinary shares, which until now had been a languishing section of the market. The public responded avidly. In *Le Populaire* of 6 December 1928, Léon Blum wrote how surprised he was to see the driver of the taxi who was taking him to the Chamber buy *L'Information financière* and how he thus learnt that 'nowadays everyone speculates, everyone gambles'. (Cited in A. Sauvy, *Histoire économique de la France entre les deux guerres*, vol. i, p. 398.) This situation and state of mind helped on the machinations of several adventurers: Marthe Hanau, for instance, who made extravagant promises and went bankrupt at the end of 1928, or the banker Oustric, who arrived poor from the provinces and made a fortune through shady dealings and flagrant abuse of influence. So there developed an atmosphere of corruption that was dangerous for the regime.

Finally, as in the past, there was not enough priority given to encouraging savings for internal investment. An overall policy was lacking and when the international financial situation became freer, a proportion of French savings, as before 1914, found its way abroad. On the whole, however, French firms were able to find the capital they required, thanks to the positive aspects of the banking revolution. Many of them were helped on by the government's reconstruction policy.

Reconstruction

By a law voted on 17 April 1919 parliament had fixed the rules whereby the promises made at the beginning of hostilities would be honoured. Every property-owner who had suffered would receive a sum equal to the total of his loss at pre-mobilisation values. Furthermore, if he decided to recycle his indemnity in the reconstruction of his property, he would be allowed substantial extra sums to do so. However, this reconstruction had to be 'similar', i.e. it had to be designed for the same use as the old one, and it had to be in the same commune or nearby. Various commissions, reshuffled several times, made up of magistrates, civil servants, technicians and local politicians, were charged with carrying out valuations and settling disputes. After valuation of the damage the claimant received a certificate quoting the sum awarded, which was not negotiable but could be used as security.

This legislation was open to various criticisms. First, because those who did not spend it on rebuilding were paid in francs that rapidly lost their value, and so they felt cheated. Second, because the system, which enforced identical reconstruction, largely prevented rationalisation or reconversions, which a more flexible system would have allowed. Third, and above all, the law allowed valuations that were far too high. As it was accepted for a long time that 'the Boche would pay', it was patriotic to help the claimant to overvalue his property. A total of twenty-eight billion francs of 1913 value was devoted to reparations, which according to Sauvy assumed that one-tenth of French property, including land, had been entirely destroyed. Finally, the law was unable to prevent the dubious granting of entitlements to reparation, which became a source of profitable operations. A document published in the Chamber in 1924, for example, showed that Béghin, a sugar refiner in the Nord, by adding to his own claim those of several small sugar refiners which he had taken over, had managed to receive a total of 126 million francs, and thus laid the foundations of a vast and flourishing empire. Similar action had allowed the chemical firm Kuhlmann, after receiving substantial sums from the state during the war to help set up a chemical industry in the unoccupied zone, to buy up several other firms in difficulty without spending a penny themselves. (Cited in E. Beau de Loménie, *Les Responsabilités des dynasties bourgeoises*, vol. III.) However, reconstruction moved steadily forward throughout the twenties, and the speed with which towns and villages in the devastated areas were rebuilt aroused general astonishment.

In the agricultural sphere, the destruction had particularly affected the alluvial plains north and east of the Paris basin, i.e. 'the granary of France', and it was estimated that two million hectares of farm land had been put out of action by the end of 1918. The restoration of this damage involved considerable effort. Broadly speaking, it was completed by 1925 and, in many devastated regions, it led to considerable rationalisation.

As regards industry, the rebuilding of the ruins was also spectacularly rapid, and many firms took advantage of the opportunity to equip themselves with up-to-date plant.

Reconstruction, with all its mistakes, gave new strength to the regions that had been invaded during the war. As they were the departments which had been the most progressive before the war, there is no doubt that this reconstruction, though largely responsible for the financial difficulties of the nation, was a considerable fillip to its economic progress.

Rationalisation tendencies

Modernisation was not limited to firms benefiting from reconstruction. The lessons of the war were not lost, especially in the industrial sector. The nineteen-twenties were the time for what was then called 'rationalisation'. By this was meant everything that could favour specialised and standardised mass production. This was achieved partly by the concentration of firms and partly by the adoption of the 'scientific organisation of labour', which had been pioneered around 1900 in the United States by the engineer Taylor.

Where concentration was concerned, the discipline imposed on French entrepreneurs by the war economy had overcome their reluctance to enter into agreements, no doubt in order to maintain or increase their profits. This concentration also enabled them to compete effectively with the enormous combines which were being set up in other countries. In this connection Clémentel's action had been decisive.

It is true that at the end of hostilities, although the administration made the difficulties of the times an excuse to maintain its role, some very vigorous attacks were made against all sorts of state intervention, and there were cries for a return to liberalism pure and simple. Many economists instanced the errors and abuses of the war economy to show up the state's incompetence at management. In *L'Etatisme industriel*, Carnot denounced the muddle and mistakes of state industry, and Gignoux examined in a severely critical manner the functioning of the Roanne arsenal in his doctoral thesis of 1920. Then Delemer in his *Bilan de l'étatisme* showed up the commercial and industrial failings of the state by examining the finances of the maritime transport system, the food supplies and the consortium for oils and petroleum (1922). Olphe-Gaillard's *L'Histoire économique et financière de la guerre* (1925) also came to much the same conclusions.

Yet something of the experience acquired remained in the outlook and doctrines of certain politicians, economists and young businessmen. Without accepting the structural reforms which were the basis of socialist or near-socialist doctrine, they hoped to jettison certain dogmas of classic liberalism and counted on energetic state action to breathe life into the country's development. Thus evolved the tendency which was called 'neo-capitalism'. It recommended the regrouping and organisation of the employers, which classical liberalism had always viewed with some suspicion, while the parallel existence of powerful unions of employees was now seen as absolutely natural. In imitation of certain leading American employers, the principle of high wages was now accepted as bringing solid benefits to everybody. It was natural, therefore, to look for dialogue with the world of labour. Proposals of this sort were supported in parliament by François-Poncet, who in 1928 favoured 'neo-capitalism' as 'supple, intelligent and perfectible', and by Loucheur, who went so far as to ask the state to play the part of an orchestral conductor charged with 'harmonising the diverse elements of production'. At the same time Giscard d'Estaing (father of the future President) and H. de Peyerimhoff, president of the Comité des Houillères, promoted similar ideas in articles in *La Revue des deux mondes* (1 August 1928 and 15 March 1929, respectively).

While the business right was influenced by this new spirit, members of the political left also often inclined the same way, although they showed a rather less scrupulous attachment than did the 'neo-capitalists' to the inviolability of privately-owned means of production and to the exclusive authority of the manager. Among the radicals, for instance, Bertrand de Jouvenel argued for an economy directed and controlled by the state and led a campaign against vested interests, while leaving the job of production to individuals. On his side Pierre Cot defended similar ideas at the Angers radical congress in 1928 and, to achieve the necessary reforms, pleaded for the integration of trade unions into the reformed state through a national economic council and through other independent bodies in which unions were to take part. ('Rapport sur la réforme de l'état', *Cahier des droits de l'homme*, 29 August 1929.) Among the socialists themselves a certain number of young intellectuals like André Philip, then a professor at Lyon, of technicians like Jules Moch, of union leaders like Hyacinthe Dubreuil and of parliamentarians like Charles Spinasse disowned the outright condemnation meted out to industrial rationalisation within the party, which only saw in it the extension of the power of capital and the 'organisation of overwork' (as it was called in a CGT pamphlet of 1914). So they arrived, with the help of the American example, at a profound revision of their attitude. For Philip, rationalisation and socialism combined to prove the bankruptcy of free competition and the necessity of a rational organisation of industry. (See *Henri de Man et la crise doctrinale du socialisme*, p. 22.) He drew the conclusion that a revision of Marxism, inspired by the thought of the Belgian Henri de Man, was overdue. But he feared that, as a result of this rationalisation, the workers might lose their class-consciousness and slide towards corporatism. None of these reservations were to be found in Hyacinthe Dubreuil, who had acquired direct and practical experience of rationalisation in the United States and expressed his enthusiasms in his book *Standards* (1917).

Within the traditional currents of thought, young iconoclasts, 'neo-socialists', 'young radicals' and 'neo-capitalists' questioned the certainties of their elders, without ceasing to disagree among themselves. However, one can clearly see that they had one thing in common – a new confidence in expansion, the source of all social progress. But, while they theorised in these terms, others, who may or may not have been influenced by their ideas, were putting the rationalisation into practice in the firms which they were creating or developing.

Employers' organisation

This same spirit was to be found in the way the employers came together. Their motives were mixed, for they wanted to defend themselves in the most traditional manner against competition and union demands, while at the same time freeing themselves from the iron rules of economics and making a real contribution to progress. In this way, 'neo-capitalists' and hard-line bosses found common ground. Ernest Mercier's movement Le Redressement Français, drawing inspiration from Saint-Simon, prospered in the nineteen-twenties. Above all, the Confédération Générale de la Production Française (CGPF) was created in 1919 with the decisive encouragement of Clémentel, who saw in a powerful employers' organisation one way of coping with the difficulties of reconstruction. This brought together the professional groups that had hitherto been independent and in competition with one another, e.g. the Comité des Forges, Union des Industries Metallurgiques et Minières, Comité des Houillères, Union des Produits Chimiques, etc. It was much more firmly established in the heavy industries such as chemicals, mining and iron and steel than in textiles, though even there it attracted most of the large firms. (Cf. G. Lefranc, *Les Organisations patronales en France*, p. 424.) However, up to 1936 at least, this organisation did not gain as much influence as had the old bodies, which it claimed to link together.

The success of the advanced technology industries

Generally speaking, the employers' organisation was less Malthusian at this time than has sometimes been claimed. In fact its activity helped to start the second industrial revolution, which was founded on the applications of electricity, the internal combustion engine, chemical science and the scientific organisation of labour. In these sectors France had hitherto been notably backward.

If we take 100 as the 1913 base, the general index of industrial production was fifty-seven in 1919 and even fell to fifty-five in 1921 because of the crisis. It passed the 1913 level in 1924 at 109, and reached 127 in 1928. The rate of growth from 1924 to 1929 was 5 per cent per annum, as compared with, at the most, 3.4 per cent for the last fifteen pre-war years. At this pace there was hope of making up for the war years within one generation. This remarkable expansion was accompanied by a no less remarkable increase in productivity, which largely accounted for it. It progressed between 1917 and 1924 at an average of 1.4 per cent per annum for production per active person and 2.5 per cent for production per hour of work.

This progress, of course, was not uniform throughout all branches. Sauvy's calculations enable us to pick out the capital industries (iron and steel, engineering, building), for which the increase in production from 1914 to 1929 was of the order of 50 per cent, while it was only 10 per cent in the consumer industries (textiles, leather, food and drink). To understand better the nature of this advance, it will be useful to consider four branches where the energy of the entrepreneurs, the speed of innovation and rationalisation in every sense brought spectacular progress, which was to make important changes in everyday life: electrical equipment, oil and motor-cars, iron and steel and the chemicals industry.

Electrical production, which amounted to 3,500 million kWh in 1920, reached more than 14,000 million kWh in 1928, of which nearly 6,000 million kWh was water-generated. Development on this scale would not have been possible in the atmosphere of classical liberalism which still held sway before the war. It had provoked ruinous rivalry between small firms that were incapable of producing the investment required for the building of power-stations and grid-systems. It was here that the state came in, but at first only to control the action of private companies, granting concessions to the most powerful. These companies 'rationalised' themselves, e.g. Ernest Mercier, with the help of the Rothschilds, amalgamated the companies of the Paris region and linked up with other large companies such as the Compagnie Générale d'Electricité (CGE) and Alsthom. In this way the mines and approaches to large towns were supplied by power-stations, while the mountain regions were exploited for water power. Many dams were constructed in the Alps, where electro-chemical and electro-metallurgic industries had considerably developed because of the war. In the Pyrénées the Compagnie des Chemins de Fer du Midi was amalgamated with the Union des Producteurs d'Energie des Pyrénées Occidentales in order to introduce the electrification of the local railways, which had been handicapped by the absence of coal in the south-west. However, private enterprise on its own was not capable of introducing the necessary modernisation in the Massif Central or on the great rivers like the Rhine and the Rhône. The only solution was to marry state and private capital in the form of mixed companies such as the Compagnie National du Rhône and the Compagnie de la Moyenne Dordogne. There was, however, plenty of opposition. Among many others, Emile Mireaux, editor of an organ of propaganda and documentation, *le Bulletin quotidien de la Société d'études et d'informations économiques*, saw a 'socialist formula' in all this and was largely responsible for the slowness with which the Compagnie du Rhône was formed despite the passing of the law that set up the company. These installations helped the development of industries making electrical equipment, especially the CGE and, after 1928, Alsthom, which was the result of the amalgamation of the Société Alsacienne de Constructions Mécaniques and Thomson-Houston, a subsidiary of General Electric.

The motor-car industry before the war was a sector of industry in which France had achieved brilliant successes. The French manufacturers, however, had not been able to achieve the rational organisation of labour by which the Americans, and Ford in particular, had won an overwhelming lead, although starting later. (For the causes of this inability, see P. Fridenson, 'Une Industrie nouvelle, l'automobile en France jusqu'en 1914', *RHMC*, October–December 1972, pp. 575–7.) This deficiency was all the more serious in that the period of major technical innovation in the industry was almost over. Consequently, it was only by the rationalisation of work and the creation of new markets that entrepreneurs could now find the means of fresh expansion.

The war had given French industrialists an unhoped-for market and had also provided conditions for mass-production. At the same time it had multiplied the number of armaments and aircraft firms of various sizes, and many of these, when peace came, saw a profitable reconversion in the motor-car industry. At the beginning of the twenties the number of firms increased greatly – there were said to be 150 in 1921. However, of the 250,000 vehicles that were made in France in 1928, more than 130,000 came out of the three giants of the industry, i.e. Renault, Peugeot and the newcomer Citroën. It was the last-named enterprise that showed the most dynamism. The son of a diamond merchant of Amsterdam who had settled in Paris, André Citroën, after leaving the Ecole Polytechnique, founded a firm for the manufacture of gears based on a patent brought back from Poland after a family visit to the Warsaw ghetto. Then he took over the management of an automobile firm, Mors, that was in difficulties; and when war broke out he was fighting against bankruptcy. He had visited the United States in 1911 and had watched a production line in action. He proposed in 1915 to apply the system to the manufacture of shells and, due to the support of Loucheur his fellow-student at the Ecole Polytechnique, he got the necessary orders and built a new factory on the gardens of the Quai de Javel. By 1917 he was thinking again of cars and requested Jules Salomon to design a small economical two-seater. At the 1919 Motor Show the Citroën A1 was launched in a blaze of publicity and proved to be a stunning success at the unheard-of-price of 7,200 francs. Citroën was able to pull ahead of his European rivals by acquiring a clientele that, if not quite popular, was much less rich and so more numerous than the aristocrat–sportsmen for whom his rivals catered. Yet, unlike his inspirer Ford, he was passionately interested in technical innovation and in 1923 he produced the famous 5CV, then in 1925 the 'all-steel' B12. He was, therefore, never able to pay off his investment. In addition, the loudest and most expensive publicity campaigns followed one after the other. In 1922, he organised the 'Black Rally' across the Sahara. In 1925, at the *Arts décoratifs* exhibition, the Eiffel Tower was illuminated with the name of Citroën in letters of fire. As André Citroën was a big spender and lost money in the Deauville casino, the firm's overdraft was bound to increase dangerously, and in 1928 he had to accept the proposals of the Banque Lazard, who took the business over. However, for some time yet the old master was able to gratify his passion for novelty. The other manufacturers, Renault, who had accumulated vast profits during the war, and Peugeot, who had managed to free himself from the supervision of the bank, remained much more cautious, but also kept

The French metals industry from 1913 to 1929

	1913		1929	
	Production[1]	Index[2]	Production[1]	Index[2]
Iron ore (metal content about 30%)	21,918	402	50,731	931
Pig iron (first melt)	5,207	192	10,360	382
Crude steel	4,687	295	9,717	611
Bauxite	309	524	666	1,100
Aluminium (1st and 2nd meltings)	13.5	1,350	29.1	2,910

[1] In thousands of tonnes.
[2] 1900 = 100.
Source: INSEE, *Tableaux de l'économie française*, 1956.

the old habits which hindered any real leap forward in the motor industry. There was too great a choice of models at excessive prices, little standardisation and the survival of anarchic competition between car manufacturers. The French motor industry was the second in the world with 5 per cent of production as compared with the American share of 90 per cent, but it was showing unmistakable signs of exhaustion.

The motor industry involved many other industries in its wake. There was the rubber industry for a start, whose production in 1929 stood at 861 (1913 = 100). Michelin was the name associated with this remarkable growth. It was a firm which, without enjoying a full monopoly, was on the way to becoming a sizable empire, entirely owned by the founder's family. Second, the spread of the internal combustion engine led to the growth of petrol refineries in France, for during the war she had woken up to the dangers of depending exclusively on the import of refined oil. When peace came, several sources of crude oil came under French control, and not only the modest reserves of the old Turkish Petroleum Company, in which France obtained 23.75 per cent of the German shares at the San Remo conference. In order to exploit these reserves the government in 1924 set up a mixed company, partly state, partly private, called the Compagnie Française des Pétroles (CFP), in which Ernest Mercier played a considerable part. This company then proceeded to prospect, and it succeeded in discovering the Baba Gurgur field in 1927. It then only remained to build refineries, and to this end a subsidiary of the CFP was set up – the Compagnie Française de Raffinage. In 1928, the Poincaré cabinet managed

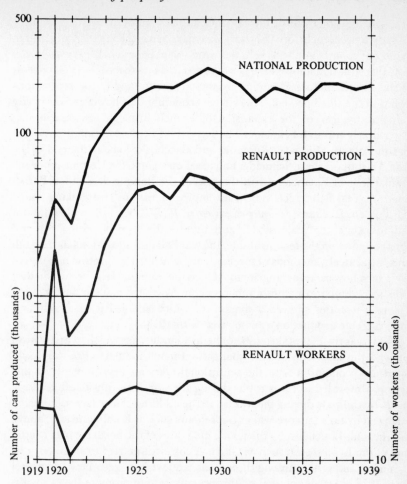

National car production: production and workforce at Renault, 1919–39. (P. Fridenson, *Histoire des usines Renault.* I. *1898–1939*, Paris, Editions du Seuil, 1972, p. 306.)

to push through some imaginative and effective oil legislation which has, broadly speaking, remained in force to this day.

The iron and steel industry also showed signs of vigorous growth. It had of course suffered from war damage, though the way the factories in the Briey basin had been spared despite the proximity of the front had caused comment at the end of the war and later. The industry benefited handsomely from reparations. The return of the lost provinces and the purchase at a very low price of confiscated firms by the big French companies proved very profitable and led to a considerable increase in French supplies of iron ore. On the other hand, the lack of coal, and more particularly coke – already a problem before the war – was more acute than ever. The solution could not come from the Saar mines which were poor in coke. We have seen how this situation allowed the German steelmakers to mount a real boycott of the French industry, hoping by this action to modify the reparations policy of the allied powers. This virtual economic war, however, was partly inspired by fear of the expansion of French firms in central Europe, particularly through Schneider's activity. This firm set up many subsidiaries in Poland, Hungary, Rumania and Czechoslovakia at the end of the war. To support these Schneider had to set up a bank, the Union Européene Industrielle et Financière with the help of the Banque de l'Union Parisienne. A 'real Schneider industrial empire in Europe' was taking shape (C. Fohlen, *La France de l'entre-deux-guerres, 1917–1939*, p. 78) which did not fail to excite the jealousy of, and indeed the fear of, Hugo Stinnes. Furthermore, on the technical side, the war had encouraged much research on special steels, methods of forging, etc., which led to improvements. We have seen how cartel arrangements solved the frictions. In general, whether iron, steel, bauxite or aluminium were concerned, the metal industry in the nineteen-twenties showed a dynamism which enabled it to double and indeed treble production as compared with 1913.

Yet it was the place taken by the chemical industries which in many ways showed the most spectacular change in French industry. Pre-war backwardness, compared with the sensational German developments in this sector, almost led to catastrophe during the war. The considerable efforts made by the state during the war led to the building of new factories, which were run by the main pre-war entrepreneurs such as Kuhlmann and, above all, through Loucheur, by the textile magnates of the north such as Motte, and of the Lyon region such as Gillet. A consortium tried to share out raw materials and orders among these firms, and we have seen how Clémentel from 1916 onwards counted on this organisation to promote the rationalisation of production. At the end of the war these industrialists, due to a clause in the treaty of Versailles, were able to exploit German patents without payment. It proved necessary in fact to solicit the help of the state in order to exploit some of these patents. After much debate, parliament at the end of 1924 passed a law creating the Office National de l'Azote, which was to have a monopoly of the manufacture of nitrogen products by the Haber-Bosch process for agriculture, and which set up factories in Toulouse. But very often these windfalls found their way to private enterprise. The factories of the Société du Rhône, controlled by Swiss capital and exploiting patents for the manufacture of asprin, soon became extremely prosperous. The Motte and Gillet families created the Société de Produits Chimiques Gillet et Fils (Progil) to make the most of this good fortune. Finally, three important groups in this way found a means of continuing the progress made during the war. There was Kuhlmann, who in 1923 took over the Compagnie Nationale des Matières Colorantes et de Produits Chimiques founded by the Banque de Paris et des Pays-Bas in 1919 with government help, and whose factories spread to the Nantes region, Normandy, Franche-Comté and Lorraine, while at the same time diversifying into fertilisers, copper sulphate, pyrites, etc. There was Alais, Frogues and Camargue, founded in 1925 to concentrate on salt and its derivatives, which soon became Péchiney and built up its empire by developing electro-metallurgy in the Alps and aluminium processing. It also took up other lines such as sodium and chlorine. Finally, there was Saint-Gobain, successor to the ancient royal factory and unequalled for all types of glass. This firm now interested itself in all aspects of the chemicals industry and particularly in cellulose and paper, as well as in oil refining. So, by 1928, France was no longer a poor relation where chemicals were concerned.

Black spots

This dynamic expansion, whose spectacular performances we have just been considering, was unable to hide obvious weaknesses. These we must now examine.

Agriculture lagging behind

The most serious weakness was the continuing backwardness of French agriculture. Production stagnated: over the three-year period 1927–9 its overall value in constant terms was just about equal to that of the last three pre-war years. (A. Sauvy, *Histoire économique de la France entre les deux guerres*, vol. I, pp. 249–50.) Yields over the whole country for the main crops were far inferior to those of other similar European countries. For the period 1929–31, the yields were 14.2 quintals per hectare for wheat against 13.3 before the war, 20.5 for Germany, 21.9 for Great Britain, 29.1 for the Netherlands. In potatoes the yields were 104 quintals per hectare against 149 for Germany, 163 for Great Britain and 191 for the Netherlands. Productivity, on the other hand, went up by 20–5 per cent, but this resulted to a great extent from the departure of inefficient farmers to the towns, and not simply from increased productivity on the part of those who stayed on the land. It is true that this relative stagnation was not universal, so generalisations should be avoided. For instance, as we have seen, reconstruction in the devastated areas was often made the occasion for positive renewal, e.g. redistribution of land, mechanisation and the introduction of more advanced methods. (cf. G. Duby and A. Wallon (eds.), *Histoire de la France rurale. IV. La Fin de la France paysane, de 1914 à nos jours*.) These cases, however, were no more than exceptions in a sea of general mediocrity.

France's agricultural production, in spite of her low population, was still far from satisfying the food requirements of the country. So there had to be recourse to imports up to 15 per cent of national farm output. But, just as before 1914, the reasons for this situation were sought where they were not to be found.

The flight from the land

The rural exodus was regarded as an evil, not because it clearly reflected the low standard of living in the country, or because the departing countryman found it difficult to adapt to town life, but because, according to landowners hungry for cheap labour at rush periods such as harvest, vintage time and haymaking, there was a serious shortage of labour. At the same time there was denunciation of the town's false attractions and pitfalls for the peasant, who was duped by people who despised the old values and beliefs. Nevertheless, the exodus gathered considerable momentum in the twenties, for there were 950,000 departures between 1919 and 1931, i.e. nearly eighty thousand a year. Emigration was often no longer linked to survival. Those who went could have stayed if they had accepted a static standard of living and an existence that was no less primitive than in the past. In this respect the war had a truly revolutionary effect in that it encouraged in the country an awareness of new needs for comfort, culture and progress. Owing to the slow development of the countryside and France's chronic inability to foster a truly peasant culture because of the indifference of local leaders, these cultural needs could only be satisfied in the towns. In former days the flight from the country had removed the incubus of the weakest elements by a kind of natural selection, but now it affected the youngest and most enterprising. (P. Ariès, *Histoire des populations françaises et de leurs attitudes devant la vie depuis le XVIIIe siècle*, pp. 297–9.) In spite of all this, the drift to the towns cannot be considered the basic cause of agriculture's relative decline. This theory is contradicted by the agricultural boom following the Second World War, which took place at a time when every year removed more and more peasants from the rural areas.

Protectionism

Inadequate customs protection was the second theme developed by the defenders of agriculture. Indeed post-war tariff policy protected industry more than agriculture. As we have seen the country's food requirements were not satisfied by national production and imports were vital, so that a government charging too much duty could soon be accused of raising the cost of living. Furthermore, the farmers were in those days less well organised than the industrialists when it came to putting pressure on the authorities. The relatively low duties on farm produce were all the more resented in agricultural circles because the industrial products which they needed were heavily protected and so became very expensive. There were few who, on the contrary, saw in the protectionist policy prevailing since Méline one of the factors that allowed the survival of marginal farm holdings. It also gave to the wealthier farmers the unearned income which made them disinclined to effort and risk-taking. They were in any case discouraged by the government through its failure to provide agricultural education.

The weight of traditional firms

Agriculture held no monopoly of this conservatism. The dynamism which we have noted in certain industries, though not exceptional, was far from being general. France remained the country of the small family firm, investing little and making small profits, in spite of the spectacular progress achieved by concentration. Although by 1930 the number of firms with more than five hundred employees had nearly doubled since the beginning of the century, the number of industrial or commercial businesses with no employees at all remained at about one and a half million. In many industries – food, building, public works, timber – less than one-quarter of the wage-earners worked in establishments of more than one hundred employees. These small businesses generally showed little enterprise. They were not interested in expansion for fear of losing family control, and in particular they refused to put their shares on the market. They were keener to reduce risks than to increase profits, and they even kept their savings in cash as an insurance against bad times rather than invest it. Secrecy and suspicion characterised their attitudes to banks, tax authorities and, of course, their clients. They kept their prices high which suited the large firms, who thereby had an interest in their survival. Although it would be excessive to saddle French family businesses with all the responsibility for the country's backwardness, as has sometimes been done, there is little doubt that they were a very effective brake on a real 'take-off'.

The deficiencies of applied research

It is also characteristic that the number of firms really capable of organising applied research remained very small. 'In France', said Henry Le Chatelier, *membre de l'Institut*, a chemist of international repute and a founder of modern metallography, 'we have only a small number of decently organised research laboratories. In the main mineral industries there is the laboratory of the Comité des Houillères, which has a right to a special position because of its exceptional quality and the services it has rendered to the nation. In iron and steel we have the laboratories of Montluçon, le Creusot, Saint-Chamond and Imphy. For engineering we have Dion et Bouton, and for chemicals Saint-Gobain, Alais et la Camargue, la Société d'Electrochimie, Messrs Lumiére and Messrs Michelin, and the Compagnie du Gaz de Paris. For cement there are the laboratories of Teil and of Boulogne-sur-Mer. Yet in French industry there would be room for about 100 similar laboratories.' (*Science et industrie*, pp. 172–81.) The lessons of the war were forgotten because heads of firms, who had hoped to make fabulous profits quickly out of such research, soon got discouraged when 'sensational discoveries that could lead to lucrative patents' did not emerge from the laboratories which they were financing. The engineers, even though they were familiar on graduation with the methods of the most advanced science, soon moved away and let themselves be absorbed by commercial and administrative matters, neglecting to keep up with scientific literature. In fact, the French system of recruitment to the *grandes écoles* by competition, where more importance was attached to the content than to the methods of science, diverted the élite from research careers, which were few and badly paid, and led them to administrative functions in the public and private sectors.

As for the state, it did not think of making up for the failings of private enterprise. The experiences of the war, during which for a time there had been a ministry of inventions, had no sequel. University research, criticised clearheadedly but to no purpose by Caullery in 1933, was more and more weakened by its defects; for it was paralysed by prejudices that were hostile to all practical notions of science.

Generally speaking, where technical innovation was concerned, only a small fringe of French industry matched the international level.

The birth of the 'French desert'

The contrast between a dynamic minority of firms and an archaic majority was matched by a regional contrast, which certainly did not date from the war but was much increased by it. This was caused in the first place by war industries being concentrated on the whole in a few regions, i.e. the Alpine south-east, a few ports on the west coast, and above all the Paris area. Indeed everything had contributed to the uncontrolled development of war industries round Paris: the closeness of the government and the ministries that handed out the orders, the transport structure and the presence of abundant reserves of manpower. It is true that in 1918, during the second battle of the Marne, there was some anxiety about the development of vital industry in such a vulnerable area, and for a time decentralisation became the order of the day in the deliberations of the government and the parliamentary commissions. But all this was forgotten once the storm passed. After the war, as we have seen, the rebuilding of plant that had been damaged or destroyed was only allowed in its place of origin. Only the old industrial regions of the north and east benefited from the inflow of capital and the innovations that resulted. With very few exceptions, the west, the centre and the south-west remained apart and were caught more than ever in a blind alley of chronic underdevelopment. The most spectacular aspect of these changing conditions was the excessive growth of the Paris region. An enormous industry of production had fastened itself round the old town, attracting the masses of a new industrial proletariat, while the traditional activities of the capital declined, at least relatively. Between 1906 and 1931 the number of workers increased by 262 per cent in engineering, by 489 per cent in the manufacture of electrical apparatus and by 220 per cent in the dyeing industry, while there was a reduction of 32 per cent in clothing, 80 per cent in textiles and 68 per cent in glove manufacture. Hand in hand with this violent change went the rapid and uncontrolled growth of a vast suburban area. Hitherto, it had been confined to ribbon development along the railways and the main roads of the Seine-et-Oise, but Paris now became a vast, almost spherical, zone.

In general two phenomena, which were going to characterise the human and economic geography of France from now onwards, date from the war and the post-war period. First, there was the contrast between an active and progressive France north of a line stretching from Le Havre to Marseille, and a backward France becoming poorer and poorer to the south of this same line. Second, imposed on this contrast was the swollen, cancerous growth of the Paris region, devouring the national wealth.

The failure of repopulation

Another major worry was the country's inability to reverse its decline in population, which most observers regarded as disastrous. Between 1921 and 1931 net immigration into France amounted to 1,953,000 persons, i.e. 74.4 per cent of the overall increase in the resident population of France. A little less than half of these immigrants came from nearby countries, and especially from Italy, where there was chronic unemployment at the time. Before 1914 these immigrants had been confined to the south-east and south-west, where they were mostly involved in agriculture; but during the nineteen-twenties they settled in all the industrial regions, e.g. Lorraine, the north, the Paris area. Others came from distant countries, particularly Poland. In 1928 there were more than five hundred thousand Poles in France who had not been naturalised. Most of them worked in the agricultural regions of the north and north-east, in the coal and iron-ore mines, and as labourers and specialised workers in the Paris region. This immigration, which was desired both by the country of origin and by French industry, was officially controlled. Contracts were negotiated between the Polish emigration department and the French employers' organisations. But there was also free immigration on the part of traders, artisans and members of the liberal professions, very often emerging from the ghettos of Polish towns. They came with other Jews from different central European countries together with Greeks and Armenians, and they piled into the first four *arrondissements* of the old Paris, which the native working class then tended to leave.

This extra source of population, although it was valuable and indeed necessary for a country that had just lost so many men in their prime, was only a stopgap, as everyone agreed. The nation could only avoid catastrophe by reversing the demographic trend, which from before the war had been downward. 'France must have lots of children', cried Clemenceau in front of the Senate on 11 October 1919, 'If not, you can put what you like into the treaty – France will be done for.' But the population policy was a total failure, for no positive measures were taken to help families. The only government action was a negative one which made for involuntary procreation. In this spirit the famous law of 31 July 1920 was passed that punished very severely those guilty of abortion or intention to abort, and it even forbad all publicity about contraceptive methods.

At the same time, positive measures to help families were extremely limited. For the most part they came from private initiatives taken by employers. During the war, Romanet, a Grenoble industrialist in metals, had given bonuses to workers with families. His example was followed in the region, but it was soon seen that certain rivals systematically took on bachelors only. New arrangements were made by which the employer's contribution remained the same whatever the family status of the employee. The system spread after the war through the voluntary acceptance of certain entrepreneurs such as Michelin, so that by the end of 1929 1,800,000 wage-earners were involved. It was only then that the Poincaré government proposed a law making the allowances general, but there were vigorous protests from many employers. The state did not give much in the way of example. It limited itself in 1919 to prolonging the allowances made during the war to minor state employees with families, and in 1920–1 started small birth grants to parents who did not pay income tax.

In addition, families, and especially young families, were very much the victims of the housing shortage caused by wartime legislation that was prolonged unduly. In this sector, price control, which had been quickly abandoned after the war in the name of liberal principles, was kept in force so that rents fixed by law remained far below the general level of prices. The aim of this, as Loucheur admitted in his 1923 report, was to avoid a rise in salaries, which would certainly have taken place if rent control had been removed. The result was that inhabitants of ancient blocks saw them turning into slums, while the disgruntled owners did nothing to repair them. The rents of the new buildings which went up in quite large numbers in the twenties were far too high for young married people. Social action proved necessary to cope with the situation, but there was much shilly-shallying. The Loucheur law took seven years to reach the statute book in July 1928. It provided for the building of two hundred thousand dwellings at low rents, mostly in the Paris area. This was quite inadequate to deal with a crisis that was becoming more and more serious.

All this encouraged Malthusian ideas in the minds of the general public, and this could not be prevented simply by the 1920 law. For the great amalgam of men and ideas caused by the war had eliminated the last remains of that fatalistic attitude towards life and death which for centuries had favoured a high birth-rate. After a brief recovery during 1920–1 following the return of demobilised troops, when the rate exceeded twenty per thousand, a steady decline set in. Since the mortality rate, despite some reduction, still remained high at seventeen per thousand, the rate of natural growth was about two per thousand. So the population was static, any growth being the direct result of immigration.

12

Illusions of consensus

After the divisions that characterised the electoral periods starting in 1919 and 1924, the ruling classes on two occasions put Poincaré in charge and professed to revive the national unity that the former President of the Republic had inspired in 1914. In giving the name of Union Nationale to these political coalitions the men in power maintained that they were only excluding the marginal groups who were enemies of both society and La Patrie. In effect, all the organisations of the world of labour, whether reformist or revolutionary, were cut off from the community. It was as if, in spite of shared ordeals, industrialisation, urbanisation and the experience of other countries, one could go back to the 'good old days' when the workers, apart from a few militants and hotheads in the large towns, accepted without a murmur the domination and values of the reigning bourgeoisie. Life was lived in an illusion of social consensus which gave free rein to sectarian rancour.

A blocked society

French society was turned upside down by the war, and during the peace and expansion which followed would not recover her pre-war equilibrium. The peasant, the middle and the working classes were transformed, but in such a variety of ways that in the present state of knowledge we can do no more than stress certain clear lines of change.

The rural world

As far as the peasant masses are concerned, our ignorance is still profound. The men of the land rarely expressed themselves. Those who professed to interpret the rural classes described them as they wanted to see them, obeying their own ideological or political prejudices. Their incomes remain almost unknown, and so they never feature in statistics. Their electoral behaviour, which is more clearly discernible, varied so much from place to place that it does not help much to illuminate the sociological realities of the countryside. As we have no comprehensive series of regional and local monographs at our disposal, we can only distinguish a few general traits.

Everyone at the time freely admitted that the rural areas had made greater sacrifices of human life in the war than the rest of France. One could see proof in the long lists of dead in the most remote villages. The rural folk were well aware of this fact, and certain politicians made a point of reminding them of it. But, in the eyes of many town people, the peasants had made large profits out of the war and had enriched themselves. The high price of farm products had allowed them, it was said, to pack away in their *bas de laine* considerable savings, which they refused to display in broad daylight because of their suspicion of all unusual expenditure. There was some evidence for these allegations. Those who had run up debts to set themselves up or expand their holdings often paid them off in the twenties; but in doing this they were only taking advantage of the inflation that favoured all debtors. Furthermore, new forms of consumption appeared after the war in the rural areas. Coffee became a habit and red meat was no longer a rarity at table. Consulting a doctor became more common, whereas up till now a resigned attitude in the face of suffering and death made such a move unthinkable. Jules Romains might well have made people laugh at this new fad in *Knock ou le triomphe de la médecine* (1923), but his play reflected a reality. It was also during the twenties that motor-buses appeared and helped to break the isolation of those villages which the railways did not reach. In general, by allowing many countrymen to compare their lot with the life of the towns and by creating new needs, the war weakened the apparent resignation with which many of them accepted their fate.

It was a fact that the rural masses, although they had shrunk in numbers, still made up about half the total population. Furthermore, the electoral systems, in the Chamber and even more in the Senate, favoured the country areas, so that the rural electorate was an element that no coalition government could alienate with impunity. But despite appearances the country interest had no proper organisation. The local leaders, who professed to speak for the masses, were in practice either landlords or members of the liberal professions, and were rarely working farmers. They had little difficulty in dominating the agricultural unions and co-operatives, and without any overall plan tried through their influence to obtain small subsidies or such services as were required, e.g. electricity, roads, main water, etc. The 'agrarians' of the left and right continued to hold sway in the countryside, praising to excess the merits of the small holding. (See P. Barral, *Les Agrariens français, de Méline à Pisani.*) As for the two million farm workers, neglected by the social laws of the time, they were hardly touched by the union movement (1 per cent were members), except where some outstanding militant such as Renaud Jean in the Lot-et-

Garonne, succeeded in bringing them together with the sharecroppers, who were more impatient than ever to shake off the yoke of the landlords. (P. Gratton, 'Mouvement ouvrier et question agraire, 1870–1947', in *L'Univers politique des paysans*, pp. 174f.)

The workers

The war, and then the economic changes caused by the expansion of the nineteen-twenties, had an even more spectacular effect on the mass of workers in industry. The mixing of people in the war had here too opened up new horizons and had more or less dislocated the old structures. The most striking case was that of the miners in the Nord and the Pas-de-Calais. Before the war these were nearly all native-born. With a high birth-rate they made up a homogeneous block under the paternal authority of the companies. Their chances of promotion were practically nil. Many of these miners had been scattered far and wide in the services and never returned. The ones who remained were less under the influence of the society around them. They were more critical, more thoughtful and no longer satisfied with their old horizons. Their fertility diminished and many of them saw their children's future outside the mines. The companies had to resort to foreign labour, especially Poles, who provided 64 per cent of the total population growth in the area between 1919 and 1927. (P. Ariès, *Histoire des populations françaises et de leurs attitudes devant la vie depuis le XVIIIe siècle*, pp. 104–18.)

Still more remarkable was the increase in unskilled workers, alongside and often to the detriment of the skilled workers of the preceding period. They were employed on the factory production lines which were increasing in number with the adoption of the Taylor system. Whether they came directly from the country, or from abroad, or whether they were formerly skilled workers rendered useless by the new work system, they were condemned to fragmented tasks of a particularly demoralising kind. Such workers were without real qualifications because they could be trained in a few days for mass-production jobs. At the slightest misdemeanour they could easily be replaced, or dismissed if the economic situation demanded it.

Yet this new proletariat did not abolish the old ways of work. Even in the most modern firms there was need for skilled labour, for the production line could not be used everywhere. Furthermore, some factories and industries continued to produce by traditional methods. The skilled worker, proud of his role as a 'producer' and conscious of his social usefulness and of his exploitation at the hands of capital, had not disappeared from the scene, far from it. But he was worried by the way he saw things going. He tried therefore to defend his interests either individually by moving into the 'middle class' or collectively by militant action in the labour movement, which was still led by people like him and did not lack fighting spirit.

Contrary to what the bourgeois and the bosses said when they readily denounced the luxurious tastes of the lower classes, the workers had profited only relatively from the war and the benefits of 'prosperity'. The salary rises in the second half of the war had not been enough to catch up with a rise in prices: real wages in 1919 were in fact 15 per cent below those of 1914. A solidly based labour movement was needed not only to catch up the arrears quickly but also to claim a fair share of the fruits of expansion; for there were very few employers ready to put into practice theories that favoured a high-wages policy to maintain that expansion.

The strikes of 1920

In these circumstances the rift in the working-class movement that occurred in 1920 and 1921 was particularly damaging. It resulted from the illusion that revolutionary change would be possible in France once the war was over. It was this illusion, as we have seen, that led the socialist party in 1919 to adopt disastrous election tactics and in consequence to suffer a defeat that was keenly felt. Certain trade unionists thought that they could carry on the policy into 1920. Jouhaux, together with most of the CGT leaders, was inclined to prudence because of the political defeat of the year before. They looked for possible progress in exploiting the existing laws on collective bargaining, while at the same time promoting the nationalisation of industry, which had been adopted as a policy at the federal congress in 1918. However, the 'revolutionaries', although they were in a minority, found an audience among the members who had recently joined and were impatient for action. This allowed them to embark on a trial of strength with bourgeois society. The action started with the powerful Fédération des Cheminots, where an amalgamation of unions in 1917 had built up a dynamic centre. In February 1920 the first strike broke out in the PLM company. A very tough reaction on the employers' part spread the movement to the other lines, which led the government to propose arbitration. The companies were very loth to accept this solution, and their reluctance encouraged the congress of the Fédération to adopt an extreme policy in April. They proposed a general strike from 1 May onwards and requested the support of the CGT. The secretary-general Jouhaux, although he himself was very sceptical, ended by giving in to those who accused him of treason, or at least suspected him of collusion with the employers. The plan was to call other workers out on strike in successive waves in support of the railwaymen's action.

However, the employers, well organised and well supported by Yves Le Troquer, the minister of public works, had time to prepare for the struggle. The strikers were replaced with spectacular effect by young men of the *bonne bourgeoisie*. Even among the railwaymen the strike did not catch on as expected, particularly on the Nord line where the vote went against strike action. Hardly anywhere did the strikers amount to more than half the workers, and the movement could not be saved by the wave of stoppages started by other branches of industry on 8 and 11 May in its support.

On 28 May work was resumed without any claims having been met. The companies in their triumph took a savage revenge – eighteen thousand railwaymen, i.e. 5 per cent of the workforce, were dismissed. The minister for commerce and industry, Isaac, even thought the time had come to get rid of trade unionism. He started an action against the CGT and found magistrates who were willing to request the dissolution of the organisation – a drastic move. Millerand, more realistically, gave assurances to Jouhaux, who immediately appealed against such a decision and the matter was dropped. Millerand could afford to be generous as he had little to fear from a confederation which had been reduced to impotence by its defeat. Within a few months union membership dropped by half, and internal strife was resumed in the weakened CGT. Indeed trade unionism had followed the socialist party into bankruptcy.

The congress of Tours

By contrast, the success of the bolsheviks seemed all the more remarkable in that they had pushed through the proletarian revolution in Russia, overcoming all opposition. The continuing disturbances in the whole of central Europe in the summer of 1920 still led people to hope for a revolutionary wave to sweep in from the east. This resulted in the split of the socialist party at the congress of Tours in December 1920.

The question of the Communist International had dominated all discussions for over a year. At the Strasbourg congress in February 1920 the majority, led by Longuet, had broken with the Second International, which had clearly failed in its mission in 1914. But it did this in the hope of rebuilding the unity of international socialism within the Third International based in Moscow. This majority was not trying to differentiate itself from the centre group with its opportunist, reforming tendencies, as was the aim of Loriot and his supporters of the Comité de la Troisième Internationale, who mostly originated in revolutionary syndicalism. It was in this spirit that the party sent two important leaders to Moscow in July – the deputy Cachin, for a long time a 'majority' man during the war and now a 'reconstructionist', and the new secretary-general Frossard. Their mission was to negotiate the socialist party's entry into the Third International, on condition that the latter ceased to deal solely with the 'so-called French communist parties' and Loriot's minority Comité de la Troisième Internationale.

On arrival in Moscow, Cachin and Frossard were received coolly and learnt that the said Comité had appointed Lefebvre, Vergeat and Lepetit, together with Rosmer, as delegates; and that these delegates had received a much warmer reception from the bolsheviks than they had themselves.

However, after explaining the French socialist party's stance to the second congress of the International, the two socialist delegates were invited to the congress debates as observers. After some anxiety about the rival delegation's reception, and after being reassured by the concessions made by Zinoviev after very tough opening conditions, they promised to call for membership from the French socialist party.

Suddenly there was a split among the 'reconstructionists' who had been in the majority since the Strasbourg congress. Cachin and Frossard, who were now in favour of membership, were opposed to Longuet, who rejected any division imposed by Moscow. This was made easier for them by the fact that their rival, the Comité de la Troisième Internationale, lost its leading figures, mostly imprisoned after the May strikes, and its delegates in Moscow, who were drowned at sea on the return journey. However, 'constructionists' and 'ex-reconstructionists' were not in disagreement about doctrine or the way to regard the Russian revolution. The supporters of the Third International were carried away by tactical and sentimental considerations, and understood the true nature of bolshevism and Marxism–Leninism as little as their rivals. At the congress in Tours Blum put up sound theoretical arguments against them, refusing membership in the name of the socialist party's traditional principles. He rejected revolutionary defeatism, strict dependence on the International, total submission of the unions to the communist party's aims and organisation, a monolithic structure and strict discipline – in fact all the conditions of membership required by Moscow. But the supporters of membership themselves saw in these conditions only verbiage. It was only on Moscow's formal insistence that Longuet's exclusion was decided, for Frossard had done everything to avoid it.

Why then did a bid for membership win an enormous majority of votes (3,247 against 1,398 for the 'reconstructionists'), when it ensured a schism? The break did not reflect old party divisions, nor those brought about by the war, nor was it caused by the gulf that had for long separated revolutionaries and reformists. It seemed to be founded on a difference in appreciation of two events in the year 1920 – the relative failure of the French labour movement in its political and union activities on the one hand, and the imminent possibility of a world revolution following on the success of the Russian revolution. The defeat of the Red Army in front of Warsaw in December in no way damaged that army's credibility. There was a double accident, according to Annie Kriegel's thesis, and many thought at the time that the check would be purely temporary.

The trade unions split

The rift grew wider during the nineteen-twenties. In 1921 it affected the trade unions. At the Lille congress in June 1921 the militants of the Comités Syndicalistes Révolutionnaires (CSR), which with Moscow's support tried with some success to infiltrate the CGT, were roundly censured by a small majority. In December, as the CRS had not given in and continued to fight against the leadership of the CGT, the administrative commission of the CGT took note of the dissidence. In the following June, the left wing of the CGT held its first congress at Saint-Etienne. There were violent disagreements between the anarcho-syndicalists, passionately attached to the Amiens charter, and the communists who supported a strong link between trade unionism and politics, and immediate membership of the trade-union International in Moscow. Although the communists managed to impose their ideas, the congress led to the departure of many left-wing union members, who would not be converted to bolshevik ideas on trade union/communist party relations.

As for the old CGT, now rid of most of its divisive elements, it was strengthened by taking into membership the state employees' unions, whose legal existence was approved in 1924 by the Herriot government. Preceded by the primary teachers in 1922, these unions joined Jouhaux's confederation in 1928. While it did not give up the traditional struggles, for which the left-wingers showed more energy and flair, the CGT tried more moderate tactics, partly under the influence of the new recruits, and did not refuse discussions with the employers and the government. It elaborated the programme sketched out in 1919, particularly the nationalisation of monopolies and public services. It demanded the establishment of an economic council of labour, to group together producers and consumers and to take part in the political and economic decisions that concerned the nation. The radical party, egged on by the neo-radicals, expressed interest in the scheme, and the Conseil Economique was created in January 1925, which was supported by the CGT in spite of its disappointment with the limited powers granted to the council. But, side by side with this rich harvest of ideas, what feeble results! The actions taken and the results achieved were unimpressive, whether in promoting strikes or in negotiating collective agreements. In general, the trade-union movement, faced with employers' organisations that were both agressive and well organised, could not or did not know how to take advantage of a situation that was after all most favourable to it. The weakness of the labour movement arising out of its divisions was certainly one of the main causes of this situation.

The communists

The split that occurred at Tours became deeper and deeper. Most of the militant socialists, who at the end of 1920 believed that a social revolution of Russian origin was imminent, joined the young communist party with enthusiasm. But the failure of revolutionary action in Germany in March 1921, the Soviet Union's self-absorption and the quarrels between bolsheviks soon led to disappointment of these hopes. The communist party began to find its place in a bourgeois republic that showed no signs of tottering. Ambiguities which had led to a massive membership at Tours had now to be removed. According to the bolsheviks, there was no question of gaining the greatest number of recruits at the price of concessions on doctrine and discipline; rather, following the example set by Lenin and his supporters before 1917, they must forge a hard core of tried militants who would be prepared, when a revolutionary situation presented itself in France, to exploit it effectively.

The Communist International in Moscow increased its urgent directives. At the end of 1921 it published its ideas on 'the one proletarian front', which meant vigorously fighting the leaders of the social democratic parties and winning over the working-class masses who had followed them. Many members of the new party jibbed at this pressure, and Moscow's orders became more demanding. When in 1922 Trotsky requested the exclusion of all communists who would not abandon Freemasonry or the Ligue des Droits de l'Homme, which in his view were centres of 'petit-bourgeois' ideology, Frossard gave up being secretary-general and then left the party at the beginning of 1923. With him departed most of the 'right' wing that had been anxious to rebuild the unity of the workers and was ready for discussions with the socialist party. From now onwards, under the leadership of Treint, former schoolmaster and army officer, 'the epitome of the bureaucrat, narrow-minded and full of himself' (Humbert-Droz), the communist party was to pursue its bolshevisation, everywhere fighting the other parties, including those of the left, which in their eyes were no less dangerous and open to criticism than those of the right. During Poincaré's occupation of the Ruhr, the communist party made common cause with the passive resistance of the Germans and fought tooth and nail against Poincaré's action. At the 1924 elections it gained nine hundred thousand votes or 8 per cent of the poll, and there arose the bastions of communism where its influence would be permanent, i.e. the Paris suburbs, the Cher and the Lot-et-Garonne, and the 'red crescent' of the Massif Central. The party fought against the Cartel des Gauches with as much vigour as against the right. At the 1928 elections it refused to follow the usual republican procedure for the second round: by keeping its candidates everywhere in the ring against the socialists and the radicals, and despite its better score (1,060,000 votes or 9.3 per cent of the poll), it helped the right to win on occasions, which led to much criticism. In 1927 it adopted a hard line, 'class versus class', at the instigation of the Communist International which prophesied the coming crisis in capitalism and a war against the Soviet Union. This disconcerted many of the militants, so that numbers fell and quarrels broke out among those who remained within the party.

The SFIO

As for the SFIO (the Section Française de l'Internationale Ouvrière), i.e. the minority excluded at the congress of Tours and reduced in

December 1920 to about thirty thousand members, it kept 'the old firm' (Blum's phrase) going, and to it would certainly return those who were disappointed in the bolsheviks. Its doctrine remained Marxist, and it saw itself as a proletarian party preaching the socialisation of the means of production. It still proclaimed itself revolutionary, admitting that the transition from a bourgeois to a socialist society would involve a short period of lawless confusion and a dictatorship of the proletariat. While waiting for this to happen the SFIO accepted reforms that would hasten on the progress of socialism. It abhorred the use of violence and condemned secret action. The positive value of 'bourgeois' liberties was admitted and should be defended. If called to take office by the operation of existing institutions, the SFIO even considered that its role should be to follow the example of the Scandinavian and British social democrats and to 'manage the affairs of bourgeois society to the greatest interest of the working classes' (Blum).

All this emphasised the divorce between revolutionary doctrine and reform in practice, which gave the SFIO an effective flexibility in public life and at the same time gave rise to virulent internal debates. It made considerable headway, unlike the communist party, which was isolated and weakened by its growing sectarianism; for most of the parliamentarians of the undivided party elected in 1919 remained loyal. From 1920 to 1924 the SFIO had a beneficial spell of opposition to the Bloc National. In 1924 it claimed more than 110,000 members, and at the national elections its alliance with the radicals enabled it to win 101 seats in the Chamber. But only a minority on the right contemplated a lasting understanding with the radicals. In the opinion of Léon Blum and his supporters, who were haunted by the fear of leaving the workers' movement open to unlimited communist influence, the SFIO could only take on government responsibilities if it were in full control. All this was getting too much for men of the left like Bracke and Zyromsky, who objected to Léon Blum's subtleties and hoped that unity of doctrine would soon allow the workers' movement to regain its cohesion.

At the same time, the social make-up of the party was changing. The workers, especially those of the industrial north, were certainly a large element; but the SFIO also attracted some members of the middle classes, particularly state employees, e.g. primary teachers and postal workers, and a number of small farmers, either sharecroppers or smallholders, in the regions that were traditionally republican. It also welcomed young intellectuals, who ignored the squabbles of their elders. All this no doubt explains (though it requires confirmation) the importance, especially after 1924, of 'revisionist' currents, e.g. the 'neo-socialism' of Philip, Dubreuil and Spinasse, and even the interest that began to be shown in Mussolini's fascism, e.g. Marquet. (Cf. Tony Judt, *La Reconstruction du parti socialiste, 1921–1926*, p. 232.)

The struggle between the two Marxist parties never flagged, and insults were constantly being exchanged. No reconciliation seemed possible between the *moscoutaires* and the *sociaux-traitres*.

The middle classes

The socialist party, in spite of its collectivist beliefs, now saw many middle-class folk joining its ranks, and their influence began to affect its reform policy. The middle classes, who in France had been richer and more numerous than in other countries, had been most affected by the general impoverishment of the country. At the end of the war *rentiers*, members of the liberal professions, landlords and civil servants often felt that they were ruined. The many people whose carefully hoarded savings had been invested in foreign and state bonds were more or less dispossessed. As for industrial shares, they lost most of their value, with certain exceptions. Railway shares, for instance, which figured in most sound portfolios before the war, had fallen in value so dramatically that J. Bainville, in a booklet for the 'capitalist' or small investor, described them as 'without any interest whatever'. (*Après la guerre, comment placer sa fortune*, Paris, Nouvelle librairie nationale, 1919.) Marc Sangnier was certainly exaggerating when he wrote: 'the proletariat, organised and aware of its power, is no longer the nation's most underprivileged class, it is even sometimes the most favoured. In the lower depths beneath it can be seen crawling a whole social swarm of different upbringing and temperament – the mass of those whom the proletariat used to regard as bourgeois, now reduced to extreme penury.' ('Le Retour à la paix', *Revue hebdomadaire*, 30 August 1919, p. 593.) However, the founder of *Le Sillon* was reflecting the post-war sentiments of those small *rentiers* who before 1914 had been representative of French society.

Naturally, inflation, then the stabilisation of the franc, only hastened their impoverishment or their ruin. Some of these small capitalists had in fact continued to subscribe to treasury bonds or fixed-interest stocks, encouraged by the tax concessions granted to holders of French securities and undeterred by their recent bad experiences. They imagined that the parity and stabilisation of the franc would be restored as before 1914. There were relatively few who learnt from experience and invested their savings in ordinary industrial shares, either French or foreign, which were now forging ahead in the current prosperity. The successive governments up to 1926 promised the recovery of the franc and the defence of savings. But not one kept its promises and the result was a certain disillusionment among those sectors of society that had been pillars of the regime. This was dangerous and stressed the artificial and often absurd character of the political game.

The essential France of the small capitalist, entrepreneur and shop-keeper, of the liberal professions and much of the public service, feared above all being converted into a proletariat. The fate of the German *petit-bourgeois*, ground down by inflation, provided a grim warning. The French equivalent clung to his privileges and tried to strengthen the barriers that blocked the social advancement of the lower classes; and he criticised as scandalous their new consumption habits, considered responsible for the inflation that was causing his ruin. The marked reduction in the number of domestic servants, which dropped from 930,000 in 1911 to 784,000 in 1926, was proof of bourgeois impoverishment and became a favourite topic for jokes in theatrical revues.

Nowhere was this touchiness more clearly demonstrated than in the debates on the re-organisation of education. In 1918 the mixing of the social classes caused by the war had brought a number of ex-service university teachers together into a group of *compagnons*, notably Carré, Brunschwig and Loretti, to propose fundamental reforms. They criticised the system which put up an impenetrable barrier between primary and secondary education and blocked any real equality of opportunity. They recommended a single school in which the children, irrespective of social origins, received the same basic education through the same methods and programmes.

Apart from the hostility of the right, which was quick to confuse the single school with the university monopoly and so saw in this campaign a prelude to the disappearance of private education, these plans met with much opposition. There was the more or less vocal opposition of most secondary school teachers, the educational administrators, the parents; in brief, of all those who in one way or another had benefited from a system which reserved for an élite that secondary education which alone opened the way to the *grandes écoles* and universities, and from there to the upper ranks of the civil service, most of the liberal professions and the leading posts in the private sector. The exceptions to this iron rule were the scholarship winners, who came from the ranks of the people and who were able, thanks to good luck and exceptional gifts, to surmount all the obstacles to advancement. Their existence quietened the consciences of those who claimed to hold left-wing libertarian views but at the same time remained firmly attached to this flagrant social selection. In this situation, the efforts in 1926 of Edouard Herriot, minister of education in Poincaré's Union Nationale, which were limited to an increase in the number of scholarships and, above all, to the mixing of pupils of various educational levels in some 150 *collèges communaux*, could not achieve much change. Although the reforms did not lead to the disappearance of the barriers between different educational ladders, they were a step in the direction of free secondary schools, which came to be an objective from 1928 onwards. However, in the élitist system, which these reforms hardly touched, the payment of very small school fees was only a minor obstacle to creating equality of opportunity. Among ordinary French people there were very few who saw what the real obstacles were.

In spite of increased contact between classes and the collapse of large fortunes brought about by the war, the social and psychological barriers at work in French society, which was always more rigid than other advanced countries at the same stage of development, created a community that was in no way open to all talents.

The political scene

The fundamentally conservative attitudes in much of French society help to explain the disturbed political scene of the time. The agitation was due to governments being entirely at the mercy of unstable majorities in parliament. This instability was increased by the inconsistent attitude of most parties, which were made up of deputies and senators deeply attached in their various ways to those obstacles to progress which we have discussed. Over and above the noise of political strife, it is now usual to highlight two main tendencies at work: *movement*, which overcame the divisions and barriers of a frozen society, and *order*, which by a variety of means adapted itself to the status quo and also assured its survival. It was this second tendency which dominated the exercise of power during the whole post-war period.

The extreme right and the right

Among leading conservative politicians there were few who accepted the description of 'right-wing'. The provinces, where the descendants of legitimist catholic leaders kept their old influence over pious peasants, e.g. the west, and the southern part of the Massif Central, gladly sent to parliament men who proclaimed themselves conservative. They were hostile to the ideology and principles of the French Revolution, and made no attempt to hide their dislike of republican institutions. Some of them refused all compromise and sat as independents. Others, readier to make concessions in the interests of effectiveness belonged to the Fédération Républicaine and formed the bulk of the Entente Républicaine Démocratique groups in the 1919 parliament and the Union Républicaine Démocratique groups in the 1924 parliament. These made up a considerable element in the 'national majorities' and provided several ministers in the 1919–24 governments and after 1926, but without providing a prime minister. The energetic and rather muddled leadership of their chief Louis Marin did not pass without opposition among parliamentarians who were by tradition jealous of their independence. (Cf. J.-N. Jeanneney, *François de Wendel en République, l'argent et le pouvoir, 1914–1940*, pp. 427–39.)

On the extreme right the Action Française was out on its own. Thanks to

Maurras it possessed a firm dogma embracing, with certain contradictions, the ancient traditions of the French, e.g. legitimism, nationalism, and certain shady aspects of Orléanism. To these were added the founder's positivist agnosticism, which combined strangely with the more or less *intégriste* catholicism of most supporters of the movement. It called itself 'the intelligent party' and claimed to bring together an intellectual élite. Indeed, it numbered in its ranks some talented writers and brilliant pamphleteers, adept at the invective which the right had always favoured. The break-up of the Union Sacrée in 1917 and the resultant anxiety won it a much larger audience than before. It gave unwelcome support to Clemenceau and was able in 1919 to slip a few of its members, notably Léon Daudet, into the lists of the victorious Bloc National. In parliament, its members defended the principles of pure nationalism, but in the country at large kept up a frenzied agitation, which became the delight of the gutter press. The murder of Marius Plateau, a collaborator of Maurras, by an anarchist woman in 1923, the mysterious events in which Léon Daudet's son Philippe lost his life, also in 1923, and finally the police's siege of the *L'Action française* offices, where Léon Daudet took refuge, and his amusing escape from the Santé prison in June 1927, all provided unexpected copy for the journalists. The movement was glad to recruit young students, who were at that time exclusively bourgeois, as shock gangs who harassed professors suspected of left-wing tendencies and broke in on meetings of Marxists and their supposed sympathisers. The Action Française movement had a lot of support from the clergy who, in the fight against the anti-clericals, chose to ignore the atheistic positivism of the movement's leading thinker. It was a traumatic moment when the Vatican authorities, alerted by the christian democrats whose pacifist tendencies the movement fiercely denounced, decided to ban the Action Française movement and put its daily paper on the Index (1927). Its decline became more evident because part of the militant youth who had followed Maurras found a new home in the Jeunesses Patriotes movement. This association had been founded at the time of the 1924 elections by a Paris deputy, Pierre Taittinger, to counteract the rise of the left. It revived the ancient tradition of the Ligues showing 'that mixture of calculation and generosity, illusion and demagogy that sprang from Bona-partism'. (R. Rémond, *La Droite en France de 1815 à nos jours* (1954 edn), p. 202.) It added a military wing that was in fact inspired by the example of Mussolini's fascism. This body gathered remarkable strength in a few years and claimed three hundred thousand members in 1929.

Meanwhile the liberal right, although it did not scorn on occasion to use the help of these activists, completely ignored them when it came to the serious side of politics. It was the heir to that Orléanism and moderate republicanism whose alliance had brought about the triumph of the Republic. It wholeheartedly accepted the institutions in which it was certain to find the means of political supremacy. To distinguish itself from the pugnacious and sectarian extreme right, the liberal right wing did not hesitate to give itself a suitable label to hoodwink the naive. The Alliance Démocratique, Républicains de Gauche, Indépendants de Gauche, Gauche Républicaine made up the bulk of the ruling right. Poincaré, Barthou, Briand, Tardieu, Laval, Reynaud and Flandin were all members of it. They did without any party organisation, for by temperament as well as doctrine they shrank from all regimentation, quite unlike the British conservatives in this respect as in others. They owed their election and their strength to their influence as regional leaders. They were not above accepting the financial aid of big business, particularly during election campaigns, in order to avoid digging into their own pockets. This aid reached them through such channels as the Union des Intérêts Economiques. Apparently very different one from the other, they found their unity when it came to preaching the classic tenets of economic liberalism, even when, as we have seen, the 'neo-capitalists' tried to apply certain correctives. They also fought against all extension of state intervention, although the hard times were making it necessary, and they were parsimonious when it came to the budget and the payment of their state servants, who were considered to be greedy consumers of public funds. In the old days they had been divided on the religious issue, but after the war this source of contention quietened down. The liberal right did not seek an impossible revenge against 'lay power' such as the *intégristes* and extremists demanded, but rather agreed to the maintenance of the status quo and even to a few concessions to the Church that would help to heal old wounds, e.g. restoration of diplomatic relations with the Vatican, observance of the terms of the Concordat in the recovered provinces, etc. In fact it was only on foreign policy that the group was seriously divided. Some of its members loudly proclaimed their strong nationalist convictions and inclined to a strong arm policy 'à la Poincaré'. But what they considered to be political realism pushed most of them towards more or less pacifist doctrines of which Briand, one of their number, was soon to become the main champion.

The radicals

With the introduction of income tax, which was adopted before the war and began to operate after its end, the radical party achieved nearly all the objectives which it had set itself. The question now was whether it could renew its programme for a further spell.

The limits of the party's ideology were vague, but the essential content was clear.

> The members and electors come from the middle class with a leftist tradition embracing the party's ideals as summed up in an accumulation of historic references, which serve as a doctrinal base, from the French Revo-

lution up to the Bloc des Gauches, passing by the 1848 revolution with Ledru-Rollin, the republican opposition to the Empire with Gambetta, the defence of the republic with Waldeck-Rousseau, and so on. The party believes in two ideals which have governed the radical programme since 1907 – loyalty to the institutions of the Third Republic, and particularly to the parliamentary system, and social reform which makes radicals liberal interventionists, opposed not only to a *laissez-faire* outlook, which crushes the 'little man', but also to collectivism which aims at the abolition of private property. Finally, in international affairs, a belief in peace guaranteed by the League of Nations is combined with real attachment to a national defence policy. (Serge Berstein, in *L'Information historique*, May–June 1977, p. 128.)

As the socialist party after 1920 tended to steal part of the radicals' support, the party's point of balance moved somewhat to the right as compared with before the war. But the radicals distinguished themselves clearly from the liberal right by their defence of the 'little man', by their uncompromising secularity and by the special nature of their patriotism, which made most of them from 1918 onwards support with enthusiasm the Wilsonian principles of collective security. This enabled them at appropriate moments to work with the socialists, whose unfailing internationalism and secularism could draw a veil over their collectivist doctrines, or with a part of the liberal right, at least that part which damped down its uncompromising nationalism. With their solid base in the country the radicals could take advantage of all possible combinations allowed by the voting system. In the Chamber they always formed a substantial group, which was indispensable for a majority, so they continued throughout the post-war period to provide ministers for every government.

Although the radicals were much better organised than the rightist groups and formed a real party, complete with congresses at which the militants regularly expressed their hopes and fears, they were a motley crew and lacked discipline. Their committees and federations looked much more like the electoral supporting teams of the local leader than centres of thought and action for the militants, who were in any case much less numerous than their left-wing equivalents. The party members in parliament could also take great liberties with the principles and strategies worked out in conferences, where the power struggles of the main leaders could be detected: Albert and Maurice Sarraut, impregnable in their Languedoc estates, on the one hand, and Edouard Herriot, assured of a position of first importance by virtue of being mayor of Lyon, on the other. It was under Herriot's guidance that the radical party was thoroughly overhauled between 1919 and 1924.

The political game and the collapse of the Cartel des Gauches
In 1919 most of the radicals elected (fifty-seven out of eighty-six) figured on lists which both refused alliance with the socialists and also with

the rightist elements in the Bloc National, even though a minority of the party had committed itself to the latter. Although they were fewer in number because of this (eighty-six deputies instead of 172 in the last parliament), the radicals could draw advantage from a spell in opposition and, at the same time, from the participation in the government of some of their number, e.g. Steeg at the ministry of the interior in the Millerand government. During this period the radicals stepped up their criticism of the Bloc National. In 1921 there were various appeals to the socialists for a Union des Gauches, but in view of the danger into which the country was plunged by the crisis of the franc, Sarraut, Strauss and Laffont were allowed to be members of Poincaré's Union Nationale government.

There were more pressing and effective appeals to the socialists during 1923 because of the drastic budgetary measures taken by Poincaré and the disagreeable impression made by the Ruhr operation on the supporters of collective security. A coalition called the Cartel des Gauches was set up, which thanks to the lesson of 1919 was able to take advantage of the electoral law of 1919 and was really successful at the elections of May 1924. Bringing 139 radical socialists and about one hundred socialists to the Chamber, this success kindled great hopes in the French left (now forgotten because of the meagre results) and caused anxiety, of course, among the rich. The rich were particularly threatened by a capital tax and never ceased to hope for an end to the triumph of the left. They had little to fear because the coalition was weak. The socialists supported it only in a limited way and would not take part in the government. Furthermore, the Cartel, in order to govern, had to make up their majority from the right among the *radicaux indépendants* (or *radicaux de gauche*) who were very lukewarm towards their programme. Another adverse factor was the clumsiness of the radical leaders, who did not perceive the necessity of acting quickly and speaking clearly to the country. Nor did they know how to master (as we have seen above) the technical side of the financial situation which they inherited.

The Millerand affair brought a first sign of these disturbing weaknesses. The President of the Republic, breaking with all precedents, recommended on the eve of the elections a reform which made for the strengthening of the executive, and at the same time he showed himself openly hostile to the Cartel. The result was that the Cartel majority forced him to resign by preventing him from forming any government at all. Parliament did not choose the scholarly Painlevé, the Cartel's candidate, to succeed him, but preferred Gaston Doumergue, a radical of the old school and president of the Senate, who was supported by all the 'moderates' of the Chamber and the whole Senate, and who was to do all he could to bring down the Cartel. For nearly a year the Herriot ministry held a majority, which became more and more precarious. Then, after its overthrow, several ministries with different majorities succeeded each other for a year, until the Cartel finally broke up and a new crisis of the franc led to the return to power of 'Poincaré-la-confiance'.

While the former President of the Republic left a free hand to Briand in international affairs, a new Union Nationale, which excluded the working-class parties and paralysed the right wing that hankered after a more anti-German foreign policy, again put power into the hands of a coalition favouring law and order. This majority was further strengthened at the 1928 elections (where the *scrutin d'arrondissement* was restored) thanks to Poincaré's success in stabilising the franc and Briand's success after Locarno. Most of the victorious radical candidates, who were elected either without any standing-down or thanks to the support of the liberal right's 'moderates', continued to favour this Union Nationale, even though it was resisted, under the young Daladier's leadership, by all those who owed their seats to a socialist standing-down. Poincaré, with this access of strength, remained in power until he was forced out by illness in July 1929. So there appeared this paradox that, in two successive elections since the end of the war, one brought in the most right-wing chamber that the Republic had ever known, and the other was the triumph of the left; yet both governments ended with the arrival in power of the same man, the symbol of that moderate France, which not only refused all risks but even resisted any major change at all. At least the regime, for the last time before the onset of the world crisis, could show a certain ministerial stability, running its day-to-day affairs with efficiency.

The cultural scene

The ordeal of war, the fears and illusions of the period which followed, could not fail to have their effect on the work of artists, who in most spheres continued to spread the renown of French culture. France, and notably Paris, was a centre from which ideas and fashions that set the tone spread throughout the world. Painters, musicians, architects and writers from everywhere came to seek at least some of their inspiration in 'La Ville Lumière'.

Scientific research: a failure in renewal

It was not, however, the same for science. It is true that Paris had long ago lost the brilliant position which she occupied at the beginning of the Industrial Revolution. Gradually paralysed by the stifling heritage of the Napoleonic university system, French science became marginal and out-dated, a worrying situation which only got worse despite periodic cries of alarm. One might have hoped, here as elsewhere, that the ordeal of war would bring home certain lessons; and, indeed, during the hostilities the basis of a national policy of fundamental research had been laid. In 1915, a directorate of inventions was created at the ministry of education, even becoming a ministerial department for a short time. Jean Perrin and Paul Langevin, amongst others, did important research there; and many scientists were enthusiastic about keeping on an organisation of this kind once peace was restored. In 1922 an Office National de Recherches Scientifiques, Industriels et des Inventions was created, whose brief was to 'stimulate, coordinate and encourage research of every kind'. This body was given, among other things, the management of the Bellevue laboratory, which had been set up during the war for the needs of national defence. But the scope of this ancestor of the CNRS (Centre National de la Recherche Scientifique) and other institutes, where in a more or less secret manner and without adequate funds key research was carried out, did not compensate for a general decline in performance. Certainly French scientists continued to play an important role in the startling developments of physics, and at the Institut du Radium Marie Curie, Frédéric Joliot and Jean Perrin explored the atom. In 1925 a young independent scientist, Prince Louis de Broglie, published a fundamental work on quantum theory, which laid the foundations of wave mechanics. But there was no equivalent to the heady atmosphere of the English and German universities or the institute which Niels Bohr directed at Copenhagen. In the traditional scientific institutions, old-fashioned ideas and a conformist outlook tended to neutralise research. In the name of common sense, and even the national genius and its peculiarities, the scientific establishment rejected all unorthodox discoveries, and even the most advanced teaching bodies spurned anything novel. Didn't Berthelot (though he later recanted) equate Einstein's new hypotheses on time and space with alchemy and spiritualism, and explain it by the author's membership of the Jewish race 'so arrogantly regarded by its sons as the chosen race of God . . . a disturbing and disturbed race'? Thus pettiness and narrow nationalism added to the sclerosis of the institutions.

The surrealist revolution

On the other hand, France remained the 'mother of the arts', except in the sphere of architecture and urban development. The innovators of the Bauhaus and the American School met with nothing but obloquy and sarcasm in French academic circles, while the country became covered with shapeless suburbs and graceless monuments. Tony Garnier's pioneer work was ignored and his urban projects, e.g. plans for the town of Lyon in 1919, remained on the drawing-board. Auguste Perret in his church at Raincy abandoned the rationalism of his first works for a 'modernist' neo-classicism which was broken up by cornices, mouldings and a Gothic style brought up to date by the use of reinforced concrete. Le Corbusier was neglected and had to use an empty site in the 1925 exhibition to build a villa that caused an uproar.

Paris, however, even during the war, was a meeting-place of great importance for artists from all over the world, who found patrons to rescue them from obscurity, colleagues to admire or fight with, and a select public anxious to remain at the forefront of the avant-garde well away from the common herd. One of the greatest of these leading spirits died at the end of the war – Guillaume Apollinaire, who was wounded in 1916 and died in November 1918 of Spanish influenza. In publishing his *Poète assassiné* (1916) and *Calligrammes* (1918), he foresaw the importance of movements that were about to be born. He even launched the word 'surrealism' to describe *Les Mamelles de Tirésias*, a play produced in 1917 in which he took over from Jarry and tried to discover profound reality under the cover of burlesque and nonsense. In the same year, 1917, Jean Cocteau, a talented young man who had made a number of experiments, presented a ballet *Parade* to the Parisian public, for which he obtained the collaboration of Diaghilev, Picasso and Erik Satie. He was in his turn to become a discoverer of talent and a promoter of new ideas – one of those links with high society which are indispensable to all cultural movements.

In the same way, Paris took over the heritage of Dada, an iconoclastic movement born in Switzerland during the war. Its members were made up of those who, in the face of the war's absurdity, cast more doubts than ever on the old world and its values. However, in 1921 the students of the Beaux-Arts school cast the effigy of Dada into the Seine, and André Breton gathered around his revue, *Littérature* (1922–4), most of those who, on the ruins of Dada, wanted to rebuild a revised humanism, liberated from the pedestrian, the practical and the common-sense outlook. Writers and poets, such as Aragon, Eluard, Soupault, Radiguet; painters, such as Picasso, Max Ernst, Picabia, Salvador Dali, Miró, Tanguy; playwrights, such as Antonin Artaud – many creative spirits who are still remembered – became more or less part of the surrealist group. From 1924 onwards, André Breton, having now become the movement's pontiff and having outlined its aims in the first manifesto, proceeded to expel in the noisiest way any disciple who had become too famous or had been touched by Christianity or Marxism. But these parish-pump quarrels did nothing to damage the surrealist group's reputation.

The great men of the pre-war generation kept clear of this revolution and were often its victims. There was Anatole France, who by his momentary rally to the communist cause became the butt both of the surrealists for his decadent classicism and of the communists for his bourgeois idealism on the occasion of his sumptuous funeral in 1924. There was André Gide, who in the name of the same classicism was fluid in his thoughts, oscillating from the pleasures of art for art's sake to political commitment as reflected in his severe condemnation of colonialism in *Le Voyage au Congo*. There was Paul Claudel, who pursued his solitary quest for a soothing faith (*Le Soulier de satin*, 1924); Marcel Proust, winner of the Prix Goncourt in 1919, who was isolated by the illness that led to his death in 1922 and who finished *Le Temps retrouvé* (1927) in his solitude; Jules Romains, starting his great epic *Les Hommes de bonne volonté*, which was destined to be a great success with a whole generation; and finally Paul Valéry, equally admired by Gide and Breton.

One finds Jean Cocteau again in the world of music. After destroying the idols of the previous generation, both Wagner and Debussy, in his brilliant little work *Le Coq et l'arlequin* (1919), he conferred his praise on Stravinsky and Satie and preached a return to the severity of Bach. He helped to launch the Groupe de Six – Auric, Durey, Honegger, Milhaud, Germaine Tailleferre, Poulenc – who together wrote the music of his *Mariés de la Tour Eiffel* before separating to follow their own often most successful ways.

Fashion in the 'mad years'

Cocteau's name was also connected with the remarkable 'art décoratif' movement which from 1900 onwards expressed the good and bad taste of the whole European and American bourgeoisie. Here, too, after the war France set the tone. The great *Arts décoratifs* exhibition of 1925 showed the whole varied range of artistic tendencies at work in day-to-day life. It was a huge shop-window of 'trinkets, little bits of furniture, *art déco* trifles, all specious and eye-catching' (Le Corbusier) where Edgar Brandt, Maurice Dufresne and others displayed a neo-classicism, either simplified or decorated. Side-by-side with a collector's villa furnished by Ruhlmann, which gave the public an example of the Parisian *haute bourgeoisie*'s domestic taste, the large Paris stores showed in their pavilions a choice of 'modern' objects suited to more modest purses. Over all this loomed buildings designed by Tony Garnier, Mallet-Stevens and Le Corbusier, together with some foreign pavilions, e.g. Russian and Swedish. *Art déco* went into a decline after this exhibition, but, with some weaknesses and hesitations, it had given birth to a real 1925 style.

Should we see in these developments, as did certain contemporaries, signs of the decadence of the Parisian *grande bourgeoisie*? The class had to a certain extent revived thanks to the war, but the new generation had not acquired the natural good taste of the heirs to the great ancient families. The society journals of the post-war era were full of the noisy and ostentatious luxury of the *nouveaux riches*, all the more criticised because hard times were the rule elsewhere. The vogue for negro art discovered by Paul Guillaume just before the war, the craze for jazz brought in by the many American residents of Paris, the 'garçonne' who cut her hair, abolished her bust and raised the hem of her skirt – all these things made the solid middle class cry with horror and talk of decadence.

The masses: the popular press and cultural change

The masses for the most part were not involved in this 'élite' culture. The press, much assisted by the spread of elementary education, was the only means of general communication that really counted. But the press that sought a wide public showed every sign of sacrificing news and commentary to sensational stories and titillating scandal. It is true that a few papers kept up a good standard, e.g. Gustave Téry's *L'Oeuvre* on the left and *Le Temps* on the right. But the efforts of the Cartel's supporters to launch *Le Quotidien* did not survive the break-up of the coalition and the rash connection with Madame Hanau. As for the political press, *L'Humanité* for the communists, *Le Populaire* for the socialists, *L'Aube* for the Christian democrats, *La Nation* for the republican federation, they usually survived with difficulty. Most provincial papers, in spite of their small scale, jogged along precariously. Only a few such as *L'Ouest-Eclair* and *La Dépêche de Toulouse*, by modernising themselves, built up strong positions and competed effectively with the large-scale Parisian press. Among the latter the Big Five, *Le Petit Parisien*, *Le Petit Journal*, *Le Journal*, *Le Matin* and *L'Echo de Paris*, having become vast businesses backed by substantial capital, tended to limit competition among themselves and to crush any rival. For instance, they managed with some difficulty to eliminate *L'Ami du peuple*, which had been launched by the perfume millionaire François Coty in 1928. This mass-circulation press spread a sort of bogus sub-culture, which soothed its readers and subtly reduced them to inaction on the political level.

The popular strata of society, who normally had so little leisure that it was often equated with unemployment, continued to be subjected, both in town and country, to a kind of cultural brainwashing which made them lose the richness and variety of their ancient culture. In the towns, the cinema, which was more or less despised by the élite, and sporting events broke up the monotony of daily existence. The country people were still turned in on themselves and were generally despised in spite of the propaganda of those people, mostly reactionaries, who commended their simple and natural lives.

In this way, deep divisions, which for a time had disappeared in the comradeship of the trenches, again began to separate the different classes and ways of life.

13

France in 1929

On the eve of an unprecedented crisis that was to shake the whole world, France, as represented by the archetypal average Frenchman, sure of his rights and traditions and confident in the virtues of work and saving, gave the impression of having surmounted one of the grimmest trials of her history.

In spite of a low population, weak alliances, economic backwardness and strategic errors, she had succeeded by a concerted, almost miraculous, effort in holding and then repelling a formidable invader. She was ruined by her exertions but was successful in avoiding the convulsions and resulting bankruptcy which shook her defeated neighbour. She had almost avoided dreaming, British-fashion, of a return to pre-war conditions and had, by devaluing, resigned herself to the loss of her former wealth.

France, therefore, seemed to adjust herself to the disappearance of a world where she had played her part in the concert of nations throughout the nineteenth century. The 'prosperity' of the nineteen-twenties, the undoubted progress of her industrialisation gave the impression that the country had outgrown her traditional Malthusian outlook and was going to come to terms with the new era by ceasing to regard her archaic economic and social organisation as proof of her virtue and balance.

However, she was not rid of certain illusions. First, there was the illusion of her power in the world, which made her play the same role of guide and arbiter as she did before the war, sometimes aggressively touchy and sometimes rashly credulous. Second, there was the illusion of social harmony, too often no more than the continuation of a blocked society, which aroused all the more bitterness and rancour because the mixing of classes during the war, the sacrifices willingly made and the upheavals in the rest of the world were a trumpet-call to change. Third, political illusion grew out of this state of affairs. The system had triumphed over the trials of war, so why change things, thought the politicians? However, the system was showing the first signs of going downhill. The feebleness of the executive, a shifting parliament in which parties without discipline or consistency made all majorities fragile and transitory, all prevented successive governments (apart from the rightist one during the three years of Poincaré's last cabinet) from coping in a vigorous and determined manner with problems which were surprising the world by their novelty.

Among the causes of these prevailing illusions, two were outstanding in importance. First, there was the egoism of the rich, who refused to pay taxes, even in wartime, and saw an attack on morality in all efforts to share out financial sacrifice. They were incapable of accepting any more just distribution of the fruits of expansion, and thereby made certain that there would be a class war, though they were at pains to deny the possibility.

In the second place, there was a Malthusian phenomenon which was certainly not new, but which was aggravated by the war and added to a very old demographic tendency. There is no doubt that, after a victory too dearly bought in lives, the disappearance throughout society of many men, who would have been capable of taking over from those who were naturally weighed down by conservatism and illusion, was an irreparable disaster.

PART III

The slump

14

The approach of the crisis

The year 1929, which historians regard as a turning-point, was not considered as such by the man in the street of that time. The great prosperity did not appear to be in danger. Poincaré's retirement, which had earned him the gratitude of the country, gave no cause for concern as it left his successors with a very comfortable majority, based on the right centre parties. The policy of Briand, 'the pilgrim of peace', seemed to be doing well, assuring both a *rapprochement* with Germany and the security of France – the country that was soon to be made invulnerable by an impregnable defensive line. 1929 was the year of the Young plan, the beginning of the evacuation of the Rhineland and the idea of a European federation proposed by Briand at the League of Nations. This federation provided for the establishment of economic links and collective security agreements. 1929 saw within France the start of work on the Maginot Line and of the social laws voted the previous year, e.g. the Loucheur law on low-cost housing and social insurance for wage-earners. It was the 1929 and not the 1930 call-up (as planned in the Paul-Boncour law) that was the first to do only twelve months military service. All these events led to a feeling of confidence, and were often indeed the product of that confidence. The Wall Street crash of 25 October in no way affected the public's quiet optimism or the government's general satisfaction.

The peak of French prosperity

In his ministerial statement of 25 November 1929, Tardieu forecast prosperous times at the very moment when the worst economic crisis of all time was breaking on the world. However, the crisis spared France for the moment and only hit her at the end of 1930. It was thought that she was immune from a disease that only affected others and even seemed to make her richer. 1929 and 1930 were the peak years of French prosperity between the wars.

The budget surplus was close to four billion francs and justified generosity on the part of the state. The stock of gold in the Banque de France went on growing, rising from twenty-nine to fifty-five billion francs between May

1929 and May 1931. Nobody noticed that this wealth was due to floating capital seeking shelter in a stable currency, or to returning capital which had left the country between 1923 and 1926 and might do so again just as suddenly if the situation demanded it. This brilliant financial position reflected continuous progress in all economic sectors, agriculture excepted. But here again nobody saw that the progress was simply due to momentum from the past; for the activity indices began to decrease between the beginning of 1929 and July 1930.

Production of iron and steel, 1929–30 (million tonnes)

	Cast iron	Steel
1929	10.0	9.6
1930	9.6	9.0

Industrial production was maintained by orders up to the end of 1930 and prices were held in check at home by the poor harvest of that year. Indeed the 1928 devaluation brought the advantage of very competitive prices in the world market. Exports remained high and the traditional trade imbalance was compensated for by tourism and profits from foreign investments. All this explains the following records achieved in 1930, which were never equalled until the advent of the Fourth Republic:

Coal   55 million tonnes (coke = 5 million tonnes)

Iron ore   48 million tonnes: ranking first in the world. A workforce of 300,000 miners

Aluminium 29,000 tonnes

In spite of technical backwardness, the textile industry also obtained excellent results, for it took advantage of the American crisis. There was no unemployment, and only immigration made it possible to delay salary increases, without actually preventing them. Consumption was high, and fell very little afterwards. The later crisis affected production much more.

The workers who earned their living by working for the few American concerns established in France might have suffered from the crisis as early as 1929. This was probably not so; in fact the opposite was the case. For instance, General Motors had, between 1927 and 1929, set up a lorry and private car sales network throughout France under American management but with Belgian and French staff. Suddenly, they stopped operating and laid off all their employees. The prestige of the American economy, reinforced by the writings of the trade unionist Hyacinthe Dubreuil (read by what today are called executives, rather than by workers) was such that Renault within a few weeks hired all the technicians and sales representatives who were willing to work for them. As for the individual garages, who had been blinded enough by ambition to become their dealers, they found themselves immediately relieved of one-sided contracts.

The French thought that they could look to the future with great confidence and reject the advice of the few pessimists. Yet a few important facts did presage imminent danger. The budget showed a deficit from 1930 onwards. The colonies were far more involved than the home country in the world economy and, with the exception of Algeria, were far less well protected; so they were immediately hit by the crisis, Indo-China in particular. These warning signs called for vigilance, but parliamentary life went on up to 1932 in the illusion of prosperity, while in fact this prosperity was in the process of collapsing. Furthermore, no one grasped the transformation which Poincaré's withdrawal was bringing to political life.

The hardening of the political opposition

France was used to the rhythm of parliamentary elections every four years, and so failed to see the importance of Poincaré's retirement. The Union Nationale, which had gained power in 1928, seemed to survive under Briand, whose last ministry, however, only lasted for three months. While the left had already renewed its leadership immediately after the war, it was only ten years later that the centre and right carried through the same change. A political generation was on its way out. The old stagers Briand and Barthou, both born in 1862, were confined to ministerial posts where their competence stood out, and they saw their influence decline long before their deaths in 1931 and 1934 respectively. Between Briand's defeat and the 1932 elections, there was no prime minister who had led a government before 1929. The centre and the right entirely changed their leaders at this time, and this affected the general conditions of political life. Although Poincaré 'the warmonger' was hated by his opponents, he was respected by them for his honesty. Briand's belated acceptance was due to his having won the Nobel Prize. Whereas Tardieu and Laval, who were going to replace them, were looked upon as shady politicians by the left. Every old Paris socialist claimed to have slipped a coin to the renegade Laval thirty years ago, so that he should be able to buy himself a meal or a suit. The young Auvergnat had turned into a millionaire. Tardieu, adored by the right but caricatured as a shark or a pike by his opponents, was exposed as a racketeer – a German agent before the war who, like Mandel, became one of the hired men of Clemenceau's dictatorship.

Ever since Urbain Gohier, the left's last great pamphleteer, had gone over to the right, the left conducted its polemics through the muted wit of de la Fourchardiére and the *Canard enchaîné*, making ironical remarks about people, but attacking ideas rather than men. It respected people's private lives and left *ad hominem* attacks and incitements to murder to the press of the right. The arrival of the new generation reversed this situation. From now onwards it was the characters of the leaders of the right that became suspect and corrupt in republican eyes. The morality of the new leaders was attacked, which made any idea of a Union Sacrée against dangers from abroad, or even any form of national union, quite unthinkable. In spite of the apparently limp and sleepy leadership of the right and the radicals, the conditions for civil war were developing at the beginning of the thirties without anyone being aware of the fact.

Moreover, the 'moderates' no longer existed, except among the radicals and the small centre parties. A wing of the right called itself 'republican', but it was not much attached to the political system. The Catholics, who made up the majority of that group, could no longer follow Maurras, but they continued to be conditioned as were their opponents of the Grand Orient Freemasons, by the consequences of the Dreyfus affair and the pre-war period. The authoritarian extreme right, therefore, continued to attack La Gueuse (the Third Republic) with its invective.

Louis Marin was a rare exception. Leader of the Union Républicaine Démocratique (URD), he was a sort of Jules Ferry, born fifty years too late, 'a moderate republican who is not moderately republican'. No one divined this before 1940. Ten years earlier he appeared to be a fascist and just as much an enemy of the democratic system as Tardieu.

Tardieu's failure

The period 1929–32 was dominated by André Tardieu, who enjoyed the support of President Doumergue but was opposed by the Senate. Born in 1876, a graduate of the Ecole Normale Supérieure, he had been an *attaché de cabinet*, a journalist and a minister since 1926. In November 1929 he became president of the Council after Briand's downfall had proved that Poincaré's majority, ranging from URD to the radical left, would not serve under the 'pilgrim of peace'.

A strong personality and brilliantly intelligent, Tardieu loathed the parliamentary system and wanted to transform the institutions by abolishing the traditional left–right confrontation. His aim was to build up a strong state by annihilating the parties. He wished to incorporate the socially conservative radicals into the majority and so govern in opposition to the Marxists, the SFIO and the communist party, winning over the radicals' electorate by reforms in economic distribution which would leave the social structure intact.

The strong executive power of which Tardieu dreamt would have reduced parliamentary control to nought. Tardieu claimed to admire the Anglo-American system, although it was totally inadaptable to French historic tradition. His two-party scheme was pure façade as it excluded any form of alternation. For the left and for a great part of the parliamentary world, this so-called 'toryism' without any partner was nothing less than the French road to fascism. As early as November 1929 the radicals refused to join Tardieu's cabinet, and a few years later they saw through his schemes and got rid of him. Even before 1936 Tardieu no longer expected to achieve his ends except by a popular rising, which he encouraged with subsidies while minister of the interior. (P. Machefer, 'Tardieu et La Rocque', *Bulletin de le société d'histoire moderne*, 15, 1972.) He ended up like Deschanel, leaving Laval and Flandin, who had far less stature, to lead the right. But from 1929 to 1932 as president of the Council, minister of the interior, of agriculture and of war, he held power in his own right or by proxy.

Reduced to Poincaré's majority, that is to say the right, Tardieu announced on 25 November 1929 that youth had come to power and that economic and social prosperity were the broad policy of the day. Defeated a few weeks later, he returned almost at once after Camille Chautemps had intervened with a left-wing cabinet that lasted for one day.

Due to the budget surplus Tardieu started up a programme of large-scale public works, and put into operation the social insurance schemes that had been voted in 1928. At the same time he ran his own personal politics by bribing the Ligues with secret funds to arrange cheering crowds and tough security forces. The Senate, worried by this training of mob power and by the restriction of parliament to merely technical debates, got rid of Tardieu in December 1930, taking advantage of the banker Oustric's fraud and bankruptcy. Raoul Péret, the Garde des Sceaux, was seriously involved in this with other leading figures, such as the under-secretary of state Gaston Vidal and the ambassador René Besnard. Steeg formed a left–centre coalition government which only lasted for a few weeks. Then Doumergue called on Laval to form a government with Tardieu's majority. Tardieu himself became minister of agriculture and inaugurated a price-support policy; for the crisis had finally struck France.

Laval was in power for a year. In May 1931 Doumer replaced Doumergue as President of the Republic. He was elected against Briand, who had been accepted by the right only grudgingly because of his slovenliness and his policy of conciliation – a policy which had been shown to be useless by the Nazi advance in 1930 and the revival of the German peril.

In order to force the radicals to make their choice or disappear, Laval, Mandel and Tardieu got parliament to vote the establishment of a one-name, one-round voting system. Then, in February 1932, an angry Senate overthrew the government and Tardieu returned to power for a very short time, as the elections changed the majority.

While this right-wing government lasted, there were no street riots and the extreme communist left was harshly persecuted. The Senate never succeeded in imposing a centre government. It was, therefore, nearly always the same men who were photographed on the steps of the Elysée, either exchanging portfolios or keeping them with a certain stability: Tardieu and Laval as presidents of the Council, Briand at foreign affairs, Maginot at war and Leygues at the navy ministries. Nothing was done to forestall the crisis, in spite of Reynaud's most unwelcome pleas. On the contrary, the burden of taxation was considerably reduced by reliefs and even cancellation of taxes on land, real estate and moveable property, as well as on industrial and commercial profits. The only incomes which did not benefit from this largess were earned incomes. But the use of budget surpluses was not all waste. The resulting social measures, even if they did not protect employment, did materially relieve the wage-earner of the sufferings occasioned by anxiety, sickness and old age.

The abolition of school fees at the level of the *sixième*, i.e. the first year of secondary education, by the finance law voted in the spring of 1930, was a forerunner of free secondary education, which was achieved in 1933. An ex-servicemen's pension scheme completed these measures, the most important to have been passed since Millerand's programme thirty years earlier. It was the political right that put this social reform into practice. The five billion francs invested in public works such as the Maginot Line, the Kembs barrage and the Grand Canal of Alsace sustained the economy and the labour market. But this expenditure mortgaged the future and made itself felt during the last two legislatures because the crisis had by then reached France. This explains why the right lost the 1932 elections.

15

The economic crisis

It was only in 1931 or 1932 that the French realised that they had been hit by a slump, though it had already started to affect them at the end of 1930. It was then that the indices of production started falling. Only 12,000 unemployed were recorded in that December, but by the following spring their number had reached 50,000. There was a slight recovery in 1932, although nobody noticed it. The devaluation of the pound sterling administered another shock to the world economy; but while the slump was coming to an end elsewhere in 1934–5, stagnation in France lasted right up to 1938, kept going by the minor American crisis of 1937.

Nothing like this had been seen before, even in the 'great depression' at the end of the nineteenth century. The slump was not as bad as in the other industrialised countries because in France the capitalist system was less developed. France was less involved in the world economy, and therefore the home market counted for much more. The country produced no raw materials and was underpopulated, hence there were fewer unemployed; and the banking system was solidly established, with credit control tighter than in other countries. But, even if the depression was less severe and brought in its train none of those upheavals that devastated other countries, it was more serious in the long run because the recovery, which came to the rest of the world after 1935, never reached France. Her economic activity in 1938 was still lower than in 1929.

The character and effects of the depression

The initial effect of the slump was the collapse of overseas trade, although the part it played in the French economy was less significant than in other advanced countries. There was also a huge balance of payments deficit. Trouble started with the failure of the Credit Anstalt and the collapse of credit in central Europe. The Hoover moratorium and the end of reparations from Germany were a more serious blow; and finally came the devaluation of the pound. Between them these factors caused or served to intensify the slump in 1931. French exports, up till then rather low in price, ceased to be competitive in world markets. The heavy fall in exports, not

Volume of gross domestic production in France (1929 = 100)

Year	Index of production
1929	100
1930	97
1931	93
1932	89
1933	93
1934	93
1935	90
1936	91
1937	96
1938	96
1939	100

Source: Taken from J. J. Carré, P. Dubois and E. Malinvaud, *La croissance française*, Paris, Editions du Seuil, 1973, p. 35.

matched by a fall in imports, resulted in industrial stagnation. It is reckoned that between 1929 and 1938 French foreign trade in manufactured goods was halved.

The balance of payments, which was about three billion francs in surplus between 1927 and 1931, was in deficit for the same amount up to the war. This was aggravated from 1931 onwards by a flight of capital, caused by fear of war and social upheaval. Even so the reserves of the Banque de France grew from forty-six to eighty-three billion francs between 1929 and 1932. Initially, this flight of capital was due to the difficulties of French banks directly involved with industry; for example, the government had to come to the rescue of the BNC and the Banque d'Alsace-Lorraine. This loss, which drained off some thirty-five billion francs between 1931 and 1937, added to the balance of payments deficit, seriously diminished the national revenue and caused a collapse of investment.

The banking crisis of 1931 did much damage to lesser firms, and in the smaller towns it entirely removed from the scene that Balzacian figure – the banker. One hundred and eighteen banks failed in 1931.

The fall in production

All industrial production was hit, falling by 17.5 per cent in 1931: steel production fell by 29 per cent. The export of finished goods was hit particularly badly by falling price levels on the world market. There was a 60 per cent increase in bankruptcies; the number of unemployed reached 190,000 by the end of the year. The great engineering cartels were in deep trouble and did not recover until 1933. The chemicals industry was hit by

A

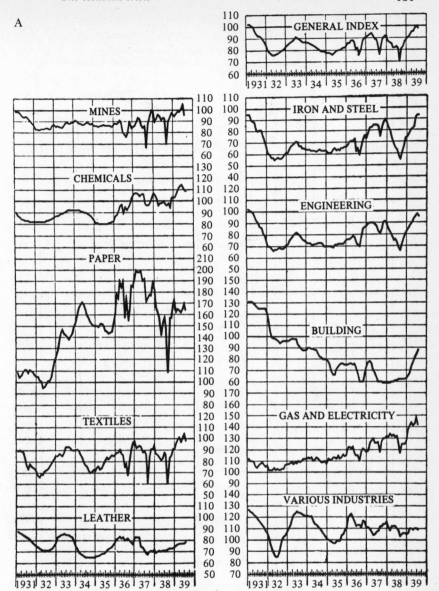

A. Industrial production (1928 = 100). B. Industrial activity, 1931–9. C. Economic movement: exports and imports (average = 6 months; 1928 = 100). D. Wholesale prices (weighted indices; 1919 = 100). (A. Sauvy, 'Evolution économique de 1929 à 1939', in *Le Mouvement économique en France de 1929 à 1939*, Ministère de l'Economie nationale, Service national de statistique, Paris, 1941, pp. 96, 104, 108, 112.)

B

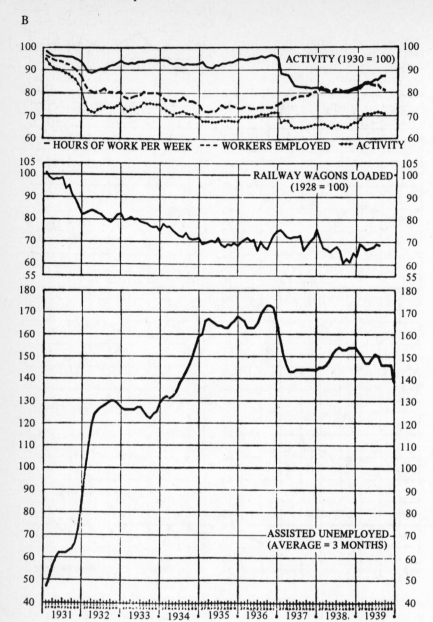

ACTIVITY (1930 = 100)

- HOURS OF WORK PER WEEK   --- WORKERS EMPLOYED   ••• ACTIVITY

RAILWAY WAGONS LOADED
(1928 = 100)

ASSISTED UNEMPLOYED
(AVERAGE = 3 MONTHS)

1931   1932   1933   1934   1935   1936   1937   1938   1939

C

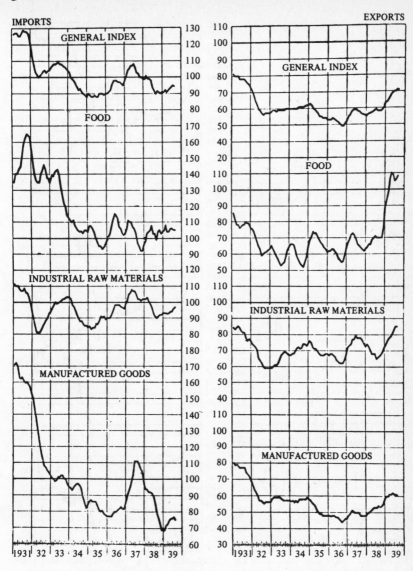

D

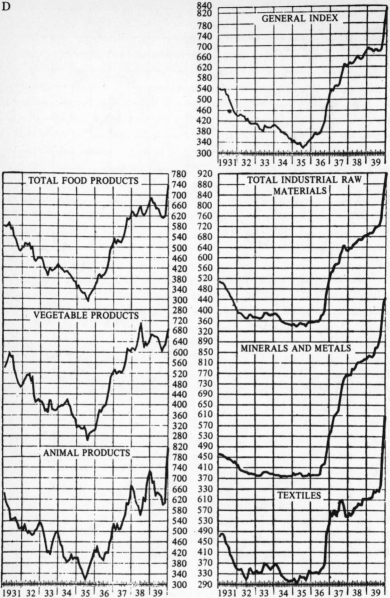

the loss of its export markets and by the slump in agriculture. The textile industry, facing heavy Japanese competition, was the worst affected of all: the wool industry more than cotton and less than silk. Between 1929 and 1934 wholesale prices fell by 46 per cent. Because of the monetary policy, this did nothing to help exports and had very little effect on retail prices, which only fell by 20 per cent. This was largely due to a sluggish distribution system and to taxes on consumption. After 1932, agriculture was in the doldrums, severely affected by falling prices and overproduction. The earnings of the peasant population, a vital part of the home market, fell from forty-three to eighteen billion francs between 1928 and 1934. Even in a progressive department like the Isère there was a huge increase in bankruptcies after 1931.

Following the bank failures came the disappearance nationwide of old family textile businesses, small firms with limited resources. Even very large firms had a rough time and were driven into mergers. The Compagnie Générale Transatlantique and the Aéropostale, both on the verge of bankruptcy in 1931 and 1934 respectively, were saved by state intervention. Citroën, in compulsory liquidation, was rescued by Michelin in 1934. The Ford company, boosted by recovery in America, took over Mathis, but the most famous name in the motor industry, Bugatti, succumbed.

However, the slump was not totally overwhelming. The big, old-established firms stood up to it better than the upstarts of the war years, and crisis speeded up economic concentration. The big iron and steel firms, Schneider and de Wendel, actually gained in strength. The large, heavily capitalised oil companies were establishing themselves, and refineries were appearing on the main river estuaries. The French motor-car industry was the second largest in the world, ahead of Great Britain, Canada and Germany, until 1933. There were nearly two million vehicles on the road. The old textile managements made common cause against the unions. Some of the entrepreneurs of those days remind one of the tycoons of nineteenth-century America, e.g. Michelin in tyres and Mercier in electricity. Even a complete newcomer achieved temporary success – Rosengart, who launched the first really cheap car. Such were a few of the factors that might have brought recovery, but they were not followed up. Moreover, productivity increased, even in agriculture where the working population diminished by half a million during this period, while the number of tractors grew from 27,000 in 1929 to 35,000 in 1938. Contrary to general belief, mechanisation was further advanced than in some parts of Germany. Productivity in industry increased by 10 to 20 per cent, and in the mines by 25 per cent.

Another phenomenon of the time was the appearance of large selling organisations, such as Monoprix, Uniprix, Prisunic, which might have done much to improve the retail trade. If only governments had had an

Annual rate of growth of French production (as percentages)

	Industry	Total productive output	Productive output and non-productive services
1896–1913	2.4	1.9	1.8
1913–1929	2.6	1.7	1.5
1929–1938	1.1	−0.4	−0.3
1938–1939	0.8	0.9	1.1

Source: Taken from J. J. Carré, P. Dubois and E. Malinvaud, *La Croissance française*, p. 35.

Growth of industrial production by branches over long periods (average rate of growth as per cent per annum)

	1896–1913	1913–1929	1929–1938
Agricultural, and food industries	1.4	2.1	0.3
Solid mineral fuels and gas	2.2	2.2	0.8
Electricity and water	8.9	12.9	3.3
Construction materials	2.4	2.5	−5.0
Iron and steel	6.5	4.0	−4.5
Engineering	4.5	4.4	−8.9
Chemicals	5.9	7.5	0.9
Textiles, clothing, leather	1.4	0.8	−1.4
Others	2.5	2.4	1.9

Source: Taken from J. J. Carré, P. Dubois and E. Malinvaud, *La Croissance française*, p. 32.

economic policy, the slump would not have been able to quench the spirit of enterprise displayed by one group of industrial leaders in the Confédération Générale de la Production Française (CGPF).

The government and the depression

State enterprises, such as the post office, the potash mines, etc., were all exposed to the depression, and governments were even harder hit by falls in the receipts from taxation.

Government attempts to cope with the situation were feeble and belated. Up to 1932 no firm action was taken beyond the Tardieu plan, which was devised to cash in on prosperity and did serve to mop up some unemployment. At the beginning of 1932 the impending elections made any unpopular measures out of the question. In fact more largess was handed out, as in the law of 11 March 1932 on family allowances. This sort of charge on the budget did at least help to maintain consumption. It was only after the elections of May 1932 that measures of economic stringency were adopted, first of all by the left until 1934, then by the right from 6 February 1934 until the accession of the Front Populaire. Neither provided a comprehensive economic policy, only monetary measures.

In fact, official measures to defeat the depression amounted merely to a strict maintenance of the level of prices. A stringent agricultural protectionism insulated the home market. Duties on grain were increased in 1929 and 1930. Animal products were protected, butter after 1930 and meat in 1933. Tariffs were imposed on a large number of manufactured goods. This was not a simple, straightforward system like Méline's; for there were also quotas, bans, anti-dumping rules and compensatory surcharges because of currency changes after the devaluation of the pound in 1931 and of the dollar in 1933.

This tightly closed market was supported by the government, which also helped big firms in difficulty, bought alcohol to mix with petrol (*carburant national*) and stockpiled wheat. These autarchic moves, which were also applied in the overseas empire, were accompanied by a mainly agricultural interventionism. There were numerous regulations against the overproduction of wine – a tax on yields, compulsory distillation, a ban on the planting and irrigating of new vineyards, and subsidies for ploughing up vines. These were all codified in the law of 4 July 1931. A minimum price for wheat was imposed in 1933, acreage under cultivation was limited and excessive yields forbidden. For industry the government preferred compacts, which simply meant that the interventionist policy was run by the chiefs of the firms concerned. This sort of commercial Malthusianism helped to keep up retail prices by protecting the most backward methods and their entrenched practitioners against the big stores. It was forbidden to set up any new Uniprix. These determined efforts to limit competition and production favoured middlemen at the expense of primary producers and consumers. As retail prices could not fall, neither could wages or costs.

Governments thought that their habitual prosperity, interrupted by the erratic behaviour of other countries, would be restored by the laws of nature. All that was needed was to defend the currency and balance the budget. This was just basic liberal thinking, and notably the creed of all top civil servants. Their pride and confidence were rooted in the recovered stability of the currency, while others went bankrupt. In spite of its ruinous effect on trade and the tourist industry, they were as little worried by the rise in prices as by the increase in unemployment, which was relatively small. The stability of the franc had become a national cult preached by the press and the authorities. Between 1932 and 1935 eleven governments put forward fourteen plans for financial recovery, all of which were simply budgetary economies. The three principal attempts were those of Herriot (July 1932), Daladier (early 1933) and Chautemps (December 1933). During this period several cabinets came and went, while the devaluation of the dollar created more difficulties.

At the London conference in 1933 France proposed all-round monetary stabilisation and a universal restrictive policy to support prices. Not surprisingly Roosevelt did the opposite – he devalued the dollar and embarked on modest inflation to stimulate consumption. Caught between the autarchy of the totalitarian states and the inflationary policies of the Anglo-Americans, the gold bloc was isolated and its action stifled. All the countries gradually abandoned gold, and France was left in 1934 with the choice between further deflation or devaluation. Devaluation was almost unanimously rejected as a form of bankruptcy which would undermine the moral basis of society. It was opposed by all the chiefs of business and industry, all the legal and academic pundits, from the radical Jèze to the right-winger Barthélémy, and not surprisingly by the more serious-minded newspapers, *Le Temps, Le Journal des Débats* and the main dailies.

Reynaud took the opposite view, although his perspicacity, so much praised today, revealed itself late in the day, for he did not express himself before the summer of 1934. Blum, in March of that year, was the first to ask in *Le Populaire* 'whether or not the fetish of monetarism, like the fetish of balanced budgets, is not a hindrance to economic recovery'. He had been challenging the advantages of deflation ever since the beginning of 1933. But, although they were quite aware of the sort of action other countries were taking, the socialists remained irresolute, incapable of deciding on any policy, leaving Reynaud to fight alone against general ridicule.

The cost of defending the currency and the budget was borne by the wage-earners, and after 1934 mainly by public officials, who, together with the social welfare legislation, were blamed for all the troubles. Under Doumergue's government salaries and pensions were cut. In 1935 there were signs of recovery, promptly aborted in July by Laval's deflationary measures, which imposed a statutory cut of 10 per cent on salaries, interest rates, rents and pensions – a saving of fifteen million francs in a budget of fifty billion francs. The concept of 'budget-guzzling' civil servants reminds one of the myths of 1787: the monarchy ruined by Marie-Antoinette's extravagance on shoes or the Polignacs' greed. The result of deflation was to reduce the French economy to its lowest level in the years 1935–6. The depression was kept going by the decline in purchasing power, which was required to sustain deflation. Meanwhile other countries were pulling out of the crisis.

It is sometimes said that the science of economics was unknown in those days. This is incorrect. Keynes' theories existed, but French economists either knew nothing about them or despised them. Those in authority clung to the ancient theories of Bastiat, which prevailed on both left and right. The communists had no native economist and relied on translations of the Soviet Russian Varga. The socialists, on the other hand, had a good team on *Le Populaire* – Marc Joubert, Spinasse, Moch, Monnet, together with the Austrian Marxist Lucien Laurat (Othon Maschl). Delaisi and Duret were the economic advisers of the CGT. The socialist Philip and the radical Mendès France were too young to command a hearing, and in any case the whole weight of academic and university thought was in the other camp, with two exceptions – Rist and Nogaro – who were more concerned with economic distress than the stability of the franc. It is profitless to blame the men of that period for not employing methods that were either as yet unknown or which were psychologically unacceptable. The history of economics is full of anachronistic judgments. If the right answers were unknown, there was no lack of wrong ones. The wealth of Utopian ideas bears witness to the intellectual ferment stirred up by this disruptive economic and social turmoil. The writings of Jacques Duboin and Jean Nocher (and his team, *Jeunes*) are the best known; but there were endless others. One deserves to be mentioned for its original approach – Robert Eisler's *La Monnaie, cause et remède de la crise économique* (Paris, Librairie Valois, 1932). This work advocated a form of currency that diminished in value, as a stimulus to consumption, an idea that was savagely ridiculed by both liberal and Marxist economists. The best study of the crisis, published in the heat of the moment, is *La Crise et l'Europe économique* (Paris, Rivière, 1932, 2 vols.) by Dimitri Navachine, a Russian refugee, later murdered by the Cagoulards.

16

The impact of the depression on society

The fight against inflation brought economic growth to an abrupt halt and caused much human suffering that was inequitably shared.

The working class

Although artificially supported, retail prices fell more than wages. According to Alfred Sauvy the cost of living fell by 10 per cent in 1932. From this economists have deduced a rise in the standard of living for the working class. The real problem, however, was unemployment. Jean Lhomme reckons that, at the beginning of 1935, there were two million unemployed out of a workforce of 12.5 million; he also reckons that, between 1930 and 1935, purchasing power fell by about 15 per cent, even after taking account of a price–wage ration that was favourable to consumers. ('Le Pouvoir d'achat de l'ouvrier français au cours d'un siècle, 1840–1940', *Le Mouvement social*, 63, April–June 1968.) Governments would have been quite satisfied with these figures had they known them, for average purchasing power had not fallen very much. That would only have confirmed their optimism, for their calculations were based on the much lower (though increasing up to 1936) figures for those actually receiving unemployment pay. The dole paid by the state or the local authorities to the registered unemployment helped to arrest the fall in purchasing power. As a result, the government could regard the unemployment caused by its own monetary policy as a problem of secondary importance.

Better still, from the government's point of view, the first victims of unemployment came from groups that were considered in every way unimportant: women, whose 'natural' place was in the home, and immigrants, who had only to go back to their own countries. Neither had a vote. The government thought it enough to set a quota on immigration in August 1932. So far as budgets allowed, Tardieu's plans for large-scale public works also helped in the fight against unemployment.

Although statistically it seemed to be reassuringly under control, the personal situation of those affected was catastrophic. In Belfort, two large firms reduced their workforce by half between the beginning of 1931 and the beginning of 1936. Opinions differ as to which groups were worst hit. Sorlin reckoned that workers in small and medium-sized firms suffered most (*La Société française*, vol. II, p. 108), but this is not the view of most historians.

Building firms and steelworkers were badly hit. Makers of consumer goods escaped lightly, which accounts for the fact that those employed in this sector largely maintained their standard of living. The employers, supported by *Le Temps* and *Le Journal des Débats*, took advantage of the weakness of the working-class movement to try and get social insurance and family allowances abolished. Marguerite Perrot has shown that in 1930 Laval's deflationary policy was linked with a great drive by the employers against this legislation, which they found very costly and did their best to evade. (*La Monnaie et l'opinion publique en France et en Grande-Bretagne*, p. 231.) The depression was not without its advantages for employers, for it strengthened their hand against the workforce. The latter had very little power of resistance. Even in prosperous times, union action was hampered by ideological divisions, and, as time went on, it was to become even more so by the weakness of those menaced by unemployment or the sack. The depression reduced the number of strikes. According to Roger Dufraisse, between 1922 and 1929, 54 per cent of strikes achieved their aims, but only 37 per cent between 1930 and 1935 (see his article in *Mouvements ouvriers et dépressions économiques de 1929 à 1939*). Unemployment was a great strike-breaker. The growing proportion of unskilled workers from the countryside or abroad had considerably weakened the revolutionary spirit of pre-war days. The rate of increase in union membership was low – 10 per cent in 1929, and only 5 per cent in the iron and steel industry.

The only really large organisation, the CGT, had 700,000 paid-up members at the beginning of the depression, and its numbers were falling. Many came from the public sector where membership of a union did not put one's job at risk. The presence of such a multitude of public servants, especially teachers, gave the CGT a rather middle-class outlook. Its members wanted reform, not revolution. They dreaded strikes and violence, and the irresponsible behaviour of the communist Confédération Générale du Travail Unitaire (CGTU) militants. They were influenced by British trade unionism and, although they had much less power, they wanted to be seen, like their British counterparts, as valuable accessories to the employers and the government. In the belief, shared with the CGTU, that the depression resulted from rationalisation, their principal aim was to protect wages and jobs. In 1931 they began to call for a forty-hour, five-day week, holidays with pay, unemployment insurance, a higher school-leaving age and a programme of important public works. Although they were deeply interested in Roosevelt's New Deal, their involvement after 1931 with the political aims of the SFIO obliged them to make the defence of democracy their principal consideration. Henceforward, they were to become the think-tank of the Popular Front, due to the influence in their midst of young socialist planning experts. *Le Peuple*, a solid and serious newspaper, was a sort of working man's *Le Temps*. Unfortunately, for this reason, it was not much read. The other principal unions had fewer members and less influence. The Confédération Générale du Travail des Syndicalists Révolutionnaires (CGTSR) founded in 1926 by the last remaining revolutionary trade unionists, only survived in a few unions such as the Trélazé slate-quarry workers. The membership of the CGTU reached 300,000 in 1929, but declined heavily thereafter. Most of the members were working-class public servants. The union supported the adventurist policies of the communist party, hoping to foster the class war by exploiting poverty. But this made little appeal to the sort of highly skilled worker they recruited to their ranks.

Outside these big unions there was an increasingly fragmented collection of autonomous bodies such as the railwaymen, while on the fringe, Christian unions, long considered as 'scabs', were beginning to grow. The turning-point for these came about when Liénart, the bishop of Lille, intervened in the dispute at Halluin in favour of the striking members of the Confédération Française des Travaillers Chrétiens (CFTC). The employers complained to the Pope, who rebuffed them. In 1929 the Pope received the strikers in Rome and gave them his blessing; and in 1930 he raised the bishop of Lille to the cardinalate. After 1920 Christian trade unions took part in some defensive strikes, with the support of certain bishops. But they remained rather unaggressive, taking no part in the defence of the Republic in 1934. The other unions continued to regard the CFTC with suspicion and refused to treat it as a representative body.

So we see that the workers' organisations confronting powerful groups of employers were fragmented, weak and paralysed by unemployment. Their financial resources, which in France, unlike other great industrialised countries, had never been very substantial, were still further weakened by their members' inability to contribute their support. With the exception of the CGTU, the unions were all moving towards acceptance of an official role within the state, and would have liked this to be recognised. After the events of 1934, the CGTU, without changing its principles, relaxed them in practice in favour of joint action. The powers that be had little to fear from a working class so battered and bruised. Nevertheless, although they were weak, divided and without a clear policy of their own, the trade unions joined battle on the side of the left-wing parties and played an important part in the coming of the Front Populaire.

Employees and civil servants

Many employees and minor executives lost their jobs. They had no organisation to protect their interests, but being professionally more adaptable than the working class they found it easier to change their occupations. School leavers could join the army, where a second lieutenant on the reserve could after 1935 rejoin in the same rank, whereas previously he would have had to accept non-commissioned rank.

Between the wars the number of public employees increased by one-fifth as a result of the expansion of state education and the postal services, and in spite of the curbs on recruitment during the depression, especially in Laval's administration. The right hated them for political reasons and the small tradesmen for social reasons. They were denounced as 'budget-guzzlers', as if they alone, together with the welfare legislation, were responsible for deficit budgets. They were accused of idly occupying lucrative sinecures instead of doing useful work. In reality they were still few in number, always underpaid, generally doing work of some economic (e.g. postal services, public works) or technical (e.g. teaching) importance. French agriculture might have been less backward if there had been more managers with agronomic training.

Besides suffering from attacks levelled at them by the popular press, civil servants saw their standard of living considerably eroded by pay cuts. Of all social groups they endured the most harassment and humiliation from the authorities, from the general public and from the world of small tradesmen. Although official figures show retrospectively that their purchasing power had not dropped prior to 1934, the opposite seemed to them to be the case. When the depression came, their pay, which, like state interest rates, had remained unchanged since 1919, had only just been increased. In the spring of 1927, secondary-school teachers had refused to take part in the bacca-laureate examinations.

Although they were slow to join unions, public employees played a traditional role in the SFIO and an increasingly important one in the CGT. The Front Populaire was to give a tremendous boost to their unionisation, and in the period leading up to it the parliamentary left, which needed their votes, became well aware of their grievances. Moreover, the measures which threatened their interests contributed to the instability of the governments of the time.

Life on the land

Prosperity had not brought much gain to the peasants, and with the depression came a fall in prices after 1930, which hit their earnings very hard. While wheat production remained steady and that of wine increased, the excess of supply over demand grew with unemployment. In 1929 a quintal of wheat and a hectolitre of wine fetched respectively 184 and 154 francs, but in 1935 no more than seventy-four and sixty-four francs. That year saw the bottom of the trough, and prices did not really pick up until 1938. There had to be some rent revision for the benefit of tenant farmers caught by the widening gap between the prices of farm and factory produce, and this caused a fall in the price of land. The farmer therefore had to live off his capital and the peasant proprietor was reduced to subsistence farming. All the same, the government paid more attention to the farmers than it did to the wage-earners in the towns. The rural vote mattered a great deal to all parties, but most of all to the conservatives and radicals in power. Tardieu and his successor Queuille saw to it as a matter of course that their economic policy with all its controls was framed for the benefit of agriculture, though not even this could prevent the poorer peasants from being one of the hardest hit social groups.

The peasants' reaction to these afflictions was violent, and there was even some rioting in the Somme, the Eure-et Loire and Normandy. The large-scale farmers, their strength depleted by the slump, had to face new kinds of ultra-right political groupings. With Le Roy Ladurie, Salleron and Roger Grand at their head, they preached a sort of corporatism, made up partly of Maurras' ideas and partly of a social–agrarian catholicism. The Parti Agraire, founded in 1928, and the Defense Paysanne of Henri Dorgères and Marcel Braibant, which joined to form the Front Paysan or 'Green shirts', indulged in a lot of anti-parliamentary talk and some violence. The rural 'fascists' could bring out the crowds, but with only one or two members of parliament they never managed to command votes. Those they did elect, some radical senators and deputies, were ringleaders of the farmers who occupied the prefecture in Chartres in January 1933.

Electorally, the left gained more from peasant discontent than the right – the left consisting of the radicals, the socialists who were trying to start a peasant trade-union movement in the famous tradition of Guillaumin and the 'paysans du Centre'; and the communists with Renaud Jean and Waldeck Rochet and their following in the Cher, the Limousin and the Lot-et-Garonne. Peasant response to the depression was a good deal more diverse and disunited than the agrarian lobby would have liked. The extreme left took up the cudgels on behalf of evicted tenants and sharecroppers. The key issue of Bergery's election campaign at Mantes was the battle between the grain producers and the wealthy millers. Finally, in many places the growing influence of the extreme right was curbed when the Catholics started to desert the cause. The Jeunesse Agricole Chrétienne, founded in 1929, helped to start an educative form of trade unionism in areas where Christianity still had a hold which was quite independent of the big landowners. This movement was slow to take off and only really made itself felt in the last days of the Third Republic.

The impoverishment caused by the depression reached the middle classes through the considerable fall in the standard of living of the peasants and the *petite bourgeoisie*, while wage-earners were hit by unemployment. The big capitalists actually gained, and, those engaged in business or the liberal professions were unscathed, although deeply troubled by fears for the future and the threat overhanging their traditional privileged status. The 'time of hate' was setting in. Several factors that had led to fascism in other countries seemed to be building up.

17

The colonies and the depression

The French were so distracted by the threatening aspect of international politics that they failed to notice at the outset how the depression was hitting the colonies. This was because colonial problems, although they boded ill for the future, hardly affected the daily lives of the majority, weighed down as they were by more immediate, mainly financial, problems. Their attention, too, was diverted by incessant and enthusiastic reminders of the advantages of having an empire. It is not surprising that the fear of bad times, born of troubles at home, should have been compensated for by the myth of imperial power – an idea that was shrewdly put across by experts of the time. 'Imperialism is the only course open to mature peoples to avoid sinking into incurable decadence, to atone for sacrificing their birth-rate in favour of the pleasures and comforts of luxury, and to preserve the élite of their population from extinction.' (P. and M. Clerget, *La France dans le monde*, p. 8.)

Imperial pride
The celebration of the splendours of the French empire did not just spring from blind vanity, as was said later on, but had a mainly educative aim 'to interest the masses in the idea of empire', and for those who cared deeply, like the authors just quoted, the aim was to achieve 'a fundamental imperial unity, intellectual, moral and cultural'. Such were the reasons for celebrating the one hundredth anniversary of the conquest of Algeria in 1930, and for the colonial exhibition organised by Paul Reynaud in 1931. The Paris exhibition of 1937 also had a large colonial section.

In the schoolroom, France was still studied within the framework of her empire, now become *France d'outre-mer* or *la plus grande France*, with an area of four million square miles and eighty million inhabitants. This was the France that had provided the best soldiers, the ones who had contributed heroically to victory and could once again save the country that was supposed to be theirs.

The economic sinews of empire could help to overcome difficulties in the homeland, contributing to a real self-sufficiency, with tropical foofstuffs, oil, meat, coffee, tea and cocoa. Bananas were a French export and had made a fortune for Dieppe. France was finding in the colonial world the raw materials she lacked for modern industry: wood, rubber (120,000 hectares in Indo-China producing 40,000 tonnes), anthracite from Tonkin (25,000 tonnes), the mines of North Africa. It was an economic Utopia kept going by the prospect of wonderful projects, e.g. Niger was to rival Egypt or Turkestan in the production of cotton, which would be transported by a Trans-Saharan railway.

The Ligue Maritime et Coloniale, the vehicle for this propaganda, had 500,000 members. They were almost entirely recruited from colleges where adolescent boys dreamed of heroism and escape inspired by the novels of Mac Orlan or Malraux, or by films like Feyder's *Le Grand Jeu* (1934) or *La Croissière jaune*, a documentary based on the Citroën expedition in Asia (1933). On the whole, the influence of these works was all the greater for their total lack of any propaganda element.

The left was particularly susceptible to these warm-hearted ideas which went back to the days of Brissot, inducing in them a fraternal urge to absorb these peoples, entrusted to them by history, into 'the great nation'. With the coming of the Front Populaire, this trend was carried still further in education under the influence of Jean Zay. Anti-colonialism, limited to an informed and committed minority, had little support. However, if the benevolence of French colonialism (so different from the inhumanity of other countries) was a widely accepted belief, it was simply based on unthinking sentiment; for the colonies were far away, out of sight, out of mind, and little known.

Colonial problems

The colonies' contribution to the metropolitan economy was rather more apparent than real. Their share of French foreign trade, which in percentage grew considerably through the collapse of world trade (28.5 per cent of imports and 33 per cent of exports in 1936) was in fact very low in comparison with 1929. To make profits out of selling cotton goods and motor-cars to the colonies, it was necessary to have local prosperity, and this aim was not pursued. The colonies were too poor to buy luxury goods and, as Henri Hauser has remarked, there was no fear of trade reprisals from that quarter; hence they were subjected to anti-colonial customs duties aimed at protecting wine, wheat, fruits against similar products, rice and bananas. All this added to their difficulties. By 1929 the slump had reached French Indo-China with a collapse in the price of rubber, and this was where the French empire suffered its first blow.

The standard of living among the native peoples of Indo-China was very low, with high infant mortality and a short adult expectation of life, made worse by migration to the marshes of the south. There were some tens of thousands of French, including a proportion of Eurasians. There were a great many more Chinese, who flocked out of the country because of the depression. The nationalist movement was provoked by poverty, but there were other causes, as travellers have described. The military rebellion led by Yen Bay, which cost the lives of members of the French establishment, was ruthlessly suppressed. Left-wing intellectuals were stirred by the writings of Louis Roubaud and Andrée Viollis just as they had been by Gide's accounts of black Africa some years earlier. There were beginnings of an anti-colonialist trend, exemplified by the writings of Challaye, Viot and Viollis, but it was still marginal. The violent attack on the *Exposition Coloniale* by the surrealists undoubtedly influenced the literature of the colonised; but how far did it touch society at large? The intellectual left and the Catholic paper *Esprit* criticised the civilisation versus barbarism argument. Some wanted Catholics to dissociate themselves from colonialism. The idea of partnership, so dear to Freemason and Christian colonial administrators, made some headway. But none of these ideas had much political effect. The socialist left was alive to them, but had no power. The communist party, whose anti-colonial feeling was well known and loudly proclaimed by Doriot, closed down its anti-militarist and anti-colonial activities when it joined the Front Populaire. Besides, Hitler's and Mussolini's support for colonial revolt was all too plain. Most French people knew nothing about the trouble brewing up in the colonies, all of whose discontents were attributed to the greed of foreign powers.

The North African situation

North Africa was even more important for France than Indo-China. The European element of the population was relatively large and youthful. There were 940,000 in Algeria, according to the 1936 census, 210,000 in Tunisia and 200,000 in Morocco. The various Mediterranean races were thoroughly intermixed and, except in Tunisia, largely Gallicised. School geography texts extolled these Frenchmen of the Maghreb whose vitality and pioneer spirit showed up the sluggishness of the mainland French; and they were all the more jealous of their colonial privileges in that they were poor, their average income per head being everywhere, especially in Algeria, much lower than in France.

There had been a shortage of labour in the Maghreb, but after 1930 the indigenous population grew rapidly. In 1936 it reached 5.5 million in Algeria, distributed more or less as at present, mostly country folk with uprooted city dwellers. The population grew rapidly after 1935, but employment prospects remained poor. The largest industry, mining, employed only 42,000 people in 1938. The result was that an indigent proletariat of unskilled workers emigrated to the industrial suburbs of mainland France.

But the problems were not entirely economic, for the depression did not begin to affect North Africa until 1932. Recovery started in 1935 due to state intervention which concentrated on the strongest sectors, at the expense of the weakest, which was the opposite of what happened in France. The troubles were, above all, political. The Africans reacted vigorously when they felt that the foundations of their civilisation were threatened by the attitude of the Catholic prelates, which was shared by the Academician Louis Bertrand and backed consciously or unconsciously by the pundits of Algiers University – the geographer, Augustin Bernard and the historians of Christian Africa, Gsell and Albertini. The endless series of Eucharistic conferences was seen as a deliberate provocation, while the traumas of 1930 marked a sort of turning-point. This year saw the Eucharistic Congress of Tunis, the celebration of the capture of Algiers, and in Morocco (where armed resistance was not to end until 1934) the *dahir* which removed Koranic law from the Berbers. Among intellectuals, discontent and alienation manifested themselves in various quite different directions. In Algeria, where the marabouts who had submitted to colonial rule were losing their influence, Ferhat 'Abbās began publication of *Le Jeune Algérien* in 1931 and called for political assimilation with France, a proposal that was rejected by Ben Bâdis and the ulemas. In Tunisia, the conservative Destour party suffered the breakaway of the reformist neo-Destour wing, led by Bourguiba. The leaders of Action Marocaine were divided equally into pan-Islamists and westernised socialists. These local movements never succeeded in concerting their actions. After 1933 they were severely curbed, increasingly so as time went on, but with occasional lulls when French authority was vested in a liberal-minded resident or governor.

In Algeria, an increasingly repressive policy was pursued, especially after the riots of 1934 in which the ulemas were involved. Spurred on by Augustin Bernard, French conservatives and colonists of all shades of opinion, the government brought in special measures with the Décret Régnier. The same course was followed in Tunisia under President Peyrouton, and in Morocco, where the nationalists had the moral support of Sultan Mohammed V. Here the depression had been more severe than elsewhere. It arrived late but with more effect. It is easy to understand what hopes were placed in the Front Populaire; and we shall see how deeply they were disappointed.

Metropolitan France could hardly fail to notice the presence of immigrants – a downtrodden class, politically unstable, ready recruits for the Ligues, or else doggedly faithful supporters of Doriot in his Saint-Denis domain. The nationalists banded together in the Etoile Nord-Africaine, founded in 1926 by Messali Hadj, dissolved in 1929, secretly re-organised in 1933, and coming back legally into the open in 1935. It was to take part in the Front Populaire and extended its activities to North Africa, but there it only increased the splintering tendency of local nationalism. This weakness diminished the impact of colonial national consciousness so that it played hardly any part in the French political scene.

18

The political ferment

The economic crisis faced the politicians of the thirties with problems which they felt unable to solve, try as they might. Poincaré's devaluation after a period of inflation made it hard for the teacher of history to censure Philippe le Bel for debasing the currency, though he could still deride the financial expedients of Louis XVI. The stabilisation of 1928 had felt like a return to normal, i.e. to the seemingly stable economic regime that had characterised the nineteenth century and that shaped contemporary modes of thought. It is not surprising that, in the face of this economic and social turmoil, there was no remedy that the powers that be could bring themselves to adopt. They were in agreement with public opinion, that is to say with the leaders of industry, and so of course the press, and could go no further than wait for things to return to normal. It seemed to them suicidal, and so out of the question, to make really drastic changes; and for this it would be absurd to blame them. All the same it was inevitable that this intellectual lethargy, or perhaps cautiousness, on the part of the traditional parties should have been challenged by certain younger or more impatient members. Inevitable too that those on the fringe of the establishment, who blamed the whole social set-up for the mess they were in, should have tried to organise revolt, either by action or in the realm of ideas.

Confusion among the radicals
It had been the vocation of the radicals to govern France under the Third Republic since 1900. They were in power during the economic crisis from 1932 to 1934, and even after that it came naturally to them to be represented in right-wing cabinets up to the time they joined the Front Populaire. The reality of power meant for them the tenure of the ministries of the interior, education and agriculture. But up to 1934 Chiappe, the prefect of police, their own appointment, regularly betrayed them, and the peasants in protest against their inability to cope with the depression started to vote heavily for left and right extremists. The radicals as a group probably had less idea than anybody how to cope with the crisis. One of its leaders of that period, Jacques Kayser, tells us: 'The radical is history's

familiar spirit, in touch with events, of unquestioned experience, accepted as the great arbiter of controversies.' (In *Tendances politiques dans la vie française depuis 1789*, p. 71.) In the face of the crisis of capitalism, references provided by the French Revolution were inadequate – the disastrous *assignat* which led to an ill-considered defence of the currency and the controlled economy of the Year II were unwillingly borne by the Convention, but accepted for form's sake by the congresses of 1931 and 1932 under pressure from the Jeunes Radicaux.

Under the leadership of Edouard Herriot and Edouard Daladier, the radical party improved its organisation; but it was so shaken by this period of crisis that its militants felt with some reason that the party was in decline through its inability to adapt to modern times. As with the socialists, its parliamentary representatives often disagreed with the party line; but the party was powerless to control its deputies. Its senators, radicals of the old school with a majority in the Senate, disagreed with the deputies, who no longer had a majority in the lower house. Undeclared war, called jokingly 'the war of the two Edouards', broke out between the leading chiefs of the party, who succeeded each other in the leadership according to their varying fortunes in the party congresses. These battles were reported in the various radical newspapers, over which the party had no control – the Sarraut brothers' *La Dépêche de Toulouse*, Daladier and Roche's *La République*, *L'Ere nouvelle* and even *L'Oeuvre*, which was not a radical paper.

The party expelled its right wing led by Franklin-Bouillon, for its inherent Jacobinism had caused it to side with the nationalists in rejecting Briand's pacifist policy. After the expulsion the party was rocked by the struggles of the Jeunes Radicaux ('Young Turks') against compromising associations with elements of the centre. They succeeded, with some hurt feelings, in keeping the radical party in opposition until the victory at the 1932 elections, when Daladier, whom they had been backing, lost the party leadership to Herriot. Their next move was to rebel against Herriot's overtures to the republican centre. But most of them, such as Pierre Cot, Jean Zay, Mistler, Kayser and Mendès France (who had been head of LAURS, the party's student body) remained loyal to the party organisation. Gaston Bergery left the party in 1933 and resigned his seat in the Chamber as a protest against what he alleged to be a betrayal of the electoral promises. For the same reasons, Gabriel Cudenet and the militants of the extreme left formed a new group, the radical–socialist Camille Pelletan party, but it was destined to be of little influence. In contrast, other Jeunes Radicaux, such as Pierre Dominique and Bertrand de Jouvenel, went the same way as the neo-socialists and soon became openly fascist.

These important secessions show how badly the radicals, devoted as they were to the institutions and modes of political behaviour that were woven into their party's history, felt the need of some sort of rejuvenation. But they found it hard to see how to achieve it.

The impatient socialists

We have already observed that the SFIO was the only party that saw the harmfulness of the measures taken to cope with the economic crisis; but alarmed by the political implications of its discovery, it left Paul Reynaud to be a lone voice damning the ill-considered defence of the franc. Backed by two million votes, the SFIO was on the way to becoming the largest party, having benefited from the collapse of communism in the towns and a decline of radicalism in the country. Yet it was restrained from joining the government by the wishes of its militant rank and file, although its most brilliant deputies were longing for cabinet office. It was divided into factions grouped around the small private reviews which fought bitterly for power in the party congresses and for seats on the permanent management committee. On the right, there was *La Vie socialiste* with Ramadier, Renaudel and Déat, who wanted alliance with the radicals and acceptance of ministerial posts. On the left, there was *La Bataille socialiste* of Bracke and Zyromski, sticking obstinately to the rigid postulates of pre-1914 socialism of the Guesde variety. On the extreme left, a small minority of neo-communists founded *L'Etincelle socialiste*, while around Marceau Pivert there were grouped some very working-class elements keeping true to the socialist traditions of Jean Allemane (1843–1935).

The result of these conflicting forces was that power in the inter-war period became vested in the centre in the hands of Léon Blum, Paul Faure, Jean-Baptiste Séverac (who inclined to the left) and Vincent Auriol (more to the right). The intellectual superiority of Léon Blum, the real basis of his authority, irked some of his colleagues, who were open to different new ideas. The Belgian Henri de Man, with *Au-delà du marxisme* and *L'Idée socialiste*, created a new sort of revisionism, popularised in France by André Philip. It had an immediate effect on the right wing. In the face of the threat of fascism and Nazism, the Jeunesses Socialistes tried to find out why resistance to these menaces had so far failed and by what means they could be defeated. A great deal of theoretical research was carried out by the Etudiants Socialistes (ES) and the planning group Révolution Constructive which developed from it. But, although their ideas accorded with some of those of the CGT, they were suspect in their own party, which still clung to its Marxist links. Moreover, the leaders of the Jeunesses Socialistes, Pierre Bloch and Daniel Mayer, both very ambitious, were hostile to the ES whom they feared as electoral rivals. In fact only two of the Etudiants Socialistes achieved success in politics, almost without meaning to – Max Lejeune and Maurice Schumann. The ES were, additionally, rather handicapped by having no journal of their own, but only a few pages in the publication of the Belgian organisation, *L'Etudiant socialiste*.

There was one man who was determined to gain ascendancy over the party by exploiting the disillusion provoked on the one hand by prophecies of revolutionary days of reckoning that never arrived, and on the other by the illusory hopes of the neo-revisionists. This was Marcel Déat, who was in too much of a hurry. He incited with his friends the revolt of the parliamentary group that had given the radical governments their majority, even when they cut civil servants' pay. This breach of discipline was severely censured by the Paris Congress in 1933; but Montagnon, Marquet and Déat in three important speeches from the floor denounced the inability of the SFIO to adapt to the critical days of the twentieth century, obsessed as it was by its outmoded ideologies. Marquet went furthest in the direction of a *socialisme national*, even a form of Nazism, with his triple slogan 'Order, Authority, Nation', which he offered provocatively to the party. This was to be called neo-socialism.

As they continued to reject party discipline, the deputies on the right of the party, followed by numerous militants, were expelled at the beginning of November 1933. A month later they founded the Parti Socialiste de France (PSF), which merged with the older dissident groups of the Union Socialiste Républicaine in November 1934. The expelled members did not remain united for long and their group broke up in 1936, while some rejoined the SFIO. The PSF were a very mixed lot. The right-wing supporters of the government merely wanted seats in the cabinet. Déat, Marquet and Montagnon had more exalted objectives. They repudiated Marxism and even Jaurès' compromise synthesis. Convinced that capitalism was capable of overcoming economic crises by the rationalisation of production, and equally convinced that socialism in Italy and elsewhere had shown itself incapable of overthrowing capitalism, they had come down on the side of capitalism's economic superiority. They merely proposed to steer it politically towards the social changes they deemed necessary. Neo-socialism has been labelled fascism of a left-wing variety, but perhaps it was nearer to Nazism.

Déat and Marquet were probably Hitlerians before Doriot. Anti-semitism certainly played a part in their personal dispute with Blum. Openly avowed as part of their nationalistic creed by the extreme right, anti-semitism was also vaguely and rather shamefacedly endemic in the extreme left. It appeared among the neo-socialists from the beginning, when Salomon Grumbach's application to join was insultingly rejected. An Alsatian patriot, a socialist of the extreme right, a French agent during the First World War, Grumbach was naive enough to think that his place was with the dissidents, who included Renaudel as head of the group. Renaudel, a rather mediocre character, was in no way interested in Déat's *socialisme national*, but Jaurès had died in his arms and this had a great sentimental effect on the militants. The neo-socialists despised the leaders of the right and only accepted their company in order to get some voting fodder and backing at party conferences. Frossard, also a supporter of the government and of Jewish descent, showed more acumen than Grumbach and escaped embarrassment by forming his own *attentiste* ('wait and see') breakaway group. This put him somewhere between the SFIO and the neo-socialists.

One might suppose that this schismatic behaviour would have weakened the socialist party, and it actually did for a time. The neo-socialists won control of municipal and departmental councils and of various political federations. But the majority soon returned to the fold. In the Chamber the elections of 1936, with the triumph of the Front Populaire, swept away the dissident deputies. The party was thus purified of those elements who had been shaken or won over by the success of fascism, and of those who had never recovered from their failure to become junior ministers. Déat's defection hardly affected party philosophy. The *planistes* of the ES stayed with the SFIO. In their day and in the historic context of that time they were responsible, in a quite disinterested way, for the most active research aimed at refurbishing socialist ideas. In fact they were not recognised by their own party, for they were up against a traditional mistrust of academics. They had no backing in the Latin Quarter, the domain of the Austrian Marxist Zyromski and his alter ego Paul Coliette, a former anarchist who, convinced of the need for party unity, had joined the socialists in 1905. Not much has been written about the part they played, but it was considerable. The CGT persuaded the Front Populaire (and that meant the socialist party) to accept many of their ideas. And one could say much about the use made of their ideas by the reformers of liberal capitalism. But the SFIO, to protect itself against accusations of reformism, preferred to give their favour to the Trotskyists, who were finally to ill reward their patronage.

The communist dilemma

'When our great party followed the party line ... ' Such was the ritual phrase by which the leaders and the communist press recalled the period when, under the leadership of Maurice Thorez, the party became the country's second largest, and sometimes even the largest. Without ever being in danger of total disappearance, like some of the small groups, the communist party proceeded to shrink, victim of the policies of the Third International, of energetic repression and of the economic crisis. It was successful in the 1928 elections, partly no doubt because of the prestige it had gained by opposing the colonial wars; but with its meagre numbers it had no influence in the Chamber, which could only serve as a platform for its spokesmen. Even with an increased poll it had few members, thanks to the return to the system of single-member constituencies (*scrutin d'arrondissement*), and most of them found themselves in prison, either together or one after the other. In 1932 the electoral catastrophe (Cachin, Duclos and Marty all beaten) reduced the representation of the communists to ten deputies, of whom eight had been rescued by socialist voters – so they no longer counted.

The external causes of their decline were the tactics of 'class against class' and 'the defence of the workers' fatherland', two suicidal slogans which made communism a ghetto between 1928 and 1935. The first, which was quite out of line with the national republican tradition of the left, was responsible for the outrageous success of the right or extreme right in the three-cornered election. It collapsed in 1932 when the unemployed rallied, on the second round, to support the radicals and the socialists in order to beat the candidates of the Comité des Forges.

The second slogan was imposed by the Sixth International congress held in Moscow in the summer of 1928. 'The defence of the workers' fatherland' amounted to a permanent conspiracy, not merely professed but proclaimed, against national security, and hence provided the authorities with a good excuse for a thoroughly repressive policy. Any hint of a public demonstration was treated as an incitement to insurrection and resulted in the preventive arrest of leaders and their associates, frightening their militant supporters off the streets.

The first blow was delivered by Tardieu who, with the help of Chiappe, the Paris prefect of police, broke up a national anti-war demonstration planned for 1 August 1929. Thenceforward the practice of preventive arrest, used in earlier days against anarchists, was regularly employed. Even when the elections of 1932 returned a left-wing government, this sort of persecution continued unchanged. In 1933 the 'Fantomas' conspiracy, involving espionage in military establishments, afforded an opportunity to suppress the *unitaire* cells in the navy and in the dockyards, which were particularly daring and active, often consisting of former mutineers of the Black Sea squadron.

The internal causes of the crisis in the communist party were that its strategy called for strong, even dictatorial, leadership, and this inevitably led to private feuds and tensions. The Barbé-Célor group, put in charge of the party by the International from 1928 to 1931, applied the two principles – class warfare and the defence of the workers' fatherland – rigorously and fanatically when they claimed that the French and the British were planning armed intervention in Russia. All their energies were devoted to attacks on the principal enemy of the proletariat, the SFIO. Any influence those 'social cops', 'social traitors', 'social fascists' might bring to bear on the working class was marked for destruction as the one great obstacle to the revolution that the crisis of capitalism had now brought so close. The party thereby went into deliberate isolation and, though lacking adequate means, launched into direct action. Abuse and violence were its chief methods.

This kind of strategy not only cut the communists off from the mainstream of national politics, but had other results as well. They denounced as police spies anybody outside the party who professed socialist or communist views, but in fact their ranks were infiltrated with informers right to the top. These in turn spread rumours that discredited even the most irreproachable members such as the secretary-general Sémard. This resulted in mutual suspicion all round. One imagines that some *provocateurs* were unmasked, and indeed one of the top men, Crémet, seems never to have returned from a trip to Russia.

The active members inevitably melted away, especially as the depression continued. It became the party of the unemployed, rubbing shoulders with the militants of the CGTU, which was recruited from the élite of the working class. The defection of key people, begun in 1922, continued with increasing speed. The founders of the party, brought up within the SFIO, began to find the latest tactics alien and hard to accept. Those who remained loyal, e.g. Cachin, Vaillant-Couturier and Renaud Jean, were used according to their abilities but excluded from any part in overall direction. Those who had been expelled either rejoined the socialist party or formed dissident groups, the most important of which was the Parti Ouvrier et Paysan, founded in December 1929 round Louis Sellier and that former white hope of the communists, Garchery. It became the Parti d'Unité Prolétarienne (PUP) and did a lot of damage to the communists in Paris and the suburbs in the elections of 1932 when all their old leaders were beaten. Some of the *pupiste* dissidents ended up by joining the SFIO.

After 1931 the Barbé-Célor group was ousted. Doriot regained influence and started his campaign against the class-war tactic. He failed and was expelled from the party in 1934. Thorez, who had become a member of the party secretariat in 1930, was on his way up. Without impugning the party line he did his best to modify it. His influence grew, with a good deal of help from the Czech Fried, an emissary of the International, who called himself Clément. It was another Klement who had published a pamphlet against Jaurès and his tradition, with the aim of breaking any connection between the party and the French type of socialism. 1931 saw the faint beginnings of a movement that was to go far, but it was not until 1934 that the party was to climb back under the joint leadership of Fried and Thorez.

In spite of its total commitment to the working class between 1928 and 1931, the party attracted and recruited many intellectuals. It also had a student organisation, the Union Fédérale des Etudiants (UFE) with its journal *L'Etudiant pauvre*, round which formed various groups who were distinguished for their extraordinary determination and self-sacrifice.

The Trotskyites

The Trotskyites never had much influence, and they proved to be more of a nuisance to the SFIO than the communists. Expelled one after the other from the communist party, they were slow to organise themselves, partly because the more important of Trotsky's personal French friends such as Rosmer and Souvarine only hovered on the edge of organised Trotskyism. Their paper *La Vérité* was founded in 1929, but it was during the Russian revolutionary's stay in France in 1933–4 that the Ligue Communiste became a reality. When Doriot was expelled from the communist party it seemed for a time that he wanted to build up a new group embracing every kind of dissident from the PUP to the Trotskyites, but he failed. The leading members of the Ligue were young – Pierre Frank, Pierre Naville, Yvan and Maria Craipeau, Fred Zeller and David Rousset. Trotsky was deported to the Alps in the spring of 1934, and before the end of the year he gave his blessing to the mass entry of his supporters to the SFIO.

The SFIO, rather ashamed of its lack of ideological background, welcomed these new arrivals, deeply imbued as they were with Marxist culture and too young to have played any part in the schism of Tours (1920). If they had played their cards properly and been in rather less of a hurry to take over, they might have played an important role in a great party. Split up among the various Jeunesses Socialistes groups, they set up their periodical *Révolution* as a rival to the unreadable *Cri des jeunes*. By the summer of 1935, the leaders of the SFIO had expelled the Jeunesses Socialistes branch of the Seine, who then formed the Jeunesses Socialistes Révolutionnaires (JSR). Others were also attracted to this body, and this forced the SFIO to carry out periodical purges of their organisation. Just as Trotsky was being expelled from France, his followers were being expelled from the socialist party.

After this there were constant disagreements and divisions into small rival groups and solitary snipers. Frank and the older members founded the Parti Communiste Internationaliste (PCI) with its own organ *La Commune*. The younger ones, around *La Vérité*, founded the Parti Ouvrier Révolutionnaire (POR), which later became the POI.

It is evident that the Trotskyite presence was, as Craipeau remarked, 'essentially Parisian and composed of intellectuals' (*Le Mouvement trotskiste en France*, p. 105). It had no influence among communist members of the working class. But it is equally noticeable that in the Paris area the SFIO was always threatened with infiltration or doctrinal 'contamination'. Intellectuals, led by the surrealists, were particularly attracted to Trotskyism. In the provinces it only appealed to the teaching profession. Under the influence of the Dommangets, the Fédération Unitaire de l'Enseignement was steered into trade unionism through the Ecole Emancipée movement, which made life hard for the communists.

One must not confuse the Trotskyites with the ultra-left. This comprised the anarchists, the groups that had left the communist party and the surrealists. The anarchists, no longer having any influence among the unions, were inconspicuous until their fortunes were revived by the Spanish Civil War. Splitting hairs over doctrinal niceties and personal animosities had reduced them to a collection of mutually hostile groups. They had various news-sheets such as *Le Libertaire* and *L'Anarchie* and reviews like *L'Idée libre*. A symptom of their sclerotic inability to adapt was their incessant reprinting of outdated pre-1914 pamphlets.

The communists who opposed the party never succeeded in becoming more than a series of cells. Yet France had welcomed former bolsheviks of the 'working-class opposition' as Russian anarchists. Small 'Luxembourgist' groups existed for a time. André Prudhommeaux, before joining the anarchist ranks, was a genuine personification of a left-wing bolshevik opposition with the numerous papers he ran between 1928 and 1933 – *Le Réveil communiste*, *L'Ouvrier communiste*, *Spartacus*, *La Correspondance internationale ouvrière*. During 1933 Lefeuvre, editor of *Masses*, took over from him. But this ultra-left movement made even less impression on the workers than the communists; although it does go to show how deeply intellectuals were involved in politics, both before and after February 1934, as we shall see below.

The right and its Ligues

The parliamentary right, which one may take as stretching across to the centre, remained unscathed by the depression, since the members of its various constituent bodies were largely people of rank and substance. Its real strength was hidden behind the scenes – the 'two hundred families', the Comité des Forges and, rather on the outside edge of overt political action, the Roman Catholic church. The unifying forces were clericalism, nationalism, liberal orthodoxy and anti-communism. All the same there was no love lost between reactionaries and moderates. 'Belonging to the same social sphere they follow totally divergent lines in questions affecting their fate. In this polemic the reactionary's defence is to suggest that the moderate is a traitor to his class, and that of the moderate that the reactionary is living in the past. So an accusation of moral inferiority counters one of intellectual inferiority.' (A. Bonnard, *Le Drame du présent, les modérés*, Paris, Grasset, 1936, p. 117.)

In practice the moderate parliamentarian was prepared to serve in a cabinet under Herriot, while the reactionary would not have sat in one under Poincaré. The reactionary Academician found it hard to take in a parliamentary situation in which the moderates in the Senate, like the radicals in the same place, were very ready to come to an agreement on the sharing out of ministerial responsibilities. Meanwhile in the Chamber the right, even the moderate right, would accept the ruling of Tardieu, who forbade such combinations. This created an atmosphere in which the Ligues could proliferate.

Under the Third Republic the left never tried to sabotage the result of an electoral defeat. Its very ideology prevented such action, and in any case it did not have forcible means of doing so at its disposal, not having sufficient trade-union muscle to bring the country to a standstill. The right disliked the constitution, but made no attempt to upset it while they had the running of it. The people with real power were not going to help in subverting the state while their own side made up the government; but it was a different matter when they lost an election. This accounts for the growth of the Ligues after 1932, when their existence raised the possibility of a French version of fascism.

Some historians have simply ignored the existence of the Ligues on the grounds that they were an old phenomenon only serving to prolong anti-Dreyfusard nationalism, offering no threat to capitalism and the liberal economy, and having no support from the working class. For the left at that period and for a small handful of historians, the authoritarian right was fascist inasmuch as Mussolini's defeat of the working classes made him their hero and a pattern to follow. To aim at an anti-parliamentary dictatorship could only be fascist. The very absence of ideology played a part in the origins of Italian fascism and even if the right was characterised only by violence, hatred of the Third Republic, and anti-communism, the left could still see it as fascist. It could see Nazism in it, too, when there was an outbreak of xenophobia and anti-semitism. Before 1940, fascism was far from being a dirty word among the right, and many, especially intellectuals, professed a French fascism, perhaps harking back to Bonapartist or Boulangist traditions. This all sprang from disillusion over the lost victory of 1918 and the feeling that the country was going to the dogs, the very feelings that had helped Mussolini to success.

The Action Française (AF) movement was certainly not fascist, although Daudet admired Mussolini as the saviour of the monarchy. It already had enough financial backing to be beyond suspicion of seeking foreign subsidies. Although weakened by papal denunciation in 1926 and disowned by the Pretender in 1937, it had set an example by street violence and attempts at a *putsch*. Although the AF had its own distinctive ideology, which its enemies despised without understanding it, in the eyes of the left it was, by reason of its methods, the absolute embodiment of fascism. The Camelots de Roi were undoubtedly the best street fighters of the time. Taittinger's Jeunesses Patriotes (JP), like the AF, made no pretence of fighting capitalism. By 1928 their influence was waning since a right-wing government had no need of their activities. This movement was of a rather Bonapartist character and regained importance with the coming of a left-wing government in 1932, due to the support of some extreme right-wing deputies such as Philippe Henriot and Xavier Vallet. But outside Paris the JP had little influence, and although they were much stronger in numbers than the Camelots, their fighting abilities were far inferior.

Besides these groups of fairly recent origin, others had shot up as an immediate result of the slump. The scent manufacturer Coty had already given financial backing to many ultra-right organisations and had in 1928 founded a demagogic, anti-parliamentary, anti-semitic daily, *L'Ami du peuple*, priced at ten centimes instead of the usual twenty-five. In 1933 he founded Solidarité Française under the leadership of Jean Renaud. It was organised on Nazi lines and recruited its storm-troopers from North African immigrant slum dwellers. Unfortunately for him his private papers were sold by a member to a left-wing group which published them under the title *Les Ennemis du peuple*. Coty's movement had quite a following among the lower middle classes, small shopkeepers in particular.

Francisme was led by Marcel Bucard, former secretary to Coty and collaborator in 1932 with Gustave Hervé in *La Victoire*, a journal in which the cult of a 'Pétain mystique' was called upon to inspire a vague sort of national socialist party. Founded at the end of 1933, Francisme had an ideology that was clearly inspired by Italian fascism, and it was generously subsidised by Mussolini. But it had no fighters, had marooned itself on the extreme right by its doctrinal rigidity and had even had the name of its movement scooped by Jolivet and Coston's *francistes*.

These various movements – royalist, Bonapartist, fascist – boasted of tens, even hundreds, of thousands of adherents. In fact, they ranged from a few people to a hundred thousand for the Jeunesses Patriotes. In any case only a small number could actually be mobilised on the streets. As with the extreme non-communist left, their influence was confined to Paris and a few large towns. But they had the backing of certain leading personalities – the surviving marshals of France, the army chiefs such as Castelnau, a large proportion of the officers, some Academicians. Coty himself spent five hundred million francs. However, on the whole, it was to the traditional right that the establishment gave its loyalty, up to the time of the Front Populaire.

Before the Front Populaire came to power the only mass movement of the extreme right was the Croix-de-Feu. This organisation of ex-servicemen, started in 1927 and of course subsidised by Coty, was unimportant until it was joined by Colonel de la Rocque, who became its president in 1931. It grew steadily and threw out offshoots such as Fils et Filles de Croix-de-Feu and the Ligue des Volontaires Nationaux. After the attempted coup on 6 February 1934 the movement probably reached 150,000 members. With tactics like Mussolini's, e.g. his technique of mobilising gangs to throw people off the streets and of hunting down communists, de la Rocque's movement preached the usual extreme right-wing ideology in its Bonapartist guise – 'esprit combattant' as he called it. Heavily subsidised by secret government funds, if we can believe Tardieu and Laval, he patrolled the streets in support of the government and cracked down on communists. After the events of 6 February he supported Doumergue's government which was dominated by Tardieu, then fought his successors. Such was the prestige of the Croix-de-Feu that it appeared to be the principal movement of the extreme right and certainly the most active. To oppose it was the main *raison d'être* of the Front Populaire. But de la Rocque's book *Service public*, written in 1934, was not at all fascist. On several occasions he had even displayed some nervousness. So he was deserted by some of his really fascist-minded members such as Pucheu and Pozzo di Borgo. The coming of the Front Populaire was to bring about a change in his behaviour and that of his rivals and competitors. On the whole, up to the time of the Front Populaire, the Ligues only stood for neo-Bonapartism. They were still under the spell of obsolete ideas and not at all keen to go in for the outward anti-capitalism of foreign fascism. Loyalty to their paymasters made it impossible for them to appeal to the working class, while the middle classes were too well looked after by the state to commit themselves to risky ventures of that kind. However, the apparent threat to the Republic was sufficient to make the left in its turn mobilise and unite against the Ligues. So, unwittingly, they did assist the coming of the Front Populaire.

A new fascism then developed with a more assured philosophy and with different patterns of action; but always with the same dream of a strong executive, which would supress the left and put a stop to constant changes of government and the social upheaval they provoked.

19

The young intellectuals and the crisis of civilisation

Ever since the Dreyfus affair there had been a specifically intellectual commitment in political questions. Those who were thirty years old in 1900 could still be alive in 1930. For many of them the clock had stopped in 1914, and they were still faithful to the idols of their youth: André Beaunier, Paul Bourget, Henri Bordeaux, Paul Claudel and the Académie Française on the right; Henri Barbusse, Jean-Richard Bloch, Victor Margueritte, Romain Rolland and the Sorbonne on the left. André Gide stood apart. His travels in black Africa and his own secular version of Christian ethics had caused him to turn to communism. Later, under the influence of the Trotskyite brothers Pierre and Claude Naville he had renounced Stalinism. Whether or not these ageing figures were great creative writers, they had nothing whatever to contribute in the way of political ideas.

Different types of rebellion

During the thirties young intellectuals took a lively interest in politics. Not many, apart from scholars and academics, were drawn to socialism and radicalism. The traditional right had few recruits. 'Commitment', a period word, expressed revolt against post-war society, against the impotence of political institutions and against the spinelessness of the political class. This was the generation born between 1890 and 1910. If there was ever a French fascism, it was a fascism of intellectuals obsessed by what seemed to them a crisis affecting all civilisation. They alone tried to transcend the antiquated Bonapartist and nationalist ideas that made up the programmes of the Ligues. Drieu la Rochelle was the outstanding member of the earlier generation. Starting from a position somewhere between left and extreme left, he first expounded his ideas in *La Lutte des jeunes*, founded by Bertrand de Jouvenel, a former radical, then in Doriot's *L'Emancipation nationale*. He was the mind behind the Parti Populaire Français and one of the best writers of his generation. It is above all in his novels, which unceasingly reflect his personal beliefs and his obsession with suicide, and most obviously in *Gilles*, that he betrays the roots of his fascism: 'violent rejection of contemporary France, a longing for the return of a golden age, and a rather ill-defined dream of a new order' (M. Winock, *'Gilles* de Drieu la Rochelle', *Le Mouvement social*, 80, July–September 1972).

This golden age came from medieval myth, the Christian corporatist order, to be found at its best in the works of Maritain, and at its worst in Walter Scott. It derived also from Barrès, who was such an influence on the generation of Drieu and Aragon, but whom the younger generation found unreadably insipid. Joan of Arc and the Year II were, as with Barrès, the two significant moments in history for those who dreamed of uniting the extremes of the political spectrum for an assault on bourgeois France; and in this he was not alone. Coming from communism, others such as Camille Fégy and Ramon Fernandez followed the same route.

L'Ordre nouveau was a review launched at the end of 1933 by a group headed by Robert Aron. He and Arnaud Dandieu (who died in that year) wrote a book which at the time caused a great stir, *La Revolution nécessaire*. Both capitalism and parliamentarism were rejected by *L'Ordre nouveau*, a clear sign of fascist leanings. Its supporters were young engineers, managers, avowed followers of Proudhon, but it would be wrong to class them as fascists. The eldest son of Péguy also had his periodicals and his group, the Front National Syndicalists. Jean Touchard has made a study of these little reviews which reveal what he calls 'the spirit of the thirties'. For him this spirit of revolt against an intolerable society is simply fascism.

The chief protagonists of this way of thinking were former students of the Ecole Normale, old readers of *L'Action française*, who, together with J.-P. Maxence, had remained under the influence of Massis and Maurras – Robert Brasillach, Maurice Bardèche and Thierry Maulnier. Massis introduced them to the *Revue universelle* in which Brasillach published his 'Funeral oration for Monsieur Gide'. But it was *Je suis partout*, a monthly with a large circulation, founded in 1930 and edited by Gaxotte, that enabled them to reach a large audience.

Planisme, backed by *L'Homme nouveau*, was far from being fascist, though coloured by neo-socialist equivocations. It owed a good deal to nineteenth-century varieties of socialism, and especially to Henri de Man. Most of de Man's disciples kept aloof and, if anything, tried to reform the SFIO. In contrast to these dreamers the group Révolution Constructive, which we mentioned earlier, had a genuine working-class base, the CGT.

The challenge to society was not made by any single movement. Although its wish was to eliminate the traditional differences between left and right, as time went on *Esprit* steadily moved towards the left. Started by Mounier in 1932 with a Catholic orientation, its founding members included some Protestants and unbelievers, and it repudiated clericalism. It almost immediately decided to fight against colonial repression. The aim of *Esprit* was to take a global view of all aspects of the crisis in civilisation, in order to help the Church and Catholics detach themselves from subjective judgments coloured by the compromises of worldly life. It inevitably became political and revolutionary in a spiritual sense. However, even though one genuinely political movement, the Troisième Force, drew inspiration from it (moving away later), Mounier wanted neither leadership nor membership of any party. His role, which he never sought, was to be the conscience of the Christian democrats, as Marc Sangnier had been before him.

It was natural that left-wing extremism should exercise a strong pull on rebellious young intellectuals who, despite the presence of working-class elements, made up the real core of Trotskyism and the ultra-left. But they also were split into autonomous groups with different political allegiances. Young poets, historians, communist philosophers, graduates of the Ecole Normale like Jean Bruhat or Paul Nizan, and teachers like Georges Politzer or Valentin Feldman attacked bourgeois culture, 'the corrupter of mankind' (Nizan). Their media were *La Revue marxiste*, where the influence of Rappoport sometimes made the Party suspicious of it, and a small publishing house Les Revues, where Pierre Morhange, Gutermann, Georges Altman and Henri Lefebvre congregated. Boris Souvarine was the leading light in a discussion group started by him which published *La Critique sociale*. The twelve issues of this review constituted in their day a remarkable expression of Marxist thought (leaning towards Trotskyism) on the subject of fascism and the failure of revolution. The principal members of Souvarine's group were Gérard Walter, Georges Bataille, Raymond Queneau; also Pierre Kaan, Simone Weil and Jean Dautry, who were younger.

Jacques Soustelle was the great man of the *Masses* group, led by Lefeuvre. He was close to being a member of the communist party, and many young intellectuals came to learn their Marxist doctrine from him. Edith Thomas used to say she owed to him her conversion to communism.

The surrealist movement, which had in 1928 produced two of its most important books – Breton's *Nadja* and Aragon's *Le Traité du style* – was ready to put itself, as Aragon's book said it should, at the service of revolution. Its great weakness was its capacity for dissension and the sort of rows that drove Breton into isolation and Crevel to suicide. Aragon and Sadoul became communists while the rest, however divided, remained generally Trotskyite. Much of the vigour of the surrealist movement was concentrated in the review *Le Surréalisme ASDLR* and in the poetry of those years; but the most significant act of the most significant movement of the inter-war period was its production (1930–9) of the tracts attacking the colonial exhibition and the expulsion of Trotsky, and Breton's *Position politique du surréalisme*. A number of young recruits were also picked up by surrealism at the time of the 'Aragon affair', when the author of the poem *Front rouge* was prosecuted. It is difficult to understand Touchard's conclusion that: 'In 1930 surrealism was on the way out and had nothing more to offer than a dubious shelter for young folk in search of a cause.' (In *Tendances politiques dans la vie française depuis 1789*, p. 115, n. 57.) Of course the movement had always followed a policy of internal purges and had never had anything to do with any *union sacrée* of revolt ganging up with reaction against bourgeois civilisation, on which Touchard laid so much stress and which was now to be put to the test.

Temporary alliances against a stultified establishment

A common rejection of the established order, says Touchard, and the will for change led the extreme left and the extreme right to come to an understanding – not in the streets, where they were still exchanging blows, but in the realm of ideas. Bernanos, a former member of the Action Française, produced in *La Grande Peur des bien-pensants* an apologia for the Commune. The more enlightened members of the extreme left were desperately looking for a way to beat fascism, whose victories made them distraught. The references for both fascism and *surfascisme* (i.e. fascism defeated) led to the same authorities, Sorel and Nietzsche; but, as everyone took from them what best suited his case, the entente could only rest on the disgust felt by both sides for existing society. Mutual aid could only be given in elections, given the impossibility of a joint constructive programme. Similar anomalous situations could be seen in the political life of other countries – in Germany with the Strasser brothers, and in England with Mosley. In France it was to be the intellectuals who were to shift most frequently from social and national revolution to national and social liberation, and the reverse. Communist intellectuals turned to fascism, while student members of Action Française in 1930 became communists in 1936. Furthermore, the irrationalism common to both fascists and certain non-communists of the extreme left made them jointly opposed to both Marxism and Maurrasism, and the different shades of opinion could on occasion join together in a display of indignation.

In March 1932, a communist cabinet-maker, Edmond Fritsch, who was haranguing some workmen on a building-site at Vitry-sur-Seine, was cold-bloodedly shot down by two policemen. This event, which might seem fairly insignificant, caused much indignation in the Paris region. Although totally forgotten today, it is worthy of record for two reasons. The first is that the young people of the extreme right, of the 'little reviews', were just as indignant as those of the extreme left. This was not the only time that these extremes acted concertedly, for it went on happening more or less up to the time of the attempted coup of 6 February 1934. But such behaviour was more uncommon in French than in German political life. Moreover, it coincided with the period during which Mussolini was encouraging a leftish fascism among students. The young Frenchmen of the extreme right had quite close relations with the Milanese groups who published *Il Cantiere* and *Camminare* in the early years of the decade.

The other reason why Fritsch's death was significant was that the communist party published a pamphlet, 'Ils ont tué Fritsch!', which was produced by the editorial and art staff of *L'Humanité*, symptomatic of a working-class trend. The articles were anonymous, the collective signature at the end – 'Compiled by the first shock brigade of the association of revolutionary writers and artists in the service of the building unions and strike committees'. It did not last. Less than two years later the same group's pamphlet which paid homage to those who died on 9, 11 and 12 February bore the signatures of Romain Rolland, Vaillant-Couturier, Ramon Fernandez, Jean-Richard Bloch, Aragon and Jean Giono.

More than a year after Fritsch's murder, Pierre Andreu returned to the subject, publishing an article about it in *L'Assaut*, which shows that the feelings it provoked were no mere pose. Pierre Andreu was a follower of Sorel, a historian with Raoul Girardet of these contemporary movements, a former member of Mendès France's LAURS, a friend of Marcel Péguy and the Black Sea mutineers, a disciple of Drieu la Rochelle and an editor on *La Lutte des jeunes*; and yet he voted communist. He was a typical case of that uncertainty and loss of direction that characterised the youth of this period, underlying their paradoxical collusions, deep friendships and all-pervading fanaticism.

The events of February 1934 put an end to these uncertainties. People had to decide where they stood. Many who had professed to reject society stood up and rejected fascism. It became obvious how impossible was Drieu's hope of an alliance of extremes, so left-wing intellectuals started to coalesce. The Association des Ecrivains et Artistes Révolutionnaires (AEAR) published *Commune*, which was founded in 1932 and continued right up to the war. Its contributors included Barbusse, Gide, Giono, Malraux, Chamson, Guéhenno, Nizan and a few stalwarts of the communist party. It was the real stronghold of the intellectual extreme left. Vaillant-Couturier imposed the party authority. To compete with it the ultra-left had its own organisation in 1935–6, Contre-Attaque, which included the surrealists and, led by Georges Bataille, the majority of Souvarine's former followers.

A rather different type from Mounier who chose to move to the left was Georges Valois. It is impossible to over-stress the importance of the Librairie Valois. Those who grew up in the thirties acquired most of their political, economic and social education, not to mention culture, from the many series and books published by the Librairie Valois. After the *Documents bleus* from the house of Gallimard and the *Documentaires* of Editions Kra, the Librairie Valois was, and still is, a remarkable symbol of the 'spirit of the thirties'. Here, as elsewhere, the birth of the Front Populaire was to bring about decisive changes, posing questions that had to be answered about the political attitudes of young intellectuals of whatever class, whose extremism, left or right, was as much aesthetic and moral affectation as political conviction.

20

6 February: day of crisis

The incompetence of the Union des Gauches

The firm hand of Tardieu was succeeded in 1932 by the feeble grasp of the left. The Union Nationale lost the elections of 1 and 8 May. In contrast to 1928 the radicals applied strict electoral discipline in the second round, and the communists were deserted by half their voters. The result, due to the discontents caused by the depression, gave the Union de Gauches 335 deputies and the right 230 deputies. Tardieu campaigned with great energy and was the big loser. Because of the *scrutin d'arrondissement*, the SFIO polled more votes than the radicals, but returned fewer deputies. The Union des Gauches was not like the Cartel des Gauches of 1924, but simply an alliance for electoral purposes. Herriot did not want to be at the mercy of the collectivists, and they, as we have seen, were divided on the question of joining the government. The parliamentary group of the SFIO presented the radicals with a minimum programme drawn up at the Salle Huyghens congress on 30 and 31 May. It was a moderate programme, but the radicals could not swallow a ban on the arms trade, the forty-hour week or the nationalisation of insurance and the railways. They wanted to run a centrist government.

Between the two ballots the President, Doumer, was murdered by a madman. In an atmosphere of general unity he was replaced by the president of the Senate, Albert Lebrun, an honourable but colourless character, who on 3 June invited Herriot, leader of the largest left-wing party in the Chamber, to form a government. Herriot formed his cabinet with radicals, members of the radical left (left of centre) and left-wing republicans (right of centre). The economic portfolios were allotted to people from the world of business and finance – Germain-Martin and Raymond Patenôtre. Tardieu resigned from the left-wing republican group and became the leader of all those on the right who were hostile to centrist coalitions. In spite of the support of the radicals and the Senate, Herriot's attempts at coalition were a partial failure, and he was forced to seek support from the SFIO deputies.

The radicals had no alternative economic or social policies to offer, but simply continued to apply, in a more drastic way, the unpopular and unsuccessful measures introduced by the Union Nationale. Socialist support, even with the help of an undisciplined section of the SFIO parliamentary group, could only be intermittent. It was during this period that the sarcastic remarks often made about radicals were most justified: 'election by the poor, government by the rich' and 'hearts on the left, wallets on the right'.

During the seven months of Herriot's ministry, the international situation deteriorated rapidly. The Lausanne conference in July 1932 reduced the amount of reparations due from Germany from thirty-seven billion francs to three, payable after a moratorium of three years. In fact this marked the end of the era of reparations. Germany, however, demanded additionally, as her price for continuing to negotiate, the recognition of her right to rearm. This was granted in principle in a joint declaration by France, Great Britain and Italy, thus ruining a vital part of the treaty of Versailles.

The government of the United States still insisted on the repayment of war debts, money borrowed, in their view, with no strings attached; and they had always refused to link them to reparations – in their view immoral distraints imposed by the victors on the vanquished. The French people were overwhelmingly of the opposite opinion. The Americans refused to accept postponement of the instalment due on 15 December 1932. Herriot chose to stake the existence of his ministry on making the payment, and was defeated in the Chamber on 14 December. This was inevitable, given the prevailing anti-American feeling. It has been suggested that, under the stress of trying to govern with such obviously inadequate support, he deliberately chose to be turned out, allowing himself to 'fall to the left'. His decision was not solely taken for this reason. He was clear-headed enough to foresee what disastrous consequences to national security could ensue from a break with America.

This setback was far from marking the end of Herriot's career, though he was never again to be prime minister. From 1934 to 1936, when he was elected president of the Chamber, he continued to wield considerable influence both in parliament and at the Elysée.

Between 14 December 1932 and 7 February 1934, there were five governments under radical or republican–socialist leadership: Paul-Boncour, Daladier, Albert Sarraut, Chautemps and Daladier. The first three were turned out because of their economic policy; the other two were victims of the Stavisky affair. Budgetary policy was carried on unchanged, a deflationary policy which simply perpetuated the depression, making the wage-earners, mainly civil servants, bear the brunt. During this period the ministry of finance was occupied by Chéron, former collaborator with Poincaré and Tardieu, then by Georges Bonnet, supported for the budget either by Lamoureux or Gardey or Marchandeau. All were supporters of strict economic orthodoxy, even Bonnet, who a few years earlier had been rather more daring. This repeated massacre of governments by the Chamber bore witness to an institutional crisis and executive impotence. Then to this crisis of democracy was added the threat to peace.

On 30 January 1933 Hitler became chancellor of the German Reich. Less than a month later the Reichstag fire consolidated his power. In October Germany withdrew from the Geneva conference on disarmament, and later from the League of Nations. The Japanese had already done this in March. These were grievous blows to collective security, and the end of Briand's policy for peace. Attempts to patch things up by diplomatic means were unsuccessful, although the Petite Entente, which gave France some Danubian allies, was reaffirmed. Mussolini was responsible for the Four Power pact between Germany, France, Great Britain and Italy, drawn up in Rome and intended to last for ten years. But one Italian alternative policy was incompatible with the previous policy. It had threatening implications for Poland and for France's small client states, since it involved territorial changes in favour of Germany and Italy. France never signed the pact, and it came to nothing. Hitler, however, while continuing to discuss rearmament with France, signed an agreement with Poland at the beginning of 1934, thus trumping a French card. The Poles, rather than depending on precarious support from France, were trying to divert German expansion elsewhere.

The failure of the world economic conference which took place in London between June and August 1933 showed how incapable the liberal nations were of co-operating in the fight against the depression. The New Deal seemed an incomprehensible monstrosity, while devaluations were crimes in the eyes of orthodox French economists. Roosevelt had scuppered the conference. The world economic crisis had now become a terrible indictment of all the values of a liberal society.

Street action

The hardships inflicted by the depression, and the absence of any cure that was not actually worse than the malady, caused increasing social unrest in the shape of demonstrations, often violent, and strikes, despite the growth of unemployment. In January 1933 textile workers in the Nord went on strike; in April it was the miners in the Nord and the Pas-de-Calais, farmhands in the Languedoc, and later engineering workers in Citroën in Paris. The miners staged a hunger march in December, and in the same year there were violent demonstrations by farmers. The Ligues, with their memberships swollen by the increased number of unemployed white-collar workers, were naturally very active, since their role was to win back on the streets the power the right had lost at the polls. But the employment situation made it possible to step up anti-parliamentary action considerably by summoning unemployed and tax-paying citizens alike to harass those incompetents of the Palais-Bourbon.

The deteriorating economic situation fuelled hatred of the Republic. In Paris, especially, the street became the battlefield between extreme left and extreme right. The police were far from neutral. Although many superin-tendents and inspectors, often radicals and Freemasons, disliked all troublemakers, Chiappe, the prefect of police, used the uniformed branch only against the left, while the radical ministers turned a blind eye. Hated by the masses, Chiappe was the idol of the well-to-do. His friends were those Parisian municipal councillors who took a leading part in anti-parliamentary action. He even got on well with the Action Française, handling them with tact. By means of preventive arrests among the extreme left, which was deeply infiltrated by informers, he managed to avert the sort of violence that had led to bloodshed in Berlin before 1933. One must give him credit for having no hesitation in saying which side he favoured. In 1930 he wrote: 'it is intolerable that young Frenchmen, whose political attachments are not my concern, but who belong to the nation's intellectual élite [presumably he meant student members of Action Française and Jeunesses Patriotes] should be beaten up and risk their lives in defence of the national cause'. Further on he makes it fairly clear whom he sees as his and their enemies in the following curious statement: 'the streets are meant for everybody, and we will never allow demonstrations to be staged there by professional rioters and the enemies of our country'. (See *Paroles d'ordre*, Paris, E. Figuière, 1930, pp. 190, 197.)

The Stavisky scandal brought new allies, the war veterans, to the side of the indignant rate-payers, small shopkeepers and unemployed in their fight against the Republic. Now that the inefficiency and muddle that had caused so much hardship was compounded by the disgrace of corruption, it was right and proper to call upon those living symbols of self-denial, self-sacrifice, heroism and honour – the war veterans. Naturally 'the fighting spirit' formed part of right-wing mystique. In fact quite a lot of ex-servicemen held left-wing, or extreme left-wing views, sometimes anti-militarist and anti-patriotic. They identified with characters in the novels of Henri Barbusse and Jean Bernier. It was just at this moment that the second wave of war literature was appearing with books by Gabriel Chevalier and André Thérive and translations of German novels by Remarque and von Unruh. The revulsion from bloodshed was reinforced by the films that portrayed it. According to Grenadou's memoirs, ex-servicemen living on the land, farmers, peasants, country schoolteachers hated war; and it was from this that grew that powerful spirit of uncon-ditional pacifism which ended in national capitulation. In the long term this was undoubtedly the most important group.

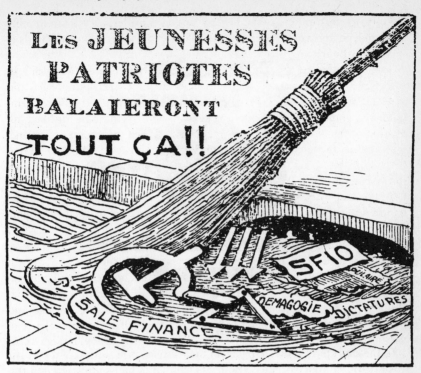

In the short term it was to pacifism that the electoral success of the SFIO was attributed by Georges Lefranc. Its campaign had simply ignored the depression, for which it had no solution, and concentrated on an anti-war campaign. 'Never again', said its posters.

The ex-servicemen mobilised by the Ligues and by the Croix-de-Feu belonged to the Union Nationale des Combattants (UNC), an extreme right-wing body. Fascism claimed to stand for the aspirations of the ex-servicemen, but this was totally fraudulent. There were just as many on the other side (communist or socialist). There were other bodies, too, that had no political colour and simply devoted themselves to acquiring material advantages, e.g. the war pensions established by Tardieu. But on 6 February the dynamism in the Ligues was provided by the old soldiers of fascist persuasion.

The Stavisky scandal

Since the time of the 'decorations', there had been plenty of scandals under the Third Republic. They were particularly numerous, doubly so one might say, between 1928 and 1932 during the Union Nationale ministry. Madame Hanau and *La Gazette du Franc* and the Oustric affair had been the principal ones. The latter more or less caused the fall of Tardieu's second ministry, three of whose ministers, including Chancellor Péret, were convicted of corruption. Other former ministers were also to appear before the Senate sitting as a supreme court, or before ordinary courts. These scandals revealed how the most dubious financial schemes could gain self-interested protection from the highest in the state. Legal action was not on these occasions exploited for political ends. To do so was not in the interests of the right, while the left could not sanction a campaign that might discredit the Republic. By comparison the Stavisky scandal was a minor affair. The parliamentary protectors of this swindler were obscure radical deputies, who were hardly known outside their constituencies. But the situation was different because this time the radicals were in power. This was the only reason why the affair caused such an unprecedented uproar.

Alexandre Stavisky, a Ukrainian Jew and naturalised French citizen, had brought off many frauds. Attempted prosecution had always failed due to the permissive attitude of the public prosecutor's office, which had allowed his bail to be renewed nineteen times. He led a flashy social life, moved in political circles and consorted with top figures in the police, including Chiappe. In December 1933 another of his frauds came to light, the case of the bonds of the Crédit Municipal de Bayonne. This body, started by the swindler, had issued bonds with a total face value of two hundred million francs, for Stavisky to pocket the proceeds. He disappeared, and his accomplices and front men, who included the deputy mayor of Bayonne, were arrested. On 9 January, the police, who had his Alpine hide-out under surveillance, announced that they had found him dying, by his own hand. This story was greeted with general disbelief.

On the same day Dalimier, colonial minister in Chautemps' cabinet, was forced to resign because, when he was minister of labour, he had put his name to a circular recommending the bonds. Up to this point the government had tried to keep the matter quiet and to treat it at a purely judicial level. This proved impossible, especially as a row broke out between Prince, a member magistrate in charge of the financial section of the public prosecutor's office, and his superior, the public prosecutor Pressard, who was Chautemps' brother-in-law.

In trying to make sense of these events there was just one point on which there was total agreement between left and right. The police were telling lies about Stavisky's death: he had not committed suicide; he had been killed to stop him talking. According to the left he would have compromised Chiappe and Prince, who was blamed by Pressard for blocking all earlier prosecutions. In the eyes of the right, Stavisky was a typical foreign Jewish financier mixed up with crooked parliamentarians and Freemasons. Chautemps and Pressard were high up in the Freemason hierarchy. It was Chautemps, therefore, who had given the order to kill Stavisky; and it was Pressard who had stopped Prince from prosecuting Stavisky. Then it was the Freemasons who abducted and murdered Prince, who on 24 February was found dead on a railway line. The left said he had committed suicide.

It is interesting to see how the extreme right managed to rally round all its old themes – anti-semitism (Madame Hanau and Oustric both conformed to the mythical Jewish type), xenophobia, anti-parliamentarianism, hatred of the Republic. In the Chamber the attack on the government was carried out by Philippe Henriot and Ybarnégaray, without success since the majority (radical and SFIO) combined and passed a vote of confidence against the right and the communists. But Chautemps was unable to survive the agitation whipped up by the so-called informed press (particularly *Paris-Soir*), by street demonstrations in Paris and by the revelation of yet another scandal, not connected with the Stavisky affair, but enough to cause the *Garde des sceaux* to resign under pressure from the Jeunes Radicaux and the socialists. Chautemps resigned on 27 January 1934.

6 February

Action Française was the moving force behind the revolt against parliament. On 7 January it issued a summons to the people of Paris to demonstrate in front of the Palais-Bourbon for the reopening of parliament on the 9th, to the cry of 'Down with the thieves!' On the 10th the Camelots du Roi held their first demonstration, but after that there were demonstrations every day – in the Boulevard Saint-Germain, Place de la Concorde, and on the main boulevards – with little interference from the police. The most serious, prior to 6 February, was on 27 January on the Boulevard des Italiens, the day on which Chautemps resigned.

On 29 January President Lebrun summoned Daladier, an honest man, supposedly brave and energetic, the leader of the Jeunes Radicaux. He formed a government just like the previous ones, stiffened, so he thought, by some members of the right, and with a dissident socialist, Eugène Frot, as minister of the interior. Chiappe, thanks to his connections with the extreme right, managed to help Daladier by getting a demonstration that had been announced by the Ligues for 4 February called off; but the left wanted to get rid of a prefect of police who was intimate with the right and was compromised by his friendship with the swindler Stavisky. He was replaced by Bonnefoy-Sibour, but he refused the post of resident in Morocco. This resulted in the resignation of the right-wing members of the cabinet, while the municipal councillors of Paris, who were hand in glove with the Ligues, called for a demonstration with the Union Nationale des Combattants on 6 February, the day the new cabinet appeared before the Chamber. The Association Républicaine des Anciens Combattants (communist) decided to mobilise on the same day against 'the regime of profiteering and scandal', and to demand Chiappe's arrest

Daladier, backed by Blum, easily won a vote of confidence in the

Chamber at 8 o'clock on the evening of 6 February. Against the opposition of Tardieu, who called for the government's resignation, he appealed for a union in support of the Republic. But by now the Palais-Bourbon was beleaguered. The Union Nationale des Combattants, Solidarité Française, Jeunesses Patriotes, Camelots du Roi and the Association Républicaine des Anciens Combattants were converging on the Place de la Concorde. The Croix-de Feu were advancing through the Faubourg Saint-Germain. Shots were exchanged between 7 o'clock and midnight. The rioters used every sort of missile and slashed the legs of police horses with razor blades. The Gardes Mobiles held firm on the Pont de la Concorde. The thin screen of police guarding the Chamber on the left bank would almost certainly have been forced back if de la Rocque had not called off the attack by the Croix-de-Feu. There were fifteen dead and more than two thousand wounded. On the morning of the 7th several of the riot leaders were arrested. However, not only the right-wing press but even the big dailies attacked the 'government of assassins', and Daladier, despite the vote of confidence of the previous evening, resigned towards noon. The magistrates and other top officials refused to carry out the government's disciplinary measures. Herriot, who was then the official head of the prime minister's own party, also refused to co-operate. A majority of ministers pressed for the government's resignation.

A historian of the Year II of the French Revolution, General Herlaut at the time commanded a tank regiment near the capital. He later stated that he had telephoned Daladier during the night offering to move on Paris. Daladier could not govern with only the socialists to support him, so he had to capitulate. It was the first time in the Republic's history that a cabinet had yielded to street disturbances.

Colonel de la Rocque was responsible for the failure of the coup. Perhaps he was unwilling to pull other people's chestnuts out of the fire. Historians in general have not seen 6 February as a fascist *putsch*, but simply as a display of anger against parliamentary corruption and inefficiency. This was certainly the case with the rank and file of the marchers, though it is undeniable that they willingly followed their leaders, the municipal councillors of Paris. The councillors' reputation was pretty shady, as shown in Pagnol's best-known play, at this date only six years old; and many of them made no secret of their admiration for Hitler and Mussolini. The Republic would hardly have survived a successful attack on the Palais-Bourbon; but there were too many different subversive groups, and they were too weak and lacking in genuine popular support to set up a fascist state. Moreover there was too much rivalry between the power seekers – the financial backers like Coty and Mercier, and the men of action like Taittinger, de la Rocque, Renaud Jean and others. No single insurrectionary party existed as in Italy and Germany.

The moment the right was back in power under the auspices of the former President of the Republic, Doumergue, summoned by Lebrun to be the saviour of his country, the Ligues melted away and the press changed its tune. In the evening of 7 February the area bounded by the Place de la Concorde, the Etoile and the Madeleine was closed and put under strict police control. Anyone found in the street between 8 o'clock and midnight was roughly handled by the police. There were many wounded and one or two more deaths. This time demonstrators or bystanders of the previous day who returned to the scene, but not as organised marchers, were described by *Paris-Soir* as 'criminals come in from the suburbs'. Only the day before the same paper printed a picture of a woman and a police officer with the caption: 'A foreign lady congratulates an officer of the Garde Mobile.'

One sentence explains the curious reversal – Tardieu was back in power as minister under the nominal premiership of Doumergue ('beaming Gastounet'). During the day of 6 February, Tardieu had unsuccessfully called for the capitulation of the Chamber while it was being besieged from the streets. Daladier's resignation had given it to him, reversing his defeat of the previous day. It was not surprising that the Ligues should be dissolved by the man who had backed them with secret funds in 1932. This was in fact their traditional role: in winning back for the right the power it had lost in the elections, they had fulfilled their mission. On 7 February Tardieu regained what he had lost in 1932. What he failed to realise was that the left had seen in the rising the mirror image of German and Italian fascism, and was frightened. At directing staff level its reactions on 6 and 12 February were totally unorganised, but the ranks understood at once that the menace of fascism obliged all those it threatened to unite. Whether or not the rising of 6 February was a fascist *putsch*, its historic role was to have prepared the way psychologically for the anti-fascist Front Populaire.

PART IV

France in the thirties: change and stability

21

The population

The general trend

The population – between forty-one and forty-two million – changed remarkably little during the last years of the Republic. It increased by 72,000 between the 1931 and the 1936 census. The density of seventy-six people per square kilometre was far lower than in the other industrialised European countries. The birth-rate was low, but not as low as some others, perhaps because there were still a few rural strongholds sticking to Catholic traditions, which, as Philippe Ariès has shown, had a braking effect on the general downward trend. This higher rate was not reflected in the annual number of births, which was always less than 620,000 in the period. The old influence of Malthusianism and the casualties of the First World War had a cumulative effect. In 1936 there were 180 children per hundred families, in comparison with 197 in 1911 and 182 in 1926. There were fewer families without any children (228 per thousand) than in 1926 (233 per thousand). This last figure undoubtedly reflects the slaughter of the only sons of peasant families between 1914 and 1918.

The growth of the secondary and tertiary sectors at the expense of agriculture may have affected the birth-rate. Whether he was acquiring middle-class tastes through a rising standard of living, or simply because he was unemployed, the urban working man had fewer children than some of the country folk of western or central France.

It is impossible to calculate the effect of the depression because it is indistinguishable from the much more serious effect of the war. However, the falling off in the number of marriages can be attributed to it – for how can one marry if one has no job? The decline in the birth-rate coincided with the arrival of the 'hollow groups' in the population pyramid at the age of fecundity. As in other countries the mortality rate fell, and was not affected by the depression, so that increased longevity made for an older population. Correspondingly, the social charge on the state per adult was never so low, for there was no increase in the number of children.

After 1935 deaths exceeded births every year, and the shortfall grew from 18,000 in 1935 to 35,000 in 1938. In 1939 there were more deaths than births in sixty departments. At this rate the French population seemed doomed to extinction before 1980, or so it was said by those who demanded measures to encourage procreation, ignoring the possible effects of immigration. This had been discontinued during the depression, but for the previous thirty years it had been the one factor that offset the fall in the native population. This demographic weakness was the most important factor in the history of the period and outweighed all others. There was a slight increase in 1936, and between 1938 and 1939 the birth-rate started to rise again. Was it the result of legislation, i.e. tax reliefs and increased family allowances for wage-earners in 1932, extended to small farmers in 1938 and the entire working population in 1939? Or was it, as Sauvy suggests, the result of much heavier penalties for abortion? If the latter, it would be the only time such penalties had ever been effective! A more likely explanation is that the rather large number of children born in 1919 and 1920 had succeeded the 'hollow groups' and had arrived at the age of procreation. What still needs explaining is why this upsurge in the birth-rate, though it could not take immediate effect, should have been destined to last. One can hardly expect to find specifically French causes for a universally observed phenomenon.

However, the Front Populaire seems to have had a beneficial effect. It was after 1936 that the gross rate of fecundity, though distorted by the low birth-rate of the 'hollow groups', actually increased. Perhaps the working class felt a slight lessening of the worries of everyday life. All the same the death-rate, though getting lower, was not low enough to make up the deficit. The age of the population should suffice to explain this. But, at every age level, masculine mortality was higher in France than in any other industrialised country. Widespread tuberculosis claimed many victims, so did alcoholism, especially in Brittany and Normandy. This catastrophic situation was a prime cause of economic decline, political and intellectual decay, and military weakness. 'Frenchmen are getting scarce', remarked Jean Giraudoux. In 1936 only 31 per cent were less than twenty years old, and about 15 per cent were over sixty. Conservatism was thereby reinforced.

When the 'hollow groups' grew up, the working population inevitably decreased: 52.4 per cent of the total in 1931, 49.2 per cent in 1936, 20,300,000 in all, of whom 7,300,000 were women. The latter tended increasingly to take up work in trade, the liberal professions and the public sector. But they were up against public opinion as well as unemployment, and although there were many war widows at work who had not remarried, the number of working women fell continuously. The exception was the tertiary sector where there was an increase.

Agriculture was carried on by an older workforce because of the departure of the young to the towns; but there was a rejuvenation of farming thanks to modern methods. The case of Picardy shows that the departure of young workers and craftsmen between the wars only affected the overpopulated regions, resulting in a more evenly spread population, perfectly adapted for efficient land utilisation. Only technical backwardness could prevent the countryside from benefiting from depopulation.

Philippe Ariès reckons that the fertility rate remained stable in the traditional middle class and in the rich farming regions. In the Beauce the eldest son inherited the farm, while the three or four other children, boys or girls, were set up with *dots* as tenants in farms of equal value, where all that had to be provided was the rent and enough working capital. Things were very different in Aquitaine, as described by Lagardelle (*Sud-Ouest*, Paris, Librairie Valois, 1929), where the sharecropper could acquire his little property as a going concern without ever ceasing to be poverty-stricken. In such areas the birth-rate continued to fall.

All this goes to show that demographically, as in other respects too, France was a country of very marked contrasts. But the overall impression remains that only immigration could compensate for the decline in population caused by war, the Malthusian tradition and national demoralisation.

The foreigners

Immigrant labour was essential to the economy, but many of the young unmarried workers sent their earnings back home, which was bad for the balance of payments. Foreigners had a higher birth-rate than the French, even those who became naturalised. However, because of the depression and the measures taken in 1932 to protect the jobs of French nationals, the proportion of foreigners in the population fell steadily in the last ten years of the Third Republic. They were very numerous in 1931, in all 2,900,000, of whom about two-thirds were in employment. As evidence of French prosperity, in contrast with stagnation elsewhere, immigration increased after 1927. But by 1936 their number had fallen to 2,200,000 and went on falling, in spite of the dire conditions in central Europe. Between the two censuses, the number of those actively employed fell by 700,000. This decline partly resulted from the depression, but also helped to prolong it, for the key industries, such as mining and building, became short of labour on their departure. In any industry the foreigner is the first to be made redundant. Then came the threat of war. The large number who acquired French citizenship obviously diminished the official figures for foreigners. Between 1931 and 1936, 155,000 were naturalised, the total of those naturalised by 1936 being 517,000 – 125 per 1,000 inhabitants – of whom 100,000 had been born in France, and 160,000 were Italian born. In 1928 55 per cent of the men conscripted in Hyères were Italian born, and 65 per cent in Massigny (Meurthe-et-Moselle). Some were reluctant to take

French citizenship through apprehension about military service for their children, assimilated though they would be both by education and egalitarian social laws that benefited the foreign worker. The Polish and Italian clergy did their utmost to impede this process of assimilation which was generally fairly rapid, though it varied inversely with their numbers in the locality and the character of their work. Down on the farm Gallicisation for the Poles was faster than in the mines. A consequence of the huge number of war dead was numerous mixed marriages, which greatly speeded up the process of assimilation. In 1936, there were 720,000 Italians (33 per cent), 425,000 Poles, 255,000 Spaniards and 195,000 Belgians. The greatest concentrations of foreigners were in the Paris region, the Mediterranean coastlands, the Belgian frontier and the industrial regions of the east.

Belgians and Spaniards mostly worked on the land, Poles and Italians in the basic industries. When the political situation worsened, an exodus began, mainly of Italians and Germans. Rates of pay were very little affected, since competition was minimal, and French workmen were remarkably tolerant, except in one or two places where clashes occurred because of a surplus of manpower (e.g. with Italians on building sites in Brittany). However the depression brought xenophobia and racialism among the lower middle classes, technicians and workers in hotels, restaurants and show business. These feelings were encouraged by German and Italian propagandists, professional or otherwise, who found plenty of channels through which to give expression to them. Traditional French liberalism succumbed to economic stringency, while a debilitated people might well feel some unease before such a large peaceful invasion.

Population patterns

The working population had indeed diminished. In 1936 it amounted to 19,400,000. The three sectors of the economy – primary, secondary and tertiary – employed, respectively, 37 per cent, 32 per cent and 31 per cent of the population. The proportion of town and country dwellers remained fairly stable. The depression had brought the rural exodus to an abrupt halt, with some returning who had only just left. But the Front Populaire restarted the rush to the towns because of the social advantages enjoyed by industrial workers and the increase of jobs in nationalised industries. Hence the growth of the towns. In 1936 there were twenty with over 100,000 inhabitants, as opposed to seventeen in 1920. Fifty-three had over 50,000 inhabitants. The big cities grew most, except Paris itself; but the Paris conurbation became enormous. There was a huge difference between this overpopulated region and the 'French desert'. This sort of situation could lead to serious demographic and hence social imbalance. The north, north-west and north-east regions, being very much alive, were fairly stable demographically, as were the backward parts of the

Massif Central. Things were very different in the Midi and especially in the south-west, which suffered from age-old weaknesses.

At this time not many people were interested in population questions. The appearance of stability and the slow rate of change, combined with a certain fatalism, all helped to distract the minds of politicians from the gravity of a situation that was leading France to a state of decrepitude. Actually there were two Frances, one alive and kicking, the other asleep. The maps of birth-rate, of population, of agricultural output were not totally coincident, but overlapped to a considerable degree, and showed up the differences between north and south. The north and north-east were densely populated and had a high birth-rate. The Midi and the south-west were thinly populated and underdeveloped. The birth-rate was low in the Paris conurbation, but the population density was high owing to a constant influx of the surplus from regions with a high birth-rate and little industry. Such were Brittany and the more backward parts of the Massif Central. The fact that the rural exodus was so long delayed explains this illusory equilibrium and the extraordinary political influence exerted by the most retrograde areas. There was a powerful school of thought, including most teachers, which glorified the balance and variety of French productiveness, agriculture and industry contributing equally to the national income. The ancient tradition persisted, keeping home industries in the Vosges, the Vimeu and the Cambrésis and giving French products their wonderful finish. This patriotic ecstasy over a beautifully balanced national economy was based on an illusion. Flanders and the plains of the Paris basin, the industries of the north and east were paying heavily to support a 'douce France' and a picturesque countryside with its unproductive inhabitants.

22

Aspects of rural life

The rural population, which was slowly declining, still amounted to almost half the country's total and provided one-third of its workforce. But it only produced one-quarter of the revenue, its share falling from forty-three billion francs in 1928 to 18.5 billion francs in 1935. Agriculture played a major role in the economy, far more so than in any other industrialised European state. Because of the massive size of the rural electorate and the influence of the farming interests that claimed to represent it, agriculture was carefully cherished by governments, particularly by the Senate. The combined result of traditional Malthusian habits and the slump in farm prices was that French yields increased absurdly slowly in comparison with England, Germany, Belgium and Scandinavia. The productivity rate, because of the huge number of small family holdings, was even worse.

On the whole, peasant incomes were badly hit after 1931. By 1935 they had probably fallen by about one-third, for the prices of farm produce had fallen far more than had the cost of fertilisers, while the cost of farm machinery had hardly changed. Of course, small and unprofitable farms began to be squeezed out, to the advantage of medium-sized ones. Large landowners were also hit by heavy costs, aggravated by the slump and the fall in receipts from let property. The medium-sized estates benefited from the flight from the countryside and other difficulties. A further trouble was the Colorado beetle which in 1930 affected eighteen departments and by 1939 had spread throughout France. This also contributed to the fall in farm incomes, though it was not as catastrophic as the phylloxera sixty years earlier.

The peasants

Most peasants owned their land, especially in the poorest regions, and they were sometimes very sad cases. Their mentality was very old-fashioned, characterised by deep attachment to the soil, soil which up to the war had kept them often in poverty, and in any case yielded all too little income. There were about two million of these rural artisans, working their family holdings, owned or rented; or five million, if families and hired labour are included. The paid hands of these small concerns, themselves often owning small plots, nourished hopes of one day setting up on their own in a small way, and so shared the mentality of their employer. They could not be said to form a proletariat. The absence of a managerial class and of any technical training ensured an unchanging way of life. Mechanisation promised a better future, and the obstacle in its path was not so much these traditional methods of working as the multiplicity of small and scattered holdings belonging to individual proprietors.

In regions where small farmers followed in the wake of the large operators, they learnt to adapt and enrich themselves by a complete change in their way of life. The single-crop agriculture of the Bas Languedoc, the Loire valley and the plains of the lower Rhône was managed as a series of purely commercial projects. Between 1930 and 1940 these areas were entirely given up to fruit growing. No region was to suffer so much from food rationing as the wine-growers of the Languedoc. The surge of exports of fruit and vegetables to Great Britain from the 'French California' showed that the peasant was not always incapable of finding outlets for his produce.

One cannot put much faith in statistics or figures of average earnings in trying to find out if the lot of the small peasant was improved or worsened in this period, and if peasant unrest was more acute than general unrest or just one aspect of it. One can only conclude that there were wide disparities. What did occur during the depression of the thirties was the development of a group consciousness that was prepared to exert pressure on the state through the agrarian parties. The people behind these parties, however, had very different social affiliations and, whether fascists or monarchists, were enemies of the Republic. Their leaders were townsfolk who had little idea of what peasant life was like and had stepped into the shoes of the landowning upper middle class now reduced to a few property owners, decayed gentlefolk living in their Aquitaine villages on the revenue from one or two small farms. Typical of their successors were doctors and *notaires*. The local vet and either the priest or the schoolmaster, depending on the region, still retained their influence. It was towards 1930 that the break with old traditions began. In some areas the co-operative movement, the trade unionism of the Confédération Nationale Paysanne (CNP), founded by Calveyrac in 1933, and the Jeunesse Agricole Catholique (JAC) threw up young leaders who later on became of some importance. Communism and socialism took root in places where there was an old-established radical tradition, and genuine men of the soil were elected, such as Renaud Jean and Waldeck Rochet. One of the youngest socialist deputies elected in 1936 was Tanguy-Prigent, a small farmer from the Finistère. After the Liberation he was the first peasant ever to become minister of agriculture.

The farmers

Sixty per cent of all land consisted of large farms, either rented, or, less often, owner-occupied. They were worked by half a million farmers or farm managers. The riots in Chartres in January 1933 showed that agriculture was suffering from a slump, but certainly not as seriously as was made out. Grenadou's memoirs (*Grenadou, paysan français*), even allowing for a few errors, show that farmers were just as ignorant of economics as everybody else.

In fact the big farmers lived comfortably and well. Their economic initiative was on a par with their demographic drive, which we have already noted. There was a capitalist mentality not unlike that of the city businessmen; yet the image that the farmer from the Beauce liked to project, namely that of a gambler, still derived specifically from the land. To decide whether or not to fetch in a crop on a particular day is to bet, just as much as winning or losing a flock of sheep in a game of cards to enliven a dull train journey. Between 1930 and 1940 the large-scale agriculturalist was certainly much nearer his American opposite number in outlook than was any other sector of the French economy.

The social and economic behaviour of the big farmer was radically different from that of the 'Malthusian' peasant, with whom rural myth sometimes lumped him. His productivity and his income were on a level with any in the rest of Europe. His standard of living rivalled that of the urban middle class. Because of the mileage he had to cover on his lands, and for appearances' sake, he always had a fairly expensive car, which he frequently changed. He belonged to the local farmers' union, the Syndicat Agricole de l'Eure-et-Loir, and would not have had much schooling, but his children went to a *lycée*, usually up to the age of sixteen, going no further than the school-leaving exam. This general education was finished off with a 'winter course' in agriculture organised locally. The next generation, after the war, went to the Institut Agronomique.

The Beauce farmer worked between 250 and 500 acres, most of which was not his own property; but the amount of capital he deployed was equivalent at this period to about half the value of the land. He employed a fairly large seasonal labour force, a genuine proletariat with mental processes similar to those of their urban brethren. They were unionised, having fought for and won a better standard of living, becoming consumers of meat and coffee. The mechanisation of large-scale farming and the introduction of the forty-hour week tended to make the threshing-hand a creature of the past. Nevertheless, in 1936 the Senate, which had slumbered through the wave of strikes in June, suddenly woke up, as if for a life-and-death struggle, when the farm labour of the Paris basin decided to join in. Fear of the distributionists still lived on, even after the absorption into industry of the surplus rural population. Alongside this wage-earning class there existed another with a life-style verging on that of the small farmer. These were the skilled workmen, such as carters, shepherds and cowmen, working in close association with their employers, at least in the Beauce. In Brie and the northern part of the Paris basin, where farming was on a much larger scale, they were separated from their employers by a protective screen of bailiffs or foremen.

It is widely believed that social advancement could only be achieved in a town. The idea was plausible and, though certainly true of regions of small-scale farming, it was much less so on the alluvial plains of the Paris basin. Grenadou's father was a 'haricotier', a bean-grower, who farmed a few acres in the valley. The son, who started with nothing, became 'someone', with at least 250 acres on the plain. One of the basic conditions for rising in life was not to be among the very poor, to have some small means to get started with or to get the highest wage in one's own activity. Grenadou was a carter; he was ambitious and hardworking. All through the depression, farm rents and the price of land were low; and people were not investing very heavily in either fertilisers or machinery. A slight indebtedness could be paid off in a few years. Grenadou managed to take advantage of the depression of the thirties and, without realising it, repeated the family success of his deputy, Triballet, whom he admired. Triballet's grandfather, a tobacconist, had managed to beat the 'great depression' of those days by taking advantage of the fall in land values.

Politically, the Syndicat Agricole de l'Eure-et-Loir, which largely consisted of this sort of person, ran the department. Unlike the peasants, who were nearly always represented by strangers, the Beauce farmers between the two wars always (except in 1919) elected local colleagues to the Chamber and the Senate. The only exception was Violette, whose career went back to pre-war days.

The agrarian technocrat Ricard, a former minister of agriculture in the cabinets of Millerand and Leygues, lost his seat in the Senate in 1922 to Bouvart, a farmer. Triballet had been elected to the Chamber in 1924 and made no great impression there. After 1930 he made himself felt both in committee and in debates. He proposed and won the adoption of a minimum price for wheat in 1933, and he was one of the creators of the Office du Blé in 1936. His career, however, demonstrates how hard it was for the farming middle class, with its taint of peasantry, to be accepted in political circles. The republican socialist Triballet never rose to be a minister in either radical or socialist governments, as were Quenille and Monnet, fluent speakers from liberal professions. And it was the lawyer Violette who in the Eure-et-Loir led the left, and not one of the parliamentary farmers.

Regional contrasts

There is a discrepancy between what we have said above and the apparent existence during the thirties of a contrast between regions of small-scale cultivation like Aquitaine, where 'farming doesn't pay' and where the peasant proprietor could only make a living because contraception and rural depopulation left him with fewer mouths to feed, and those parts of the Paris basin where massive productivity saved the farmer any worry about providing for a large family. These great differences in attitude to family and finance coexisted with similarities of behaviour imposed by nature and by long-established traditional customs.

Family life everywhere was still very close and much more extended than in the towns. There were still some extraordinary survivals such as the daughter's primogeniture remarked by Strabo in the Barèges district of the Pyrénées and still existing in 1940. People were living longer, and longevity in heads of farming families made some impatient sons head for the towns. In some places there were communities of old men whose sons had died on the Marne or at Verdun. The head of the family, who ran the farm, still had great authority, and it was only in war-time that the farmer's wife took over. On very small farms his status might be somewhat diminished by the earnings of the poultry run, which went into the wife's purse; hence, in the country, an ex-serviceman's modest pension could mean a lot for a man.

However, this world was now educated, thanks to primary education, extended in more prosperous regions by complementary courses in agriculture, by the higher primary schools, colleges, *lycées* or religious establishments. Basic education to the age of fourteen was the same in town and country; and the only illiterates were a few old people born under the Second Empire. The level of culture was much the same as in the towns. Typical reading matter would be *L'Almanach Vermot, Le Chasseur français, Le Catalogue de la manufacture de Saint-Etienne*. Different regions had different local newspapers, departmental gazettes and a different religious atmosphere: *Le Pèlerin* and other such publications in Catholic areas, little evangelical tracts in Protestant ones.

Folk customs, not yet cheapened by tourism or commercial exploitation, still survived, even in the most developed regions. In Beauce, less than ten kilometres from Chartres, lovers were still in 1940 fixing a symbolic green branch, 'le mai', in their sweetheart's window on the eve of May Day. On the local feast day the mobile dance hall would arrive, with its booth and polished floor. At Easter the family would open the doors and windows of the house built thirty years earlier for the lad who never returned from the front – but for less than two days, so as not to pay any rates.

Keeping up old customs did not stop town and country getting closer to each other, where food, clothing and speech were concerned. But, although France was supplied with electricity in the period, the rural household was totally devoid of comfort and the peasant's home was often a slum. This was why towns appealed to young women and the main reason why they wanted to leave the country. The peasants probably ate better during the depression, but they were very badly housed. Increased uniformity meant that the countryman's visits to the local town became less frequent than they had been before 1914. Fairs and markets began to die out. But the town came to him via the travelling salesman, often with a van, and the touring cinema, while the voice of Paris was transmitted by radio.

In contrast to these aspects of rural life which varied but little from place to place, there was a great diversity of political and religious convictions. Between the wars, most of the rural population were practising Christians in the Nord, the Pas-de-Calais, the Caux region, Brittany, Alsace and Lorraine, in the mountainous eastern parts, in most of the Massif Central and in the Pyrenean west. We have already remarked on the fact that there were unexpectedly fewer births than formerly. But the birth-rate remained fairly high and the traditional overpopulation of the most impoverished regions caused a migration into the left-wing suburbs; and paradoxically Brittany's penetration by communism started from within.

The rest of rural France was either unconcerned or hostile to government – red since 1848 or won over since 1875 by the radical co-operative movement, and even, in the west of the Massif Central, by a sort of communism which really stood for the jealousy of the 'have-nots' for the 'haves'. Anti-clericalism was common to all areas where there were rich and poor. Grenadou, a violent anti-militarist, also loathed country priests; and in this he was typical of the well-to-do farmers of the Syndicat Agricole de l'Eure-et-Loir.

Rural France between the wars displayed the uniformity and variety of an archipelago, with some islands rich and full of life, and other apathetic or still bleeding from the carnage of 1914. On the whole, in spite of their lamentations, the farmers' lot had improved. The war had wiped out their indebtedness; their standard of living, though still lower than that of townsfolk, had risen and their general status had improved. The state, whether personified by a Tardieu, a Queuille or a Monnet, in spite of clumsiness and some incompetence, was always devoted to their interests and gave them priority treatment.

23

Urban society

The workers

The urban population had just become the majority in France – 51 per cent in 1931 and 52.5 per cent in 1936. The workers formed the largest group. Yet between the wars the total number in industry had increased by less than those in trade or the public services. Only the workforce in technologically advanced industries such as chemicals, engineering and the metal industries had grown, whereas in the traditional industries and especially textiles, it had shrunk. The technicians, the managers and the clerical staff had come to matter most in the actual running of industrial businesses and were therefore increasing in numbers more rapidly than those on the shop-floor.

The working conditions of the employee in large-scale industry were considered appalling by those who had been at work before the days of the production line. Their indignation, put across in films like *A nous la liberté* or *Modern Times* appealed to the public conscience of the time and served to justify a corporatist reaction as well as to provide a motive for social revolution. What they complained of was certainly true, but what was equally true was that production was raised to unprecedented heights. Mass production did not prevent the efficient worker on piece-work from getting ahead of his schedule, which would have been impossible later.

The worker was manipulated most on the human relations side. The tyranny of the timekeeper and of management affected him socially and morally more than economically. The heads of large industries tried to boost their skilled workers' and technicians' pride at the expense of those who worked with their hands. Among these there was a strictly maintained ranking order, from the floor sweeper to the unskilled operator up to the highly qualified. Factory society was very like army life, with all its varieties of paternalism, pleasant and unpleasant. It involved strict discipline, meticulous timekeeping, a ban on smoking and no slackening of pace. In the larger factories, a well-organised spying system saw to it that any trade-union official, any militant socialist or communist, any reader of a left-wing newspaper, however moderate, was sacked as soon as he was found out. It was as unwise to bring *L'Oeuvre* into the Citroën works as it would have been to bring it into an army barracks, even in the days of radical governments, whose views the paper closely reflected.

In contrast, working conditions in the smaller industries were as they always had been, generally free and easy. This was true even of the small modern workshops, which had revitalised the towns and to which work from the large firms, especially in various kinds of metal-working, was contracted out. But, with oppression on one side and friendliness on the other, neither provided an opening for the intrusion of trade unionism, even after 1930.

Class divisions were much wider than thirty or forty years later. The manual worker was isolated from the rest of the nation, and the very small-scale employer's way of life hardly differed from that of the working class, which accounted for the latter's variegated character. But the militants were probably less isolated than those of the CGT before 1914, and class-consciousness was more widespread. Undoubtedly, between 1931 and 1939, life was hard for the French working man.

It has been calculated that the average earnings of the French working class were less hurt by the depression and less helped by the Front Populaire than was once thought. They remained almost unchanged, falling by about 15 per cent between 1930 and 1935, then rising by about the same amount with the easing of unemployment. The family budget of the Parisian working man (1930–9) shows a rather low standard of living but a development in the style of living. The amount spent on food fell, though less than in the rest of the industrialised Europe, because, recently, people had been eating less bread and more animal products – a change common to all classes. There was a general increase in the consumption of meat, wine, eggs, butter and tobacco. Sugar was no longer a luxury and had become a normal part of the working man's diet with cocoa, cake and jam. Far more oranges, lemons and bananas were being eaten; twice as many as in the preceding decade.

The proportion spent on rent, as in all classes, was not high, and less was spent on clothing. But there was a marked increase in miscellaneous expenditure, mostly personal: the new-fangled 'perm'; visits to the doctor; transport; bicycles; motorbikes; the occasional second-hand car, more commonly indulged in by the young mechanic than the peasant. More was spent on travel, largely thanks to holidays with pay. People spent more on reading, various subscriptions, amusements and, of course, the ever-increasing taxes. New sorts of needs and demands on the purse arose, e.g. radios and children's toys; and most of this was the result of the Front Populaire. Up till then the only pleasures had been a Saturday night visit to the cinema or a Sunday outing to the Bois de Boulogne or the banks of the Marne. But there was not much change for the better since food and

Working-class family budget, Paris, 1930–7 (percentages)

	1930: Typical working-class budget (4 in family)	1936–7: Budget of 4 working-class families (average 5 in family, all women at work)
Food and drink	60	52
Rent	10	7
Miscellaneous expenses	10	23
Heat and light	5	7
Clothes	15	11

Source: After A. Sauvy and M. Halbwachs, 'De la France d'avant-guerre à la France d'aujourd'hui', *Revue d'économie politique*, January–February 1939; and M. Auffret, *La France de l'entre-deux-guerres, 1919–1939*.

clothing still bore too heavily on the budget, while the very small proportion devoted to rent merely reflected the vast number of run-down slum dwellings which their owners, ruined by inflation, no longer bothered to maintain. Town-planning hardly existed, and there were dozens of unhealthy pockets in old Paris and Lille, with the result that city centres became depopulated while suburbs flourished between 1920 and 1930. At the same time there were increasing numbers of poor living in places without services and often liable to flooding. After 1930, as a result of the Loucheur law, efforts were made to remedy this situation. Town councils built HBM (*habitations à bon marché*), building estates for workers in concrete or brick. But the apartment blocks erected on the sites of the old fortifications of Paris were too expensive for the working man, and on the surrounding waste ground there developed 'la zone', a slum belt even more squalid than the slums of the centre.

Workers were outraged by working conditions that their children were to find quite tolerable, but they put up with housing conditions that no other industrialised country would tolerate, unequalled even by Poplar or Whitechapel. In such circumstances, for right-wing thinkers to complain about the 'self-indulgence of the working class', much encouraged by the Front Populaire, was rather absurd. What probably annoyed them was the spectacle of the young working man giving up his cloth cap and dressing just like them, and his wife doing the same; so unlike their parents.

The middle class
The term 'bourgeoisie' covers such a variety of living standards that it is hard to avoid providing a collection of vague generalisations. Any attempt to match the working-class budgets, shown above, with one for the well-to-do bourgeoisie will reveal enormous differences.

Bourgeois family budget, Paris 1919–39 (percentages)

Food and drink	21.5			
Housing	9.8			
Clothes	8.5			
Miscellaneous expenses	60.2	*including*	Children	4.9
			Wages	7.2
			House	6.7
			Taxes	8.0
			Various	33.4

Source: After M. Perrot, *Le Mode de vie des familles bourgeoises.*

The low percentage for food and drink and the high one for miscellaneous expenses (which include heating and lighting) underline the great difference in living standards. Before 1914 taxes and servants' wages were even lower. This was a specifically French situation – low rents and low taxes. The budget shown above is based on a collection of averages and only gives a very rough idea of the differences between the standards.

The bourgeoisie included the 'new poor', people living on small fixed incomes or rented property, as well as the modern technician who was on his way up and the old one who was on his way down because of industrial concentration. The 'Roubaix tailors' could produce a suit of clothes for five hundred francs, while the bespoke tailor had to charge at least 1,500 francs. Changes in linen underwear had put the little sempstress and the small city workshop out of business.

These victims of economic and technical change were joined by those hit by changes in personal habits. The small manufacturer of curling irons was ruined by the invention of the 'perm'. But, from this large group of impoverished *petite bourgeoisie*, the small shopkeeper emerged successfully. Between the wars there was a great increase in the retail trade, and during the depression the small shopkeepers were favoured by the government at the expense of the big firms, just as were the peasants. They were a class that made money and rose in the social scale; through it one could aspire to the middle and upper ranks of the bourgeoisie. The vast expansion of this intermediate social group was a burden on the economy and depressed the wage-earner's standard of living; but it was good for the middle classes. The government looked after them because the small shop was a bastion against socialism and communism, and, if this group were neglected, its hatred of the state could make it a breeding ground for fascism.

The higher strata of the middle class consisted of owners of businesses, civil servants, magistrates and members of the liberal professions. The thirties saw a considerable change in this last category. Since the nineteenth century, and even before, medicine had been a hazardous occupation.

Except where there was a real vocation or a family tradition, only people of rather mediocre attainments had gone in for it. For the last hundred and fifty years, the leaders of revolution had been lawyers without briefs and doctors without patients. Social insurance transformed the medical profession, which immediately became risk free. But it thereby also abolished treatment as a form of charity, the basis of many a political career.

At the top of the bourgeoisie were the 'two hundred families'. First, 'la Haute Banque', represented by the Vernes, the Mallets, the Rothschilds, who until 1936 occupied the directorships of the Banque de France. Next were the great industrialists whose wealth dated back to the eighteenth century – the Peugeots, de Wendels or, from the nineteenth century, the Schneiders. Beside these old, powerful families there were several parvenus, who sometimes failed to keep up and went bankrupt – like the Citroëns.

These families controlled all the big firms, and through the Banque de France, of which they were directors, they dominated the government and the administrative civil service. The most important bodies of the latter – the Conseil d'Etat, the treasury, the foreign office – they managed to pack with their most brilliant dependants. They played a less conspicuous part on the political scene than in the nineteenth century, having abandoned the Chamber; but they maintained their power in the Senate and, up to 1936, bore entire responsibility for the economic and monetary policies of successive governments, which they controlled through the Banque de France, the administrative services and the press.

The nobility

This class presents a rather similar picture to that of the bourgeoisie. The constant assumption of unwarranted titles assured their continued existence. There were not more than four thousand families of genuinely noble descent, but ten times as many who had pretensions to it. This period of the Third Republic was remarkable for the disappearance of the world of Proust, the idle aristocracy. Its members were idle no longer. By the end of the nineteenth century they had begun to leave the countryside, even when they still had a family mansion there. They became city dwellers, in Paris or the provinces. The laws of inheritance tended to cause the break-up of large family fortunes, but by judicious internal arrangements certain great landed estates had remained intact and their personal wealth preserved or restored by marriage with rich heiresses. However, some families more recently ennobled under the empire, or earlier, had enriched themselves only during the Restoration, and were now ruined by the fall in value of the franc. It is thought that one-quarter of those with genuine titles renounced them for lack of means to live up to them.

In the higher reaches of French social life the aristocracy and the wealthier bourgeoisie tended to intermingle, as in England from the eighteenth century onwards. Both were to be found among the heads of the administrative services, both practised a generous patronage of the arts, something to the credit of the ruling classes but hardly noticed at the time. Such were the Wildensteins and the Deutsch de la Meurthe family, or the women endowed with wealth who married a great name. All of which goes to show that ten or twenty years of income tax had inflicted no more damage on capital than one hundred and fifty years of the Civil Code had on the great landed estates. Sport too had its wealthy patrons such as the Peugeots, the Michelins, the banks and the state-owned industries.

Although one can identify a specifically working-class way of life, there were such wide differences in the other classes and such vast disparities in incomes that precise generalisations become impossible. Daily life obviously became rather more comfortable, but although the vacuum cleaner appeared early on the scene, the refrigerator sold by General Motors during their brief stay in France was as rare as the electric shaver. Many middle-class people had motor-cars and everyone had a bicycle, but prices were too high for the arrival of a high consumption society such as already existed in America. Nevertheless, even for the very poor there had been great improvements in diet over the last thirty years, both in variety and calorific value; and prices had fallen. We have already seen that rents had been getting lower since 1914. Hence in the towns all classes had had a certain proportion of their incomes to spare that could be devoted to saving or recreation. In the depression this margin was reduced or abolished, but food consumption was largely unaffected. In fact, it increased steadily from 1930 to 1938: the same amount of bread but more milk and meat was consumed. The daily average intake of 3,700–800 calories was markedly higher than in the preceding decade. But averages can hide wide differences. It seems that in Paris people ate less well; but, although in 1936 the unemployed worker's daily intake was down to 2,700 calories, it was reassuring that this was well above his vital needs. Perhaps all this explains the gradual move of the workers and their organisations towards reformism.

24

Some victims of traditional society

We shall have little to say about the real misfits. The pressures of industrial society were sometimes unbearable; but the tramp and the down-and-out had always been there. The life of the delinquent has long been glamourised in literature, and some who have lived on the fringe have contributed to it, like Poiret and Orwell. In his autobiography, published after 1945, Julien Blanc paints an appalling picture of what *maisons de correction* were like. No doubt this sort of thing will give historians good material for case studies, but contemporaries already knew about the horrors of penal settlements and children's prisons through the classic reporting of Albert Londres and Louis Roubaud. Obviously the sub-proletariat of the colonial workers' world would also find a place in this chapter, were it not deliberately confined to those whom we traditionally respect – women, children and the aged.

The elderly

In 1936 nearly 15 per cent of the population were over sixty and 10 per cent were over sixty-five. Up to 1919 nobody had realised that increased longevity created a social problem. According to Sauvy the elderly had, up to the time of the depression, been working past the normal retirement age, the reason being the gaps caused by war deaths and the erosion of savings. But when the depression came, the elderly workers were, with women and foreigners, the first to become unemployed. The problem was how to turn them into retired people. The law of 1930 set up a pensions insurance scheme to which all wage-earners had to contribute, but it only applied to those who were over sixty at that date. In spite of the efforts of the Front Populaire no help was forthcoming for the 'old workers' during that period. However, the position of those in official retirement was constantly bettered by numerous government measures, except at the time of Laval's *décrets-lois*, which cut their purchasing power as drastically as it did that of public servants.

In 1939 about one million people were receiving retirement pay, probably about twice the pre-1914 figure. This was a great improvement, but even so only about one elderly person in four got it. Also the sum was so small that those who received it were often forced to accept jobs at any sort of pay. This had a dire effect on the pay of those in regular employment, as did the clandestine work of those receiving unemployment relief. In the absence of statistics it is hard to say whether the general rise in the standard of living helped the aged. It probably did, for most of them managed to live and die among their own offspring; in which, it is safe to say, they were more fortunate than succeeding generations.

Women

The position of women changed very little between 1930 and 1940. Though it varied according to social status, it was always inferior – more so than in almost any other industrialised country. As elsewhere in Europe, the urge towards matrimony was strong, though the result was not necessarily enduring. There were 270,000 marriages annually and nearly 25,000 divorces. As a result of the First World War there was an excess female population of 300,000 widows and spinsters.

Women had no political rights and, although between the wars the Chamber had three times voted in favour of female suffrage (the last occasion in July 1936), it was a sham, for the deputies knew quite well that the Senate would endlessly postpone its appearance on their agenda. The radicals could never forget that, if women had had the vote in 1898 and 1902, the Republic would never have survived. Some left-wing municipalities co-opted female deputy councillors, naturally without any voting rights. Others appointed women to education or social aid committees. For the first time in French history, Léon Blum brought three women into his government.

There was no strong feminist movement in France at this time. There had been an active one before 1914, on the lines of the English suffragettes. Since the war it had been feeble and divided, at a time when women increasingly needed to earn a living. The most important body was the Union pour les Suffrages des Femmes, led by Mme Brunschwig. Campaigns were launched at the time of general elections. *L'Oeuvre*, the left-wing intellectuals' paper, opened its columns to the battle for women's rights, particularly to Séverine. Women who called for more forceful action, social rather than political, like Louise Weiss, had no following. The feminists had papers like *La Française* or *Minerva*, most probably read by women who had previously known La Fronde and been involved in its activities. The young mostly joined movements aiming at female emancipation through social change, e.g. Jeunesses Communistes and Etudiants Socialistes. It was hardly surprising that, being without proper legal status, women should have shunned militancy or even membership of a political party. Even as wage-earners they rarely joined a trade union.

Their economic situation was no better. Almost all the legislation regulating women's working conditions had been passed before 1930. The Front Populaire did nothing. Women were more adversely affected by the depression than were men. Unemployment among the better educated men severely limited women's chances of jobs in the civil service. Diplomacy, the magistrature and all senior posts in departments of state were, of course, closed to them. In 1930, Mme Bertrand-Fontaine became the first ever female hospital consultant – a landmark in women's ascent to the top rungs of the professional ladder.

Legally a woman could not run a business without her husband's permission. Even in her professional life a married woman remained a dependant. She only won separate civil status on the eve of the 1939 war. The need for a husband's authorisation to apply for a passport was abolished in 1937. But this was not the end of the Napoleonic heritage of male supremacy. A woman's adultery was treated differently from that of her husband, to whom she continued to owe obedience. In marriage she had no share of paternal rights, and even as a widow her rights were limited. Another feature of this antiquated legal system that shocked many foreigners was state control of prostitution.

Although the political and legal position of women lagged far behind contemporary standards of behaviour, class differences in clothing and fashion were narrowing both in Paris and the provinces. The world of *haute couture* was at its most dazzling during the thirties. Doucet and Poiret, the latter bankrupt, had gone, but others had taken their place and, in spite of the depression, were playing an outstanding role, artistically, economically and socially. The fashion leaders of the world came to Paris to get their clothes from Jean Patou, Molyneux, Chanel, Jeanne Lanvin, Madeleine Vionnet and later Schiaparelli. As compared with the previous decade, tastes were simpler, more refined and less extravagant. This was an advantage socially, for it made it possible to be elegant without being rich. Except in the country, the working-class girl no longer had to be badly dressed. Only the elderly still went about in their aprons and shawls. The 'perm' imposed a certain uniformity on hair-styles. In the streets of a city it was now almost impossible to place a girl socially at a glance, except by her way of speaking.

Children

The life of a child and adolescent gave very little room for independence. In the country his early upbringing was traditionally much overshadowed by his grandparents, but elsewhere families tended to be confined to the couple and their offspring. However, all had to be drawn into the melting-pot of school. In 1936 compulsory education was extended to the age of fourteen. Free secondary education came gradually after 1930.

Bringing the syllabus of girls' secondary education into line with that of boys, together with the policy of free education, made for democratisation and for an equality of opportunity to which governments paid lip service and which the Front Populaire undoubtedly wanted. Looking back one can see that governments were themselves to blame for the obstacles that stood in the way of the rapid and wholesale fulfilment of their aims. For instance, as a result of the reforms of the previous ten years, the standards of school syllabuses were raised to an extent that put them beyond the intellectual capacity of the masses, who were gathered in by free schooling. One can see that new social barriers were deliberately being erected that stood in the way of more democratisation. The sudden enormous influx of children, born just after the war, into the now free secondary schools was used in 1933, a time of financial difficulties, as an excuse for introducing an exam into the lowest form. At university level, the obstacle of compulsory Latin was introduced into certain degrees, which was a discouragement to pupils from modern schools who were often of modest origin.

Perhaps it is true that secondary education was class-oriented, with its own social pecking order, but there were local differences. In the Nord the children of the local bigwigs – top management, magistrates and higher civil servants – always went to Church schools. The children of the middle classes – the prefects, army officers, teachers – would go to *lycées* and colleges. But in the Paris region, where even the wealthiest were immune to the pressures of clericalism, children of the middle and even the upper classes, and of the large farmers, were divided equally between both *lycées* and private schools. Some might move annually from one to the other as a result of underachievement or bad behaviour.

Scholarship children, who between 1920 and 1930 included very many war orphans, were not looked down on, as has often been said. The young inevitably form groups based on birth or schooling, country children and farmers' sons always being boarders and the children of foreigners or civil servants often day pupils. But what made a boy, whether subsidised or not, a natural leader was his skill at ball games or athletics. Moreover, the chosen few, heirs to the future, paid dearly for their future privileges and might well envy the ones whose backwardness in class had set them free at the age of thirteen. In spite of reforms the drum-beat that told the time of day in boys' *lycées* up to 1940 was not the only Napoleonic relic. For those who endured boarding-school life, sometimes coming straight from a nursery school at the age of five or seven, the routine was hopelessly ill-designed to inculcate civilised behaviour. Getting up at half past five in summer, 6 o'clock in winter, frozen dormitories, vile food that was worse than barrack-room fare, the unimaginable boredom of disciplined walks in crocodile, made *lycées* unspeakable prisons, occasionally rocked by rebellion. Vigo's autobiographical film, *Zéro de conduite*, gives an exact picture of what they were like.

All the same, secondary education did become more democratic between 1930 and 1940. This is shown by the figures. In 1938 there were 195,000 boys and girls in *lycées* and colleges as against 107,000 in 1930. The Ecoles Primaires supérieures and the *cours complémentaires* grew proportionately, but technical education was still badly provided for, in spite of the efforts of Fernand Dubief and Charles Spinasse and many other politicians between 1900 and 1940.

To sum up, democratisation was no superficial phenomenon, but it was limited in scope. First, it only benefited townsfolk. Among the masses the *certificat d'études primaires* kept its prestige. There may have been no more illiterates, but the peasants seldom got past the elementary level. There were few *cours complémentaires* in agriculture. Furthermore, although the school population explosion and free secondary schooling had made the French a more educated nation, the great gulf between the *baccalauréat* and the certificates of primary and secondary education ensured a social segregation within the system as wide as that created in Great Britain by an Oxford accent.

25

Spiritual powers

In theory, France was mainly Catholic with very small Protestant and Jewish minorities. The state and the churches were separated, except in Alsace and Moselle where the government complied with the Organic Articles. In actual fact agnosticism predominated throughout the greater part of the country, and in the course of a century had probably reduced the Jewish and Protestant communities by one half.

The Catholics

The last ten years of the Republic were for Catholics a time when all their political and social attitudes were in a state of doubt and confusion. Since the pontificate of Pius IX there had been continuous opposition to Modernist thought. By 1930, however, the crisis of Modernism may be considered to have been resolved. The textual critics and historians infected with Positivism were almost all either dead, returned to the fold or expelled from it. Those who survived had left the Church, often rather belatedly like Joseph Turmel. They had produced under the imprint of the firm of Rieder the series *Christianisme*. Bergsonism was now the fashionable school of thought and nobody worried about the scientific pretensions of Modernism. Fliche and Martin's *Histoire de l'Eglise* was a key work of the period, and all the volumes published before 1939 were very conservative. This sort of atmosphere encouraged an increased degree of ostentation in pilgrimages to Chartres, Lourdes, Lisieux and other more obscure, newly re-discovered shrines.

After this recent history of indecision and crises in relations between Church and state, it was not surprising that the political loyalties of Catholics should favour either reaction or conservatism, while socially there was a connection with rather exalted anti-republican circles. Nevertheless, the papal denunciation of *L'Action française* also involved the disavowal and rejection of the *intégristes* and a distressing change of outlook for the majority of Catholics, who had to acquiesce in this revival of *ralliement*. But they continued to vote for the conservative right. They concentrated their bitterness on the policy of the single school and the extension of free education, both of which harmed their own private schools. The associations of parents of pupils in private schools began to be founded after 1930, and throughout all this period the schools controversy raged in the west of France. In the rest of the country it quietened down, except for brief and violent outbursts in 1930 and 1936. Just before the war Daladier and Cardinal Verdier negotiated secretly to try and settle the question. In spite of the moderation, discretion and even the advice of Church leaders, Catholic sentiment and behaviour were still bitterly hostile to the left, a survival of the anti-Dreyfus tradition. The Front Populaire horrified them, even though it had no anti-clerical policies. Anti-semitism was condemned in theory, but in practice it was excused and tolerated, and in 1936 there was an outburst of it in Alsace. Their only objection to Nazism was that it went a little too far. The political mouthpiece of the Catholics continued to be *L'Echo de Paris* or *La France catholique* and their spokesman, General de Castelnau.

Opposing this current of opinion were the Jeune Republique, offspring of the Sillon, who supported the Front Populaire and managed to elect one or two deputies, and the Parti Démocratique Populaire, who took a few seats off the royalists in the west. But the influence of these movements was to be seen much later.

The denunciation of *L'Action française* had a powerful effect on Catholic intellectuals, many of whom were long-standing followers of Maurras, and some began to shed their political commitments in favour of more social ones. There was some movement to the left, with the idea that pluralism was not altogether to be condemned. Maritain was one example. Bernanos managed to remain royalist while expressing views on the Spanish Civil War which were similar to those of the left. The influence of Emmanuel Mounier was felt beyond the confines of the Church. *La Croix* changed its political views just before 1930 and lost some of its readers. *L'Aube* and *Esprit* were started in 1932, then came *Sept* in 1934. This was shut down in 1937 for having published an interview with Léon Blum, and was replaced by *Temps présent*, since the Church was unwilling to see all its intellectuals, so recently right-wing, deserting to the left. The Christian democrats were also deeply suspect. The bishops decided that a social approach offered more hope than a political one. With their backing the Jeunesse Ouvrière Catholique (JOC) started to gain ground in 1926. It served as a model for the peasants' JAC in 1929 and the student JEC in 1932. In 1936 came the foundation of the Paroisse Universitaire for Catholic teachers of every kind and at all levels. This Catholic revival was to have effects which have lasted up to the present day.

Christian trade unionism really originated, as we have seen, during the troubles in the textile industry in the Nord in 1928. But, apart from Cardinal Liénart and a few bishops, the episcopate generally remained rather cool, while the majority of the clergy and their congregations were totally hostile to a movement that was in fact less politically committed than the JOC. Nevertheless, the Confédération Française des Travailleurs Chrétiens (CFTC) was recognised as a genuinely representative body by various collectivist conferences in the spring of 1936 and at a national level in August of the same year. It had just over 300,000 members, which meant that its appeal was limited; and the corporatist ideas of some of its leaders foreshadowed those of the Vichy regime. In 1936 bishops in working-class areas were much more worried and embarrassed by strikes than actually opposed to them. In 1932 Monsignor Verdier raised a loan of twenty million francs to build churches in the working-class quarters of the great industrial regions. This evangelical movement was evidence of a form of catholicism which, even if it numbered few adherents, was genuinely alive and less rigid in its way than before the war of 1914.

Missionary work was an essentially French activity – one-third of all the missionaries in the world were French. The chief reason for the Church's social approach was that both its leaders and its younger members were aware of the widespread 'dechristianisation', or simply paganism, of parts of the country. The sociological research carried out between 1930 and 1940 by Gabriel Le Bras and Canon Boulard caused consternation. According to Le Bras two to three million had not been baptised; according to Boulard, seven to eight million. Probably one out of five French people had no religion. For many, catholicism was merely social conformism. Only 50 per cent went to church at Easter, and less than half of these attended mass regularly.

These figures were an average. Le Bras balanced the Catholic areas (the north-west, west, Alsace, Flanders and a few scattered regions) against the 'missionary' areas (the Paris region, Champagne, Limousin, Périgord, the Mâconnais and the working-class suburbs of industrial towns). The remainder were parts of France where church attendance was minimal, limited to special occasions and almost uniquely indulged in by women and children. The fact that women seemed to be more devout than men may explain the significant part they played in Christian social work and trade unionism, and also the faint aura of feminism in the Church and in its practical work.

From a social point of view the return of the bourgeoisie to the Church, which was accelerated by the 1914 war, increased the alienation of the working class. There were many working-class Catholics in Alsace, Moselle and the Nord, while the peasants of the Yonne and the Creuse were irreligious. However, the adverse effects of town life on religious observance are well known. Hence, as more people left the countryside, the towns acquired a larger proletarian pagan population, and the extreme left a larger body of supporters. At election time the priests nearly always campaigned for right-wing candidates.

There were too few clergy and of too low calibre. The Church gained few recruits all through this period, far fewer than at the beginning of the century, and not enough to replace the previous generation. One-third of all priests were over sixty. As a teaching body, the Church was staffed by old men and was untouched by the intellectual and social revival. The Catholic universities, which preached a neo-Thomist philosophy, were offering a better education to their young clerics. These were no longer country folk but came from the urban middle class, awake to forms of Catholic art and literature as represented by Claudel, Francis Jammes, Mauriac, Maurice Denis and Rouault, and informed about social problems through the pages of *La Croix*, less often through *Esprit*. But what about the remaining two-thirds – elderly priests, ardent followers of Action Française ever since their seminary days? Often they were intellectually incapable of dissociating catholicism from anti-republican nationalism, an idea that had been inculcated from earliest days and was reinforced by the Great War of 1914–18.

Typical of this spirit was the Abbé Bethléem, a self-appointed mentor of Catholic reading habits. He proscribed or advised against anything written by Jews, Protestants and left-wing writers 'who abuse all decent Frenchmen'. He excluded a number of Catholics whose orthodoxy was in doubt – Bernanos, Max Jacob, Louis Martin-Chauffier, Mauriac. He condemned the *L'Action française* writers, rather regretfully, for they had been good patriots. He even had a soft spot for the purveyors of pornography such as Léon Daudet and Binet-Valmer. He recommended René Bazin, Henry Bordeaux, the anti-semitic Jean Drault and his colleague the Abbé Loutil, who wrote under the pseudonym Pierre l'Ermite: 'The harrowing scenes of *Les Deux Mains* reveal the sinister influence of Freemasonry. *Restez chez vous* is an eloquent defence of country life ... *La Grande amie* ... and *L'Empire* put us right in the thick of heart-rendingly moving and melodramatic scenes in the struggle between the land and the factory, the land owning nobility and the cosmopolitan Jew, the kindly rustic home and the incessant exodus which sucks the peasant into city life.' (*Romans à lire et Roman à proscrire*, Paris, Editions de la revue des lectures, 11th edition, 1932.)

This sort of thinking was evidently prevalent among the clergy, and it led them into some extraordinarily ill-advised behaviour at election times. In a pastoral letter the bishop of Dax, writing in 1942, said 'For us the accursed year has not been that of our external defeat, but the year of our internal defeat, the year 1936.' (C. Langlois, 'Le Régime de Vichy et le clergé', *Revue de science politique*, August 1972.) This was why the efforts of Pius XI, of prelates like Verdier, Liénart and Saliège, of *La Croix* and *L'Aube*, to put an end to the link between the Church and the right wing, found themselves blocked by deep-rooted social prejudice on the right and suspicion on the left. But their work was to show results much later.

The Protestants

These made up a minority that is hard to measure, probably not more than about 600,000 in all. As they moved away from the country they dwindled in number, because town life had a more paganising effect on minorities, which lost touch with each other in the crowd. There were still a fair number in Alsace, in Moselle and the Doubs; in the Gard, the Drôme and the Ardèche; in parts of south-west France and the Cévennes and round Paris. There were a few scattered households in the Nord, in Normandy and north Brittany.

Protestants tended to belong to the bourgeoisie; there were few in the working class. The Protestant peasants of Saintonge and the Cévennes suffered heavy losses during the war; some villages seem almost to have disappeared. The Protestants were not only dispersed, but also divided into various sects. There were Reformed and Lutheran, and many splinter groups, whose converts came mostly from the Catholics. Although scattered and few in number, the Protestants wielded a lot of influence in the banking world and industry, for there were many of them in the higher reaches of the civil service, in politics, in education and cultural life. Their small sects were often at loggerheads over questions of dogma or politics, yet, supported more by devotion than cash, they managed somehow to publish their books and journals both in the Midi and Paris. The great clash during the 1914–18 war, which divided the Protestants into pacifists and 'nationals' lasted a long time and broke out again with the Front Populaire. For many right-wing Protestants, fear of communism had taken the place of fear of the Germans. However, Christian socialism was making headway, and further to the left there was a pro-bolshevik group, Terre Humaine. Georges Lasserre and André Philip, who were law students and who later became professors of economics, were active in discussions on socialism and conscientious objection. André Philip began his career in Christian socialism by popularising Henri de Man's ideas.

On the other side, Maurras' brand of monarchism, which had always had its Protestant adherents, began to win followers (often not for long) among some of the leading intellectuals of the Reformed Church, e.g. Auguste Lecerf and Charles Westphal. One can interpret this either as a result of the condemnation of *L'Action française* by the Vatican, or else as a rather perverted reaction of the Reformed conscience to national decadence.

There were, in addition, various constitutional disagreements. In Alsace and Moselle only one French-speaking person in forty was a Catholic, but one-third of the population were Protestants, of whom the majority were

Lutherans. They were grouped under two churches, still regulated by the Organic Articles of 1802 – the Church of the Augsburg Confession and the Reformed Church of Alsace-Lorraine. This situation had survived Herriot's failed policy of assimilation. But the Protestants as a whole were opposed to home rule. The deputy Dahlet was always a patriot, and it would be wrong to class him as an agent of pan-Germanism. All through this period the problem was to find German-speaking pastors to replace those who had been installed in livings under a thoroughgoing Germanising policy prior to 1918. Various attempts were made at this time to bring the different groups closer together. The Fédération Protestante united the principal churches in France and the newly recovered provinces. Starting in 1929 Marc Boegner presided over the organisation for thirty-one years. Other French Protestants have become famous, nationally and even internationally, but he was the only one to be famous for this alone. It was through his efforts that French Protestantism played such an important part in the œcumenical movement. 'French Protestantism was so small, so divided, so isolated and tormented by its terrible history, that participation in the œcumenical movement was of fundamental importance in making it feel it really stood for something in the world.' (S. Mours and D. Robert, *Le Protestantisme en France au XIX*e *et au XX*e *siècles*, p. 385.)

The division between 'orthodox' and 'liberal' grew less acute as the influence of Kantian rationalism declined. Negotiations carried out between 1933 and 1938 resulted in the unification in the Eglise Réformée de France of all sects stemming from Calvinism, except the most uncompromising 'orthodox' wing, which remained obstinately apart. So ended a schism which dated back to 1872. 'Fundamentalism', itself a fruitful begetter of sects, made headway. Contemporary trends of thought encouraged the move towards unity, initially a return to the origins of the Reformation inspired by the 'neo-Calvinism' of Auguste Lecerf and his disciples. In 1930 the ideas of Karl Barth reached France and were disseminated by Pierre Maury, the review *Foi et Vie* and the Fédération des Etudiants Chrétiens. Protestant beliefs were soon to be deeply affected by existentialism. As André Siegfried observed: 'One is tired of this all-pervading God who, in the end, becomes indistinguishable from either man or nature, and one wants to go back ... to transcendental ideas that are consistent ... with concepts not only of intelligence and doctrine, but also of man and the life of man.' (*Ibid.*, p. 391.) These disciples of Barth, mostly born between 1890 and 1920, were the heirs of the Protestant positivists of the Second Empire.

In a totally different connection it is worth noting that the expulsion of German missionaries from the Cameroons and Togoland extended the field of action of the French Protestant missions.

The Jews

There were about the same number of Jews as of Protestants, and in many ways they played a similar role. The economic, social and intellectual influence of the older communities was out of all proportion to their size and numbers, even among their own people. But while the humble Protestants were largely country folk and peasants, their Jewish equivalents tended to be artisans and proletarian town-dwellers. Furthermore, a large majority were recent immigrants.

Up to 1914 the French Jewish community absorbed any new arrivals without difficulty. They were concentrated in and around Paris. But between the wars they were swamped by masses of new arrivals from North Africa, the Levant, eastern Europe and Germany. After 1939 the German Jews were simply using France as a staging-post for America. In 1939 the Jewish population was about 350,000. Half of them were in Paris and only about one-third of these were of French descent. This accounts for the rise in anti-semitism in all classes, directed as much at the motor mechanic in the IVth *arrondissement* as at the banker, doctor, lawyer, artist or politician in the XVIth.

It is difficult to get at the realities of Jewish religious practice. Judaism was one of the three religions recognised and supported by the government in Alsace and Moselle; elsewhere it was of course independent. It suffered from sectarian divisions. The Ashkenazis and the foreigners were constantly growing in numbers, except, obviously, in North Africa. Among French Jews liberals were in opposition to traditionalists and were anti-Zionist, in spite of the emotional appeal of the Palestinian homeland. To them Judaism was simply a religion. They maintained their traditional observances and their literature; their press dated back to the nineteenth century. As with Protestants, their primary schools were in decline, but their secondary colleges were on the increase (the Ecole Maimonide was founded in 1930). Politically, the upper-class Jews were mostly right of centre, though some were of the extreme right, providing members in 1934 of the Union Patriotique des Français Israélites and the Groupe des Croix-de-Feu Israélites.

Nobody in this ancient community had any idea of the dangers that threatened it, though the massive influx of foreign Jews was disturbing. The immigrants learnt the French language, but there was a clash between the two cultures. Between 1930 and 1939, the Consistory made great efforts to assimilate the new arrivals by a vast increase in religious centres. There was also heavy expenditure on social aid. When assimilation did take place in the second generation, it happened outside the Jewish milieu through the secular schools.

The Sephardic Jews, who were untouched by Yiddish culture and usually French-speaking, conformed fairly quickly; but the Ashkenazi proletariat and artisan class, badly hit by unemployment, were very much under the thumb of societies that deliberately resisted conversion to French ways. It happened all the same, either through school or mixed marriages. There was an extreme left group that opposed Zionism. The Yiddish press, which included dailies, could be communist, Trotskyite or Zionist. Without the help of Christian or so-called Christian organisations the French Jewish community would never have been able to absorb the vast numbers of east European refugees fleeing from persecution.

Generally speaking, both the churches and synagogues were up against new problems arising from urban congestion, political insecurity and the depression. This seems to have encouraged the growth of atheism or at least religious indifference. But at the same time a prevailing strain of anti-rationalism in contemporary thought brought about a vigorous theological revival as well as a new attitude towards social questions.

Freemasonry

Between the wars, the more the Roman Church shed its anti-republicanism, the more the Republic's own 'church' declined. Free-masonry found it hard to recover from its war wounds. During the thirties the lodge of the Grand Orient had 35,000 active members, with 20,000 in the other lodges. Many politicians were Masons, though not the left-wing leaders, Herriot, Daladier and Blum. The Blanquist Groussier, several times a deputy for a Paris constituency, was one of the principals of the Grand Orient between wars, but all the same Freemasonry was not socialist. The Presidents of the Republic, Doumergue, Doumer and Lebrun, all members of the right and all Masons, were elected to office against candidates of the left who were not Masons. The brotherhood was very moderate in its politics, but was all-powerful in the very anti-Blum, anti-Front Populaire Senate. It was not actively anti-clerical during this period. It did, however, continue to recruit from among prominent militant socialists and radicals, and to act as a pressure group, using the Ligue de l'Enseignement and the Ligue des Droits de l'Homme. It may claim some credit for the initiation of social insurance and for the democratisation of education.

One interesting aspect of Freemasonry was its influence in the postal workers' and other public service unions, where it rallied workers to resist communism. Baylot's and Lacoste's militancy in this sphere launched them later on into brilliant careers in administration and politics respectively. The magazine *Syndicats* was dominated by Masons, and there were many gendarmerie officers in the fraternity. Although only one of many pressure groups, Freemasonry was one of the right-wing's traditional bugbears. The Prince affair, which was closely linked with the Stavisky scandal, gave rise to extraordinary and ridiculous attacks on Freemasonry.

As we have seen, Prince, who was a Mason, had been suspiciously slow to prosecute Stavisky, and his death, probably suicide made to look like murder, was laid at the door of the Freemasons. The whole incredible affair did them a great deal of harm.

Affected by the decline of positivism, they had little to contribute to contemporary thought, although the writings of René Guénon, little noticed at the time, were to receive some recognition later. Some Masons turned to spiritualism, with a revived Masonic ritual. Albert Lantoine's lasting friendship with the Jesuit Berteloot finally ended the anti-Christian tradition of French Freemasonry. There were no longer any dark sinister forces in the brotherhood. Those that existed were on the right, trying to undermine the Front Populaire: the 'two hundred families', and Comité des Forges and the Cagoulards.

26

Leisure and culture

In 1936 the working week changed from forty-eight hours to forty. The 'English weekend' had already become a widely accepted habit. The working class won holidays with pay, but the middle classes gained little more leisure. Holidays for them, when they existed, tended to be very short, except for women, children and teachers. It was only at weekends that men appeared at the seaside. Country folk worked continuously, except in the winter when they went shooting. Time off simply meant a few hours a day or week to spare for the newspapers, sport, shows or the cafés. The upper crust and the habitués of Parisian artistic and literary circles frequented the night life of Montmartre and Montparnasse, went shooting, had holidays in the mountains, at Deauville or the Côte d'Azur, the latter becoming more plebeian during the summer. Race meetings and casinos were full of people of all kinds and classes.

From the lonely reading of a novel to mixing with 50,000 people at the Colombes stadium, the uses of free time were becoming so varied that one can only cover a few of the activities with which the French diverted themselves.

The media

The daily press was the principal source of information, with a total output of ten million copies. The daily budget for a working man, plastered on walls by the CGT, included a morning and evening newspaper as necessities. The Parisian press, with a print number slightly greater than that of all the provincial papers put together, went all over the country, particularly *Paris-Soir*. Its circulation rose steadily between 1930 and 1938, at which time it increased its price and lost sales. The great number and variety of papers bore witness to a dislike of concentration, while, apart from *Paris-Soir*, the French press was technologically backward. But it must have been fairly prosperous, seeing that in the middle of the depression many of the big newspapers modernised their plant.

The Parisian right-wing press comfortably outmatched its rivals, for after 1934 the big dailies of general information became more and more

Range of newspapers, March 1939

I Main Parisian newspapers (current affairs)

Paris-Soir (evening)	1,750,000
Le Petit Parisien	1,000,000
Le Journal	410,000 (pro-Mussolini)
Le Matin	310,000 (pro-Hitler)
L'Intransigeant (evening)	135,000 (right-wing)
Excelsior	130,000 (illustrated; fashionable)
Paris-Midi	100,000
Le Temps (evening)	70,000 (Comité des Forges)
L'Information (evening)	50,000
Le Journal des débats (evening)	35,000 (De Wendel – Compagnie de Suez)

II Main provincial newspapers

L'Ouest-Éclair	350,000 (Christian democrat)
La Petite Gironde	325,000 (radical)
L'Echo du Nord	300,000
La Dépêche de Toulouse	260,000 (radical)
Le Progrès de Lyon	220,000 (radical)
Le Réveil du Nord	200,000 (socialist)
Le Petit Dauphinois	200,000 (left-wing)
La France de Bordeaux	150,000
Le Petit Marseillais	150,000
Les Dernières Nouvelles de Strasbourg	150,000

III Parisian newspapers (political)

L'Humanité	340,000 (PCF)
Ce soir (evening)	260,000 (communist)
L'Œuvre	235,000 (radical and socialist)
Le Jour-Echo de Paris	185,000 (Catholic right)
Le Petit Journal	180,000 (PSF – La Rocque)
Le Populaire	160,000 (SFIO)
La Croix	140,000 (Catholic)
L'Epoque (founded in 1937)	70,000 (anti-Hitler right – Kérillis)
L'Action française	45,000 (monarchist)
Le Peuple	16,000 (CGT)
La Liberté (evening)	15,000 (Doriot)
L'Aube	14,000 (Catholic democrat)

IV Important weeklies

Gringoire (1928)	650,000 (maximum) (pro-fascist; anti-semitic)
Le Pèlerin (1873, monthly)	550,000 (Catholic)
Candide (1924)	500,000 (maximum) (Maurrassite)
Ric et Rac (1929)	340,000 (escapist)
Détective (1928)	250,000 (escapist)
Regards (1932)	100,000 (communist)
Je suis partout (1930)	100,000 (maximum) (pro-Hitler)
Marianne (1932)	60,000 (moderate left)
Vendredi (1935)	100,000 (maximum) Front Populaire
Le Canard enchaîné	275,000 (85,000 in 1929) (anti-communist left)

anti-left. Radicals and socialists got much better hearing in the regional press. Serious reviews dealing with intellectual or economic affairs were badly supported and poor in quality. It must be added, however, that a paper could survive with few readers and modest financial backing.

The ideas of the extremists were the most skilfully propagated – those of Maurras via *Candide* rather than via *L'Action française*, those of communism via *L'Humanité*, which became very prosperous after a great struggle for survival between 1929 and 1935. In the provinces a departmental press coexisted with the big regional newspapers. The right-wing *La Dépêche d'Eure-et-Loir* had a circulation of 30,000, the left-wing *L'Indépendant d'Eure-et-Loir* only 10,000, though the department as a whole voted for the left. There were even some papers that catered only for an *arrondissement*, like *Le Nouvelliste de Châteaudun*, or a canton like *Le Messager de Bonneval*, or *Le Journal de Brou*, which survived the war and is still alive today.

The notorious financial instability of the press was not healthy. Many papers were only kept going by means of hidden subsidies – from secret government funds, from banks, from the Union des Intérêts Economiques and other capitalist organisations, from foreign dictatorships and sometimes from mere crooks. Even the biggest depended on the Havas agency, the monopolist of news-gathering. On the whole, the French press was corrupt, biased, anti-parliamentarian and xenophobic, and much of what it printed was noxious. The more widely circulated right-wing weeklies were irresponsible and violent to the extent of occasional incitements to assassination. Béraud and Maurras were no worse in this respect than Rochefort and Cassagnac had been; but the law of January 1936 made incitement to murder a penal offence. However, due to the opposition of the big newspapers and the Senate, the Front Populaire failed to clean up the press.

Despite this gloomy picture, between the wars, and particularly after 1930, the literary and intellectual level was occasionally raised by the contributions of a group of outstanding correspondents, such as Albert Londres, Louis Roubaud, Edouard Helsey, Andrée Viollis, Jacques Viot and of distinguished writers who turned to journalism, like André Salmon, Joseph Kessel, Pierre Mac Orlan and Saint-Exupéry.

During this period a new sort of periodical appeared, new both in its aims and in its techniques of presentation. *Vu*, founded by Vogel in 1928, was the first great photographic news magazine, and its issues on the Soviet Union and the United States were exciting events. In 1931 *Lu* began to provide a monthly review of the world press. The *presse du cœur* or women's magazines really took off in 1937 with *Marie-Claire*, which had a print number of just under one million and many imitators. Lower down in the scale came *Confessions* and *Confidences*. New children's magazines quickly sprang up. Those born at the time of the 1914 war disappeared before that of 1939, displaced by *Le Journal de Mickey* and the Del Duca magazines.

The new media as yet offered no serious competition to the newspapers. Whereas today we see the news on television before we read it, at that time news-films came after the event and simply illustrated it. Actually radio developed fairly rapidly, the number of sets growing from half a million in 1930 to five and a half million in 1939. Radio was used by Tardieu in 1932 and Doumergue in 1934 through the state broadcasting stations and others owned by the big newspapers. In 1936 it figured for the first time in an election campaign, with time allotted on the air to all parties. As in the daily press, sports reporting held an important place in radio.

The entertainment world

Shows could be artistic or the reverse, expensive and of high quality or cheap and popular. Ballet, opera and music held a less prominent place than before. With changing tastes, opera shed the portentousness it had shared with historical painting in the previous century. That kind of opera was out of fashion, in Paris at least; but the Opéra-Comique was producing pieces like *Pelléas et Mélisande* and *Les Noces* that were admired. Dance was very popular with sophisticated and discriminating audiences both in Paris and Monte Carlo. Diaghilev died in 1929, but the tradition of Russian ballet was carried on by Lifar, Ida Rubinstein, Massine and others. Different traditions were represented by Argentina, Teresina and Josephine Baker.

There were many orchestras in Paris – the Orchestre Symphonique de Paris, the Société du Conservatoire, Pasdeloup, Colonne, and in 1934 the Orchestre National was founded for broadcasting. But the attraction of America was strong and many conductors emigrated, among them Monteux, Munch and Paray. Some small orchestras were kept going by wealthy patrons; one such was La Sérénade which performed the work of young composers. Chamber music became popular in Paris for the first time, while instrumentalists such as Casals and Marguerite Long could fill the Salle Gaveau with solo performances, while Kreisler, with a rather popular programme, could fill the Opéra. Wanda Landowska, performing at her house in Saint-Leu-La-Forêt, set a fashion for the harpsichord and early music. In spite of all this, music was in decline. It had become too esoteric for the general public. Stravinsky was still hissed at a Pasdeloup concert in 1935. Music-lovers were more knowledgeable, but there were fewer of them. Improved gramophone recordings helped, but ordinary people still found classical music inaccessible.

Music halls, cabarets and *chansonniers* were what the public liked. It was the golden age of the revue, a sudden flowering which contrasted sharply with the mediocrity of the previous decade. French song was brought to life by Mireille, followed by Trénet. The realist tradition, both lyrical and comic, was well exploited by Damia, Fréhel, Piaf, Marianne Oswald,

"LA SÉRÉNADE"

Société de Musique de Chambre

❖◆

COMITÉ : YVONNE de CASA-FUERTE, Georges AURIC,
Roger DESORMIERE, Igor MARKEVITCH, Darius MILHAUD,
Nicolas NABOKOFF, Francis POULENC, Vittorio RIETI,
Henri SAUGUET.

◆

COMiTÉ FONDATEUR

Princesse Ed. de POLIGNAC
Comtesse J. MURAT
Vicomtesse de NOAILLES
Comtesse A. J. de NOAILLES
Comtesse J. de POLIGNAC
Comtesse G. POTOCKA
Comtesse PECCI-BLUNT
Madame MANTE-ROSTAND
Madame René DUBOST

Mme G. IMANN-GIGANDET
Mlle O. de la PANOUSE
Mlle Gabrielle CHANEL
Comte E. de BEAUMONT
M. DAVID-WEILL
M. Pierre BOUVET
M. Paul GOLDSCHMIDT
M. Edward JAMES

◆

MEMBRES D'HONNEUR

Mlle Nadia BOULANGER, M. Edouard BOURDET,
M. MAINBOCHER, Vte de la PANOUSE

◆◆

Secrétariat : Mme *Rose CELLI,*
10, rue des Feuillantines, (V·)

Famous patrons

Lucienne Boyer, Jean Sablon, Chevalier and Georgius. There were others too who were a good deal coarser. Itinerant street singers and musicians, who wandered from town to town, managed to survive against the increasingly widespread gramophone record.

Jazz was discovered in the thirties. Before then there had been syncopated dance music that people thought was jazz, performed by the Jack Hilton and Paul Whiteman bands, and by Wiener and Doucet at the Boeuf sur le Toit. Ray Ventura carried on with it after 1931. The key dates for real jazz in Paris were 1933 with Louis Armstrong at the Pleyel, 1934 with Duke Ellington at the Pleyel, and the début of the Hot Club de France quintet. In 1937 the Cotton Club started performing at the *Moulin Rouge*, at which point jazz ceased to be just an entertainment for the sophisticated few. Hugues Panassié was a pioneer in all this.

The middle classes much preferred the theatre to music and its related arts. The sort of plays they liked were 'boulevard' plays, the popular successes of Bernstein, Bourdet, Pagnol, Jacques Deval, Stève Passeur, Marcel Achard and Sacha Guitry. Baret's touring company, hopelessly behind the times, went on producing plays by Henry Bataille, de Flers and Caillavet in provincial theatres. The common people had no use for the theatre and much preferred to watch boxing.

As with music, the general public could not stomach anything at all difficult. At the Théâtre de l'Œuvre, Lugné-Poe produced Claudel or Crommelynck, with Madeleine Lambert, before a half-empty house, whereas Jouvet and Baty in the Cartel des Quatre had no financial difficulties with plays by Jules Romains or Giraudoux. Life was harder at the Atelier where Dullin was bringing on young actors like Barrault and Marchat, and wanted to put across plays by young writers like Salacrou, Anouilh, André de Richaud, as well as the Elizabethans. As for the Pitoëffs, who made no concessions to the groundlings with their productions of Chekhov and Bernard Shaw, their hardships are well known. Georges Pitoëff put on Schnitzler's *La Ronde* with a cast of his wife and Louis Salou. Two was just enough and three would have cost him too much. There were two theatre-going publics, each deeply contemptuous of the other. The loyal followers of Dullin and Pitoëff would have scorned to be seen in one of the boulevard theatres where poor Ludmilla Pitoëff was forced to earn her living.

The cinema

Music and drama were middle-class diversions, catering for a wide variety of tastes and ages. All classes went to the cinema, except the peasants, who only saw a film when a travelling fair passed their way. Seats at new films, to be seen only at the Champs-Elysées or the Boulevard de la Madeleine, were expensive. Society no longer looked down on a form of entertainment which had once been thought common and without any claim to be an art. All the same, the courts had just given a verdict against Léon Moussinac, who had found fault with Paramount Films, for a breach of commercial law just as if they had been a brand of noodles or motor-car.

In the *quartiers*, the suburbs and the provincial towns the cinema was very cheap and all sorts of people flocked to it every weekend. The silent film came to an end early in the thirties; then came sound, followed by speech, putting hundreds of musicians in small cinemas out of work. Henceforward film-making became much more expensive, and equipping picture palaces with sound systems also cost money. French companies had to pay royalties for foreign licences and often got into serious financial difficulties, which were only increased by the depression. There was an invasion of foreign films, with German and Russian films, always of good quality, being shown in the more adventurous cinema houses such as the Vieux Colombier, Studio 28 and Ursulines. After Chiappe's departure Russian films were shown publicly. Certain French and American films were also shown exclusively in a few Parisian cinemas, whose policy was rather like that of the Cartel des Quatre in the theatre. A number of cinema clubs in provincial towns followed suit, and because of them the silent film never disappeared.

The advent of the talkie was a great shock to those for whom the art of the cinema was far from being simply an inferior form of cheap entertainment, and it had a damaging effect on French production. The avant-garde producers who disappeared during the late twenties into journalism (Germaine Dulac), foreign parts (Cavalcanti) or simply silence (Jean Epstein) had always refused to admit that film had any connection with theatre. René Clair in his talkies stuck to the idea that cinematic art was an art of movement and was closely allied to a musical performance. But the general public just liked to see theatre performances of the boulevard playwrights transferred to the screen. All of which was bad for those with real creative talent.

In other words, there were several different publics. There were those people who went to the local cinema as they might to a café, regardless of what was being shown, and they were the largest and most proletarian group. Next came the fans of particular stars, e.g. Raimu, Milton, Chevalier, or of a particular kind of film, e.g. a comedy or an American musical with Fred Astaire and Ginger Rogers. Finally, there were those who looked down on anything that seemed bourgeois and flocked to see films directed by Buñuel, Pabst, Pudovkin or Vigo.

However, these divisions were not nearly so lasting in the world of the cinema as they were in the theatre, and by 1935 the great film-makers were getting their work across to all sectors of the public. The result was that the cinema in the last years of the Third Republic, like compulsory education in the previous period, or the spread of the French language in much earlier days, had a culturally unifying effect by its diffusion of Parisian tastes and values, unlike other forms of visual entertainment which merely served to reinforce cultural diversity.

Sport

Like the cinema, sport had great importance for the social and cultural history of this period, for it was then that it asserted itself in opposition to traditional attitudes. It had its own daily, *L'Auto*, printed on yellow paper, with a less successful rival, *l'Echo des sports*, printed on pink paper. Cinema had no daily, but they both had weeklies. This does not however mean that sport had a wider appeal. The cinema was something enjoyed by the whole family, while sport was sexist and testified to masculine superiority. Women of course had their share: they rowed, they swam, they played tennis, they competed in athletic events, and they might even do rather well. Suzanne Lenglen was no longer on the scene in the thirties, but Mme Mathieu had a prize-winning career. There were brilliant female aviators. But, women were totally excluded from the two greatest national sports – football and cycle racing. The male superiority syndrome, which barred women from the world of sport, was reinforced by the sporting press which made a point of showing how massively inelegant were the Dutch female swimming champions, and how flat-chested were the German women athletes. Conditioned in this way, women kept away from spectator sports, as they did from politics and war. They thought it good form to despise sport and look after the children while their husbands were at the stadium. Twenty years earlier a little burst of feminism had resulted in the establishment in Paris of some athletic clubs, e.g. Linnettes and Fémina-Sport, but they faded out. In emulation of Wimbledon, society women went to watch the tennis championships at Roland-Garros, but this was as much a social as a sporting occasion; and they were never to be seen in the cheaper seats.

For men the 1914 war brought one extraordinary psychological change. According to people born around 1880, if a group of men was seen, in the early nineteen-hundreds, going to an open space to play with a round or oval ball, they were abused and treated as if they were mad. Between the wars, however, the football grounds were packed with people of all ages, the oldest of whom had probably never played in their lives. Meanwhile, in schools and colleges, children were rushing about kicking footballs or any sort of ball. Nobody played prisoners' base or leap-frog any more. Such games survived in the novels of Marcel Aymé, but soon they would merely be subjects for folklore specialists.

Sport did exist in France before 1914, but it was very class-oriented. Some sports, such as French boxing and swimming, indulged in by the masses and even the underworld, were considered degrading. Others indicated a certain superiority of mind or wealth. In imitation of the English, rugby was played by the sons of aristocrats or stockbrokers, and so were tennis and athletic sports. These mostly took place in the universities. The Chautemps brothers and Fernand Bouisson, considerable politicians of this period, were all outstanding rugby players; and it is well known that Jean Giraudoux was national champion at four hundred metres. Between the wars these sports became much more democratic. All over the Midi, the man in the street was mad about rugby, which became a sort of Occitanian symbol. Many activities previously looked down on were being reassessed; in fact there were some abrupt changes of mind. After 1930, apart from polo and golf, there were hardly any games that the ordinary man could not take up. The expensiveness of tennis alone made it an exception. Paradoxically one should also have added swimming, for even at a time when training for other sports was neither so scientific nor so demanding as it is today, it was already difficult to combine it with a job or a course of study.

Thanks to the prestige which now surrounded sport, for the first time it became a good way of rising in the social scale. Football, rugby and cycle racing led to jobs and helped young workers to get away from the production line. Of the twelve or thirteen world champion boxers produced by France, only three have emerged since 1945; all the others were between the wars. The vigorous condition of boxing, that terrible profession that nevertheless offers social advancement to the lowest and most desperate members of the proletariat, showed that France was still far from escaping the awful living conditions of the first industrial revolution. Admittedly several of these champions came from Africa.

Football in the winter, and cycle racing chiefly in the summer, were both followed by millions with passionate interest. The chief events were the football championship and the French Cup, the Six Day race and the Tour de France, the latter a mammoth affair involving vast sums of money and massive publicity.

The democratisation of sport and the opportunities for social advancement it offered to the lowly born gave rise to some moral problems. The rise of 'shamateurism' or concealed professionalism caused internal and external rows. The four British national rugby teams refused to play with the French, who were reduced to matches with inexperienced German clubs. Efforts were made with Rugby League and professional soccer to put an end to bogus amateurism, but without success. This is all very extra-ordinary if one considers that twenty years earlier nobody would have dreamed of subsidising somebody's education, or have given him a job or a shop, simply because he was endowed with the necessary skill and physique for some sport.

The state did not share this public infatuation and did nothing for sport. The most recent constructions dated back to the 1924 Olympic Games – the

Colombes stadium and the Tourelles swimming pool. No help was given to athletes. The winner of the Olympic marathon of 1928 is said to have died a pauper. The star French four hundred metres runner became unemployed and disappeared. All this time other countries were exploiting their athletic successes as a branch of psychological warfare, but French athletic results were very mediocre.

Between 1927 and 1932 French tennis players beat all comers; then suddenly they ceased to count. As for athletics they won no gold medals in the Olympic Games between El Ouafi's in 1928 and Micheline Ostermeyer's two in 1948. In 1932 they were still getting into the finals, but in 1936 they failed totally.

In 1932 gold medals were won for cycle racing (2), fencing, riding, yachting and weight-lifting (3); in 1936 in cycle racing (3), fencing, weight-lifting, boxing (2) and wrestling. It is noticeable that the French went on winning in two of their traditional sports, one of which was essentially a sport of the masses. In 1936 the Germans were dumbfounded by French victories in certain contests involving physical strength or combative skill, quite contrary to their ideas of Frenchmen, who were only good at tennis, a rather effeminate game in their opinion. The history of sport in France between 1924 and 1929 should not be taken too seriously. The pathetic results obtained by French athletes in the 1936 Olympic Games in Berlin undoubtedly contributed to the idea of French decadence, just when writers like Montherlant and Giraudoux were hailing sport as one of the most valuable achievements of twentieth-century civilisation.

For the older generations, still clinging to traditional moral values, the adulation heaped on the stars of show business and the sports stadium seemed to stand in the way of a more solid recognition of those whose genius had benefited the human race. It seemed to the old a real sign of moral decadence that this applause should be reserved for Maurice Chevalier and the Pélissier brothers.

27

The dazzling brilliance of the thirties

As we have seen in the previous chapter, Paris was a city of world-wide importance, as a centre of *haute couture*, fashion, stage shows, ballet, variety and music halls, especially the Casino de Paris which, like the Folies-Bergère, attracted provincials and passing foreigners alike. Artists of all nationalities were to be found living in Montmartre, and even more so in Montparnasse, as well as young English and American writers, sometimes very hard up, like Henry Miller, or in desperate poverty, like George Orwell.

This was the historic role of Paris. It had for long been the capital of the art world, but the appearance of a cosmopolitan literary Bohemia was more recent. Although German publishers had specialised in publishing English and American best-sellers, it was in Paris, in the Rue Cardinale, after 1931 that the first continental editions of books by Faulkner, Hemingway and Kay Boyle were to appear.

What attracted such people to Paris was undoubtedly the contemporary atmosphere of moral and intellectual freedom which, during these years of so-called decadence, helped to produce an extraordinary flowering of science, letters and the arts. One symptom of the widespread character of this culture and its scrupulous desire to avoid cultural narcissism was the habit of according the highest praise to the work of French-speaking foreign writers, such as the Swiss novelist Ramuz and the Belgian historian Henri Pirenne.

Science and thought

The inter-war period, and especially the thirties, saw the practical application of the theories and seminal discoveries of the last years of the nineteenth and the early years of the twentieth centuries. The followers of Freud and Einstein were multiplying, and between them were destroying long-held scientific theories.

The ferment among intellectuals, and even in high society – for relativity became a fashionable mythology – can only be compared with the reaction to natural science in the age of the Enlightenment. The theories of Einstein,

272

the Curies and Becquerel, from which sprang the discoveries of Louis de Broglie and the Joliots, led to a wave of research which was shared by foreign scholars who had been driven from their countries by totalitarian regimes. The coming of relativity made a whole new system of mathematics necessary. The work constructing one was carried out by the physicists Langevin and Perrin, and the mathematicians Picard and Borel. This revolution continued, and in 1939 there appeared *Premier fascicule d'éléments de mathématiques*, a joint work under the pseudonym 'Nicholas Bourbaki'. The effect of these discoveries on the society of the thirties was to undermine belief in traditional theories of knowledge and experimental method.

The only government to take any interest in science was that of the Front Populaire, which founded the Centre National de Recherche Scientifique (CNRS) and the Musée de l'Homme a year later. At the time of the Universal Exhibition of 1937 an attempt was made to popularise science with the opening of the Palais de la Découverte. The Joliot-Curie cyclotron was one of its show pieces.

Prevailing trends in philosophy were reinforced by the decline of positivism. Einstein and Langevin were the counterparts of Bergson and Valéry. In the thirties the writings of Bachelard provided a link between relativity and philosophic relativism, while in his lectures he developed ideas about the unconscious which took shape later, chiefly after 1940, in his written work: for example, *L'Eau et les rêves, Essai sur l'imagination de la matière*, previously sketched out in his *La Formation de l'esprit scientifique, contribution à une psychanalyse de la connaissance objective* (1938). Bachelard, both poet and scholar, was not a follower of Bergson, but rather of Freud and the surrealists. Thanks to the Nobel prize award, Bergsonism had acquired a sort of official status, and for this very reason had lost the revolutionary impetus of its early days. Nobody in 1930 could have called it 'intellectual Boulangism'! The young communist philosophers Politzer (who wrote under the pseudonym Arouet) and Nizan (*Les Chiens de garde*, 1930) launched a joint attack on the whole apparatus of university philosophy. After 1930 Bergson published only one book of any significance, *Les Deux Sources de la morale et de la religion* (1932). The loss of his influence on any group but the right caused a gap which was quickly filled. The extreme intellectualism of Alain was an anachronistic relic without significance. Emmanuel Mounier's work of pure philosophy was produced after 1940. Paradoxically these two men, who were poles apart in their ways of thought, exerted a rather similar influence by teaching an austere ethic and an intellectual rigour, which they inculcated through their own personal behaviour at a time when standards were collapsing all round them. Mounier's personalist doctrine was more significant for its political effect – the left-wing commitment of some young Christian intellectuals – than for its philosophical content.

The most remarkable phenomenon of the thirties was the emergence of existentialism. Kierkegaard had been discovered at the same moment by both philosophers and theologians. Over twenty translations of his works, of very uneven quality, competed for readers in this period. Jean Wahl, in his masterly *Etudes Kierkegaardiennes* (1938), gives a list of seventeen titles translated between 1929 and 1937, and even this is incomplete. It was by way of Kierkegaard that existential philosophy had already reached a wide public before the appearance of Sartre. The Collège de Sociologie of Georges Bataille, Roger Caillois and Jean Wahl could claim descent from him, as also from Nietzsche, whose key works, translated by Geneviève Bianquis, were appearing at just that moment. Interest in Heidegger, on the other hand, was confined to a small group of younger philosophers. (J. Wahl, *Esquisse pour une histoire de 'L'existentialisme'*, Paris, L'Arche, 1949, p. 54.)

Translations of Jaspers and Husserl were also beginning to appear. Bataille and Sartre could reasonably be accused of simply using German philosophy to construct their own systems; but for various reasons the former remained unpublished while Sartre put his views across in a novel, *La Nausée* (1938).

Having once got under way, the rejection of rationalism was not going to stop at physics and philosophy. Its last stronghold, academic history, which was dominated by a positivism that accepted academic certainties, succumbed to the violent attacks and derision of Marc Bloch and Lucien Febvre, whose review *Annales d'histoire économique et sociale*, founded in 1929, brooked no restraint in its early days. The *Annales* school of historians broke down the compartments that separated history from other research activities, but failed to fill the widening gap that separated it from the ordinary educated reader. No historian since Ernest Lavisse and Camille Jullian had been elected to the Académie Française. It was the only branch of knowledge to be kept out, and it was the thirties that confirmed the ban on history with the repeated rejection of the Byzantine scholar, Charles Diehl.

The decline of belief in scientific infallibility and in current philosophies of life was accompanied by the idea of 'political commitment' by scholars, writers and artists. Even Julien Benda seemed to go back on his old opinions in announcing the return of classical rationalism to the service of patriotic activism, in his *Esquisse d'une histoire des Français dans leur volonté d'être une nation*.

Writers and artists

Writing and the arts were neither the reflection of existentialism nor were they the source of it; but they exhibited the same turmoil. Moving between grief and despair, disgust and revolt, resignation and commitment, artistic creativity of every kind bore the stamp of the 'spirit of the thirties' which marked the political ideas of the young intellectual.

The range, of course, was a very wide one. First, the *maîtres*, some members of the Académie, some not. Claudel, aloof, isolated by his arrogance and scorn of convention; Gide, strongly disapproved of by the right-wing young, but with great prestige on the left for having, earlier in his life, been the great wrecker of conventional ideas and bourgeois family values, and for his courageous advocacy of social reform; Colette, a brilliant writer with nothing much to say; Valéry, who reached the widest public because of his universality, his verse often hard to understand and his philosophy owing something to both Bergson and Einstein, but imbued with a sense of moral decline and the death of civilisation. After the established success of Roger Martin du Gard and Jules Romains comes the younger generation of writers with their obsession with guilt. They formed part of a general movement, and it is important to note the strong influence of English-speaking novelists, e.g. James Joyce, Aldous Huxley, Dos Passos and Faulkner. German writers too, e.g. Hermann Ungar, Fritz von Unruh and Ernst von Salomon. Something of all these was to be found in the novels of Céline, Malraux, Marcel Aymé and Sartre. The re-issue of Unamuno's *Le Sentiment tragique de la vie* was an indication of the general feeling.

Giraudoux and Montherlant were already passing judgment on man's daily life. Drieu and Malraux in their novels were writers who were trying to find themselves and the meaning of the human condition. For some, political commitment led to a new sort of humanism in which the service of a cause, the feeling of activity and sacrifice, carried a verdict on a decadent society. Denis de Rougemont's absurd expression 'thinking with one's hands' is nevertheless a condemnation of culture for culture's sake.

The only writer who had enough genius to invent his own language, Céline, in *Voyage au bout de la nuit*, tries to show that despair, 'the deadly malady', can be insuperable and may lead to nihilism by way of impotence and disgust, ending up with the sort of insane racism of *Bagatelles pour un massacre*, reflecting the subconscious of the French *petit bourgeois*. At a lower level the popular writers Dabit and Poulaille, for instance, were obsessed with the same sordid aspects of life, moving between resignation and revolt. In another sense society was being weakened by a force that cut across its traditional culture – the beginnings of a revolution that combined the influences of Freud, Marx and Rimbaud.

Some writers, including Jean Touchard and Emmanuel Mounier, tried to bury surrealism with *Le Second Manifeste* and *Un cadavre*, which marked the final break with former members of the group. There was also the 'Aragon affair', in which the poet, now a committed communist, was prosecuted for his poem *Front rouge*. The artists and poets who broke away – Desnos, Prévert and Buñel – rejected Breton's dictatorial ways and damned his retractions, while still holding with the solutions surrealism offered for the problems of aesthetics and existence. The group as a whole was very active, counting among its members Picasso, Dali, Ernst, Arp, Tanguy, Miró, Char, Eluard, Tzara, Crevel, Breton, Péret and many other younger people. With such names it is hard to see much evidence for a decline. On the contrary, the international surrealist exhibition at the beginning of 1938 in the Galérie des Beaux Arts in Paris, and the publication of the review *Minotaure* on the eve of war, were evidence of considerable vitality.

As in the surrealist novels of Crevel, the Catholic novelists pilloried social hypocrisy and spiritual sickness. Bernanos, Julien Green and Mauriac scared the habitual readers of René Bazin and others who dealt in good intentions and nice feelings. Others, reacting against industrial civilisation, extolled the idea of a return to healthy country life, not in the backward-looking spirit of the Catholic Academicians, upholders of a disciplined and godly sobriety, but in a spirit of revolt and conscientious objection. Such writers were Ramuz and Jean Giono. Then there were those who sought escape in the exotic, in adventure, imaginary or real. Such were Mac Orlan and Carco, the heirs of Alain-Fournier and Louis Chadourne.

Finally, there were those who were not interested in commenting on their own times and carried on a traditional type of literature, which, though unimportant, was significant for its need to forget or refuse to recognise the existence of a world crisis of civilisation. The works of Pierre Benoit, Joseph Kessel, André Maurois and Paul Morand were all printed in vast numbers, which showed that the great majority of French men and women did not want to be bothered with questions about themselves or their society, but preferred to have their minds taken off into something quite different. By the eve of the war, when Jean-Paul Sartre was making a name for himself, a lot of rubbish was appearing from the pens of the generation that between 1920 and 1930 had been called 'the under-thirties'. This was probably an unfair judgment, for Pierre Bost, Emmanuel Bove, Jean Prévost and André de Richaud, who seemed headed for success in about 1930, will certainly be read again once more.

What we have said above can be repeated almost word for word for the French cinema, which was largely inspired by contemporary novels, such as *La Bandera, Quai des Brumes* and *Hôtel du Nord*. The birth of the talkie, which initiated a golden age for France despite financial difficulties, produced a number of escapist films. René Clair, for instance, completely ignored contemporary society (unlike Labiche from whom he drew his inspiration) or else used cinema to try and defuse class rivalries (*A nous la liberté!*). Another was Pagnol, whose Provence derived totally from the rose-coloured world of *Les Lettres de mon moulin* and *Maurin des Maures*. But there were also directors of films that dealt with real life and real people and could be crudely down to earth; such were Duvivier, Feyder, Renoir, Vigo and Carné. By their pictorial beauty and with dialogue by writers such as Prévert, some managed to achieve a lyrical quality that transcended

Summary of films produced

Contemporary newsreel and other documents

Ce siècle à 50 ans	Director:	D. Tual, 1950
Entre deux guerres	Director:	M. de Gastyne, 1952
(caricature of Parisian life)		
Les Années folles	Director:	M. Alexandresco
(pre-1929)		et H. Torrent, 1960
36, le grand tournant	Director:	H. de Turenne
		et P. Hadrien, 1969

Documentary films

La Zone	Director:	G. Lacombe, 1928
A propos de Nice	Director:	J. Vigo, 1929
Nogent, Eldorado du	Director:	M. Carné, 1930
dimanche		
La vie est à nous	Director:	J. Renoir, 1936

Films of fiction that cast light on contemporary society

Les Nouveaux Messieurs	Director:	J. Feyder, 1929
(the anti-parliamentarians)		
Zéro de conduite	Director:	J. Vigo, 1932
(boarding-schools)		
Toni	Director:	J. Renoir, 1935
(immigrant workers)		
La Belle Équipe	Director:	J. Duvivier, 1936
(the unemployed)		
La Marseillaise	Director:	J. Renoir, 1937
(despite the title, reflects 'the spirit of 1936')		
La Règle du jeu	Director:	J. Renoir, 1939
(according to Sadoul: 'the new *Marriage of Figaro*')		

---

naturalism. What we have said is true of the whole period, and it was quite wrong for Sadoul, who wanted to give all the credit to the Front Populaire, to talk about the desert of French film-making between 1930 and 1935. The whole of the period 1930–45 was the great age of French poetic realism. One has only to mention *L'Atalante* (1934), *Jenny* (1936), *La Kermesse héroïque* (1936), *La Belle Equipe* (1936) and *La Règle du jeu* (1939).

Art was also committed to the left with Picasso, Léger and the surrealists; but this was perhaps the least popularly interesting branch of art in a period dominated by elderly artists who had already made their reputations, or had had them made by speculating dealers. Picasso, the Fauves, the Cubists had all arrived. The lesser artists suffered in the depression. Max Jacob, who had done well out of his painting in 1929, much better than out of his books, was not prosperous in the thirties. There was no one to take the place of Utrillo, Braque, Marquet or Matisse. Miró, Masson, Picabia, Ernst and Gromaire were not yet established; Kandinsky, Mondrian and

Klee were simply ignored. The specialist journals *L'Art vivant* and *Le Cra-pouillot* (which meant the dealers) were pushing André Favory and Terech-kovitch, unworthy scions of the Ecole de Paris – a preference which has not been supported by later generations.

Sculpture seemed even more static, through the pre-eminence of Rodin's pupils, mostly reacting against their master: Maillol (born 1861), Despiau and Drivier. There was also Pompon, the sculptor of animals. The archi-tectural legacy is the Pont de la Tournelle and the Palais de Chaillot.

Of all the arts modern music had won the widest success before 1914; but the great composers had all gone, except Ravel, and their successors had found it hard to gain acceptance. There was Paul Dukas, who died in 1935, Florent Schmitt and Albert Roussel. Of the younger generation the Group des Six had caused an uproar with their music in 1921, and had broken up in 1930. Honegger and Darius Milhaud managed to establish themselves; Auric started composing music for films; Poulenc composed a great deal, Germaine Taillefer very little. Louis Durey, the least distinguished member of the group, was the only musician to have, like Malraux and Léger, a political 'commitment'. Without him music would have remained quite out of touch with the anguishes and activities of its age. Erik Satie was subjected to disapproval and misunderstanding, and his disciples of the School of Arcueil had become scattered. Satie had remained loyal to the communist party; other members of the school joined later; but the only one who went on composing, Henri Sauguet, never took any interest in politics (like most musicians). In the politically neutral atmosphere of Max Jacob's circle of poets, actors, painters and musicians, Sauguet was to form his friendship with Igor Markevitch.

In 1936 the Jeune France group started performing and won a somewhat limited public. Its members included Messiaen, Jolivet and Lesur. Apart from performing before small societies like Le Triton or La Sérénade these young composers, including Sauguet himself, hardly got a hearing, while Schönberg, Bartók, Berg and Varèse were either quite unknown or totally misunderstood.

Music and painting, overshadowed alike by Stravinsky and Picasso, managed to survive and flourish, and the talents of some artists won recog-nition quite quickly. It remains true, however, that in the thirties the French were quite oblivious of the innovations that were revolutionising these two arts. This could be taken as further confirmation of national sclerosis if the brilliance of literature and the cinema did not give the lie to such an idea.

Culture on the fringe

It was an age of great, often very great, poets – Valéry, Claudel, Max Jacob, Pierre-Jean Jouve, Supervielle, Saint-John Perse, Reverdy, Eluard, Desnos, Michaux and many others. Not since the sixteenth century had France produced such a stream of brilliant and memorable poetry; but it was unread and often treated with contempt.

How widespread was interest in the arts we have been discussing? Some have accused Paris of suffocating cultural life in the provinces, except in Strasbourg. The answer depends on whether one looks at the question from the provincial or the Parisian viewpoint. The accusation had long been true, but did not altogether hold at this time. It was not the fault of Paris if Toulouse clung to the old-fashioned view that music began and ended with Meyerbeer and Puccini. Yet Toulouse had a literary life flourishing round the *Cahiers libres* edited by René Laporte, Philippe Lamour and André Cayatte. There were similar circles in Lyon and Algiers. There was not one provincial *lycée* without some lively argument in its top class being carried on by two or three surrealists. Joe Bousquet, Jean Giono and their friends took absolutely no notice of what went on in Paris, while in Marseille appeared *Les Cahiers du Sud*, the most important literary review of the day, except the *NRF*. This was at a time when the old Parisian reviews, *La Revue des deux mondes*, edited by René Doumic, and the *Mercure de France*, edited by Georges Duhamel, were dying on their feet. Music and dance were also to be found outside Paris, and Jean Vigo in Nice had set up one of the first film clubs, soon to be widely imitated. It could be argued that the very liveliness of the learned provincial societies was evidence of a form of conservatism.

Paul Souday's column in *Le Temps*, which was reasonably open to new ideas, had a wide circulation all over France, while *Les Nouvelles Litteraires* and *L'Art vivant*, both published by Larousse and edited by Maurice Martin du Gard and Jacques Guenne respectively, offered a fairly popular variety of culture. They were much read by provincial adolescents. After 1930 *Les Nouvelles Littéraires* suffered from the competition of the big politico-literary weeklies. However *Gringoire* and *Candide* diffused a culture that was far from being narrowly Parisian.

There were opposing tendencies inside Paris itself, where there was a 'right-bank' culture, whose idols were André Maurois, Sacha Guitry, Marcel Pagnol, *Le Roi des resquilleurs*, Ginger Rogers and Fred Astaire, and a 'left-bank' culture, with Jean Giraudoux, Luis Buñuel, *Drôle de drame*, Gaston Baty, William Powell and Myrna Loy. Between the reader of the *L'Almanach Vermot* and the reader of Saint-John Perse stretched a huge diversity of cultures, not setting up Paris against the provinces or one class against another, but a huge mass against a tiny fringe.

Most of the names quoted in this chapter, which in the outside world are seen as the glory of France in the thirties, only interested between fifty and fifty thousand people at the time; more often, between five hundred and five thousand. Nine out of ten Frenchmen still roared with laughter at a Braque or a Picasso. At the Ursulines cinema in the middle of the Latin Quarter each showing of Man Ray's *Etoile de mer* was like the battle on the first night of *Hernani*. The two greatest film directors of the period, Vigo and Renoir, were under a sort of curse. Renoir experienced nothing but setbacks up to 1935. The Front Populaire was his salvation, by which time Vigo was dead. We have seen how the theatre-going public neglected the Cartel des Quatre and crowded into the boulevard theatres. One could construct a marvellous dunce's anthology of the critical judgments passed by the *Canard enchaîné* on Claudel, Picasso and the surrealists. This weekly, much read by elementary school teachers, was only less absurd than *L'Œuvre*, the schoolmaster's daily, in which André Billy pontificated on the literary page. There the well-polished sonnets of Edmond Haraucourt were contrasted with the absurd and incomprehensible gibberish of *Charmes*. The intellectual left, mostly university teachers imprisoned in syllabuses in which poetry stopped at Leconte de Lisle and prose at Alphonse Daudet, had absolutely no desire to understand the poetry of their own age. They formed a last stronghold of readers of Anatole France. Facing them on the right bank was the right-wing bourgeoisie, who stuck to Henry Bordeaux, René Bazin and Jean de la Brète. The least retrograde taste was undoubtedly to be found at the extreme ends of the political spectrum. Only Léon Daudet in *L'Action française* and Paul Vaillant-Couturier in *L'Humanité* took any serious interest in youthful talent.

The French middle class was sunk in intellectual torpor. The most recently acquired book in the library of the lawyer or doctor, a Paul Bourget or a Zola, would have been bought by his father. The generation that lived between the wars is apt to be given the credit for the enduring results of an extraordinary artistic and literary creativity. In reality the society of that time was just as inert and unenterprising in this sphere as it was in that of economics and politics. Art and thought had their occasional growth sectors, just as industry did. But if one turns one's eyes away from the few great figures, one is faced by the fact that the most successful book of the period was Gabriel Chevalier's *Clochemerle*, that the fashionable painters were Gabriel Domergue and Jacques-Emile Blanche, and that the state commissioned its buildings from pompous hacks, and not Le Corbusier. To appreciate an ailing society's view of its own age, one has only to see the sort of people the Académie honoured with its membership.

One may well ask how poets managed to live and write poetry, and young painters to survive. Economic conditions at the time were not all that difficult. With 1,500 francs squeezed out of grandparents, aunts and cousins, a group of young folk could put out a review which might last for two or three issues. Then one started again under another title, e.g. *L'Ours en peluche* (The Teddy-Bear), *L'Oeuf dur* (The Hard-Boiled Egg), *La Courte Paille* (The Short Straw). With a hand press, Jacques and Marguerite Maret kept *Feuillets inutiles*, the most luxurious of all poetry magazines, going for a long time. Guy Levis-Mano ran a sort of cottage industry

French intellectuals, 1928–39

Membership of the Académie Française in 1928	Recruitment to the Académie Française from 1928 to the end of the Republic	
Louis Barthou	Maurice Paléologue	1928
Cardinal Baudrillart	Maréchal Pétain	1929
Joseph Bédier	André Chaumeix	1930
Henri Bergson	Pierre Benoit	1931
Louis Bertrand	Général Weygand	1931
Albert Besnard	Abel Bonnard	1932
Henry Bordeaux	François Mauriac	1933
Paul Bourget	Duc de Broglie	1934
Abbé Brémond	Léon Bérard	1934
Eugène Brieùx	Maréchal Franchet d'Espérey	1934
Jules Cambon	André Bellessort	1935
André Chevrillon	Claude Farrère	1935
Clemenceau (absent)	Jacques Bainville	1935
Maurice Donnay	Louis Gillet	1935
René Doumic	Georges Duhamel	1935
Edouard Estaunié	Amiral Lacaze	1936
Maréchal Foch	Monseigneur Grente	1936
Georges Goyau	Jacques de Lacretelle	1936
Gabriel Hanotaux	André Maurois	1938
Abel Hermant	Jérôme Tharaud	1938
Maréchal Joffre	Charles Maurras	1938
Célestin Jonnart		
Camille Jullian	*Winners of Nobel prizes*	
Duc de la Force	*in France between the wars*	
Pierre de la Gorce	Léon Bourgeois	Peace	1920
Henri Lavedan	Anatole France	Literature	1921
Georges Lecomte	Jean Perrin	Physics	1926
Charles Le Goffic	Aristide Briand	Peace	1926
Georges Lenôtre	Henri Bergson	Literature	1927
Maréchal Lyautey	Ferdinand Buisson	Peace	1927
Louis Madelin	Charles Nicolle	Medicine	1928
Emile Mäle	Louis de Broglie	Physics	1929
Pierre de Nolhac	F. et I. Joliot-Curie	Chemistry	1935
Emile Picard	Roger Martin du Gard	Literature	1937
Raymond Poincaré		
Georges de Porto-Riche		
Marcel Prévost		
Henri de Régnier		
Henri Robert		
Paul Valéry		

publishing business to suit his taste. The scenery for Shaw's *The Apple Cart* cost Georges Pitoëff five francs.

Painters could sell their work, for they did not ask high prices. Only the great names were becoming prohibitively expensive. Max Jacob sold a drawing of himself by Picasso for ten thousand francs, while his own gouaches fetched one thousand five hundred francs and his drawings five hundred francs. An oil painting by Kisling or Pascin sold for about five thousand francs, the equivalent of one month's pay for a university lecturer or a Parisian executive at the top of his career.

The general public showed less bad taste in its appreciation of the novel than of the arts and poetry. The tally of the most widely read authors – Marcel Aymé, René Bazin, Georges Bernanos, Louis-Ferdinand Céline, Gabriel Chevalier, Pierre L'Ermite, André Malraux, François Mauriac, Marcel Pagnol and Saint-Exupéry – add up to quite a creditable collection. However, it remains true that, if one bases one's idea of the general level of culture in the thirties on what has survived, one gets a wholly mistaken impression.

PART V

The Front Populaire

28

The making of the Front Populaire

The immediate result of the events of 6 February was the formation of a government headed by Gaston Doumergue. Faced with danger, the political establishment turned to an old man, for the third time in less than twenty years. Doumergue was an old stager, whose cheerful smiling manner and apparent simplicity was reassuring. Having lived in retirement since the end of his presidential term, 'Gastounet' seemed like a Pagnol character played by Raimu. In fact he was a wily operator and, like Grévy, had generally managed to get his own way by playing rival politicians off against one another. Like all old men, he was secretly rather authoritarian and concealed a love of power behind a pretence of indifference. He was clever enough to make the collection of former prime ministers feel they needed him badly, and he was loudly welcomed by the crowd on his arrival in Paris. He took no ministerial portfolio, nor did the two ministers of state, Herriot and Tardieu, representing the two possible majorities in the Chamber, the old and the new. Barthou, Germain-Martin, Laval, Louis Marin, Albert Sarraut, Flandin and Piétri took part in this ministry of all the talents. Marshal Pétain became minister for war. There was one new face, Adrien Marquet, a leader of the neo-socialists. As in 1926 the result was a right-wing ministry, a sort of Union Nationale, which under the guise of a party truce relegated the extreme left, that is the socialists, to opposition. The comparison is not quite accurate since Poincaré had in the course of his life made only one move, from centre left to centre right, while Doumergue, like Clemenceau before him and Laval after, had moved from extreme left much further to the right. The fact that the cabinet and its leader held such views cleared the way for a *rapprochement* of the extreme left-wing parties. The immediate results of 6 February were thus to be totally gainsaid by its more distant consequences.

The impotence of government and parliament

Doumergue had first to cope with pro-republican reactions on 9 and 12 February against the Ligues and in protest over the Prince affair, which came hard on the heels of the Stavisky scandal. By the end of the month things seemed to have calmed, and Doumergue might have been able to achieve fairly easily the constitutional reforms he had in mind.

The government's economic incompetence suffices to explain its rapid loss of popularity. Doumergue started by enacting a half-year deficit budget to give him time to prepare the cuts he imposed in April, i.e. reductions in civil and military pensions, and in the number of civil servants. However, in spite of Marquet's plan for large public works, to be paid for from the reserves in the social security funds, there was total economic and financial breakdown.

Externally things were looking bad in spite of Barthou's strenuous efforts. Hitler's power had been enormously strengthened by the 'Night of the Long Knives', then by Hindenburg's death. Hitler had meanwhile on 25 July brought about the assassination of Dollfuss, the Austrian chancellor, in an SS rising, whose aim was to bring about the Anschluss between Germany and Austria. Mussolini reacted at once and the Germans withdrew. France did nothing, for fear of lending support to Italian pressure on the Danubian states. In fact, Barthou tried to strengthen and increase counterbalancing alliances by getting the USSR admitted to the League of Nations in September 1934. Unhappily for France Barthou shared the fate of the king of Jugoslavia when he was murdered in Marseille on 9 October by Croat nationalists in the pay of Mussolini. Laval succeeded him as minister for foreign affairs.

The government was already in decline when, in the autumn, at Tardieu's instigation, the prime minister put forward his plan for constitutional reform. The aim was to strengthen the executive by giving the President more positive powers. The prime minister would become no more than the chief minister. The Chamber could be dissolved without the Senate's authorisation. Measures involving public expenditure would no longer be initiated in the Chamber, and the current budget could be extended for another year if a new one was not voted at the due time.

Now that the emergency was over, the saviour was no longer wanted. The radicals strongly objected to the radio talks by means of which Doumergue reported directly to the nation. Herriot, who had been kept rather in the background while Tardieu was being petted, decided to quit. Herriot had not wanted in 1932 to repeat the Cartel of 1924; nor did he wish in 1934 to provide the same sort of alibi for the right that he had arranged in 1926. The radicals' excuse for leaving the government was the demand for special powers which would have given Doumergue a free hand for three months. Finally, Doumergue resigned on 8 November without having won any of his hoped-for reforms.

From November 1934 to 1936, the Union Nationale was kept going by an agreement between the moderates and the Radicals. Within a few hours Flandin managed to put together a cabinet, which was joined by Mandel but left by Tardieu on the pretext of ill health. The new prime minister was an upper middle-class liberal, more akin to Poincaré than was Tardieu, whose deeply anti-Marxist feeling he shared; but he differed from him in his hatred of the extreme right. He was genuinely of the centre. Perhaps Léon Blum was offering him some indirect help when he congratulated himself in the Chamber on frustrating 'an attempt to gain personal power'. Flandin needed some help from the left, but it was not forthcoming. Tardieu's career as a parliamentarian may be said to have ended at this point. From now on his ambition was to achieve power and destroy the constitution by action in the streets. The rapid worsening of the financial crisis was accompanied by a resurgence of political trouble. In order to cope with international pressure on the franc by the banking world, Flandin asked parliament to give him powers to enact the necessary measures by statutory decrees. He was voted down on 31 May. Within a few days the president of the Chamber, Fernand Bouisson, a former member of the SFIO, managed to form a broadly based cabinet, which included Herriot, Caillaux and Pétain. It was immediately voted out because of its financial policy. Laval formed the next cabinet on very similar lines. Out of sheer exhaustion parliament gave him the very same authority to govern by decree 'to defend the franc' that had been denied to Flandin and Bouisson. Laval's four to five hundred statutory orders, drawn up by the cabinet between July and October 1935, amount to the only consistent body of political, social and economic legislation between 1931 and the arrival of the Front Populaire. They ordained a cut of 10 per cent in all public expenditure, both by the state and by public bodies, in all kinds of rent and in loan interest. The price of gas, electricity and coal was similarly reduced. This was all-out deflation, cutting every form of expenditure, both public and private, and its aim was to get back to the gold standard.

This policy was a total failure and there was no end to inflation. This was because the price cuts were not accompanied by any serious attempt to improve the economy or check the survival of the economically most unfit. Laval's policy was the most damaging because it was the most systematic. The deflation of summer 1935 stifled the emerging signs of a slight recovery. The overvalued currency enfeebled the economy and perpetuated depression. Only Paul Reynaud understood that there was nothing to be gained and no prospect of recovery without a rise in prices, and hence a devaluation. The immediate result of Laval's actions was the social unrest that quickly led to the triumph of the Front Populaire. If one is to believe General Gamelin – and one must allow for his desire to escape responsibility for defeat – it was at this moment, between 1934 and 1935, that the impending war was lost on the economic front. Meanwhile, economic recovery was beginning elsewhere, e.g. in Great Britain, the Dominions and the United States from 1933, in Germany from 1935. Recovery was even faster in Great Britain in 1935 and in Germany in 1936. It was slowing up in the United States, but even there industrial activity was far greater than in France. Unemployment was falling everywhere except in France.

There was a great increase in activity of the Ligues during Laval's ministry. Blood was shed in Limoges in a brawl between the Croix-de-Feu and the Front Populaire supporters. The reaction of parliament was to give the government powers to dissolve the Ligues by decree and to stiffen the penalties for violation of the press laws. However, the attitude of the prime minister, who suspended communist mayors but remained friendly with Colonel de la Rocque, was quite ambivalent.

By now the Laval ministry was doomed, weakened by setbacks in its foreign policy. The middle classes, who voted radical, were particularly hard hit by deflation. Six months before the elections, it was obvious, from the extreme discontent throughout the country, that the Front Populaire was going to win. Herriot left the government after publicly damning it, taking the other radical ministers with him. Laval resigned on 24 January. It was to be four years before he was to be back in power as the result of France's defeat. Herriot and Delbos, both radicals, refused to form a government, but Sarraut accepted. It was to be a government of transition, which still included Mandel and Flandin but had a slightly left-wing bias with radicals predominating and Chautemps back in office. Thus the Union Nationale was succeeded by a republican grouping. The right went into opposition, and the socialists gave discreet support to this stop-gap ministry, which finally achieved nothing.

The governments arising out of the February 1934 change of majority completely failed in their efforts to restore the political and economic situation. They succeeded in making people forget the blatant incapacity of the radicals between 1932 and February 1934, but anti-republicanism continued to thrive on the depression and the paralysis of government. Since 1914 attempts had been made to give the executive more power and make the premiership a genuinely administrative office. Then the *décrets-lois* had appeared, i.e. power was given to the executive to modify laws. What had begun as war-time improvisation developed as a natural consequence of the crisis. The office of prime minister, with its attendant administrative functions, was officially recognised by a law of December 1934 and set up in the Hôtel Matignon. Neither Doumergue nor Flandin took any specific portfolio, and so it was with the four successive Front Populaire cabinets.

Décrets-lois came to be used more and more in the fight against the depression. They considerably strengthened the hand of the executive; but their effect was drastically marred by the instability of ministries, for parliament either voted cabinets out the moment they promulgated necessary but unpopular decrees, or refused to grant plenary powers to unwanted prime ministers. The Senate's role was particularly harmful. Its mode of election and self-renewal endowed it with an almost rocklike permanence. Representing only a minority of the population, and full of wealthy reactionaries, it nearly always managed to frustrate the will of the electorate and to stand in the way of all reform, except during the first weeks of Blum's first government. Between 1925 and 1938 the Senate overturned five ministries – Herriot, Tardieu and Laval once each, and Blum twice. In fact it had a paralysing effect on any leader without a very strong personality. In its opposition to all political and social change and its attachment to ideas that had been rendered obsolete by the First World War, the Senate had become the gravedigger of the Republic.

The growing threat of fascism

Peace was threatened by the breakdown of talks on disarmament and by France's weakness as a European power, while internal security was endangered by anti-republican feeling engendered by the success of fascism and Nazism. France was isolated economically by the collapse of the gold bloc, which Italy had left in 1934 and Belgium in 1935. Diplomatically, the collapse of the 'spirit of Geneva' – unregretted by the right which had always opposed it – had left the country without any allies. Poland signed a bilateral agreement with Germany after the collapse of the Locarno pact. Barthou had had the enormous merit of stimulating diplomatic action while managing to preserve simultaneously the contradictory policies of encircling east European alliances and a purely defensive military strategy symbolised by the Maginot Line. He breathed new life into the Petite Entente, which was dealt a serious blow by the assassination of the king of Jugoslavia and of Barthou himself. He had begun to seek an alliance with the USSR. This was pursued by Laval and ended with a pact of mutual assistance, signed in Paris on 2 May 1935, followed by a visit to Moscow by the French minister. At the same time Laval came to an agreement with Italy guaranteeing the integrity of Austria and reaffirming the Versailles treaty in the face of the growing threat from Germany.

The agreements with the USSR and Italy in the spring of 1935 crowned the efforts of Barthou; but his successor, Laval, was deeply aware of the contradiction between offensive diplomacy and purely defensive military strategy. A total change of direction was financially out of the question. Hence French diplomacy now tended to lean towards *rapprochement* with Germany, going along with the British, in the hope of diverting Hitler's expansionism towards the east. This policy might have pleased both warring factions at home – the left wing for its pacifism and the right because it favoured fascism. Unfortunately it was a failure. Hitler's effrontery grew with success. He tore up the military clauses of the Versailles treaty. While German rearmament was being carried out secretly, the French took no action, because the general staff was against any sort of agreement which would have legitimised it; when it came out into the open in March 1935, they still took no action. A year later Hitler denounced the Locarno pact and sent troops into the demilitarised Rhineland. Sarraut, then prime minister, did no more than utter loud protests, and the Versailles treaty now lay in ruins. The French left had nothing to say as they had always been against the treaty. They thought that now that Hitler had achieved parity, he might make no further claims. As for the cabinet, it was paralysed by the defection of its allies, Poland and Great Britain, and above all by the approach of the elections. The chiefs of the armed forces, Maurin, Gamelin, Pétain and Weygand loudly demanded violent retaliation – in effect a cover-up for inactivity. They knew well that reservists do not get called to the colours within two months of a general election. According to Paul Reynaud, the government were relieved that Great Britain withheld support because it gave them an excuse for their spinelessness. Militarily this was France's last chance, and they let it slip, at the very moment when deflationary policies had seriously damaged the economy.

Laval's pacts were without effect. No advantage was taken of the Russian alliance because it might have been too much help to the Front Populaire at the forthcoming elections. The agreement with Italy was wrecked by the Abyssinian war which resulted in the western democracies breaking off relations with Mussolini, although Laval was providing discreet support. His action resulted in a serious disagreement with Great Britain, which partly explains the latter's inertia towards Hitler's demands. On the verge of the Front Populaire's accession to power, France found herself without diplomatic backing or material resources with which to resist the claims of Hitler and, soon after, of Mussolini, threatened as she was by civil war within her own borders.

After the *journées* of February 1934 most of the Ligues began to fade out, as has so often happened in history, but the Croix-de-Feu benefited from its rivals' weakness and went on growing. Numbering 35,000 members in February 1934, by the summer it had more than 100,000 and reached 450,000 by the beginning of 1936. They had benefited most from 6 February, which is odd when one remembers that it was only the lack of enterprise of de la Rocque's forces that had saved the Chamber from invasion. It is well known that the Ligues were financed by the most politically active and anti-republican of the employers' organisations. Coty, de Wendel and Mercier were involved in the Croix-de-Feu, who later insisted that they received no subsidies. Tardieu, however, claimed that he and other right-wing governments helped de la Rocque from 1929 to 1932 with secret service money. De la Rocque is said to have had 20,000 francs a month from Tardieu, 10,000 from Laval, then later 150,000 from Tardieu. The Croix-de-Feu backed Doumergue's ministry, then at Tardieu's instigation vehemently attacked his successor Flandin. On the other hand, they supported Laval in 1935.

When historians discuss the characteristics of 'French fascism', they make the point that it was de la Rocque's collaboration with right-wing governments that distinguished his movement from its foreign counterparts. His book *Service public*, written in 1934, repeats all the well-worn commonplaces of the extreme right, such as are to be found in the creed of the Union Nationale des Combatants as well as the Ligue des Contribuables. This is why the genuine fascists in the colonel's entourage, like Pucheu, broke with him in July 1935. It is true none the less that the tactics of the Volontaires Nationaux were the same as those of all European fascist movements from the moment they became mass organisations. By March 1934 the Croix-de-Feu were mounting demonstrations in 'red' districts, e.g. the north-east of Paris, the 'black country' of the Pas-de-Calais and Lille. Mobilised in military formations, the *dispos* went in for commando-style operations. Armed and motorised they would move into places where the local authority was left-wing controlled and behave as if there were a civil war on, controlling the traffic at crossroads and pretending to occupy public buildings. If the locals objected, they would provoke a fight, and blood was sometimes shed in the ensuing brawls. With help from the police and the army, some members managed to get trained in the use of arms, although this seems to have been strictly against their leader's orders. In the face of this provocation the left managed to keep cool and to avoid street fighting as much as possible.

De la Rocque appears to have been vague about his real aims, but his policy of street demonstrations was endlessly provocative; and if socialist or communist mayors took steps to stop them, the prefects suspended their powers to take police action.

In October 1935 came the story of a plan to neutralise the 'red districts' following a seizure of power in Paris. In fact various manœuvres did take place, with the Croix-de-Feu occupying parts of Paris and strategic positions on the main traffic routes. However, through the mediation of the deputy Ybarnégaray, de la Rocque agreed to this disarming of the Ligues and submitted to the law of January 1936 authorising their dissolution. Thus the leader of the Croix-de-Feu, despite his horrendous speechifying, seems often to have behaved as a restraining influence, always stopping short of a final bid for power. As he was the only leader with a significant body of followers, his rivals, Taittinger in particular, could only rage impotently.

The anti-fascist counter-attack

For the left, argument about de la Rocque's ideas and beliefs was irrelevant; what clearly mattered were his methods. The vastly superior material backing he had, at a time when only the ruling classes owned motor-cars, was a danger to the Republic. The colonel even boasted of his own aeroplanes. There were left-wing elements in the army; there were many in the police; and they were showing signs of unrest. Whether or not the menace of fascism was exaggerated, anti-fascism was a reality and a necessity. It is almost true to say that the Front Populaire was started and established to form an opposition to de la Rocque.

In 1932, and even in 1934, an alliance of the three main left-wing parties seemed out of the question. The isolation of the communists was all the more absolute for being self-imposed. However, in May 1932 a first attempt was made to break down this isolation with the Amsterdam-Pleyel committee. Romain Rolland and Henri Barbusse, authors and communists, but above all pacifists, took the initiative with a congress in defence of peace held in Amsterdam, followed by another in Paris at the Salle Pleyel, which because of Hitler's rise to power brought anti-fascists and pacifists together. The two communist writers, who were rather scorned by the younger generation, gathered round them a large number of politicians, trade unionists and intellectuals. But any paid-up members of the socialist or radical parties or the CGT who attended were disowned by their groups and represented only themselves, as did the rest. The committee was thus crypto-communist and had no very wide-reaching effect, especially as the communists still retained their basic stance, denouncing social democracy as the arch-enemy of the proletariat.

Hitler's arrival in power had triggered off another tentative move towards an alliance from a different quarter. This was initiated by Gaston Bergery, radical deputy for Mantes and founder of the Front Commun Contre le Fascisme. Bergery was on the extreme left of his party, which he left after Daladier's capitulation in February 1934. He always prided himself on having been the real founder of the Front Populaire. He gathered round him a group of high-powered politicians – Georges Monnet, a deputy, one of the great hopes of the SFIO, who rated him as one of their best economists, and a specialist in agricultural affairs; Jacques Doriot, the most popular of the communist leaders, but already at odds with the party policy-makers; the physicist Langevin, a communist sympathiser; Benoît Frachon, who represented the CGTU; Bernard Lecache, president of the Ligue Internationale Contre l'Antisemitisme. All these helped to form the initial group. But the SFIO gave Monnet no backing and he had to resign, and the same thing happened to Doriot and Frachon. The radical party gave no support to Bergery, who was mistrusted by Herriot and Daladier. Consequently all attempts at united action by the left failed as long as the fascist threat was not too obvious. On 6 February the communist ARAC (Association Républicaine des Anciens Combattants) joined forces with the right-wing ex-servicemen, but the *rapprochement* brought about by the riots of 9 and 12 February was purely temporary.

The demonstration organised by the communist party in the Place de la République on 9 February 'against fascism and the murderers Daladier and Frot' had nothing to do with any sort of common front. Although officially banned, it took place, and counter action by the police turned it into a savage fight near the Gare du Nord and the Gare de l'Est and at Belleville. There were nine dead and hundreds of wounded. There were certainly many young socialists, lapsed communists, anarchists and members of the extreme left fighting beside the embattled communists. The big dailies, which had been enthusiastic on the 6th, angry on the 7th and more restrained on the 8th and 9th, after the 10th abruptly stopped inciting the people of Paris to rise up. The soothing influence of Doumergue, but also the fear of 'the man with a knife between his teeth', induced the agitators to preach appeasement.

It was now the turn of the CGT to order a general strike for 12 February. The socialists decided to join in and organised a march from the Porte de Vincennes to the Place de la Nation. The CGTU decided to take part in the strike and the communist party to join in the march. There had been no prior discussion between these people, who had been abusing each other daily for years; but for the first time the communists followed in the wake of the reformist group and the SFIO. During the night of the 11th there were more clashes between the extreme left and the police, with some dead. The general strike was a complete success in both Paris and the provinces. One hundred thousand took part in the Vincennes march which was not opposed by the government, and the two columns of fraternal enemies mingled in the Place de la Nation. Men who had known the schism of Tours (1920) wept with emotion. There were demonstrations all over the country – in Toulouse, Bordeaux, Grenoble, Marseille, Mulhouse, Limoges and in many smaller towns, especially in the south and in the coalmining districts of the Pas-de-Calais.

These *journées* of 9, 11 and 12 February came to be invested with great significance in left-wing folklore, for they had 'saved the Republic'. They also made the party leaders stop and think. On the 9th the communist party had attracted a following that was far more numerous than its own membership; on the 12th the leaders, who hated each other, had had unity forced on them through the fraternisation of their respective rank and file. In the long term they were going to be forced to acquiesce in this strong grass-roots urge towards union. But only in the long term because, despite everything, these events had no immediate effect. On 12 February Cachin declared in his speech that the communists had not come out to defend a rotting Republic, while Blum asserted that they had all drawn together to defend the best regime – the Republic. The only immediate and positive result was the foundation of the Comité de Vigilance des Intellectuels Antifascistes by three distinguished professors – Alain, who was pro-radical, Rivet, a socialist and Langevin, a communist sympathiser. Unlike the Amsterdam-Pleyel committee it never had a communist majority.

The key to the situation lay to all appearances with the SFIO, but in reality with the International, of which the French communist party was only a subordinate branch. Up to May 1934, and strictly in line with Soviet foreign policy, whose attitude towards Nazi Germany remained undecided for several months, the principal enemy was 'social fascism', meaning social democracy, the exploiter of the working class. Thorez went on saying that socialist workers must be won over to communism, in obedience to the ten-year-old slogan of 'plucking the chicken' (*Maurice Thorez, vie secrète et vie publique*). The go-it-alone policy continued, against the wishes of the rank and file and their communist sympathisers. Doriot dissented from the party line and stood up for the same joint action that he had organised in his own bailiwick of Saint-Denis with a committee of anti-fascist action, which included militant members of the CGT, the CGTU, the SFIO and the communist party.

Doriot's insubordination forced the French communist leaders to tighten up on party discipline and the policy of splendid isolation. Meanwhile the International had been driven to the conclusion that the victory of Nazism over the most highly organised proletariat in the world had hardly advanced the prospects for communist revolution, and that to defeat fascism they had to come to an understanding with the socialists. The attack launched by Doriot against the leadership on the evening of 9 February had won him enormous popularity in the party, and he might conceivably have become its head. But it appears that he had already decided to get himself expelled and to be independent of the International. This left the International with no alternative but to continue supporting Thorez (who was secretly controlled by Fried) but getting him to follow a totally new policy. The break with Doriot and his expulsion, between April and June 1934, left Thorez free to get rid of those who opposed a *rapprochement* with the socialists and the middle-class left, and to move from independent action towards a combined front against fascism. This virtual about-turn was officially sanctioned at the Ivry conference in June. The last group to accept the idea of joint action, the communist party, was now to be the principal driving force in the very policy advocated by Doriot, but which, paradoxically, only his expulsion a month earlier had made possible. (Cf. J.-P. Brunet, 'Reflexions sur la scission de Doriot', *Le Mouvement social*, 70, 1970.)

They now had to cope with the reservations of the socialists. These had been intensified by a communist threat to wreck a 'socialist-fascist' gathering. The CGT had been obliged to call the gathering off. In spite of the mistrust of Léon Blum, Paul Faure and Jean Lebas, pressure from the militants forced the socialists into talks with the communists. On 14 July, at the invitation of the socialists leaders, delegates from the Parisian branches of the two parties had a meeting. A short time later the national leaders negotiated the pact of combined action of 27 July. The socialists had been heaped with abuse by the communists almost until the previous day, so they were particularly anxious 'in the face of the danger presented by fascism to the world of labour ... to put an end to attacks, insults and criticism'. They wanted a treaty of non-aggression between the socialists and communists.

The communist plan made no reference to immediate past and put the accent on the fight against fascism. The first sentence of their plan, repeated in the text of the pact, said: 'The central committee of the communist party and the permanent administrative commission of the socialist party are inspired by the will to fight fascism.' (*Cahiers de l'Institut Maurice Thorez*, 1 April 1966.) In spite of the positive attack against the pauperising *décrets-lois*, this key stage in the formation of the Front Populaire was marked above all by its anti-fascist stance. From now onwards the communist party was to show much wisdom and determination. They saw that to beat fascism it was essential to prevent it from winning recruits from the middle classes, who had assured its success wherever it had attained power. At the end of October they began to woo 'the left-wing elements in the radical party'. Evidently they were thinking of Daladier, who at that time was not in the cabinet. In that month, too, the communists made some gains in the cantonal elections. After Thorez and Duclos had persuaded the central committee of the party to approve the change of policy, Thorez made a speech in the Chamber on 13 November appealing for the support of the middle classes. It is certain that the socialists, much more reluctant up till now, were having their hands forced. Among the radicals, those who supported a pact with the extreme left were still in a minority at the Nantes congress in October 1934.

The middle-class radicals to whom the communists were now appealing were antagonised by Laval's economic policy. His visit to Moscow was marked on 15 May 1935 by a celebrated episode. In their joint communiqué Laval obtained from Stalin a statement of his understanding and full approval of 'the policy of national defence pursued by France in keeping her armed forces at the level needed for her security'. Laval's aim, cunning rather than clever, was to embarrass the French communists by making their anti-militarism look absurd in the light of the Russians' need for a pact with France against German foreign policy. Contrary to expectations, this in fact made it easier for the communists to express wholehearted patriotism.

Abandoning the anti-militaristic dogma on which their movement had been founded and the pre-1914 slogans of revolutionary syndicalism, the communists turned back to Blanquism, the most chauvinistic strand in

French socialism. The spirit of Jacobinism prevailed right up to the war. It was as if a long-suppressed patriotism burst out with extraordinary force, with immense satisfaction and relief to the militant rank and file, happy to leave their isolation. The party now became a mass organisation with numbers increasing from one to two hundred thousand. It seems to have quite misunderstood the real policy of the Soviet Union, which had made a merely circumstantial alliance, implying no sort of ideological agreement nor any idea of backing parliamentary democracy against Nazism. France and Germany were bourgeois states whose disagreements were to be exploited without any preference for either. The French communists, on the other hand, really believed that the defence of the Republic and the fatherland were an integral part of all socialist values and that the Franco-Soviet alliance was irrevocable – ideas which led them blindly up the path to 1939.

For the moment all obstacles to good relations with other left-wing patriots were removed in so far as the latter were not put off by this sudden and total conversion. The socialists and communists did well in the municipal elections of May 1935. The radicals did less well in the country, where they were allied with the right, than in the towns, where they joined forces with the socialists. The election of Paul Rivet on the second ballot in a ward of the Vth *arrondissement* in Paris demonstrated the effectiveness of the alliance. This seat had been disputed between left and right since the war. The president of the Union Française des Combattants, rated a 'fascist', had won by one vote in 1929. He was well ahead on the first ballot and seemed certain to win, when the four left-wing and extreme left candidates retired in favour of the socialist founder of the Comité de Vigilance. Paul Rivet's victory made a great stir, and served as useful experience, for the Front Populaire called for by the communists had not yet taken shape.

The radical party was now split: on one side Herriot and the other ministers of the Laval cabinet; on the other, Daladier and the left-wing radicals.

The Amsterdam-Pleyel committee suggested a huge demonstration in Paris for 14 July. The executive committee of the radical party, moved by the anti-fascist mystique, decided to take part. This was the origin of the Comité d'Organisation de Rassemblement Populaire presided over by Victor Basch, professor at the Sorbonne and president of the Ligue des Droits de l'Homme. It comprised delegates from the communist, socialist, radical and neo-socialist (USR) parties, from the CGT, the CGTU, the Ligue des Droits de l'Homme, the Amsterdam-Pleyel committee, the Comité de Vigilance, from Action Combattante and from the Fédération Nationale des Combattants Républicains. The 14th of July 1935 saw the birth of the Front Populaire. In the morning there was a mass meeting in the Buffalo stadium at Montrouge, followed by an enthusiastic procession from the place de la Bastille to the place de la Nation, in which half a million people marched in a frenzy of emotion over the new-found unity of the left. The left-wing radical leaders, Daladier, Jean Zay and Pierre Cot, marched side by side with the communist and socialist leaders. The cheers for Daladier were his compensation for 6 February. This was the second stage in the formation of the Front Populaire.

Patriotism was the keynote of most of the speeches. The left laid claim to the heritage of Joan of Arc, the military glory of the Great Revolution and Verdun, all mixed up with socialism and the October Revolution. They all swore an oath 'to stay united in the defence of democracy'. Thanks to Victor Basch, the Comité d'Organisation became permanent and, in the Jacobin tradition, did its best to branch out in provincial local committees to prepare for the elections. It also set up links between the various national party headquarters to further agreement on a programme.

By October 1935 Laval was obviously losing influence. The radical congress gave Daladier a majority and voted in favour of the party supporting the programme of a Rassemblement Populaire, but the cabinet only agreed in January 1936. By this time the programme was generally known.

It had been difficult to agree on a programme, for the only thing they all had in common was anti-fascism. The radicals did not want any structural reforms and rejected all the socialists' suggestions. They believed that everything could be solved politically in a liberal economy in spite of the lessons of the last four years. The communists simply wanted the Front Populaire to come into being, and they were particularly anxious not to alienate the radicals and so push the middle classes into the arms of the fascists. They sided firmly against the socialists and the entente was launched. The Front Populaire programme had well-defined anti-fascist policies, but no economic or social proposals. Priority was given to the suppression of the Ligues, the defence of personal rights, press reform and the nationalisation of the armaments industry – in order to penalise the arms dealers.

For the economy, the radicals acquiesced in the reform of the Banque de France, the tool of the 'two hundred families' and the 'wall of money' which had broken Herriot's first ministry in 1925. Both deflation and devaluation were rejected as remedies for the depression. The need for state intervention on the lines of Roosevelt's New Deal was recognised, in order to increase purchasing power and encourage full employment. The only precise move planned was the abolition of the *décrets-lois*.

This was a reasonable programme and full of vague promises. It could serve as an electoral manifesto for a coalition, but not as a programme for a coalition government, for none of the contradictions inherent in the three parties' aims had been ironed out. None of the groups taking part was prepared to sacrifice any of its independence. The Front Populaire would never have existed without the threat of fascism. It was the patient creation of the communist party, who won great credit for it at the Third International. At the Seventh congress Thorez was acclaimed and elected to the praesidium. In two years he had made certain of the French party leadership, and he became general secretary at the beginning of 1936. During the first six months of 1936 he worked unceasingly for victory in the elections.

29

The victory of the Front Populaire

The prospect of elections, which everyone thought were bound to be won by the left, kept the government in a state of suspended animation all through the early months of 1936. As we saw earlier, Hitler knew how to profit from the situation, which added to the general anxiety.

On 13 February Léon Blum's motor-car, in which he was accompanied by Georges Monnet and his wife, got in the way of the funeral convoy of the Action Française academician and historian Jacques Bainville. The motor-car was surrounded and the socialist leader was quite badly beaten up and narrowly escaped lynching, thanks to the intervention of some workmen from a nearby site. This provoked a huge demonstration of protest between the Panthéon and the Bastille, and there were several street fights. The Action Française, as a Ligue, had been suppressed under a law passed a month earlier, but Maurras continued his incitations to bloodshed in his newspaper.

Some weeks later the trade-union merger took place. Negotiations had started back in September 1934. They had taken a long time because the leaders of the CGT had been dragging their feet, but under pressure from the militants they at last reached an agreement in principle at the end of 1935. Those in favour of union, who felt the need most strongly, made all the concessions. The new group was to keep the name CGT, and its political independence was confirmed on the lines laid down much earlier in the Amiens charter. There were to be no separately organised break-away groups. Such were the terms of unification agreed at the Toulouse congress in March 1936. Only two of the earlier proponents of the merger, Frachon and Racamond, were admitted to the group secretariat. The secretary-general, Jouhaux, declared himself pleased with the new-found unity, but many former members remained resolutely anti-communist. However, the merger was immediately greeted with great enthusiasm by the working class, and there was a great increase in union membership. The election campaign thus opened in very favourable conditions for the left.

The 1936 elections

As the *discipline républicaine* only became operative on the second ballot, each party put up separate candidates for the first. The socialists offered a programme of massive nationalisation, a return to proportional representation, abolition of the Senate and support for collective security. For them the Front Populaire was a side issue, and as the planning proposed by Révolution Constructive had been rejected, there was hardly any difference between these proposals and the ideas they had been talking about for the last eight years.

The radicals had no national programme, but Daladier, who had again become president of the party at the beginning of 1936, endorsed that of the Rassemblement Populaire.

The communists asserted as an absolute priority the need to defend the Republic against the enemies of the people, on behalf of peace, bread and freedom. The radio was quite fairly put at the disposal of all candidates, and Thorez made the best use of it. The Paris press was almost totally anti-Front Populaire. In his broadcast of 17 April on Radio Paris 'for a free, strong and happy France' the communist leader's single theme was 'unity', not just for the parties that cared about the working class, but for all the people of France: 'We offer you our hand, Catholics, workers, employees, craftsmen, peasants – we, mere laymen, because you are our brothers ... We offer you our hand, national servicemen, old soldiers who have joined the Croix-de-Feu, because you are sons of our own people.'

The policy of 'a hand held out to the Catholics' irritated the socialists, the radicals and even, according to Jacques Duclos, some of the faithful in the party. In this way the members of the Front Populaire were pushed to the right by the communists, who now appeared as the great promoters of a national left, to which they were completely integrated.

Downcast by Laval's failure and the disastrous effect it had on their morale, the right staked its whole campaign on the fear of bolshevism and on a description of the awful disasters that would ensue if the left won the election.

The elections were held on 26 April and 3 May. There was a record number of candidates:

Number of candidates in elections, 1919–36

1919	1924	1928	1932	1936
2,120	2,765	3,763	3,837	4,817

There were 618 seats as opposed to 615 in 1932. The turn-out of voters (84.3 per cent) was the highest since 1914.

On the evening of the first ballot the number of those elected with a clear majority was the lowest ever: 174 out of 424 counts. The left received 5,421,000 votes as against 4,233,000 for the right. The right had in fact only received 70,000 votes less than in 1932, the left 300,000 more.

It was an undeniable victory for the Front Populaire, but slightly disappointing. The existence of a right-wing government since 1934 had made people forget that the left had won an election in 1932, and the latter expected a landslide success. Moreover, the breakdown of votes within the left was very different. The radicals lost 400,000. The socialists polled 1,950,000 and were still the largest single party, though they lost 30,000 votes, which were more than compensated by heavy defections from the USR.

The communist party made far the biggest gains, with a total of 1,500,000 votes, an increase of 800,000. This upsurge was widespread, the exceptions being the Doubs, the Landes and the Mayenne. It gained 200,000 votes in the Paris area, 40,000 in the Bouches-du-Rhône, 38,000 in the Nord, between 10,000 and 20,000 in the Rhône, the Loire, the Alpes-Maritimes, the Var, the Dordogne, the Gard, the Allier, the Pas-de-Calais, the Somme, the Seine-Inférieure and the Gironde. One must suppose that these gains were made at the expense of the socialists, who in their turn took votes from the radicals. Very probably, in constituencies where the result was in doubt, the right voted communist in order to stop a radical from heading the left-wing vote.

In the second ballot everything went well for the Front Populaire, and the fight turned into one between the two big coalitions. Radical support held firm in spite of their losses, and the left won decisively with 376 elected members against 222. The impoverished Midi with its 'budget-guzzling' peasants and artisans had flown to the aid of the Republic, returning radicals and socialists to the Chamber.

The right and the extreme right (Fédération Républicaine, Républicains Indépendants, Union Républicaine et Nationale, etc.) gained twenty seats; the centre right lost about forty-five.

The radicals (106) lost fifty seats; the socialists (147) gained fifteen; the Communists (72) gained sixty-one; the various other left-wing parties, USR, dissident communists and independents took fifty-one seats. The USR lost about forty seats.

1936 is the most important date in French electoral history since 1877. Thenceforward, and up till today, no left-wing government could survive without the support or at least the connivance of the communist party. At the time, however, the situation seemed rather like those of 1924 and 1932, inasmuch as there were two possible majorities, which the right saw at once:

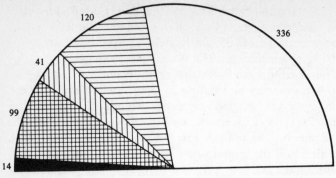

1928: elected members

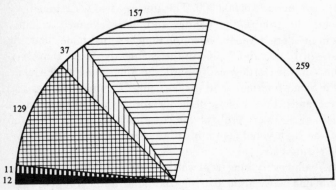

1932: elected members

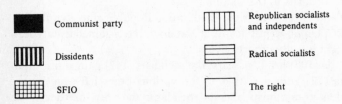

■ Communist party		▥ Republican socialists and independents	
▥ Dissidents		▤ Radical socialists	
▦ SFIO		□ The right	

The Chamber of Deputies in France, 1930–9

The balance will be held by the radical socialists, the independent socialists and the USR socialists, who, though much diminished, still muster about 150 votes. Practically all of them fought the election under the banner of the Rassemblement Populaire, which means that they made common cause, especially in the second ballot, with the communists and the SFIO. But once an election is over, alliances arranged for the purpose of winning it rarely survive. We can expect some desertions, especially in

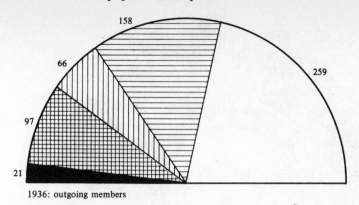

1936: outgoing members

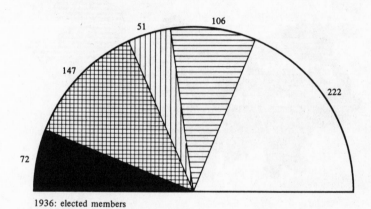

1936: elected members

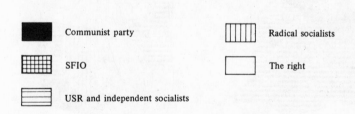

Communist party

SFIO

USR and independent socialists

Radical socialists

The right

the ranks of the radical socialists. Will they be numerous enough to stop the extremists from launching into risky experimental policies that could do much social, economic and monetary damage? That is the great question that hangs over the XVIth legislature (*L'Illustration*, May 1936.)

This is precisely what the left, and especially the communists, feared.

The radical party, having disengaged itself from the alliances of the

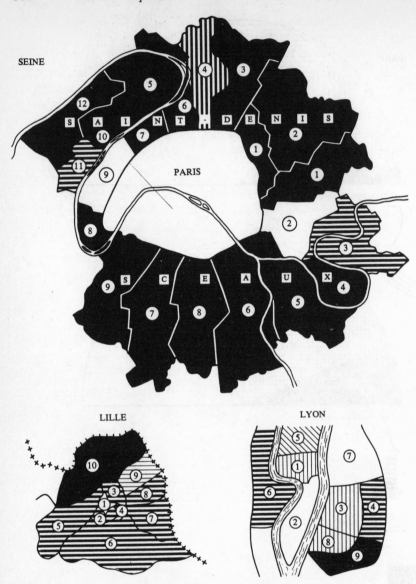

The Front Populaire in Paris, Lille, Lyon, Bordeaux and Marseille. (*Le Figaro*, 5 May 1936. The arabic numerals refer to the constituencies.)

PARIS

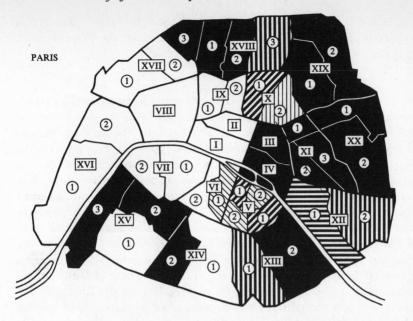

BORDEAUX

MARSEILLE

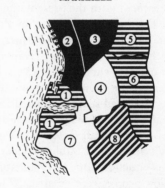

■ Communists	☰ Socialist union	▥ Radical socialists	▨ Left-wing republicans
▥ *Pupistes*	▨ Independent socialists	≡ Independent radicals	□ URD conservatives

Union Nationale, was no longer a hostage of the right. For a change, it was to play a privileged part in the Front Populaire, for the Marxists were prepared to make any concessions to preserve unity.

June 1936

Léon Blum immediately claimed control in the name of his party. It was, of course, his by right; but in taking it he felt bound by the undertakings he had made to his allies and by the need to observe constitutional legality. He was not so much going to seize power as to exercise it. Blum had for several years pondered and written in anticipation of the day when he would be called upon to form a government. If a revolution had put power into the hands of the SFIO, or it had gained an absolute majority at an election, then such power would have been won outright, and a socialist programme would be carried through. But if, as in the present situation, the SFIO was only the largest party in a left-wing coalition (ignoring the possibility of its being in a minority), the socialist leader of the government could not, without a breach of faith, impose socialism on his bourgeois colleagues, namely the radicals. The exercise of power within a capitalist state is circumscribed by the limits of existing institutions and can only follow a policy favouring the working class while at the same time respecting existing structures. Blum refused to form a government until the present one's term had expired, so it was not until 4 June that he was summoned by President Lebrun. He presented himself to parliament on 5 June. As usual there was a political vacuum lasting a month, during which the Sarraut cabinet, only too willing to give up, could only transact current business.

During the course of this month there was a wave of sit-in strikes on an unprecedented scale. It started in the Breguet factories at Le Havre, and spread to Latécoère in Toulouse and Bloch (now Dassault) in Courbevoie, all of them aircraft factories. Soon it was all over France, in every form of activity except the public services, which were the most unionised. Trade and production came to a standstill. During May and June, upwards of two million people were on strike. The wealthy classes were appalled by the widespread character of the movement and enraged at the occupation of businesses – an intolerable trespass on private property. Unlike Italy of 1920, however, or France today, employees made no attempt to run the factories themselves.

At the beginning of June the right hit on the idea that it was all a conspiracy. It was shown up by Henri de Kérillis and Jacques Bardoux. The former said it was German, the latter that it was Russian, and would be followed by a communist take-over, abetted by Blum, on 12 June. These fabrications were revealed to the public in *La Documentation catholique*.

Historians now agree that the movement was spontaneous, triggered off by the exhilaration of an election victory, which had banished fear of the bosses and dread of the unemployment which they had suffered so long. Another motive was the prison-like character of working conditions in many factories and big shops. The worker had his pride and wanted it recognised; occupation of his place of work not only demonstrated solidarity but also blocked attempts at strike-breaking. The union leaders were taken by surprise and could do very little to control the movement. In many strike-hit firms there were no union members at all. All this led to a good deal of local activity by small left-wing and ultra-left-wing groups – Trotskyites, revolutionary syndicalists and militants of the Gauche Révolutionnaire, a new movement started by Marceau Pivert in 1934, which was a mixture of Trotskyism and workers' Allemanism. Up to 11 June the communists appear to have been split. However, militant action never developed into political action.

What particularly struck contemporaries about the sit-in strikes was the extraordinarily cheerful feelings that prevailed. They seemed to be seeing a new sort of non-violent revolution, taking place in a holiday atmosphere. Henri Lefebvre had earlier recalled 'the holiday feeling' in speaking of the Commune of 1871. Those who saw Louis XVI returning to Paris after the October Revolution describe the people as jubilant. There was an illusion of unforced happiness, of a return to a golden age, mingled with the sudden realisation of collective power. But in 1936 the excitement lasted a long time; it was kept going by the entertainment world, particularly the 'October Group', which performed Prévert's *Le Tableau des merveilles* in the First Communion Counter of a major store. The infection seemed to spread to the sound of the accordion, and the lightheartedness of those making collections 'for the strikers' met with general sympathy, even from people who had no great love for the Front Populaire. This version of the events is accepted by most historians. Georges Lefranc, however, in his *Histoire du front populaire* reminds us that inside some of the businesses affected there was a certain amount of resistance by employers and managers, and strike pickets were often apprehensive of a fascist counter-stroke.

It was only after June 1936 that people flocked to join the CGT. Union membership grew from 1 per cent or 2 per cent of the labour force to 90 or 95 per cent. On 28 May, in commemoration of the Commune, 600,000 people filed past the *mur des fédérés*.

It was against this background that Léon Blum shaped his cabinet on 4 June, presented it to parliament on 5 June, and on 6 June received a vote of confidence from the Chamber of 384 to 210. The more liberal-minded employers had been impatiently waiting for this moment. Lambert-Ribot of the Comité des Forges had already on the 5th asked the government to arbitrate between workers and employers so that the factory occupations should cease. After meeting delegates of the CGT and the employers Blum got them both to come to the Hôtel Matignon, where, after two days of talks, they signed the Matignon agreements. These stipulated increases in pay, collective bargaining and recognition of trade-union rights. Although Léon Jouhaux hailed these as the 'greatest victory of the workers' movement' and in spite of the social legislation enacted soon afterwards, the return to work was slow. The CGT and the employers were in a hurry to get a settlement before things got out of control, but the workers were reluctant to drop a weapon whose effectiveness had surprised and delighted them. In the CGT, the SFIO and the communist party, the militants were saying that they had the bosses by the throat and could have got much more out of them, while others felt they could have achieved a revolution. On 27 April Pivert had written an article in *Le Populaire* under the heading 'All things are now possible'.

The radicals wanted to see a quick end to chaos. But Blum did not feel that he had a mandate for revolution. As early as 6 June he had sternly condemned the strikes in the Chamber. 'I have been asked if I think factory occupation is legal. I do not regard it as legal.' Neither the CGT nor Léon Blum could contemplate the use of force. Thorez urged a pacific approach, saying on 11 June: 'we must be able to end a strike when satisfaction has been obtained. We must even be able to compromise if not all demands have been met, as long as the most essential ones have been conceded. We cannot expect to have everything.' The communists, who were soon to expel André Ferrat because he objected to the new party line, were thus disowning their old policy of revolt in favour of keeping in step with the radicals and the *petite bourgeoisie* whom they represented.

This unity lasted for several weeks, and it is one reason why members of the left who lived through it so treasure the memory of June 1936. Yet the return to work continued very slowly, only slightly speeded up by the effect of the new social legislation, and there were new strikes. Up to the end of the year there were always more than three hundred strikes a month, as against twelve thousand in June. There were more still in 1937.

Some militant socialists have blamed Blum and Thorez for having obstructed a socialist revolution. Some historians think it would have been feasible; others think that at any rate more could have been gained. Such views are purely theoretical. In practice there could be no revolution without the communists, and these were committed to an international party line which, both in France and in Spain, meant alliance with the middle classes against fascism. This was the very essence of the popular front movements.

On their side the employers felt the workers' victory as a most damaging blow to their power. Once the panic was over the signatories of the Matignon agreements were disowned. Duchemin had to resign the presidency of the employers' organisation in favour of Gignoux, who was determined to go on fighting. Medium-sized businesses could not forgive the big ones for giving in, and they were set on revenge. For the owner of a small textile firm it was intolerable to have to stop talking and thinking in terms of 'my workforce': in a large engineering business it hardly mattered. Alongside these two indignant tendencies a third party was appearing, as yet without much influence, grouped around Nouveaux Cahiers, which understood the need for a new type of social relationship and was prepared to accept it. Lefranc tells us that Simone Weil was aware of the significance and originality of this group of employers. Unfortunately she was just on her way to join the Durutti International Brigade in Spain and had no time to lend her influence to the movement.

The Blum experiment

Léon Blum, born in 1872, came from a well-to-do Jewish orthodox family. Like Tardieu he left the Ecole Normale Supérieure half-way through his course and, at the end of the nineteenth century, worked on *La Revue blanche*, an avant-garde literary review with anarchist tendencies. His first career was in the Conseil d'Etat. He became a socialist but played no part in politics prior to 1914. He was Directeur du Cabinet to the socialist minister, Marcel Sembat. In 1919 he led the group that opposed the idea of joining the Third International, which made him the natural leader of the SFIO after the Tours congress. Blum's view was that socialist revolution could only come about in one of two ways – either a successful rising, which he could not countenance, or a victory at the polls with an absolute socialist majority. This might take time, but meanwhile the exercise of power could be obtained by means of a left-wing coalition in which the SFIO would be the largest member. This is precisely what resulted from the elections of 1936. In these circumstances the partners in the coalition were morally bound to adhere to the agreements arranged between them and not to attempt any constitutional changes. Blum was a jurist with a strict moral code and a strongly held belief in the inviolable sanctity of law. For him a 'suspension of legality' could only happen at the demand of an absolute majority. This was why, as party leader, he had always set his face against revolutionary adventurism on the one hand and participation in 'bourgeois' governments on the other, or indeed any other action that went against his principles.

One might suppose that such a man was ill-suited to a political world where any means, good or bad, justified the end. In character he was not unlike Gladstone, whose career was enormously successful. He must be counted as one of a line of great French or French-speaking bourgeois intellectuals such as de Pressensé, Jaurès, de Brouckère, Vandervelde – men whose humanity led them into socialism. He was, with Jaurès, the man most hated by the right, and probably more than Jaurès, for the followers of

Maurras saw him as Jaurès and Dreyfus combined. This incredible hatred, which screamed daily for his assassination, was not counterbalanced by the deep affection that was felt for Jaurès. He was reserved, apparently without warmth and had a horror of demagogy. The communists detested him and preferred the more easy-going radicals. Even in his own party many disliked him. He aroused the worst in some people – jealousy of excessive intellectual superiority and small-minded anti-semitism. With his stature enhanced by the very vileness of his enemies and the scurrility of *l'Action française* and *Gringoire*, he was often paralysed by his own honesty, the scruples of his legalistic conscience and his lack of pragmatism. This was immediately evident in his refusal to take action for a month after the election, a bad start for his 'exercise of power' and the Blum experiment.

Admittedly he had to face appalling difficulties. As well as those already described – a diplomatic vacuum, economic ruin, a massive flight of capital, an explosive social situation – there was at the time the refusal of the communists to join the cabinet. The socialists could hardly complain, having treated the radicals in just the same way in 1924 and 1932. According to Jacques Duclos, Thorez was in favour of joining. *(Cahiers de L'Institut Maurice Thorez*, 2, July–September 1966.) His presence would certainly have given a great boost to the government, and the decisive role he had played in the election victory of the Front Populaire seemed to demand it. But the political bureau of the communist party turned down the idea. According to Philippe Robrieux, it was Thorez who refused 'in deference to the Comintern, as well as not to cause alarm' (*Maurice Thorez, vie secrète et vie publique*, p. 199). There was certainly a feeling that the middle classes had to be reassured about the Front Populaire. It was as if the communists were saying 'the presence of a bogey like this would serve as a pretext for the enemies of the people to start a panic'. There was something in this. All through the election campaign the right had plugged the myth of 'the man with a knife between his teeth'. And the communists always supported Blum in the Chamber. The CGT, affected by another myth, the Amiens charter, also refused to participate.

The cabinet thus consisted of socialists and radicals. Next to Blum in importance and position came Daladier, vice-president of the cabinet and minister of defence. Chautemps (radical), Violette (Socialiste Français) and Paul Faure (SFIO) were ministers of state. The economic portfolios were held by socialists – Vincent Auriol (finance), Spinasse (economy), Monnet (agriculture). The political portfolios were shared between radicals and socialists, with Yvon Delbos (foreign affairs), Jean Zay (education), Pierre Cot (aviation), Salengro (interior) and Moutet (colonies). Among the remaining ministers it is worth mentioning Mme Brunschwig, Irène Joliot and Suzanne Lacore who, though still without the right to vote, became under-secretaries of state. What chiefly scandalised the right (and was blown up out of all proportion at the Riom trials) was the creation of a ministry for sport and leisure, allotted to Léo Lagrange (SFIO).

It is in the early days of their power that statesmen carry out their most lasting work. All that remains of 1848 is the work of the provisional government: the legislation of June 1936 is the sole legacy of the Front Populaire.

The Matignon agreements started with an all-round increase in wages. This was not to exceed a total of 12½ per cent in each firm, the lowest paid getting increases of 15 per cent and the highest 7 per cent. There were to be collective agreements for every industry on a national scale, involving recognition of shop-floor representation, that is of union power. The principal result of the Matignon negotiations was to increase purchasing power, in conformity with the CGT and SFIO theory that the crisis was due to under-consumption.

The government immediately tabled three bills which became law a few days later. The first laid down the procedure for collective agreements; the second gave employees a fortnight's holiday with pay: the third limited the hours of work to forty a week. There was little opposition, except from Paul Reynaud, who opposed the third bill, which became law on 12 June.

After passing these laws the government succeeded, in spite of spirited resistance by the Senate and the agrarian groups, in setting up the Office National Interprofessionel du Blé (ONIC). The state was to take over the marketing of wheat, whose stocking in the hands of the co-operatives would enable prices to be raised and maintained. The annual price was to be fixed by the Office, which had a monopoly of imports and exports. In 1935 a quintal of wheat cost eighty francs. The Office fixed it at 141 francs in 1936 and 180 in 1937. Its success was assured when it managed to absorb the whole crop of 1938, in spite of the adverse propaganda of the agrarian groups. But the big producers and the millers succeeded in getting the Office's juridical status and financial independence abolished in 1939, when it simply declined into being a service provided by the ministry of agriculture.

The only constitutional reform was the re-organisation of the Banque de France. By the law of 24 July 1936 the oligarchical general meeting of the two hundred principal shareholders was replaced by a meeting which all shareholders could attend. The fifteen-member council of regents appointed by the old general meeting was abolished and replaced by a board of twenty experts nominated by the Conseil Nationale Economique and by the government. It remained a private bank and the 'wall of money' was far from being demolished. Vincent Auriol would have liked to nationalise the bank, but the Senate would never have passed such a measure. On the other hand the law of 11 August proposed the nationali-sation of the armaments industry. The armed forces approved of this, and, beginning in October, Daladier nationalised one dozen factories, principally in the aircraft industry. The government had control of the rest.

The Front Populaire's main effort was devoted to distributive reforms intended to raise the standard of living of the working class. Between 1936 and 1939, six thousand collective agreements about salaries and holidays were signed. The increases in pay, the reduction of working hours, the improvement of working conditions and the abolition of taxes on the pay of public servants were to benefit all levels of society by raising purchasing power and encouraging expenditure on leisure activities. The question of providing recreation for the working class had been discussed by the Jeunesses Socialistes since before 1930, and the demand came from the SFIO rather than the Front Populaire. France was behind other countries in this respect, for none of her plans had come to fruition. The achievements of Léo Lagrange did more than anything else to establish the legend of the Front Populaire. 'Minister for Idleness' in the eyes of the right, an admirer of Hitler's Kraft Durch Freude, he invented the people's annual holiday ticket. Six hundred thousand people benefited by it in the first year. Yet holidays away from home were out of the reach of the working-class families, and it was mostly bachelors and young couples who took advantage of it. The CGT and the Catholics started tourist groups for the people. Various types of youth hostel sprang up; there were bicycles and tandems all over the roads, with young people singing. Lagrange also invented a general sports certificate.

Tremendous efforts were made to extend education, through the theatre, music and the cinema. The musicians of the Ecole d'Arcueil, Roger Désormière, Louis Durey, the film-makers, Renoir, the Prévert brothers and many others devoted themselves to popular culture. In the theatre the 'October Group' excelled in the art of choral speech. In addition to all this Jean Zay raised the school-leaving age to fourteen.

This was the time when the working class really emerged from outer darkness. It was fully realised both by the workers and their enemies, who objected to the arrival on their beaches of 'holiday-makers with pay' and bad-mannered 'louts in cloth caps'. The great reproach levelled at Léon Blum was that he had taught the French working man how to be idle, and his reply would be that he took legitimate pride in this:

> I did not often leave my office during the period of my ministry, but every time I went out and passed through Paris and its suburbs, I saw dozens of old jalopies, motor-bikes and tandems ridden by pairs of workmen wearing multi-coloured pullovers, which show that the idea of leisure makes even them want to 'dress up' in a natural and simple way; all of which gives me the feeling that, through my way of organising work and leisure, I have managed to inject a little beauty and sunshine into lives of hardship. (*L'Œuvre de Léon Blum*, vol. v.)

The peasants were well rewarded for the many votes they had cast for the SFIO in the money spent by the new wave of holiday-makers from the towns. The success of the ONIC, called by the right 'the bolshevisation of the countryside', the army wine ration raised to half a litre, then the 'Quartermaster's free issue' dished out in bucketfuls, rather scandalously, on manœuvres (Blum was deputy for Narbonne) all boosted peasant incomes. The allowance for appreciation and the right of pre-emption on a piece of land whose value was falling were important advantages for the small farmer. But the proposed legislation on tenant leases and share-cropping were rejected by the Senate.

The object of economic policy was to further social reform. Since the Blum government was committed to preserving the liberal economy, and the programme of the Front Populaire repudiated both deflation and devaluation, the leaders had to copy Roosevelt and encourage consumption by increasing purchasing power, which was a reflationary stimulus for production. A rise in production would lower the cost of French manufactures and make them more competitive, reducing the huge deficit on foreign trade. Prosperity would bring a higher return from taxes and help to balance the budget. Reform of the Banque de France would lead to an expansion of credit facilities. Such were the anticipated effects of the social legislation. In addition, various large public works were started up, and a programme of rearmament, all of which were intended to increase employment and production.

This was a very dangerous policy: the deficit in 1936 amounted to eight billion francs, of which six billion were due to excess expenditure. Socialist governments find it difficult to borrow money, and the deficit was financed by inflation. Another economic misfortune was a large fall in the gold reserve, which seems to have passed unnoticed. The export of capital was made all too easy by the lack of proper exchange controls.

Blum's economic gamble was a loser. Salaries rose more than was expected, but failed to catch up with prices, which rose because production failed to pick up. Increased demand led to increased imports, while French prices remained too high, and the balance of trade deteriorated. The expected increase in tax revenue failed to materialise, and unemployment was not noticeably diminished. Inflation and the flight of capital got worse.

Failure seems to have been due to the slowing-down of production coupled with excessive demand on the home market. Historians have argued endlessly and passionately about the causes for this. The right has blamed the social legislation for making people want more and work less. Jeanneney thought that antiquated equipment and the forty-hour week combined to make increased production impossible. Alfred Sauvy, followed by most historians, blames the forty-hour week for reducing the hours of work of skilled technicians, who had never experienced unemployment, thereby causing bottlenecks which deprived the unskilled of work, The CGT was wrong in claiming that technological progress caused unemployment: eight hours less per worker did not create one-fifth of an extra job, but simply means the loss of eight hours' production. In these circumstances production could only fall, and this is what lay behind the whole cycle of failure. Alfred Sauvy has repeatedly asserted in *L'Express* and *Le Monde* that the Front Populaire was a national disaster, setting back the coming of socialism by at least a generation and undermining France's ability to face the threat of Nazism. As a considered opinion this is surprising, for nobody can fix a definite date at which the arrival of socialism in France, whose appearance the author seems to favour, could have been possible, or may be or will be possible. The forty-hour week certainly had some of the damaging effects which Sauvy denounces, but it alone was not responsible. To begin with, the working week in 1936 was, on average, not forty-eight but forty-three hours: hence many must already have been working less than forty hours. In that year there were eight hundred thousand unemployed, but in 1938 only six hundred thousand, which indicates some growth in the demand for labour. If the employment of unskilled labour had not been allowed by law, the flight from the countryside would not have started up again and the agrarian parties would not have been able to blame the government for rural depopulation. What was certainly disastrous was the delay in implementing the laws which resulted in state enterprises being the first to reduce working hours and benefit from an influx of skilled hands. However, three hundred thousand jobs were created.

It is not possible to reduce *Homo sapiens* into *Homo economicus*, and the moral importance of the forty-hour week was that it provided leisure for self-education. The French working-class movement had always had a perhaps excessive belief that the emancipation of the worker depends on education. An anonymous author has well said: 'If the working class has one day to assume the highest responsibilities in government, it will be because leisure has prepared it for that task.' The CGT's Institut Supérieur Ouvrier took this preparation in hand.

In a symposium at the Ecole Normale, Mendès France confirmed Blum's assertion that the causes of economic failure were political. (See J. Bouvier in *Le Mouvement social*, 54, 1966.) Not to recognise this is simply to ignore the historical background. The forty-hour law was the CGT's absolutely basic demand; it was implicit in the Front Populaire's programme which, without putting an exact figure on it, was proposing 'a reduction in the working week with no reduction in weekly pay'. Blum was totally committed to this, as he was also to the deplorable taboo on devaluation, the very starting-point of the New Deal. If the refusal to devalue and to set up exchange controls, combined with the forty-hour law, was responsible for economic failure, it must be admitted that they were measures imposed for political reasons.

France was governed by her middle class through local assemblies, the Senate, the civil service and the press. The liberal economy was sacrosanct. But the middle class refused to create jobs or to step up production because it did not want to support the Front Populaire or increase its wage bill. Paul-Boncour remarked that the forty-hour law would have been perfect with the 'three eights', i.e. eight hours work, eight hours play and eight hours sleep, but neither the employers nor the workers wanted it and no one would have dared impose it. Everything submitted to the surge of popular feeling, and the middle class had to beg the socialists to get the strikers out of the factories. But the right quickly recovered. The enemies of the Front Populaire had every intention of exploiting to the utmost the anxieties of the rich and their not-so-rich hangers-on. That, at least, was how the left accounted for the collapse of their hopes for the start-up of production. This view has been scouted by Mysyrowicz who blames industry for being out of date and inadequately equipped, though 'quite willing to reap the fruits of a rearmament programme'. (*Autopsie d'une défaite*, p. 192.) Jean Bouvier considered that the forty-hour week had less effect than the counter-attack of the middle-class business world on all fronts.

The standstill at the factories was not simply because of the forty-hour week, but also because their owners did not want them to function. Blum's recognition of the political role played by the business world shows that he could only have succeeded after a purge and constitutional change. He was not willing to go so far. Even as early as June *La Flèche*, whose leading articles were edited by Gaston Bergery and Robert Aron, was insisting that redistributive policies had no chance of success without constitutional change. Yet, quite apart from the forty-hour controversy, Mendès France has commented on the profusion of other measures, some of which had very positive results, notably the reform of the Banque de France which enormously expanded the availability of credit.

Colonial policy was no more successful than economic policy. Nothing came of Pierre Viénot's negotiations with Bourguiba in Tunisia or with Allal el Fassi in Morocco. The government had not the courage to ask parliament to ratify the treaties of independence that had been drawn up for Lebanon and Syria. A more ambitious policy of conciliation was attempted in Algeria. The Etoile Nord-Africaine, formed in Paris by Messali Hadj, had lent its support to the Front Populaire. Violette (now a minister of state) had been governor-general of Algeria in 1924. Blum and he drew up a plan for limited assimilation which proposed to give French citizenship within the Koranic law to about fifty thousand native Algerians, ex-servicemen or people of some education. The Blum-Violette plan, put before parliament in August 1936, was a mild reform, but significant for the hopes it raised for the future. This of course was why the *colons* and the Algerian lobby in Paris attacked it viciously and managed to get it dropped.

30

The Front Populaire in trouble

Between June and October 1936 there was no sign of recovery from the depression, and economic problems were leading to incessant social disturbances. The enemies of the Front Populaire plucked up courage and attacked it violently. There was no real unity between the parties composing the Front, and the radicals, alarmed by the strikes, tried to put the brakes on.

The communists and the other parties in the Front

The communists on the other hand attacked the government for being so timid in carrying out its social and economic policies. They accused the government of not fulfilling the commitments undertaken under the pact for united action of 1934, while Blum felt himself bound by the programme of the Rassemblement Populaire, set up in 1935. In order not to jeopardise the prospect of radical participation, the communists had purposely excluded any plans for constitutional reform. They felt that Blum was incapable of achieving anything without their needling him. They approved of the rise in wages and the progressive social legislation, but protested at the lack of any financial policy to control 'the forces of money' and the owners of capital who, bent on the destruction of the Front Populaire, were undermining the franc and transferring their wealth to Switzerland. They condemned the inconsistency of harassing the capitalists and at the same time leaving them free to speculate.

The socialists did not want to frighten the radicals who were already beginning to show misgivings at their party congress in Biarritz in October 1936. No further social legislation seemed possible. Inside the socialist party there were very divided views on both home and foreign policy.

The communists were unwilling to give up their demands, but they were constantly worried by the fear of possible radical defection. As a reassurance they made a point of showing themselves to be good Jacobin and Blanquist patriots. On 10 May they held a celebration in memory of Joan of Arc, a daughter of the French people betrayed by her king. On 27 June Maurice Thorez at Choisy-le-Roi celebrated the centenary of the death of

Rouget de Lisle with a speech which he called 'La Marseillaise'. Three days later the secretariat of the party announced: 'The tricolour flag must not divide the French people.' Still in pursuit of national unity the communists started to woo the Catholics, singing the praises of the French virtues. In its issue of 14 July 1936, *L'Humanité* invited Parisians to go and cheer the army at the Champs Elysées march past with a headline 'The Army is at one with the People'. In August Thorez and Duclos suggested changing the Front Populaire into the 'Front Français'. They said they wanted to bring about 'a union of all those who were ready and willing to maintain law and order within the republican establishment'. In September the Jeunesses Socialistes were severely rebuked for producing a pamphlet objecting to two-year military service. The shop-floor cells of that period imposed a truce between the CGT and the CFTC.

In these circumstances it was impossible for the socialist party to be on good terms with the communists. The socialists thought the communists deceitful, and they were worried by the growth of the communist party and the falling off of reformists in the trade unions. The government's social legislation had given a great boost to union membership. The CFTC reached 350,000 and increased its strength in existing strongholds, e.g. Alsace, the Paris region and the Nord; and it acquired a foothold in Brittany. The CGT had four or five million members, and its Fédération des Métaux, which had forty thousand members up to June, had 750,000 by December, out of 1,200,000 workers in their industry. These new groups came under communist influence, and were gradually joined by several more Fédérations.

It seems odd that discussions about a merger of the two Marxist parties, started in 1935, should have been continued in such an atmosphere of controversy and suspicion right up to 1938. For their part the communists did not seem to feel any ambivalence in defending their own society and that of the Soviet Union at the same time. But it was foreign affairs that showed up the cracks in the ruling majority. Blum had above all to take heed of the foreign policy of the British, who had been shocked by Laval's support of Mussolini. Relations with the latter were getting steadily worse as France refused to recognise King Victor Emmanuel as emperor of Abyssinia. Meanwhile the pacifist Blum did not want to exacerbate relations with the dictators. On 25 August there was an incident when Thorez rebuked Blum in a letter for allowing Dr Schacht to pay a courtesy visit to Labeyrie, the governor of the Banque de France.

By far the most serious rifts in the Front Populaire were caused by General Franco's rising against the Spanish government on 18 July 1936. Both Germany and Italy intervened at once, and their massive support was, in the long run, decisive. Blum was at first inclined to respond favourably to the Spanish government's request for arms. The French right

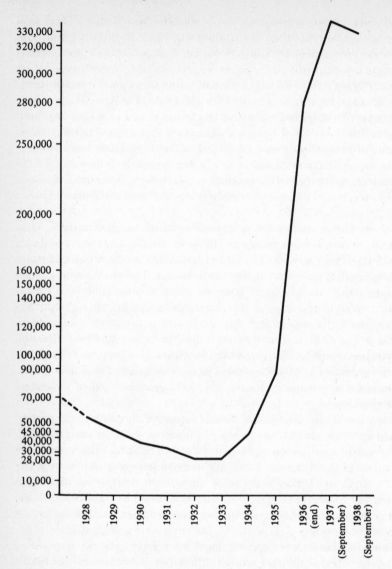

330,000
320,000

300,000

280,000

250,000

200,000

160,000
150,000
140,000

120,000

100,000
90,000

70,000

50,000
45,000
40,000
30,000
28,000

10,000

0

1928 1929 1930 1931 1932 1933 1934 1935 1936 (end) 1937 (September) 1938 (September)

Membership of the communist party, 1931–6. (*Revue française de science politique*, XVI, February 1966.)

reacted violently against this attitude. But the determining factor was Great Britain's policy of non-interference, in spite of the threat to her interests in the Mediterranean. The British, whose freedom of action was hamstrung by pacifist pressures and by fear of bolshevism, and who were aware of internal dissension in France, insisted on the latter's neutrality. A few months earlier Sarraut had been warned by the general staff that France could not oppose Hitler without calling up reservists. Blum, who was also subjected to the restraining influence of Lebrun and Delbos, considered it out of the question to pursue policies which could lead to France fighting a war without allies, probably with a civil war on her hands at home. This was why France, in a diplomatic note on 1 August, proposed that the powers should agree to observe a policy of non-intervention. Hitler and Mussolini accepted this on 9 August, but never complied with it. French deliveries of arms to the Spanish government continued between these dates. The policy of non-intervention was opposed by a minority of socialists, but was quite unacceptable to the communists, who saw it as a sham and attacked the government unceasingly for its spinelessness in the face of fascist provocation. For the communists the defence of France and of the Soviet Union meant the defence of the Spanish government. They agitated continuously in this cause, and the slogan 'Guns and planes for Spain', repeated daily in the press and shouted in the streets, found a sympathetic response among those socialists led by Jean Zyromski, Jean Longuet and Marceau Pivert who, together with the Comité d'Action Socialiste pour l'Espagne, opposed the prime minister's policy. Supporters of help for the Spanish government were to be found in the CGT, in the radical party, and even in the cabinet in the person of Pierre Cot, the minister of aviation. Blum continued to assert his pacifist convictions which, he believed, conformed with the national interest and with the wishes of the vast majority of people. Nevertheless, he allowed volunteers for both sides to go to Spain, and also a certain amount of arms and ammunition. As the republican cause steadily deteriorated, dissension in France between the communists, Léon Blum and the uncompromising pacifists of the SFIO, such as Paul Faure, grew more and more acute. On 4 December the communist deputies abstained on a vote concerning the government's foreign policy. This was the Front Populaire's first open break in the Chamber. The right, naturally followed by the majority of the press, and with one eye on its heavy investment in Spanish banks, came out in favour of Franco.

Meanwhile Hitler was carrying on with his diplomatic offensive. After raising the period of military service to two years, he demanded the return of Germany's former colonies, denounced the Versailles rules concerning navigation on German rivers and signed the anti-Comintern pact with Japan. These actions all served to confirm the government's determination to rearm. As a result of deflationary policies and orthodox budgets, hardly anything had been done since 1936, especially where modern equipment was concerned, e.g. motorisation and air defence. As early as June Daladier had calculated that the general staff's programme of nine billion francs was inadequate, and the budget for rearmament was increased to fourteen billion francs, while a four-year plan was put under way to catch up on lost time. This new resolve partly accounted for the nationalisation of the armaments industry. A start was made in October. Backwardness in manufacturing techniques, social disturbances, the unwillingness of the employers to rearm a state that was going bolshevik, all serve to explain the feeble results of this effort, especially in the most modern types of equipment, in which the general staff simply had no faith. Some historians have seen this situation in a different light. Mysyrowicz points out rather sensibly that heads of industry never objected to making profits; Renouvin agrees and puts the blame equally on the middle and lower classes in industry.

The economic and social defeat

The cost of rearmament seriously affected the financial situation; it also affected the economy as a whole, when firms that had turned over to armaments ceased to produce consumption goods, whose scarcity now contributed to rising prices. The result was to give a further boost to the inflation that had already been produced by the Front Populaire's social policies, and by uncontrolled speculation.

After September 1936 the government was obliged to give up the 'defence of the franc' policy. In June it had arranged with the Banque de France a credit of ten billion francs. This was meant to finance the costs of its reflationary policy, but even by the autumn the loan had not been very much used, because the public works and rearmament only got under way at the end of the year. By 25 September the treasury had only borrowed two billion francs. It was speculation against the franc that finally forced the government into a measure that had been rejected by all parties, especially the communists, namely devaluation. The issue of treasury bonds was not going well. The export of capital had drained away a great deal of gold. At the beginning of 1935 the reserves of the Banque de France exceeded eighty billion francs. Thanks to the crises of spring and autumn 1935 and April–May 1936, they had seriously diminished; at the beginning of September 1936 they were about fifty-four billion francs and the currency was 58 per cent covered. Between 4 and 16 September another 1.5 billion francs leaked out.

The government felt obliged to devalue, especially as the general staff told them that the gold reserves should not be allowed to fall below fifty billion francs. It was shown that they were right in 1937 when the 'neutrality law' was passed by Congress in the United States, imposing the 'cash and carry' rule which obliged belligerents to pay up for their arms purchases.

After a secret agreement with Roosevelt and Baldwin in talks held by the French financial attaché Monick in London – demonstrating that France was just as dependent on the Anglo-Americans financially as she was diplomatically – the government suspended the free convertibility of the currency on 26 September. On the 28th she signed a tripartite agreement with the Anglo-Americans and tabled the proposed measure which was voted through on 1 October. Vincent Auriol loathed the word 'devaluation' and put forward his reform as a 'monetary adjustment' carried out in full accord with the Anglo-Americans. The Auriol *franc élastique* differed from the Poincaré franc in having no fixed parity, but in having two limits in weight of gold – 43 and 49 milligrammes – between which it was allowed to fluctuate. It amounted to a devaluation of between 25 and 35 per cent. The pound sterling varied between 100 and 115 francs. The gold reserves could not be revalued. There was to be an exchange equalisation fund on the British pattern, managed by the governor of the Banque de France, which made it possible for him to intervene in the market to support the franc. The import and export of gold was forbidden: a fixed price was imposed.

Devaluation gave speculators a chance to make some profits. It was received with sorrow by the left, with rage by the communists who accused the government of reneging on its promises, of being soft on the capitalist enemies of the people and of increasing the poverty of the workers. It was only natural that the right should condemn it too. *Le Temps* saw it as the price paid for lunatic policies and the natural result of socialism, but it undoubtedly preferred devaluation to exchange control. The enemies of the Front Populaire, besides making material profits from devaluation, derived some moral advantage by adding a few monetary fictions to their arsenal.

The government felt ashamed of the move, but in fact the devaluation came too late and did not go far enough, partly because the Anglo-Americans wanted to limit it so as not to damage their export trade. All the same it had some positive results. The shock stimulated some economic revival between October 1936 and March 1937, especially in industry, and there was a fall in unemployment. The Paris stockmarket had been in a state of torpor ever since August 1930; after October 1936 there was a slight burst of activity in share speculation. But the devaluation had been so mild that the balance of trade showed no improvement; rather the opposite in fact. France still failed to export. The over-pricing of her goods – denied at the time by liberal economists – was reduced, but not really eliminated, since the previous devaluations of the pound and the dollar had been as much as 40 per cent. Also, costs of production were adversely affected by social legislation and antiquated machinery. This was why the beneficial effects of devaluation were soon eroded by the internal rise in prices, just as the increase in wages had been neutralised in the summer of 1936. The brief recession of 1937 in America also probably impeded French recovery.

The inflationary thrust of social expenditure and the cost of rearmament was very heavy as the shape of the 1937 budget shows:

1937 budget, percentage shares

Administration	11	Economic action	11
Defence	31	Social action	14
Education	7	Debt service	26

As a result of all this, capital started once more to flow out, and the country's financial situation continued to deteriorate. There seemed no end to political and social turmoil. Blum appealed to the patriotism and goodwill of his opponents in a speech on 31 December. 'Are there really people who are prepared to ruin their country in order to harm us? Does anyone imagine that it is in his interest to wreck economic recovery or stir up further social disturbance? I cannot believe this.'

Blum now decided to restore 'confidence', in other words abandon social reform in order to reassure the moneyed classes. The law of 31 December, supplemented by the decree of 16 January, made it illegal to strike without first having recourse to arbitration. On 13 February he proclaimed an official 'pause' over the radio. 'Confidence' was a right-wing expression, so like Vincent Auriol's 'devaluation', he left it out of his speech. All the same 'pause' meant 'confidence' and a return to orthodox budgets with the abandonment of pension schemes for aged workers, a national employment fund and a sliding scale for wages. A few days later 'three experts' were appointed to sit on the exchange stabilisation committee and advise the government, but in reality to keep an eye on Labeyrie, the governor of the Banque de France, a left-wing economist. These were Charles Rist, director of the Compagnie de Suez and the Banque de Paris et des Pays-Bas; Jacques Rueff, one of Poincaré's former advisers, head of the Mouvement Général des Fonds; and Paul Baudouin, director of the Banque de l'Indochine. All three were enemies of the Front Populaire, and all except for Rueff were part of the business world, and convinced practitioners of the free economy. Restrictions on the circulation of gold were lifted. With cruel sarcasm *Le Temps* of 8 March said, 'It's more than a pause, it's a conversion.'

Confidence was perhaps slightly restored, as shown by the initial success of the big *sécurité nationale* loan which was launched at that time, but there was no economic revival. Disturbances showed that the masses felt that they had been let down. The communists protested violently against this surrender to the 'trusts', while violent attacks from the right proved that the socialist leaders must be very simple if they thought that giving in to the 'two hundred families' could win them a truce. It only encouraged the enemy to smell victory in the air.

The rising tide of extremism

After the victory of the Front Populaire the frenzied expansion that had characterised the ultra-left in the early thirties began to diminish. Souvarine was deserted by his supporters and Georges Bataille lost interest in political action. After the collapse of Contre-Attaque the surrealists became divided. The Trotskyites were stagnating, broken into mutually excommunicating groups. The ejected members of the communist party, André Ferrat and the few supporters of his review *Que faire?*, had lost their readership.

The revolutionary left, however, which dominated the Fédération de la Seine of the socialist party, together with the anarchists, was extremely active. In spite of their disunity the anarchists had gained a new lease of life, thanks to the renown of the Catalan anarchists, who dazzled the French intelligentsia. When Simone Weil, who was an old friend of Trotsky and Souvarine, made her short and disastrous expedition to Spain, it was not to the Trotskyist POUM that she offered her services but to the anarchists, the Durutti International Brigade.

Another ultra-left figure was André Prudhommeau, who was then running a co-operative printing house in Nîmes and publishing a large number of anarchist papers that were financed by Spanish anarchist and labour groups. One organisation, Solidarité Internationale, which was controlled by anarchists, was in rivalry with the communist Secours Rouge. Up to the war it published its own weekly, *SIA*, which had some very distinguished contributors such as Henri Jeanson. Thanks to help from Spain the old organisations were flourishing. Fourteen anarchist periodicals appeared in 1938. (See J. Maîtron and A. Droguet, 'La Presse anarchiste française de ses origines à nos jours', *Le Mouvement social*, April–June 1973.)

The violence of communist fulmination against Blum's economic and social policy was due to their anxiety to make sure that there was nobody further to their left. Meanwhile the ultra-left concentrated its attacks on the communists. The war veterans' anti-militarism, which had contributed so much to the birth of the party, now turned against it, and the uncompromising pacifists denounced its members as warmongers. The Stalinist persecution, the liquidation of the bolshevik old guard, Stakhanovism and the revelations of Victor Serge, whom Stalin had released at Laval's request, all contributed to their repugnance of communism.

Fascism was a more serious threat to the Front Populaire. The smaller groups were gradually disappearing, and on 18 June 1936 all the Ligues were officially abolished. To the astonishment of many of his followers de la Rocque conformed and turned his organisation into a party, the Parti Socialiste de France. Renouncing civil war and abiding by the rules of the parliamentary game, he cleverly modelled his party on the lines of the SFIO. This regard for legality paid off. The PSF quickly became the largest political group in France. The Croix-de-Feu had had 450,000 members, the PSF had 600,000 and went up to 800,000. It was much larger than either the SFIO and the communist party. However, after September 1936 it resumed the para-military motorised activities of the old Croix-de-Feu, mainly for strike-breaking, and it was suspected of setting up arms dumps. There were many confrontations between de la Rocque's followers and the communists in Lyon, Clermont-Ferrand, Vienne and particularly in Paris on 4 October 1936. The movement also took root in the country in Algeria. On 1 October an enquiry opened to investigate this illegal revival of the Ligue that had been suppressed.

De la Rocque wavered between street violence and parliamentary action. He was divisive for the Front Populaire. For the communists the PSF was simply the Croix-de-Feu in disguise, whose destruction was required by the law of the Republic; for Blum and the radicals the law of the Republic bound them to respect the rights of a party that supported parliamentary institutions. But de la Rocque also proved troublesome for the enemies of the Front Populaire. His aim was to supplant the traditional right, and he had already managed to attract the bulk of fascist support into his following.

Jacques Doriot suffered most from de la Rocque's competition. He had changed a good deal between 1934 and 1936. At the time of his ejection from the communist party he still seemed to be a man of the extreme left. The whole of his Saint-Denis sector had followed him and remained loyal to him as mayor in 1935 and as a deputy in 1936. But it was only on his home ground that he had made any impression on the party. At one time it looked as if he might form a party of all the anti-Stalinists.

In *La France ne sera pas un pays d'esclaves* (1936) Doriot gave vent to his bitterness at having been ousted from the Front Populaire by the leaders of the PCF. The same people had excluded him from discussions on a union of all workers' parties. Doriot was still having discussions with the Trotskyist Zeller and the communist Duclos as if he still belonged to the Marxist clan. He claimed to be the true founder of the anti-fascist Front Populaire. 'That is the popular front we belong to.' But at the same time he was proclaiming the transformation of his Saint-Denis following into the Parti Populaire Français. The PPF was to be national and social. It asked for the recon-·ciliation of all members of the middle and lower classes, but its programme was fairly vague. Paradoxically it was, for a long time, much less anti-semitic than other versions of fascism.

The new party collected round itself former members of the communist party, trade unionists and ex-personnel of the Ligues or of the Croix-de-Feu who were disappointed by de la Rocque's moderation. Through Pucheu, one of their supporters, Doriot obtained a great deal of money (ten million francs in 1937) from the world of high finance, from the banks (Vernes, Lazard, Rothschild, BNCI) and from the big industrialists (Japy, Comptoir Sidérurgique, etc.). He copied the communist set-up, with a women's centre, a centre for farmers, a Union Populaire de la Jeunesse Française and a Union des Jeunesses Sportives Françaises, headed by the champion swimmer Cartonnet.

Drieu la Rochelle and Ramon Fernandez both joined Doriot and tried to form a rival body to the AEAR (Association des Ecrivains et Artistes Révolutionnaires). Although he wrote that 65 per cent of his party were ex-communist working class, he never succeeded in forming his own trade-union organisation. He was short of manpower, with less than one hundred thousand members scattered throughout the big cities and in Algeria. To face up to de la Rocque he tried to collect into the Front de la Liberté all the would-be insurrectionists of the extreme right. He gained the support of the agrarian agitators, Le Roy Ladurie and Dorgères, and also of Tardieu, who had given up action through parliament and hoped for nothing less than a *coup d'état*. Tardieu claimed to have subsidised de la Rocque, but the excitement was only short-lived and the PSF lost nothing thereby. In North Africa those who were inspired by Franco's example preferred the PPF to the PSF; but, if they had wanted to win the support of the native population, they should not have come out against the projected Blum-Violette reforms.

Not all the fascists who felt let down by de la Rocque and the Ligues joined Doriot. Some, in the pay of Mussolini, formed secret terrorist organisations. Foreign money was involved in all these small groups, including Doriot's. The Alsatian home rule movement was heavily subsidised by both the Weimar Republic and Hitler. Mussolini did the same for Corsica and Nice. It was only in Alsace and the Moselle that there was any significant popular support for home rule. 'A home rule movement is often nothing but the symbol of a desire to be dissociated from governments that are hesitant or in decline, from self-interest or simply a wish to be on the winning side.' (G. Mauco, *Les Etrangers en France*, p. 590.) The Front Populaire, which was backed by the combined forces of the communist party of Alsace-Lorraine and the SFIO, was faced with a violent antisemitic, pro-Hitlerian separatist movement organised by the Volksfront. This hostile body had managed to unite the Germanophile Catholics and the Parti Communiste Ouvrier, the latter being those former members of the communist party ejected by Doriot in 1929, who had become pro-Hitlerian.

Anti-semitism increased considerably under the Front Populaire government. It was disseminated not only by the partisan press *Gringoire, Je suis partout* and *L'Action française*, but also by the big dailies that favoured

Hitler and Mussolini. It existed within the pacifist left, which hated Jews and communists alike – both of them 'warmongers'. In *La Flèche* Bergery started by saying that a Jew was a Frenchman like anybody else, and ended by saying he was not a Frenchman like anybody else because the prime minister's personal 'cabinet' contained only Jews.

The right-wing press, including the big dailies, poured out the vilest and most absurd calumny on Léon Blum, Jean Zay and others in the Front Populaire, even those who were not Jews. As Claude Fohlen has said, it was truly 'a time of hate'. In the autumn of 1936 this hate was responsible for the death of Roger Salengro, the minister of the interior. Salengro, mayor of Lille and its deputy, had led the negotiations for the Matignon agreements and with Jean Lebas, deputy mayor of Roubaix, had originated most of the major social reforms. After 14 July 1936 he was accused of desertion during the First World War in *L'Action français* and by Henri Béraud in *Gringoire*. These papers endlessly exploited what they called the 'Salengro affair': a traitor, condemned to death *in absentia* by court-martial, was sitting as minister of the interior in a Jewish ministry. These accusations were gladly taken up and bandied about by other papers, notably *L'Echo de Paris*. They were totally unfounded. Depressed by the death of his wife, unable to endure these attacks alone, and worn out by overwork, Salengro committed suicide on 18 November 1936. An enormous crowd attended his funeral, and Cardinal Liénart forcefully expressed his horror and disapproval of this slanderous campaign: 'A press that specialises in vilification is not Christian.'

Marx Dormoy took over Salengro's portfolio. In December a law was passed clamping down on defamation in the press.

The end of the Blum experiment

The Salengro affair was only the most glaring example of the atmosphere of passionate animosity that enveloped France at the very moment when Blum was making his appeal to the moral feelings of his opponents and trying to appease them with his 'pause'. In spring 1937 the ministry really had its back against the wall in spite of the great success of the Paris exhibition, whose opening had been delayed by strikes. It was already in serious trouble over its capitulation to the employers and its indulgence towards the fascists, when the 'fusillade de Clichy' suddenly made things much worse. The government had refused to ban a PSF demonstration in a cinema in Clichy. Clichy had a communist council and a socialist deputy, and they called for a counter-demonstration. There was a violent clash with the police, resulting in five deaths and five hundred wounded. Dormoy, who rushed to the scene, was unable to stop the firing, and Blum's head of cabinet, André Blumel, who accompanied him, was wounded.

The 'fusillade de Clichy' was the pay-off for the 'pause'. The socialists were in despair. The communists and the revolutionary left accused Blum of being soft on fascism, and demanded Dormoy's resignation. The CGT called a general strike on 18 March. The radicals, on the other hand, saw nothing wrong since de la Rocque's meeting was perfectly legal, while the counter-demonstration was not. It seems possible that from now on the communists were considering ways of getting rid of Blum so as to bring about a change in foreign and social policies. He himself was considering resignation. Whatever the case, Blum 'the killer' was totally deserted by the working class, which had been cheering him a year earlier, while the failure of the 'pause' had not gained him a single new supporter. The levying of the March 1937 loan had been halted by the 'fusillade'; capital still left the country, production was falling, unemployment spreading. Vincent Auriol refused to increase taxes in April, that is to resort to deflation. Rist and Baudouin resigned from the exchange stabilisation committee.

Seeing that there was no way of fighting against the 'wall of gold', Blum and Auriol on 14 June asked for plenary financial powers to govern by *décrets-lois* until 31 July. The Chamber consented, conditionally, but the Senate, instigated by Caillaux, refused. Blum had on three occasions contemplated resigning – when the British opposed aid to Spain, when the communists abstained on a vote in the Chamber in December 1936, and on the morning after the Clichy affair. This time he made no attempt to fight the Senate's decision and offered the government's resignation to the President on 22 June.

The Blum experiment, an attempt to make the liberal society of 1936 accept a rather mild form of socialism, without any rules of enforcement, had actually failed some months previously, ever since the 'pause'. In the prevailing political climate at home and abroad the whole idea was utterly utopian.

31

The death agony of the Front Populaire

The Front Populaire came to grief through its own economic ineffectiveness and because of external pressures over which it had no control. However, the electoral coalition and the parliamentary majority survived the jettisoning of its programme. This was confirmed in by-elections during 1937 and 1938, and even in a Senatorial election at the end of 1938 when Marx Dormoy was successful in spite of being branded a 'warmonger' by the radicals and a 'murderer' by the communists.

The last three ministries of the Front Populaire

To all appearances the Chautemps and Blum ministries from June 1937 to April 1938 carried on the policies of the Front Populaire; but they had lost its spirit. The Comité National de Rassemblement Populaire continued to exist. The third Chautemps ministry seemed to be a continuation of the Blum ministry, the only difference being that a radical had taken the place of a socialist. Most of the ministers stayed put and Blum was deputy prime minister. But there was a different atmosphere. Bonnet, who had moved from the left to the right of the radical party, became minister of finance. The communists had offered to join the ministry and been turned down. As deputy prime minister Blum was supposed to read the ministerial statement to the Senate, but he was received with abuse and let Albert Sarraut take his place. The policy, started by Chautemps and lasting until November 1938, was one of temporisation. Plenary powers were willingly granted on 30 June. The impact of the Auriol devaluation had already faded and Bonnet did away with the minimum gold price of the franc. The 'floating' franc which now replaced the 'elastic' franc had in reality come off the gold standard. From then on there was a whole series of devaluations; no longer a nightmare, they had become a perfectly normal event. But the franc was too high relative to the pound and the dollar, and the economic situation went on getting worse up to November 1938.

The deficit in the balance of payments increased tenfold between 1935 and 1937. The gold reserves went on shrinking. All this, together with continued speculation, was responsible for a steady slide in the value of the franc.

Inflation of the franc, 1928–40

Date	Weight in gold		Value of the pound in francs	Value of the dollar in francs
1803	franc Germinal: 322.18 mg		25.221	12.181
1928	franc Poincaré: 65.5 mg		24	25
1931			31% without devaluation: real value=75 francs	
1934				41%=15 francs
1 October 1936	franc Auriol ('elastic')	43–9 mg	about 105	about 18
1 July 1937	franc Bonnet ('floating')	43 mg	about 194	about 25
5 May 1938	franc Daladier		179	about 36
12 November 1938	franc Reynaud	27.5 mg		
February 1940	franc Reynaud	21 mg	186	43.80

France's isolation in the world made it more and more necessary to rearm. In April 1937 Belgium declared herself a neutral state, just at the moment when Great Britain was trying to settle her disagreements with Germany and Italy, and when Yvon Delbos on his tour round central Europe was about to say that the Petite Entente was defunct. The budget, already heavily in deficit, was crushed by the cost of rearmament: the returns from taxation had been gravely reduced by economic stagnation, strikes and riots. At the end of July Georges Bonnet cautiously returned to the pre-1936 policy of hitting purchasing power and raising taxes, import dues and transport rates. This had hardly any effect and in October 1937 the pound sterling stood at 148 francs. The only lasting legacy of the Chautemps ministry was the creation of the SNCF (Société Nationale des Chemins de Fer Français), necessitated by the near bankruptcy of the railway companies, which were losing out to road transport. Believers in a liberal economy willingly agree to the nationalisation of loss-making concerns so long as private profit-making is allowed. The SNCF was a mixed economy type of enterprise, with the state owning 51 per cent of the equity and taking responsibility for management. The decree of 31 August 1937 created a merger rather than a take-over. For the liberal capitalist the SNCF had two advantages: the state took over the railways' debts and its management could be held responsible for them, since in the past the private companies had managed to make profits. The nationalisations of 1936–7 bore no resemblance to the 'confiscations' of the post-Liberation period. The former owners always received substantial compensation.

The economy continued to stagnate; the government was weak, the political scene was confused, but the right was encouraged by Blum's fall. The visible part of the extreme right increasingly rallied to de la Rocque.

The PSF, which evidently had wealthy backers, went on growing, and although the electorate remained loyal to the Front Populaire in the cantonal elections of 1937, a great flood of de la Rocque supporters was expected in the Chamber in 1940. The membership of Doriot's PPF began to fall away at the beginning of 1938. Its financial backers were moving over to its rival the Action française, which, dissolved as a Ligue, had got over the shock of its condemnation by the Orléanist pretender, the Comte de Paris, and still had much influence through its newspaper.

A new factor was the secret activities of various groups set up in 1936 and subsidised from abroad, of which the best known was the Comité Secret d'Action Révolutionnaire (CSAR), known to its opponents as the 'Cagoule'. Its leaders, Deloncle and Dusseigneur, were conspiratorial extreme right-wing characters disillusioned by the obvious feebleness of their own party. Their aim was to organise some highly provocative incidents, rather on the lines of the Reichstag fire, which would make people believe in a communist plot. Some believed that the Cagoulards were responsible for the 'fusillade de Clichy.' They assassinated several people, among them Dimitri Navachine and the Rosselli brothers. The latter were Italian socialists who formed a rallying-point for exiled anti-fascists and recruited the brigades who had fought in Spain against Mussolini's troups at Guadalajara. On 11 September 1937 the Cagoulards destroyed the office headquarters of the Confédération Générale du Patronat Française and the Union Patronale Interprofessionnelle. They hoped that their members in the army might persuade their fellow officers to believe that the communists were responsible and so turn the army against the Republic. In November Dormoy exposed the plot and made a good many arrests. Later this elimination of the Cagoule was to cost him his life.

The colonies were all suffering equally from the depression, and the situation was tense. In North Africa the Europeans were very divided and the natives equally so. The government pursued repressive policies in Indo-China, Tunisia and, after the riots in Meknès, in Morocco. The communists, who were violently against Messali Hadj, managed to get the Etoile Nord-Africaine suppressed, to the great annoyance of the non-communist left and the anti-semites. It promptly started up again as the PPA. The resemblance to the PPF, if only in its initials, shows up the inconsistency in the political relations between colonists and natives in Algeria.

Yet the situation in France was far the most serious. At the beginning of September there was a wave of strikes and factory sit-ins. In October the cabinet, meeting at Rambouillet, issued a special statement calling for social discipline in order to get production moving again. But in December there were more strikes near Paris, and when Dormoy sent in the Gardes

Mobiles to eject the strikers, the only result was to spread the strike movement all over the Paris region, then all over France, especially in the Nord and the Lyon area. At the end of the year Paris was brought to a standstill by a general strike of the public services.

By now Chautemps was absolutely overwhelmed, his majority split into two rival camps with parts of the SFIO in each. When the new session began on 14 January, he launched an attack on the communists, whom he accused, by implication, of fomenting strikes in order to make the government change its apathetic foreign policy. Replying for the communist group Arthur Ramette said that the 'wall of gold' was the guilty party, and that all social problems would be resolved if only the Front Populaire's programme could be fulfilled in its entirety. After this the communists withdrew their support from the government. The prime minister then told them that they were to free 'to depart. The SFIO deputies, taking this to mean that Chautemps was putting an end to the Front Populaire, ordered their ministers to resign from the cabinet. Chautemps was also obliged to resign, but four days later he constructed a new ministry, rather more to the right, as the independent socialists took the places of the SFIO ministers. But in an attempt to preserve the Front Populaire the socialists and communists gave Chautemps a vote of confidence for his fourth ministry. This lasted for three months during which he took no action and the situation grew steadily worse. By March 1938 the situation had become intolerable. The pound sterling stood at 153 francs, production was falling in spite of fewer strikes, the state coffers were empty; and in the midst of these disasters the Chamber of Deputies voted itself an increase in salary from 60,000 to 82,000 francs. The radicals now decided that they had to take over the government as soon as possible, enlisting the right against the extreme left, just as their senators had repeatedly urged them to do in 1926 and 1934.

On 9 March the government asked for plenary powers to impose a policy of austerity and deflation. The SFIO deputies made it known that they would abstain. Without risking a vote Chautemps placed his government's resignation in the hands of President Lebrun. On 12 March, taking advantage, as usual, of a power vacuum in the democracies, Hitler carried out his long-matured plan for the invasion of Austria. France, like Great Britain, took no action.

In this desperate situation Blum was called upon to form a government and decided to appeal directly to the opposition with the idea of forming a ministry of national union, running from Maurice Thorez to Louis Marin. The communists had offered to join Chautemps' cabinet in June 1937 and could hardly reject a formula that revived, in the face of the Nazi menace, the policy they had themselves advocated for a 'Front Français'. It was a policy that was admittedly out of the question for the pacifist extreme left.

Nothing like it had been tried since 1914, when Poincaré was President of the Republic. It was then called the Union Sacrée and had nothing in common with the Union Nationale, which was just a right-wing government with a group of captive radicals. On 18 March Blum spoke to a group of opposition deputies in a special session of the Chamber and in an emotional speech entreated them, as a matter of life and death to the nation, to achieve a Union Sacrée. There was certainly going to be a war, and he was ready to do anything to meet it with British support externally and a union of all parties at home. After he had finished there was a discussion among the minority parties. Only Paul Reynaud, Champetier de Ribes and the Démocrates Populaires allowed themselves to be swayed by patriotic feeling. The great majority followed Pierre-Etienne Flandin, who was backed by the senator Joseph Caillaux, and rejected the idea with contempt. This was either because they thought that a Union Sacrée, if it was to be anything like the Union Nationale, could only come to pass, as in 1914, by a total capitulation of the left to the right; or else they had already decided, in a phrase immortalised by the history books, 'Rather Hitler than Blum'. They were not going to govern with the left when there was a possibility of a right-wing government which could avoid war by agreements with Germany, Italy and later Spain.

Blum now decided to form a last Front Populaire ministry more or less identical with that of June 1936, though he knew it would be thwarted by the Senate. He received his vote of confidence, but that did not stop demonstrations, strikes and sit-ins that lasted from 25 March to the beginning of April. At this point Blum asked for plenary powers. It has been pointed out that the measures Blum intended to implement with his second cabinet were derived from Keynes and amounted to socialism, rather mild but quite genuine and consistent: a tax on capital of up to 17 per cent, exchange control, control of stockmarket dealings and currency control, with slight inflation at first to get the economy moving, followed by a sharp increase in taxation later to prevent inflation getting out of hand. The Chamber gave him his plenary powers. The radical deputies, just like everybody else, knew perfectly well that the Senate had decided to overturn the ministry. It is idle to speculate whether such a programme could have been put across in June 1936, when the opposition was panic-stricken. In the circumstances of 1936 Blum's moral code would not have allowed him to be anything other than the honest manager of a liberal Republic. What he wanted in 1938 was to use the last days of the Front Populaire to register a protest and a warning against the selfishness of the ruling class, of the right and of the radicals. In this hopeless struggle his programme was nothing more than a symbolic gesture, whose appeal might have been stronger if he had accepted a few communist ministers in his cabinet.

Persuaded by Caillaux, the Senate voted against the government, refusing to discuss the project, with a massive majority of 223 to 49. The pound sterling was now at 180 francs. The demonstration organised by Marceau Pivert and the SFIO federation outside the Palais de Luxembourg that same evening was a disastrous failure. The day was long past when working-class enthusiasm could get thousands of people out on to the streets of Paris.

Daladier took office on 12 April. There were no socialists in his cabinet. On the other hand there were some opponents of the Front Populaire, such as Paul Reynaud, Georges Mandel and Champetier de Ribes. It was a ministry that covered a wide spread. The Front Populaire had thrown its principles overboard at the time of the 'pause', but had lived on until June 1937. The Rassemblement Populaire which formed its core seemed to survive in the persons of Chautemps and Blum. Daladier received an almost unanimous vote of confidence on 13 April, which showed that in the face of the external threat the extreme left was still hoping to keep the anti-fascist front intact. In fact the Front Populaire's death certificate was to be deferred for several months, until autumn 1938.

Conclusion

So everything was going back to normal; meaning that the working class was to be put back in its proper place – outside society. Its exile seemed to have come to an end in June 1936, and its hopes had lasted a little longer than in 1848 or 1871. The death agony was more protracted, and the bourgeoisie had not had to stain its hands with the blood of the June days (1848) or of the week in May (1871); but its hatred of the workers was just as strong. It seemed intolerable that they should claim a status which put at risk all the values of the social hierarchy. Even after the fall of the Front Populaire the ruling class still thirsted for vengeance – a hangover from the fright they had had. Hence it was quite naive, or cynical, a few months later to ask the workers to die for a society that treated them as enemies.

It simply did not occur to anybody on the right that a nation in decay could be regenerated by social reform. The only exception was perhaps Tardieu, but he looked to fascism for the answer and ignored the threat from abroad. They were men of experience but they could not conceive of any form of moral firmness other than that of 1914–18, and even then they were safely in the rear, as Marc Bloch remarked in *L'Etrange défaite*. Georges Mandel, who was holding forth about the Nazi threat in 1933, and Paul Reynaud, who saw so clearly the true reasons for economic decline, were brilliant and patriotic men. One can understand that they might not have seen the possibility of national regeneration from a revolution; but when they were faced with a minute social readjustment, involving a little social justice, they were as blind as the rest. They shared the whole of the right-wing's hatred of the Front Populaire. It is true that the forty-hour, five-day week helped to prolong the crisis through the lack of economic expertise and proper statistics; but the real reason for the failure was social and moral. It amounted to hatred of the working class, hatred of the Jew, hatred of the communist and the socialist.

There were political reasons too. The Front Populaire was an anti-fascist and hence defensive coalition, whose members had contradictory ideas about how to unite the nation against Hitler; whether to appease the right by giving up their demands for social reform or to wage war ruthlessly on the home front against potential collaborators with the enemy. Mistrust had been aroused from the first by the discouragement of grass-roots committees of the Rassemblement Populaire through fear that the communists would infiltrate them and turn them into soviets. The Spanish Civil War and disappointment over the failure of economic and social measures turned political rifts into chasms. Not only did the right hate the left, but also, within the left, the partisans of resistance to foreign fascism hated those who were willing to appease it. The extinction of their 1936 hopes two years later was to shatter all the organisations, except the communists, that had participated in the Rassemblement, or else to turn them into ideological battlefields, like the CGT. The quarrels between anti- and pro-communists, between pacifists and hard-liners, weakened the Front Populaire and helped to cripple its power to govern.

There were analogous reasons for the Front Populaire's economic policies, which we find so easy to criticise today – their respect for capitalist society and the people who ran it, the lack of an exchange control policy, the lateness and inadequacy of devaluations and the timidity of their redistributive reforms. But it was not only the right whose survival depended on an outmoded political system. The radical socialists were even more dependent; and so partly were the socialists, who had ridden to power not only on the votes of the workers, but also on those of the backward farmers and peasants of the underdeveloped Midi.

With such heterogeneous support it was not possible for the Front Populaire to carry out any root and branch social reform: hence it could not get the economy moving. It probably made economic stagnation worse by shortening working hours, which in turn led to social difficulties. It was impossible for it to get out of the vicious circle in which all the governments of the previous ten years had been caught.

By 1938 the economy had barely reached the level of 1913. National income per head was very low – three hundred dollars, compared with five hundred in Great Britain and six hundred in the United States. The inflation of 1936 had not brought prosperity to anyone, though prices were higher than in 1929.

The standard of living had probably fallen little, if at all. If it had fallen, it was because France was paying for her armaments and her daily bread out of capital. Deposits may have increased in face value, but savings had fallen off, for capital and wages had diminished in real value because of the wild monetary fluctuations. There was a very low rate of capital growth, plant was ageing, and there was little new investment. The double protection of tax remissions and customs duties meant that unprofitable agriculture managed to survive with its grotesquely low yields.

Economic structure had frozen social structure in a way that made regeneration impossible, in spite of incessant state intervention. This

Price rises in France, 1929–36

	Wholesale prices	Retail prices
1929	623	621
1930	543	617
1935	347	440
1936	640	706

society was preserved by its Malthusianism: 'Having reached the age of fifty a bourgeois or *embourgeoisé* generation found itself provided with a fair amount of capital, saved through not wanting and not having children. Provided with capital and denuded of people, such a generation could only resort to lending its money abroad and transforming the profit it had made at the expense of life into shaky foreign loans.' (A. Sauvy, *Richesse et population*, Paris, Payot, 1943, p. 140.)

Alfred Sauvy attributes the decline which he depicts in these words to people succumbing during the world crisis to the temptation to live off the quick profits they had made in times of so-called prosperity. A few heads of industry such as Mercier, Detœuf and Schueler, alone of their kind, attempted some experiments in a more vigorous, new-style capitalism.

Behind the scenes of violence and strife, material and human senescence was inducing political lethargy. Those who spoke in the name of France, whether statesmen or thinkers, were visibly giving up the struggle against apathy and abdication. That candid witness, Marc Bloch, has said the last word on the intellectual torpor of that gerontocracy. The ruling classes who laid claim to a monopoly of power no longer had any idea how to use it. Contemporaries and historians were agreed on this apparently incurable state of degeneracy. But this pessimism has been controverted by the facts. Beyond the defeat that the blatant chaos in the economy, society and politics rendered inevitable, France harboured a hidden force that powered an extraordinary renaissance. The economists who were later to be most severe in their criticisms admitted that the Front Populaire's economic measures, disastrous in the short term, were ultimately beneficial. At the time no one could foresee that the future lay in the hands of those who played no part in the existing regime, but who were its most vital members. Those who examined this state of decadence and thought it irremediable could not know that youthful creativity was to be found on the shop floor, in the young agricultural trade-union movement, in a revival of social Christianity, in groups of research scientists, among the artists and militants. These were the people who would bring the country to life again after their rulers had surrended social power and the country's interests to the enemy.

This is why, although it had been unable to divert the course of history after 1930, the Front Populaire continued to bulk so large in the collective memory. A frightening memory for the aged ruling class, but a mythical golden age for the people, who had joyously realised their own strength, and were never going to forget it.

Bibliography

GENERAL HISTORY

Reference works

Agulhon, M. and Nouschi, A., *La France de 1914 à 1940*, Paris, Nathan, 1971.

Ambrosi, C. and A., *La France, 1870–1970*, Paris, Masson, 1971.

Atlas de la France contemporaine, 1800–1865, Paris, Colin, 1966.

Azéma, J.-P. and Winock, M., *La IIIe République*, Paris, Calmann-Lévy (Naissance et mort), 1970.

Barral, P., *Le Département de l'Isère sous la IIIe République, 1870–1940, historie sociale et politique*, Paris, Colin (Cahiers de la Fondation nationale des sciences politiques, 173), 1967.

Baumont, M., *La Troisième République*, Lausanne–Paris, Editions rencontre, 1968.

— *La Faillite de la Paix (1918–1939)*, Paris, Presses universitaires (Peuples et civilisations), 1967, vol. XX.

Beau de Loménie, E., *Les Responsabilités des dynasties bourgeoises*, Paris, Denoël, 1954, vols. III and IV.

Bonnefous, E. and G., *Histoire politique de la IIIe République*, Paris, Presses universitaires, 1959–65, vols. III, IV, V, VI.

Brogan, Sir Denis, *The development of Modern France, 1870–1939*, London, Hamish Hamilton, revised edition, 1967.

Bury, J. P. T., *France, 1814–1940*, London, Methuen, 4th edition, 1969.

Chastenet, J., *Histoire de la Troisième République*, Paris, Hachette, 1957–63, vols. IV, V, VI, VII.

Chevalier, J.-J., *Histoire des institutions politiques de la France de 1789 à nos jours*, Paris, Dalloz, 1952.

Cobban, A., *A history of Modern France*, Harmondsworth, Penguin, 1965, vol. III.

Crouzet, M., *L'Epoque contemporaine à la recherche d'une civilisation nouvelle*, Paris, Presses universitaires (Histoire générale des civilisations), 1970, vol. VII.

Duby, G. and Mandrou, R., *Histoire de la civilisation française*, Paris, Colin, 1958, vol. II.

Dupeux, G., *French society, 1789–1970*, translated by P. Wait, London, Methuen, 1976.

Duroselle, J.-B., *L'Europe de 1815 à nos jours*, Paris, Presses universitaires (Nouvelle Clio), 1970.

Clerget, P. and M., *La France dans le monde*, Paris, Payot, 1938.

Fohlen, C., *La France de l'entre-deux-guerres, 1917–1939*, Paris, Castermann, 1972.

Greene, N., *From Versailles to Vichy, the Third French Republic*, New York, Crowell, 1970.

Guérard, A., *France, a modern history*, Ann Arbor, Mich., University of Michigan Press, revised edition, 1969.

Histoire générale de la presse française, edition by Cl. Bellanger, J. Godechot, P. Guiral, F. Terrou, Paris, Presses universitaires, 1972, vol. III.

Johnson, D., *France*, London, Thames and Hudson, 1969.

Joll, J. (ed.), *The decline of the Third Republic*, London, Chatto and Windus (Saint Antony's Papers, 5), 1959.

Kayser, J., *La Presse de province sous la Troisième République*, Paris, Colin (Cahiers de la Fondation nationale des sciences politiques, 92), 1958.

Knapton, E. J., *France, an interpretive history*, New York, Scribner, 1971.

Manévy, R., *Histoire de la presse, 1914–1939*, Paris, Corréa, 1945.

Mayeur, J.-M., Bédarida, F., Prost, A., Monneron, J.-L., *Cent ans d'esprit républicain*, Paris, Nouvelle librairie de France (Histoire du peuple français), 1964, vol. V.

Néré, J., *La Troisième République, 1914–1940*, Paris, Colin, 1969.

Rémond, R., *Introduction à l'histoire de notre temps. III. Le XXe siècle de 1914 à nos jours*, Paris, Editions du Seuil (Points), 1974.

Renouvin, P., *La Crise européenne et la première guerre mondiale*, Paris, Presses universitaires (Peuples et civilisations), 1965, vol. XIX.

Shirer, W. L., *The collapse of the Third Republic, an inquiry into the fall of France in 1940*, London, Heinemann, 1970.

Sorlin, P., *La Société française*, Paris, Arthaud, 1971, vol. II.

Taylor, A. J. P., *The struggle for mastery in Europe, 1848–1918*, Oxford, Clarendon Press, 1954.

Tint, H., *France since 1918*, New York, Harper and Row, 1971.

Wright, G., *France in modern times*, New York, Norton, 3rd edition 1981.

Zeldin, T., *France, 1848–1945*, Oxford, Clarendon Press, 1973, 1977, 2 vols.

Biographies and memoirs

Beauvoir, Simone de, *Mémoires d'une jeune fille rangée*, Paris, Gallimard, 1959.
— *La Force de l'âge*, Paris, Gallimard, 1960.

Bloch, M., *L'Etrange défaite*, Paris, Franc-Tireur, 1946

L'Œuvre de Léon Blum, Paris, Albin Michel, 1955, vol. V.

Léon Blum ou la politique du juste, by C. Audry, Paris, Julliard, 1965.

Léon Blum, humanist in politics, by J. Colton, New York, Knopf, 1966.

Léon Blum, by J. Lacouture, Paris, Editions du Seuil, 1977.

Léon Blum et le parti socialiste, 1872–1934, by G. Ziebura, Paris, Colin, 1967.

Brasillach, R., *Notre avant-guerre*, Paris, Plon, 1941.

Briand, sa vie, son œuvre avec son journal et de nombreux documents inédits, by G. Suarez, Paris, Plon, 1938–52, 6 vols.

Caillaux, J., *Mes mémoires*, Paris, Plon, 1952, vol. III.

Clemenceau, G., *Grandeur et misère d'une victoire*, Paris, Plon, 1930.

Clemenceau, by G. Monnerville, Paris, Fayard, 1968.

Georges Clemenceau, a political biography, by D. R. Watson, London, Eyre Methuen, 1974.

Cogniot, G., *Parti pris*, Paris, Editions sociales, 1977, vol. I.

Duclos, J., *Mémoires*, Paris, Fayard, 2 vols. 1968, 1969.

Flandin, P.-E., *Politique française*, Paris, Editions nouvelles, 1947.

Le Mystère Gamelin, by Pierre Le Goyet, Paris, Presses de la cité, 1975.

Grenadou, E. and Prévost, A., *Grenadou, paysan français*, Paris, Editions du Seuil, 1966.

Herriot, E., *Jadis*, Paris, Flammarion, 1952, vol. II.

Herriot, by P. O. Lapie, Paris, Fayard, 1967.
Humbert-Droz, J., *Memoires*, Neuchâtel, La Baconnière, 1969–72, 3 vols.
Léon Jouhaux, by B. Georges, D. Tintant, M.-A. Renauld, Paris, Presses universi-
taires, 1962
Pierre Laval and the eclipse of France, by G. Warner, London, Eyre and Spottiswoode,
1968.
Lefebvre, H., *La Somme et le reste*, Paris, La Nef de Paris, 1959, 2 vols.
Liddell Hart, B. H., *Memoirs*, London, Cassell, 1965–8, 2 vols.
Georges Mandel and the Third Republic, by J. M. Sherwood, Stanford, Calif., Stanford
University Press, 1971.
Ernest Mercier, French technocrat, by R. F. Kuisel, Berkeley, Calif., University of
California Press, 1967.
Paul-Boncour, J., *Entre deux guerres, souvenirs sur la IIIe République*, Paris, Plon, 1945,
2 vols.
Poincaré, R., *Au service de la France, neuf années de souvenirs*, Paris, Plon, 1933, 10
vols.
Poincaré, by P. Miquel, Paris, Fayard, 1961.
Poiret, P., *En habillant l'époque*, Paris, Grasset, 1930.
Prévost, J., *Dix-huitième année*, Paris, Gallimard, 1929.
Reynaud, P., *Mémoires*, Paris, Flammarion, 1959–63, 3 vols.
Rougemont, Denis de, *Journal d'un intellectuel en chômage*, Paris, Albin Michel, 1937.
Thirion, A., *Révolutionnaires sans révolution*, Paris, Laffont, 1972.
Albert Thomas, trente ans de réformisme social, by B. W. Schaper, Paris, Presses
universitaires, no date.
Maurice Thorez, by G. Cogniot and V. Joannès, Paris, Editions sociales, 1970.
Maurice Thorez, vie secrète et vie publique, by P. Robrieux, Paris, Fayard, 1975.
Maxime Weygand and civil–military relations in modern France, by P. C. F. Bankwitz,
Cambridge, Mass., Harvard University Press, 1967.
Defeated leaders, the political fate of Caillaux, Jouvenel and Tardieu, by R. Binion,
Westport, Conn., Greenwood, reprinted 1975.

WAR AND DIPLOMACY

The First World War

Baechler, C., *Les Alsaciens et le grand tournant de 1918, la fin de l'Alsace allemande*,
Strasbourg, Association des presses universitaires, 1972.
Becker, J.-J., *1914, comment les Français sont entrés dans la guerre*, Paris, Presses de la
Fondation nationale des sciences politiques, 1977.
— *Les Français dans la grande guerre*, Paris, Laffont, 1980.
Becker, J.-J. and Kriegel, A., *1914, la guerre et le mouvement ouvrier français*, Paris,
Colin, 1964.
Bidou, H. and Gauvain, A., *La Grande Guerre*, Paris, Hachette, 1922.
Cassar, G. H., *The French and the Dardanelles*, London, Allen and Unwin, 1971.
Ducasse, A., Meyer, J., Perreux, G., *1914–1918, vie et mort des Français*, Paris,
Hachette, 1962.
Duroselle, J. B., *La France et les Français, 1914–1920*, Paris, Colin, 1972.
Elcock, H., *Portrait of a decision, the Council of Four and the treaty of Versailles*, London,
Eyre Methuen, 1972.
Ferro, M., *La Grande Guerre*, Paris, Gallimard, 1969.
Ferry, A., *Les Carnets secrets, 1914–1918*, Paris, Grasset, 1957.
Marshal Foch, *Mémoires pour servir à l'histoire de la guerre*, Paris, Plon, 1930, 2 vols.

General Gambiez and Colonel Svire, *Histoire de la guerre mondiale, 1914–1918*, Paris, Fayard, 1968, 2 vols.

Horne, A., *The price of glory, Verdun 1916*, London, Macmillan, 1962.

Marshal Joffre, *Mémoires, 1910–1917*, Paris, Plon, 1932, vol. II.

Kaspi, A., *Le Temps des Americains*, Paris, Publications de la Sorbonne, 1976.

Keiger, J. F. V., *France and the origins of the first world war*, London, Macmillan, 1983.

King, J. C., *Generals and politicians, conflict between France's command, parliament and government, 1914–1918*, Berkeley, Calif., University of California Press, 1951.

— *Foch versus Clemenceau*, Cambridge, Mass., Harvard University Press, 1960.

General Koeltz, *La Guerre de 1914–1918, les opérations militaires*, Paris, Sirey, 1968.

Mantoux, P., *Les Déliberations du Conseil des Quatre (24 March to 28 June 1919)*, Paris, CNRS, 1955.

Mayer, A. J., *Politics and diplomacy of peacemaking, 1918–1919*, London, Weidenfeld and Nicolson, 1968.

Miquel, P., *La Paix de Versailles et l'opinion publique française*, Paris, Flammarion, 1972.

— *La Grande Guerre*, Paris, Fayard, 1983.

Pedroncini, G., *Les Mutineries de 1917*, Paris, Presses universitaires, 1967.

— *Les Négociations secrètes pendant la première guerre mondiale*, Paris, Flammarion, 1969.

— *Pétain, Général en chef, 1917–1918*, Paris, Presses universitaires, 1974.

Porch, D. *The march to the Marne, the French army 1871–1914*, Cambridge, Cambridge University Press, 1981.

Perreux, G., *La Vie quotidienne des civils en France pendant la Grande Guerre*, Paris, Hachette, 1966.

Pingaud, A., *Histoire diplomatique de la France pendant la Grande Guerre*, Paris, Alsatia, 1938–1940, 3 vols.

Renouvin, P., *La Première Guerre mondiale*, Paris, Presses universitaires, 1967.

— *L'Armistice de Rethondes*, Paris, Gallimard, 1968.

— *Le Traité de Versailles*, Paris, Flammarion, 1969.

Revue d'histoire moderne et contemporaine, January–March 1968 (special number on the year 1917).

Rosmer, A., *Le Mouvement ouvrier pendant la première guerre mondiale*, Paris, Librairie du travail, 1936; Paris, Mouton, 1959.

Service historique des armées, *Les Armées françaises dans la grande guerre*, Paris, 1922–39, 34 vols.

Stevenson, D., *French war aims against Germany, 1914–1919*, Oxford, Clarendon Press, 1982).

Tanenbaum, J. K., *General Maurice Sarrail, 1856–1929*, Chapel Hill, NC, University of North Carolina Press, 1974.

Tardieu, A., *La Paix*, Paris, Payot, 1921.

Terrail (Mermeix), G., *Fragments d'histoire, 1914–1919*, Paris, Albin Michel, 1919–20, 5 vols.

Wormser, G., *La République de Clemenceau*, Paris, Presses universitaires, 1961.

From war to war

Adamthwaite, A., *France and the coming of the second world war*, London, Cass, 1977.

Albrecht-Carrié, R., *Britain and France, adaptations to a changing balance of power*, Garden City, NY, Doubleday, 1970.

Artaud, D., *La Reconstruction de l'Europe, 1919–1929*, Paris, Presses universitaires, 1973.

Bariéty, J., *Les Relations franco-allemandes après la première guerre mondiale*, Paris, Publications de la Sorbonne, 1977.

Beau de Loménie, E., *Le Débat de la ratification du traité du Versailles à la Chambre des députés et dans la presse en 1919*, Paris, Denoël, 1945.

Bourdon, J., *Considérations sur les causes des deux guerres*, Paris, Hachette, 1946.

Challener, R. W., *The French theory of the nation in arms, 1866–1939*, New York, Russell and Russell, 1965.

Duroselle, J.-B., *Histoire diplomatique de 1919 à nos jours*, Paris, Dalloz, 1970.

— *La Décadence, 1932–1939*, Paris, Imprimerie nationale, 1979.

Fridenson, P. and Lecuir, J., *La France et la Grande-Bretagne face aux problèmes aériens, 1935– mai 1940*, Vincennes, 1976.

Gates, E. M., *End of the affair, the collapse of the Anglo-French alliance*, Berkeley, Calif., University of California Press, 1981.

Horne, A., *To lose a battle, France 1940*, London, Macmillan, 1969.

Hughes, J. M., *To the Maginot Line, the politics of French military preparations in the 1920s*, Cambridge, Mass., Harvard University Press, 1971.

Jacobson, J., *Locarno diplomacy, Germany and the west, 1925–1929*, Princeton, NJ, Princeton University Press, 1972.

Jordan, W. M., *Great Britain, France and the German problem, 1919–1939*, London, Cass, new impression 1971.

Kaiser, D. E., *Economic diplomacy and the origins of the second world war*, Princeton, NJ, Princeton University Press, 1980.

Komjathy, A. T., *The crises of France's eastern European diplomacy*, New York, Columbia University Press, 1976.

McDougall, W. A., *France's Rhineland diplomacy, 1914–1924*, Princeton, NJ, Princeton University Press, 1978.

Maier, C. S., *Recasting bourgeois Europe, stabilisation in France, Germany and Italy in the decade after the first world war*, Princeton, NJ, Princeton University Press, 1975.

Mayer, R., *Bankers' diplomacy*, New York, Columbia University Press, 1970.

Micaud, C. A., *The French right and Nazi Germany*, Durham, NC, Duke University Publications, 1943.

Rostow, N. *Anglo-French relations, 1934–1936*, London, Macmillan, 1984.

Schuker, S. A., *The end of French predominance in Europe, the financial crisis of 1924 and the adoption of the Dawes Plan*, Chapel Hill, NC, University of North Carolina Press, 1976.

Scott, W. E., *Alliance against Hitler: the origins of the Franco-Soviet pact*, Durham, NC, Duke University Publications, 1962.

Waites, N. (ed.), *Troubled neighbours, Franco-British relations in the twentieth century*, London, Weidenfeld and Nicolson, 1971.

Wandycz, P. S., *France and her eastern allies, French–Czechoslovak–Polish relations from the Paris Peace Conference to Locarno*, Minneapolis, Minn., University of Minnesota Press, 1962.

Weill-Raynal, E., *Les Reparations allemandes et la France*, Paris, Nouvelles éditions latines, 1947, 3 vols.

Wolfers, A., *Britain and France between two wars*, New York, Harcourt Brace, 1940.

Yates, L. A. R., *The United States and French security, 1917–1921*, New York, Twayne, 1957.

Young, R. J., *In command of France, French foreign policy and military planning, 1933–1940*, Cambridge, Mass., Harvard University Press, 1978.

POLITICAL HISTORY

General history

Aron, R., and Dandieu, A., *La Révolution nécessaire*, Paris, Grasset, 1933.

Bernstein, S., *Le 6 février 1934*, Paris, Gallimard-Julliard, 1975.

Chavardès, M., *Le 6 février 1934*, Paris, Calmann-Lévy, 1966.

Dupeux, G., *French society, 1789–1970*, London, Methuen, 1976.

Frédérix, P., *Etat des forces en France*, Paris, Gallimard, 1935.

Girardet, R., *La Société militaire, 1814–1940*, Paris, Plon, 1953.

Goguel, F., *La Politique des partis sous la Troisième République*, Paris, Editions du Seuil, 1958.

—*Géographie des élections française sous la IIIᵉ et la IVᵉ Républiques*, Paris, Colin, 1970.

Goldey, D., 'The disintegration of the Cartel des Gauches and the politics of French government finance', unpublished thesis, Oxford University, 1962.

Mysyrowicz, L., *Autopsie d'une défaite*, Bordeaux, Delmas, 1973.

Néré, J., *The foreign policy of France, from 1931 to 1945*, London, Routledge and Kegan Paul, 1975

Pollès, H., *L'Opéra politique*, Paris, Gallimard, 1937.

Prévost, J., *Histoire de France depuis la guerre*, Paris, Rieder, 1932.

Prost, A., *Les Anciens combattants et la société française, 1914–1939*, Paris, Presses de la Fondation nationale des sciences politiques, no date, 3 vols.

Siegfried, *Tableau des partis en France*, Paris, Grasset, 1930.

Soulier, A., *L'Instabilité ministérielle sous la IIIᵉ République, 1871–1938*, Paris, Recueil Sirey, 1939.

Tendances politiques dans la vie française depuis 1789, Paris, Hachette (Colloques, Cahiers de civilisation), 1960.

Werth, A., *The twilight of France, 1933–1940*, edited by D. W. Brogan, New York, Harper and Row, 1942.

The right and the centre

Anderson, M., *Conservative politics in France*, London, Allen and Unwin, 1974.

Bonnard, M., *Le Drame du présent. 1. Les Modérés*, Paris, Grasset, 1936.

Bourdrel, P., *La Cagoule*, Paris, Albin Michel, 1970.

Doriot, J., *La France ne sera pas un pays d'ésclaves*, Paris, Les œuvres françaises, 1936.

— *Refaire la France*, Paris, Grasset, 1938.

Doriot, by D. Wolf, Paris, Fayard, 1969.

Laurent, R., *Le Parti démocrate populaire, 1924–1939*, Paris, Maison de la Presse, 1965.

Lèvy, B.-H., *L'Idéologie française*, Paris, Grasset, 1981.

Machefer, P., *Ligues et fascismes en France, 1918–1939*, Paris, Presses universitaires, 1974.

Maxence, J.-P., *Histoire de dix ans*, Paris, Gallimard, 1939.

Milza, P., *L'Italie fasciste devant l'opinion française, 1920–1940*, Paris, Colin, 1967.

Nolte, E., *Three faces of Fascism, Action française, Italian fascism, national socialism*, translated by L. Vennewitz, New York, Rinehart and Winston, 1966.

Nye, R. A., *The origins of crowd psychology, Gustave Le Bon and the crisis of mass democracy in the Third Republic*, London, Sage, 1975.

Pierce, R., *Contemporary French political thought*, Oxford, Oxford University Press, 1966.

Plumyène, J. and Lasierra, R., *Les Fascismes français, 1923–1963*, Paris, Editions du Seuil, 1963.

Rémond, R., *La Droite en France*, Paris, Aubier-Montaigne, 1954; 2nd edition 1982.
Soucy, R., *Fascist intellectual: Drieu la Rochelle*, Berkeley, Calif., University of California Press, 1979.
Sternhell, Z., *Ni Droite ni gauche*, Paris, Editions du Seuil, 1983.
Tannenbaum, E. R., *The Action française*, New York, Wiley, 1962.
Georges Valois, by Y. Guchet, Paris, Albatros, 1975.
Vaussard, M., *Histoire de la démocratie chrétienne*, Paris, Editions du Seuil, 1956.
Weber, E., *Action française*, Stanford, Calif., Stanford University Press, 1962.
— *Varieties of fascism*, Princeton, NJ, Van Nostrand, 1964.
Winock, M., *Edouard Drumont et Cie, antisemitismes et fascismes en France*, Paris, Editions du Seuil, 1982.

The left and extreme left

Brower, D. R., *The New Jacobins*, Ithaca, NY, Cornell University Press, 1968.
Brunet, J.-P., *L'Enfance du parti communiste, 1930–1938*, Paris, Presses universitaires, 1972.
— *Saint-Denis-la-ville-rouge, 1890–1939*, Paris, Hachette, 1982.
— *Histoire du P.C.F.*, Paris, Presses universitaires, 1982.
Caute, D., *Communism and the French intellectuals*, London, André Deutsch, 1964.
Craipeau, Y., *Le Mouvement trotskiste en France*, Paris, Syros, 1971.
Edouard Daladier, chef du gouvernement, et la France et les Français en 1938–1939, edited by R. Rémond and J. Bourdin, Paris, Presses de la Fondation nationale des sciences politiques, 1977–8.
Droz, J., *Le Socialisme démocratique*, Paris, Colin, 1966.
Estier, C., *La Gauche hebdomadaire, 1914–1962*, Paris, Colin, 1962.
Fauvet, J., *Histoire du parti communiste français, 1917–1939*, Paris, Fayard, 1964, vol. I.
Ferlé, T., *Le Communisme en France*, Paris, La bonne presse, 1937.
Girault, J., *Sur l'implantation du parti communiste français dans l'entre-deux-guerres*, Paris, Editions sociales, 1977.
Greene, N., *Crisis and decline, the French socialist party in the Popular Front era*, Ithaca, NY, Cornell University Press, 1969.
Hughes, H. S., *The obstructed path, French social thought in the years of desperation*, New York, Harper and Row, 1968.
Humbert-Droz, J., *L'Œil de Moscou à Paris*, Paris, Julliard, 1964.
Joll, J., *Intellectuals in politics, three biographical essays* (Léon Blum), London, Weidenfeld and Nicolson, 1971.
Judt, T., *La Reconstruction du parti socialiste, 1921–1926*, Paris, Colin, 1976.
Kayser, J., *Les Grandes Batailles du radicalisme*, Paris, Rivière, 1962.
Kriegel, A., *Aux origines du communisme français, 1914–1920, contribution à l'histoire du mouvement ouvrier français*, Paris, Mouton, 1964.
— *La Croissance des effectifs de la CGT, 1918–1921*, Paris, Mouton, 1967.
— *Les Communistes français*, Paris, Editions du Seuil, 1968.
— *Le Congrès de Tours, naissance du parti communiste français*, Paris, Gallimard-Julliard, 1975.
— *Le Pain at les roses, jalon pour une histoire des socialismes*, Paris, Presses universitaires, 1968.
Larmour, P. J., *The French radical party in the 1930s*, Stanford, Calif., Stanford University Press, 1964.
Lefranc. G., *Le Mouvement socialiste sous la IIIe République*, Paris, Payot, 1963.
— *Le Mouvement syndical sous la IIIe République*, Paris, Payot, 1967.

Ligou, D., *Histoire du socialisme en France, 1880–1961*, Paris, Presses universitaires, 1962.

Lorwin, V. R., *The French Labor movement*, Cambridge, Mass., Harvard University Press, 1954.

Maitron, J., *Le Mouvement anarchiste en France. II. De 1914 à nos jours*, Paris, Maspéro, 1975.

Marcus, J. T., *French socialism in the crisis years, 1933–1936*, New York, Praeger, 1958.

Pierre Mendès France, by J. Lacouture, Paris, Editions du Seuil, 1981.

Monatte, P., *Syndicalisme et révolution*, ed. J. Maitron, Paris, Maspéro, 1975.

Mortimer, E., *The rise of the French communist party*, London, Faber, 1984.

Nicolet, C., *Le Radicalisme*, Paris, Presses universitaires, 1957. *Le Parti communiste français, étapes et problèmes, 1920–1972*, by R. Bourderon, J. Burles, J. Girault, *et al.*, Paris, Editions sociales, 1981.

Pennetier, C., *Le Socialisme dans le Cher, 1851–1921*, Paris, Delayance, 1982.

Philip, A., *Henri de Man et la crise doctrinale du socialisme*, Paris, Gamber, 1928.

Racine, N. and Bodin, L., *Le Parti communiste française pendant l'entre-deux-guerres*, Paris, Colin, 1972.

Robrieux, P. *Histoire intérieure du parti communiste. I. 1920–1945. IV. Biographies, chronologie, bibliographie*, Paris, Fayard, 1980, 1984.

Tarr, F. de, *The French radical party from Herriot to Mendès France*, Oxford, Oxford University Press, 1961.

Tartakowski, D. *Les Premiers communistes français*, Paris, Presses de la Foundation nationale des sciences politiques, 1980.

— *Histoire du P.C.F.*, Paris, Presses universitaires, 1982.

Tiersky, R., *French communism, 1920–1972*, New York, Columbia University Press, 1974.

Trotsky, L., *Le Mouvement communiste en France, 1919–1939*, Paris, Editions de minuit, 1967.

Wall, I.M., *French communism in the era of Stalin*, Westport, Conn., Greenwood, 1983.

Walter, G., *Histoire du parti communiste français*, Paris, Somogy, 1948.

Willard, C., *Socialisme et communisme français*, Paris, Colin, 1967.

Winock, M., *Histoire politique de la revue 'Esprit', 1930–1950*, Paris, Editions du Seuil, 1975.

Wohl, R., *French communism in the making, 1914–1924*, Stanford, Calif., Stanford University Press, 1966.

The Popular Front

Léon Blum, chef de gouvernement, 1936–1937, colloquium held in 1965, under the direction of R. Rémond, P. Renouvin and E. Labrousse, Paris, Colin, 1967.

Bodin, L. and Touchard, J. *Front populaire, 1936*, Paris, Colin, 1972.

Bourdé, G., *La Défaite du Front populaire*, Paris, Editions du Seuil, 1977.

Chavardès, M., *L'Histoire du Front populaire*, Paris, Calmann-Lévy, 1966.

Chambaz, J. and Willard, C., *Le Front populaire*, Paris, Editions sociales, 1961.

Danos, J. and Gibelin, M., *Juin 1936*, Paris, Maspéro, 1972, 2 vols.

Delperrie, J. de Bayac, *Histoire du Front populaire*, Paris, Albin Michel, 1972.

Dupeux, G., *Le Front populaire et les élections de juin 1936*, Paris, Colin, 1959.

L'Expérience Blum, un an du Front populaire, Paris, Editions du Sagittaire, 1937.

Exposé-debat du 26 avril 1965 sur l'expérience économique du front populaire, Paris, Ecole Normale Supérieure, no date.

Grandmougin, J. *Histoire vivante du Front populaire*, Paris, Albin Michel, 1966.

Guérin, D. *Front populaire, révolution manquée*, Paris, Maspéro, 1976.

Lefranc, G., *Le Front populaire*, Paris, Presses universitaires, 1965.
— *Juin 1936*, Paris, Gallimard-Julliard, 1973.
— *Histoire du Front populaire*, Paris, Payot, 1974.
Logue, W., *Léon Blum, the formative years*, De Kalb, Ill., Northern Illinois University Press, 1973.
Prost, A., *La C.G.T. à l'époque du Front populaire*, Paris, Colin, 1964.
Quillot, R. and Chambaz, J., *Le Front populaire, juin 1936*, Paris, Editions du Burin, 1972.
Rossel, A., *Eté '36, 100 jours du Front populaire*, Paris, Editions de la Courtille, 1976.

Special aspects

Ageron, C.A., *Les Algériens musulmans et la France, 1871–1919*, Paris, Presses universitaires, 1968, 2 vols.
— *Histoire de l'Algerie contemporaine. II. De Napoléon III à de Gaulle*, Paris, Presses universitaires, 1979.
Andrew, C.M. and Kanya-Forstner, A.S., *France overseas*, London, Thames and Hudson, 1981.
Berque, J., *Le Maghreb entre les deux guerres*, Paris, Editions du Seuil, 1969.
Bourgin, H., *L'Ecole normale et la politique, de Jaurès à Léon Blum*, Paris, Fayard, 1938.
Cohen, W.B., *Rules of empire, the French colonial service in Africa*, Stanford, Calif., Stanford University Press, 1971.
Crowder, M., *West Africa under colonial rule*, London, Hutchinson, 1968.
Dreyfus, F.-G., *La Vie politique en Alsace, 1919–1936*, Paris, Colin, 1969.
Duiker, W.J., *The rise of nationalism in Vietnam*, Ithaca, NY, Cornell University Press, 1976.
Grimal, H., *La Décolonisation, 1919–1936*, Paris, Colin, 1967.
Helmreich, P.C., *From Paris to Sèvres*, Columbus, Ohio, Ohio State University Press, 1974.
Hilaire, Y.-M., Legrand, A., Ménager, B., Vandenbussche, R., *Atlas électoral Nord-Pas-de-Calais, 1876–1936*, Lille, Presses universitaires de Lille, 1977.
Julien, C.-A., *L'Afrique du Nord en marche*, Paris, Julliard, 1972.
Kedourie, E., *England and the Middle East, the destruction of the Ottoman Empire, 1914–1921*, Hassocks, Harvester Press, 1978.
Maugué, P., *Le Particularisme alsacien, 1918–1967*, Paris, Presses de l'Europe, 1970.
Moneta, J., *Le PCF et la question coloniale, 1920–1965*, Paris, Maspéro, 1971.
Morgenthau, R.S., *Political parties in French-speaking West Africa*, Oxford, Clarendon Press, 1964.
Nevakivi, J., *Britain, France and the Arab Middle East, 1914–1920*, London, Athlone Press, 1969.
Shorrock, W.I., *French imperialism in the Middle East*, Madison, Wis., University of Wisconsin Press, 1976.
Smith, R.J., *The Ecole Normale Supérieure and the Third Republic*, Albany, NY, State University of New York Press, 1981.
Von Albertini, R., *Decolonisation, 1919–1960*, translated by F. Garvie, Garden City, NY, Doubleday, 1971.

ECONOMIC, DEMOGRAPHIC AND SOCIAL HISTORY

General aspects

Ariès P., *Histoire des populations françaises et de leurs attitudes devant la vie depuis le XVIIIe siècle*, Paris, Editions du Seuil, 1971.

Armengaud, A., *La Population française au XXe siècle*, Paris, Presses universitaires, 1977.

Asselain, J.-C., *Histoire économique de la France. II. De 1919 à la fin des années 1970*, Paris, Editions du Seuil (Points), 1984.

Bairoch, P., *Révolution industrielle et sous-developpement*, Paris, Mouton, 1974.

Bairoch, P. and Lévy-Leboyer, M., (eds.), *Disparities in economic development since the Industrial Revolution*, London, Macmillan, 1981.

Bettelheim, C., *Bilan de l'économie française*, Paris, Presses universitaires, 1946.

Braudel, F. and Labrousse, E., *Histoire économique de la France. IV. L'Ere industrielle et la société aujourd'hui, 1880–1980*, Paris, Presses universitaires, 1979–1980.

Caron, F., *Histoire de l'exploitation d'un grand réseau, la compagnie des chemins de fer du Nord, 1846–1937*, Paris, Mouton, 1973.

— *An economic history of modern France*, translated by B. Bras, New York, Columbia University Press (Columbia economic history of the modern world), 1979.

Claude, H., *De la crise économique à la guerre mondiale*, Paris, OCIA, 1945.

Clément, P. et Vieille, P., *L'Exode rurale historique*, Paris, Imprimerie nationale, 1960.

Combe, P., *Niveau de vie et progrès technique en France, 1860–1939*, Paris, Presses universitaires, 1955.

Demangeon, A., *Le Déclin de l'Europe*, Paris, Colin, 1920.

Duby, G. (ed.), *Histoire de la France urbaine*, Paris, Editions du Seuil, 1980, 5 vols.

Duby, G. and Wallon, A., (eds.), *Histoire de la France rurale*, Paris, Editions du Seuil, 1975–7, 4 vols.

Ehrmann, H.W., *Organised business in France*, Princeton, NJ, Princeton University Press, 1975.

Fridenson, P., *Histoire des usines Renault*, I. *1898–1939*, Paris, Editions du Seuil, 1972.

Fridenson, P. (ed.), *1914–1918, L'Autre Front*, Paris, Editions ouvrières (Cahiers du mouvement social, 2), 1977.

Gignoux, G., *L'Economie française entre les deux guerres, 1919–1939*, Paris, Colin, 1942.

Guerrand, R.H., *Les Origines du logement social en France*, Paris, Editions ouvrières, 1967.

Guinot, J.P., *Formation professionelle et travailleurs qualifiés depuis 1789*, Paris, Domat, 1946.

Guiral, P. and Tenine, E., *La Société française à travers la littérature*, Paris, Colin, 1972.

Halbwachs, M., *L'Evaluation des besoins dans les classes ouvrières*, Paris, Alcan, 1933.

Halévy, D., *Visite aux paysans du Centre (1907–1934)*, Paris, Grasset, 1935.

Kemp, T., *Economic forces in French history*, London, Dobson, 1971.

— *The French economy, 1913–1939, the history of a decline*, London, Longman, 1972.

Keynes, J.M., *The economic consequences of the Peace*, Macmillan, London, 1919.

Landes, D.S., *The Unbound Prometheus, technical change and industrial development in Western Europe from 1750 to the present*, Cambridge, Cambridge University Press, 1969.

Le Chatelier, H., *Science et industrie*, Paris, Flammarion, 1925.

Mauco, G. *Les Etrangers en France*, Paris, Colin, 1932.

Néré J., *La crise de 1929*, Paris, Colin, 1969.

Niveau, M., *Histoire des faits économiques contemporains*, Paris, Presses universitaires, 1966.

O'Brien, P. and Keyder, C., *Economic growth in Britain and France, 1780–1914*, London, Allen and Unwin, 1978.

Pirou, G., *Les Doctrines économiques en France depuis 1870*, Paris, Colin, 1934.

Rist, C., *Evolution de l'économie française, 1910–1937*, Paris, Recueil Sirey, 1937.

Sauvy, A., *Histoire économique de la France entre les deux guerres*, Paris, Fayard, 1965–70, 4 vols.

Sauvy, A. and Defroid, P., *Salaires et pouvoir d'achat des ouvriers et des fonctionnaires entre les deux guerres*, Paris, Presses universitaires, 1940.

Touraine, A., *La Civilisation industrielle de 1914 à nos jours* Paris, Nouvelle édition de France, Histoire generale du travail, 1961, vol. IV.

Toutain, J.C., *La Population de la France de 1700 à 1959*, Paris, Cahiers de l'Isea, 1963.

Finance

Bouvier, J., *Un Siècle de banque française, les contraintes de l'état et les incertitudes des marchés*, Paris, Hachette, 1973.

Dauphin-Meunier, A., *La Banque de France*, Paris, NRF, 1937.

Delaisi, F., *La Banque de France aux mains des deux cents familles*, Paris, CUIA, 1936.

Divisia, F., Dupin, J. and Roy, R., *A la recherche du franc perdu*, Paris, Imprimerie R. Blanchard, 1954–6, 3 vols.

Hamon, A., *Les Maîtres de la France*, Paris, Editions sociales internationales, 1936–8, 3 vols.

Jeanneney, J.-N., *François de Wendel en République, l'argent et le pouvoir, 1914–1940*, Paris, Editions du Seuil, 1976.

— *Leçon d'histoire pour une gauche au pouvoir, la faillite du Cartel, 1924–1926*, Paris, Editions du Seuil, 1982.

Kindleberger, C., *Economic growth in France and Britain, 1851–1950*, Cambridge, Mass., Harvard University Press, 1964.

Lachapelle, G., *Les Finances de la IIIe République*, Paris, Flammarion, 1937.

Lévy-Leboyer, M., *Les Banques européennes et l'industrialisation internationale*, Paris, Presses universitaires, 1964.

Mendès France, P., *L'Œuvre financière du gouvernement Poincaré*, Paris, Librairie générale de droit et de jurisprudence, 1928.

Moreau, E., *Souvenirs d'un gouverneur de la Banque de France, histoire de la stabilisation du franc, 1926–1928*, Paris, Librairie du Médicis, 1954.

Neurisse, A., *Histoire du franc*, Paris, Presses universitaires, 1963.

Perrot, M., *La Monnaie et l'opinion publique en France et en Grande-Bretagne*, Paris, Colin, 1955.

Sédillot, R., *Le Franc, histoire d'une monnaie des origines à nos jours*, Paris, Sirey, 1952.

Wolfe, M., *The French franc between the wars, 1918–1939*, New York, Columbia University Press, 1951.

Social classes, pressure groups

Auge-Laribé, M., *La Politique agricole de la France de 1880 à 1940*, Paris, Presses universitaires, 1950.

Barral, P., *Les Agrariens français, de Méline à Pisani*, Paris, Colin, 1966.

Carter, E.C., *et al.* (eds.), *Enterprise and entrepreneurs in 19th and 20th century France*, Baltimore, Md, Johns Hopkins University Press, 1976.

Les classes sociales en France, edited by Maurice Duverger, Paris, Colin, 1955.

Gratton, P., *La Lutte des classes dans les campagnes, 1870–1921*, Paris, Anthropos, 1971.

— *L'Univers politique des paysans*, Paris, Colin, 1972.

Lefranc, G., *Les Organisations patronales en France*, Paris, Payot, 1976.

Lequin, Y., *Histoire des français, XIXe–XXe siècles. La Société*, Paris, Colin, 1983.

Meynaud, J., *Les Groupes de pression en France*, Paris, Colin, 1958.

Miller, M.B., *The Bon Marché, bourgeois culture and the department store, 1869–1920*, Princeton, NJ, Princeton University Press, 1981.

Mouvements ouvriers et depressions économiques de 1929 à 1939, 7e colloque internationale

d'histoire des mouvements sociaux, Comité international des sciences histori-
ques, Assen, Van Gorcum, 1966.

Pernoud, R., *Histoire de la bourgeoisie en France*, Paris, Editions du Seuil, 1962, vol. II.

Perrot, M., *Le Mode de vie des familles bourgeoises*, Paris, Colin, 1961.

Shorter, E. and Tilly, C., *Strikes in France, 1830–1968*, Cambridge, Cambridge University Press, 1974.

Talmy, R., *Histoire du mouvement familial en France*, Paris, UNCAF, 1962, 2 vols.

Weil, S., *La Condition ouvrière*, Paris, Gallimard, 1951.

Weiss, J.H. *The making of technological man, the social origins of French engineering education*, Cambridge, Mass., MIT Press, 1982.

Wright, G., *Rural revolution in France, the peasantry in the XXth century*, Stanford, Calif., Stanford University Press, 1964.

CULTURAL HISTORY

Religion

Chevallier, P., *Histoire de la franc-maçonnerie française*, Paris, Fayard, 1975, vol. III.

Courtrot, P. and Dreyfus, F., *Les Forces religieuses dans la société française*, Paris, Colin, 1965.

Dansette, A., *Histoire religieuse de la France contemporaine. II. Sous la IIIe République*, Paris, Flammarion, 1952.

Headings, M.J., *French Freemasonry under the Third Republic*, Baltimore, Md, Johns Hopkins University Press, 1949.

Le Bras, G., *Etudes de sociologie religieuse*, Paris, Presses universitaires, 1965.

Léonard, E.G., *Le Protestant français*, Paris, Presses universitaires, 1953.

Mours, S. and Robert, D., *Le Protestantisme en France au XIXe et au XXe siècles*, Paris, Librairie protestante, 1972.

Pierrard, P., *Histoire de l'Eglise catholique*, Paris, Désclée, 1972.

Rauch, R.W., *Politics and belief in contemporary France, Emmanuel Mounier and the Christian democratic movement, 1932–1950*, The Hague, Nijhoff, 1972.

Rémond, R., *Les Catholiques, le communisme et les crises, 1929–1939*, Paris, Colin, 1960.

Roblin, M., *Les Juifs de Paris*, Paris, Picard, 1952.

Schram, S.R., *Protestantism and politics in France*, Alençon, Corbière et Jugain, 1954.

Weinberg, D.H., *Les Juifs de Paris, 1933–1939*, Paris, Calmann-Lévy, 1974.

Literature, thought and the arts

Albarès, R.M., *L'Aventure intellectuelle au XXe siecle, 1900–1959*, Paris, Albin Michel, 1969.

Aron, R., *Mémoires*, Paris, Julliard, 1983.

Auffret, M., *La France de l'entre-deux-guerres, 1919–1939*, Paris, Culture, arts, loisirs, 1972.

Bardèche, M. and Brasillach, R., *Histoire du cinéma*, Paris, André Martel, 1948.

Bernard, J.-P., *Le Parti communiste et la question littéraire, 1921–1939*, Grenoble, Presses universitaires, 1972.

Brisson, P., *Le Théâtre des années folles*, Geneva, Editions milieu du monde, 1943.

Cadwallader, B., *Crisis of the European mind, a study of André Malraux and Drieu La Rochelle*, Cardiff, University of Wales Press, 1981.

Charlton, D.G. (ed.), *France, a companion to French studies*, London, Methuen, 2nd edition, 1979.

Courthion, P., *L'Art indépendant*, Paris, Albin Michel, 1953.

Cruickshank, C.G., *Variations on a catastrophe, some French responses to the Great War*, Oxford, Oxford University Press, 1982.

Dictionnaire abrégé du surréalisme, Paris, Galérie des Beaux-Arts, 1938.

Dumesnil, H., *La Musique en France entre-les-deux-guerres, 1919–1939*, Paris, Editions milieu du monde, 1946.

Fitch, N.R., *Sylvia Beach and the lost generation, a history of literary Paris in the twenties and thirties*, London, Souvenir Press, 1984.

Flower, J.E., *Literature and the Left in France*, London, Macmillan, 1984.

Fosca, F., *La Peinture en France depuis trente ans*, Geneva–Paris, Editions milieu du monde, 1948.

Gilpin, R., *La Science et l'état en France*, Paris, Gallimard, 1958.

Gischia, L. and Vedrès, N., *La Sculpture en France depuis Rodin*, Paris, Editions du Seuil, 1945.

Histoire générale des sciences, edited by R. Taton, Paris, Presses universitaires, 1964, vol. III.

Jouffroy, A., *La Vie réinventée, l'explosion des années 20 à Paris*, Paris, Laffont, 1982.

Lalou, R., *Histoire de la littérature française contemporaine*, Paris, Presses universitaires, 1953, 2 vols.

Lavelle, L., *La Philosophie française entre les deux guerres*, Paris, Aubier, 1942.

Lottman, H., *The Left Bank, writers in Paris from the Popular Front to the Cold War*, Boston, Mass., Houghton Mifflin, 1982.

Loubet del Bayle, J. L., *Les Non-conformistes des années 30*, Paris, Editions du Seuil, 1969.

McCarthy, P., *Céline*, London, Allen Lane, 1975.

Nadeau, M., *Histoire du surréalisme*, Paris, Editions du Seuil, 1945.

— *Documents surréalistes*, Paris, Editions du Seuil, 1948.

Nizan, P., *Les Chiens de garde*, Paris, Rieder, 1932.

Paul Nizan, by W. D. Redfern, Princeton, NJ, Princeton University Press, 1972.

Panassié, H., *Douze années de jazz (1927–1938)*, Paris, Corréa, 1946.

Prost, A., *L'enseignement en France, 1800–1967*, Paris, Colin, 1968.

Sadoul, G., *Histoire du cinéma*, Paris, Flammarion, 1962.

— *Le Cinéma français*, Paris, Flammarion, 1962.

Schalk, D.L. *The spectrum of political engagement, Mounier, Benda, Nizan, Brasillach, Sartre*, Princeton, NJ, Princeton University Press, 1979.

Silvera, A., *Daniel Halévy and his time*, Ithaca, NY, Cornell University Press, 1968.

Le Surréalisme, edited by F. Alquié, Paris, Mouton, 1968.

Talbott, J.E., *The politics of educational reform in France, 1918–1940*, Princeton, NJ, Princeton University Press, 1969.

Tucker, W.R., *The fascist ego, a political biography of Robert Brasillach*, Berkeley, Calif., University of California Press, 1975.

Wahl, J. *Tableau de la philosophie française*, Paris, Gallimard, 1969.

Index